Designing the Adobe InDesign Way

Explore 100+ recipes for creating stunning layouts with
the leading desktop publishing software

Andy Gardiner

BIRMINGHAM—MUMBAI

Designing the Adobe InDesign Way

Copyright © 2023 Packt Publishing

Group Product Manager: Rohit Rajkumar

Publishing Product Manager: Nitin Nainani

Senior Editor: Hayden Edwards

Technical Editor: Simran Ali

Copy Editor: Safis Editing

Project Coordinator: Aishwarya Mohan

Proofreader: Safis Editing

Indexer: Subalakshmi Govindhan

Production Designer: Vijay Kamble

Marketing Coordinators: Namita Velgekar and Nivedita Pandey

First published: July 2023

Production reference: 1200723

Published by Packt Publishing Ltd.

Grosvenor House

11 St Paul's Square

Birmingham

B3 1R

ISBN 978-1-80107-443-8

www.packtpub.com

To my parents, Margaret and Geoff, for all their support and encouragement. To my beloved wife, Ayse, who I am truly fortunate to have met, and our children, Melissa and Sami, who fill our lives with joy, hope, and endless amusement.

– Andy Gardiner

Contributors

About the author

Andy Gardiner is an Adobe Certified Instructor and CompTIA Certified Technical Trainer, delivering regular courses on the Adobe Creative Cloud tools for Highlander Training.

Based in York, in the UK, Andy delivers live online classes, as well as face-to-face training courses at clients' offices. Over the years, he has taught thousands of students from well-known organizations in industries ranging from law enforcement and healthcare to fashion and media.

Andy first started using design tools in the early 90s, when he started working on an early version of QuarkXPress. By the mid-2000s, he had settled on InDesign, Photoshop, Illustrator, and Acrobat, adding Premiere Pro and After Effects to his skill set some years later. In addition to teaching regular courses on the subject, Andy has presented sessions on Adobe Creative Cloud at industry events such as The Print Show. At the last count, he had attained a total of 20 Adobe Certified Expert certifications.

Alongside his technical expertise, Andy also has over 25 years of experience running his own training business and holds a certificate in company direction from the UK Institute of Directors.

When he's not teaching, Andy is actively involved in grassroots football coaching and can often be seen dragging goals around on a cold winter morning.

I want to thank my wife, Ayse, who has supported me throughout this process.

In addition, I would also like to thank everyone at Packt Publishing for their help during the writing process.

About the reviewer

Manan Joshi is a skilled developer specializing in InDesign plugin development, JSX scripting, and CEP development. He has been involved in various projects, such as AD workflow solutions and Custom Variable Data Merge solutions powered by InDesign Server. Some of these solutions are used by Fortune 50 organizations. Presently, he works as a freelance consultant.

With over a decade of experience, Manan has honed his expertise in leveraging InDesign's capabilities and actively contributes to the Adobe forums. Recognized as an Adobe Community Expert and a moderator on the Adobe forums, he is dedicated to sharing knowledge. Through these interactions, he fosters a collaborative environment for learning and growth within the community.

Table of Contents

2

Working with Text in InDesign 47

3

Creating and Using Tables 103

4

Using the InDesign Frame Tools   139

5

Adding Images to Your Documents   183

6

Taking Images Further   225

7

Creating and Applying Parent Pages 255

8

Working with Colors and Gradients 285

9

Formatting with Paragraph and Character Styles   337

10

Generating and Updating a Table of Contents   373

13

Preflighting and Outputting   479

Preface

When I first started working with desktop publishing tools in the 1990s, everything was output for print, and a courier would collect your files on disk and physically deliver them to the printing company. The internet was in its early days, tablet devices didn't yet exist, and mobile phones were a new thing (and the size of a brick).

Fast forward nearly 30 years and, more often than not, documents are being output for digital consumption, although print production is still a significant area. This opens up the possibility of including exciting new features in your documents, and the once clearly defined boundary between websites and other digital content has been all but removed.

Fortunately, tools such as InDesign have also evolved to reflect these changes with new features being added to every release, and interactive and cloud-based functionality becoming a significant part of the products these days. With AI and machine learning already having an effect on software such as Photoshop, it will be exciting to see how this impacts InDesign in the coming years and how the product will continue to develop.

Who this book is for

This book is ideal for marketing and communications professionals in roles such as marketing executive, marketing manager, marketing assistant, communications officer, or communications manager. Additionally, professionals such as graphic designers, publishers, bids and tender teams, PR professionals, and brand managers will also find the book really helpful.

Other computer-literate users who want to start using InDesign to create more professional content, or who already use InDesign to a basic level and want to develop their skills further, will also find the book to be a useful resource.

What this book covers

In *Chapter 1*, *Customizing the InDesign Interface and New Document Settings*, we will learn how to customize the InDesign interface, create new documents, and navigate within them. Additionally, we will learn how to use features such as grids, guides, and rulers to ensure consistency in your documents.

In *Chapter 2*, *Working with Text in InDesign*, we will look at adding text to your document and formatting it using a wide range of typography features. We will also look at using bullets, working with glyphs, and threading text frames together into a story.

In *Chapter 3, Creating and Using Tables*, we will work with tables, learning to insert, remove, and reorder rows and columns. We will learn how to format tables in a variety of different ways, place images into a table, and work with header and footer rows.

In *Chapter 4, Using the InDesign Frame Tools*, we will learn how to create different types of frames as well as how to combine frames together and adjust and align frames. Additionally, we will also look at how to generate a QR code within a frame.

In *Chapter 5, Adding Images to Your Documents*, we are going to learn how to work with images in your documents, addressing areas such as image resolution and broken links, as well as using fitting and text wrap tools.

In *Chapter 6, Taking Images Further*, we will learn some of the more advanced techniques for working with images in InDesign, including advanced text wrap techniques, hiding and showing PSD layers in InDesign, generating captions from metadata, and even anchoring image position within your text.

In *Chapter 7, Creating and Applying Parent Pages*, we will learn how to create and apply parent pages, detach objects from a parent page, base parent pages on other parent pages, and arrange parent page items in front of local page items.

In *Chapter 8, Working with Colors and Gradients*, we will gain a better understanding of color modes, learn how to create color swatches, work with gradients, merge colors together, organize color swatches, find colors in your document, customize strokes, and even set up color management settings in InDesign.

In *Chapter 9, Formatting with Paragraph and Character Styles*, we will learn how to work with paragraph and character styles, create and apply styles, redefine styles, work with overrides, and import styles. In addition, we will learn how to group styles and use features such as nested styles and next style.

In *Chapter 10, Generating and Updating a Table of Contents*, we will learn how to generate a Table of Contents from paragraph styles, format the table of contents, work with Table of Contents styles, update and edit existing tables of contents, and create story jumps.

In *Chapter 11, Creating Interactivity and PDF Forms*, we will explore the interactive capabilities of InDesign by learning how to use hyperlinks, create PDF bookmarks, include video, and use page transitions. We will also learn a number of different uses for the Buttons and Forms panel in InDesign.

In *Chapter 12, Using and Collaborating with CC Libraries*, we will learn how to work with CC Libraries in InDesign. We will add and reuse different types of content in CC Libraries, manage and rename libraries, collaborate with other users on a library, and backup and restore libraries.

In *Chapter 13, Preflighting and Outputting*, we will learn how to preflight your document to check for errors, before then going on to output your document to a wide range of formats from print-ready PDF to interactive PDF. We will then finish off with packaging and using InDesign's built-in Publish Online feature.

To get the most out of this book

To fully benefit from this book, it's important to have basic computer skills, such as knowing how to install, open, and close programs. You should also be familiar with common features in operating systems, such as menus that drop down when you click on them, menus that appear when you right-click, and using useful shortcut keys such as *Shift* and *Alt/Option*.

Software/hardware covered in the book	Operating system requirements
Adobe InDesign 2023 (or later)	Windows or macOS
Adobe Photoshop 2023 (or later)	
Adobe Illustrator 2023 (or later)	
Adobe Bridge 2023 (or later)	

You will need an active Adobe Creative Cloud subscription in order to use the Adobe programs including Adobe InDesign, Adobe Photoshop, Adobe Illustrator, and Adobe Bridge, as well as features of these programs such as CC Libraries and Adobe Fonts.

Some elements of the course will require an active internet connection and a web browser. You will also find it useful to have a PDF reader installed in order to check the files you output; I would recommend Adobe Acrobat Reader or Adobe Acrobat Pro for this purpose.

Conventions used

Bold: Indicates a new term, an important word, or words that you see onscreen. For instance, words in menus or dialog boxes appear in **bold**. Here is an example: "Select **System info** from the **Administration** panel."

> Tips or important notes
> Appear like this.

Get in touch

Feedback from our readers is always welcome.

General feedback: If you have questions about any aspect of this book, email us at `customercare@packtpub.com` and mention the book title in the subject of your message.

Errata: Although we have taken every care to ensure the accuracy of our content, mistakes do happen. If you have found a mistake in this book, we would be grateful if you would report this to us. Please visit `www.packtpub.com/support/errata` and fill in the form.

Piracy: If you come across any illegal copies of our works in any form on the internet, we would be grateful if you would provide us with the location address or website name. Please contact us at `copyright@packt.com` with a link to the material.

If you are interested in becoming an author: If there is a topic that you have expertise in and you are interested in either writing or contributing to a book, please visit `authors.packtpub.com`.

Share Your Thoughts

Once you've read *Designing the Adobe InDesign Way*, we'd love to hear your thoughts! Scan the QR code below to go straight to the Amazon review page for this book and share your feedback.

`https://packt.link/r/1-801-07443-7`

Your review is important to us and the tech community and will help us make sure we're delivering excellent quality content.

Download a free PDF copy of this book

Thanks for purchasing this book!

Do you like to read on the go but are unable to carry your print books everywhere?

Is your eBook purchase not compatible with the device of your choice?

Don't worry, now with every Packt book you get a DRM-free PDF version of that book at no cost.

Read anywhere, any place, on any device. Search, copy, and paste code from your favorite technical books directly into your application.

The perks don't stop there, you can get exclusive access to discounts, newsletters, and great free content in your inbox daily

Follow these simple steps to get the benefits:

1. Scan the QR code or visit the link below

https://packt.link/free-ebook/9781801074438

2. Submit your proof of purchase

3. That's it! We'll send your free PDF and other benefits to your email directly

1
Customizing the InDesign Interface and New Document Settings

Welcome to *Designing the InDesign Way*. In this book, we will teach you a wide range of practical hands-on techniques that will make you more efficient in InDesign and allow you to create standards-compliant content quickly and efficiently.

In this chapter, we will discover how to use the **InDesign interface** to ensure you are working efficiently in InDesign. To do this, we will be looking at the settings you need to apply when creating new documents to ensure your documents can be output without any problems.

Here, you will learn how to open and reposition panels, as well as how to customize the InDesign menus, ensuring the interface is well suited to your style of working. We will also look at how to save your interface changes into a workspace, which can then be used to easily reset the interface whenever things get a bit messy.

As we progress through the chapter, you will learn how to use rulers and guides to ensure both precision and consistency within your documents. You will also learn how to enable or disable the document and baseline grids, which can help with alignment, as well as how to change the screen mode for previewing your document more easily.

By the end of this chapter, you should be comfortable navigating and customizing the InDesign interface and setting up new documents from scratch for both print and screen use.

The recipes we will cover in this chapter are as follows:

- Changing the interface preferences
- Opening and repositioning panels
- Customizing and reordering menus
- Creating, resetting, applying, and deleting workspaces

- Creating a new document

- Navigating the document

- Zooming in InDesign

- Using the baseline and document grids

- Changing the screen mode

- Enabling and changing rulers

- Applying and deleting guides

Technical requirements

To complete this chapter, you will need a PC or Mac with a copy of Adobe InDesign installed. Depending on the device you are working on, it may be necessary to either hide the home screen that appears or disable the touch interface that is enabled by default on some touchscreen devices. We will cover those two points now, but if it does not apply to you, feel free to jump straight to the recipes.

Temporarily hiding the home screen

When you open InDesign on a regular PC or Mac for the first time, the more recent versions of InDesign present you with the **home screen**. The home screen is designed as a quick-access interface that lets you see your recent documents and quickly access presets. You can see an example of this in *Figure 1.1*:

Figure 1.1: The default home screen on opening InDesign

While the home screen can be useful, it can sometimes get in the way; when it first appears, it can hide the panels, tools, and other functionality of InDesign. To remove the home screen, you simply need to click on the **Window** option in the menu at the top of the InDesign interface and then click on **Control**. Doing this will remove the InDesign home screen until you next close and re-open the application. In the first recipe, *Changing the interface preferences*, we will also look at how to turn the home screen off permanently.

Instructions for users with touchscreen laptops

If your computer doesn't have a touchscreen, you can now jump straight to the first recipe; however, if you are working on a computer with a touchscreen, you may find InDesign detects this and brings up the **Touch Workspace** automatically, which will look like the following figure:

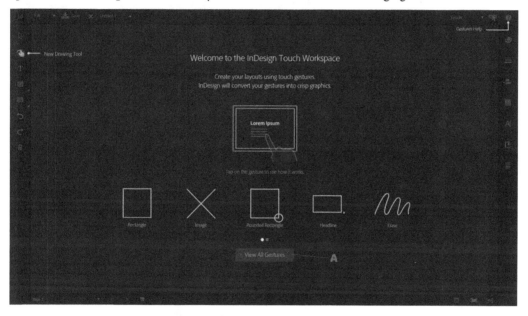

Figure 1.2: The InDesign Touch Workspace

The Touch Workspace is designed primarily for people running InDesign on compatible touchscreen devices; however, in this book, we are focused on regular desktop computers, and as a result, want to turn this functionality off. The Touch Workspace also includes a guided tour when it is first run, so we have to first complete the tour simply in order to turn off this interface.

To close the guided tour, click on the **View All Gestures** button, which can be seen at the bottom (marked *A* in *Figure 1.2*). The screen will then change to look like *Figure 1.3*.

Figure 1.3: Touch Workspace interface tour

On this screen, you can click the **Get Started** button (marked *A* in *Figure 1.3*). You will then see a **New Document** dialog box, as shown in *Figure 1.4*.

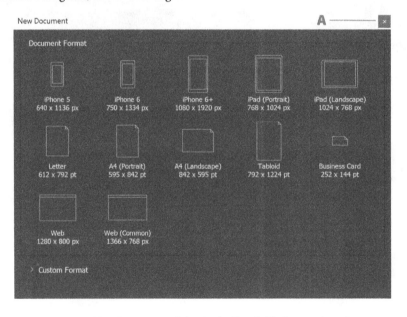

Figure 1.4: New Document dialog in the Touch Workspace interface

Close this dialog box by clicking the red x in the top-right corner (marked *A* in *Figure 1.4*). Once the **New Document** dialog box is closed, you can then click the **Touch** dropdown at the top-right of the screen and select **Essentials** instead (as shown in *Figure 1.5*).

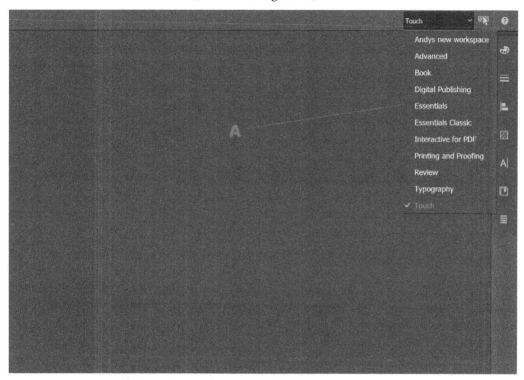

Figure 1.5: Switching to the Essentials Workspace

You will now see the standard InDesign interface with the toolbar on the left, some panels on the right, and the menus at the top of the screen. You are now ready to look at some recipes.

Changing the interface preferences

The **InDesign preferences** allow you to adjust a wide range of settings that affect InDesign, ranging from what language is used for spell-checking to what units of measurement InDesign works with. In this recipe, though, we will focus on the preferences settings that can affect the InDesign interface. We will look at how to permanently disable the home screen, adjust the intensity of the interface, change interface scaling, and alter the default grid and guide colors.

You often spend many hours staring at the InDesign interface, so being able to customize it to your personal preferences can be helpful for both your eyes and your stress levels. The skills covered here will ensure you find working with InDesign for long periods of time to be a more enjoyable and less frustrating experience.

Getting ready

To complete this recipe, simply open InDesign on your system. There is no need to create a document at this stage; we will be run through that in the *Creating a new document* recipe.

If you have the Touch Workspace enabled and are unable to access the **Edit** menu, take a look at the *Technical requirements* section for details on how to disable this and access the full interface.

How to do it...

In order to adjust the interface preferences, follow these steps:

1. The Mac and PC versions of InDesign are almost identical; however, the location of the preference information is one thing that differs between them. If you are on a PC, go to the **Edit** menu and you will find **Preferences** at the very bottom of this menu. If you are on a Mac, you will have an **InDesign** menu option (shown in *Figure 1.6*) right before the **File** menu option, where **Preferences** can be found.

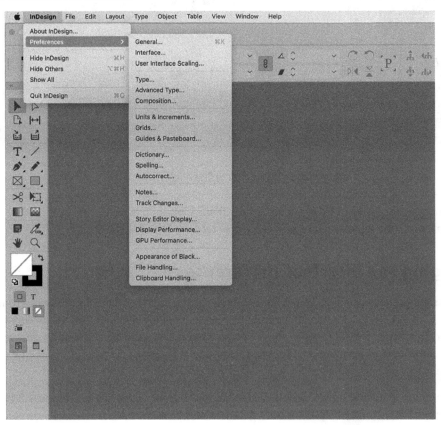

Figure 1.6: The InDesign menu on the Mac

2. When you go to the **Preferences** option in the menu, you will see a fly-out menu with a choice of 20 different options. Whichever of these options you click will still bring up the **Preferences** dialog box, but will default to the corresponding set of options within the dialog box. For example, clicking the **Interface** option would bring up the dialog box showing the **Interface** options. These various options can also be navigated within the dialog box once it is open by using the labels down the left-hand side of the dialog box (this can be seen in *Figure 1.8*). In our case, we will click on the **General** option, as seen in the following screenshot.

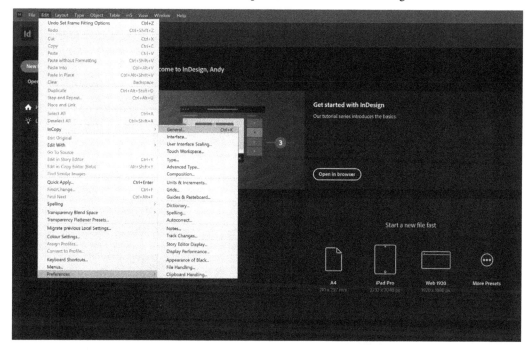

Figure 1.7: InDesign Preferences menu options

The **Preferences panel** contains a wide range of settings for InDesign that can be customized. Some of these are very obscure settings that you won't need to change, and here we will focus on the settings that primarily affect the InDesign user experience.

Note

The InDesign home screen is the initial default interface that is displayed when you open InDesign, and it offers quick access to presets, recently used files, learning resources, and a number of other features. While the InDesign home screen can be useful, it also limits your ability to customize some of InDesign's settings, so with this in mind, in *step 3*, I will disable the home screen in the preferences.

---

3. On the **General** tab of the preferences, the very top item is a checkbox for **Show Home Screen When No Documents Are Open**. By deselecting this box, you can disable the home screen, and the next time you restart InDesign, the home screen won't appear. Should you want the home screen back at a later date, you can always reverse this action by reselecting this option. In our case, we are keeping it deselected.

4. Having deselected the home screen option, we will now click on the second item down on the left of the panel, **Interface**. This can be seen in *Figure 1.8*.

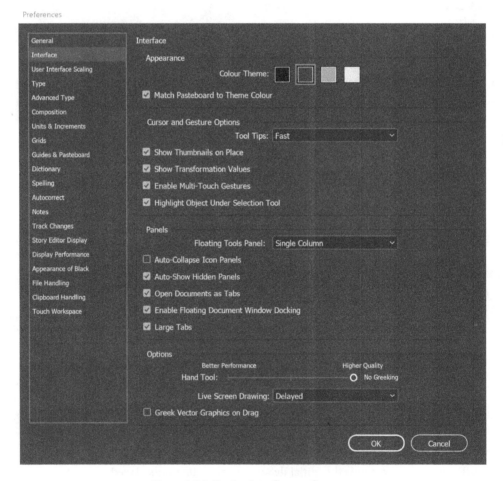

Figure 1.8: InDesign Interface preferences

5. Within the **Interface** options, you will see a section called **Appearance**; within the **Color Theme** section, you can change the intensity of the interface from dark to light. Choose whichever interface color theme you prefer.

Note

I personally find a dark interface less tiring to work with; however, throughout the rest of this book, I will use the light interface as it will be more suitable for the print version of the book.

---

6. The checkbox immediately below that setting is for **Match Pasteboard to Theme Color**, which ensures that areas around your document pages reflect your choice of intensity here. You may wish to enable this depending on whether you prefer the background area around your document to match the color theme.

7. Below **Interface** on the left-side panel is **User Interface Scaling**. This allows you to control the scaling of the InDesign UI, including changing the UI size and the size of on-screen visual aids (such as the mouse cursor and adjustment tools). In *Figure 1.9*, you can see how this would look with the **UI Scaling** value set to the middle of the slider and the **Interface** intensity set to the **Light** value. Choose an interface scale that suits your requirements, depending on your own screen size and eyesight.

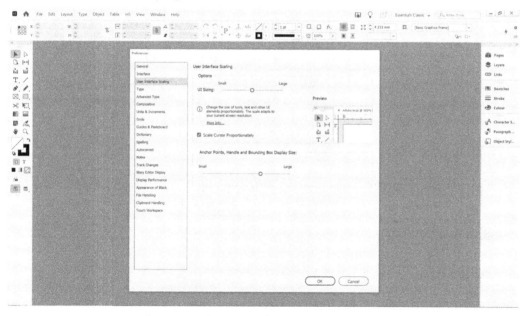

Figure 1.9: InDesign Interface with medium UI size

Note

I am going to leave **UI Sizing** set to the middle of the slider for now, which equates to a medium level of **UI Sizing**, as it will make it easier for us to see details in the screenshots.

---

8. We will skip a couple of the options on the left of the panel and jump to **Units and Increments**. Here, we are able to change the horizontal and vertical ruler units by using common units of measurement such as millimeters, inches, and pixels (plus a number of less common options). You may be working with brand guidelines, a set of predefined rules for your organization's designs, and these will often stipulate sizes using a particular unit of measurement. Being able to set the units of measurement to reflect the settings in your brand guidelines can therefore help to ensure the consistency of your brand. In this instance, we will change the measurements into **millimeters**.

9. Having made the interface preference changes that we want, we can save these changes by simply clicking the **OK** button at the bottom of the dialog box. Some changes require InDesign to be restarted before they take effect, so, depending on the changes you have made, you might find InDesign does a restart at this point.

Opening and repositioning panels

In this recipe, you will learn how to open and close panels in InDesign, as well as how to reposition panels, either by docking them in an existing panel group or by creating a new column.

Much of the core functionality of InDesign is accessed through the many different **panels**, which are interactive resizable windows that contain a wide range of options and functionality. With this in mind, being able to quickly open and reposition panels is a useful skill as it will ensure that you are able to access the features of InDesign that you need more efficiently.

Getting ready

In order to complete this recipe, simply open InDesign on your system; there is no need to create a document at this stage, which is something we will run through in the *Creating a new document* recipe. If you have the home screen enabled still, look at the *Changing the interface preferences* recipe for details on how to disable this and access the main interface.

How to do it...

To open and reposition panels within InDesign, follow these steps:

1. To access any of the panels in InDesign, simply click on the **Window** menu and choose the panel you wish to open. Some panels are hidden in submenus; for example, the **Styles** submenu contains a total of five panels, as can be seen in the following figure:

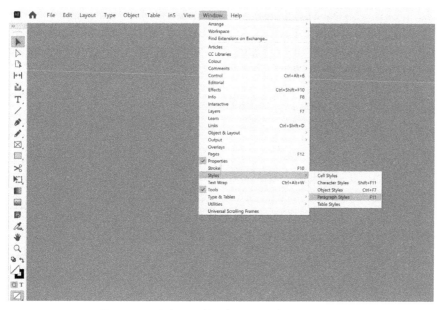

Figure 1.10: InDesign Window menu listing panels

2. In the **Window** menu, scroll down to **Styles** and click the **Paragraph Styles** option. This will open the **Paragraph Styles** panel as well as the **Character Styles** panel (as some panels automatically open in a group with closely related panels). You can see this in *Figure 1.11*.

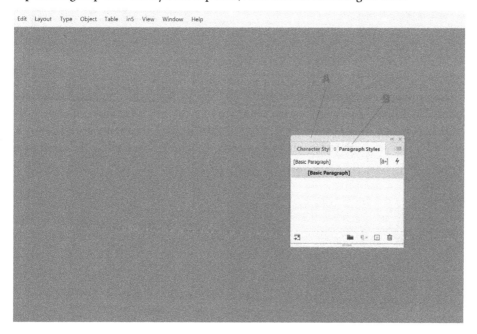

Figure 1.11: Paragraph Styles panel in InDesign

3. You can move panels around by clicking on the bar at the top of the panel group (*A* in *Figure 1.11*) and dragging them around the screen. Alternatively, if you click on the name tab at the top of an individual panel (marked *B* in *Figure 1.11*) and drag it away, the panel will be separated from the group, as shown in *Figure 1.12*.

Figure 1.12: Separating grouped panels

4. If you now drag the panel across the screen to the right, you will notice blue lines appearing and these reflect where the panel will be docked if you let go of the mouse button now. A long blue line down the side, as in *Figure 1.13*, tells us that if we let go of the mouse now, a new column containing the **Paragraph Styles** panel will be created on the left-hand side of the existing panels.

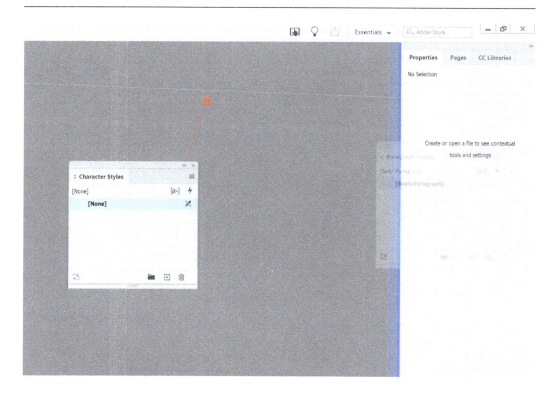

Figure 1.13: Docking a panel in InDesign

A blue line below existing panels shows that the panel will be docked beneath those panels in a separate group, while a blue square around other panels tells us the panel will be docked as part of that group of panels.

5. To close a panel, you can simply drag it by the name tab of the panel into the middle of the screen and click the small x in the top-right corner. If you wish to reopen the panel, simply select it again in the **Window** menu. Remember, every panel is available in the **Window** menu, but some might be hidden under submenus there.

6. Panels can be either expanded or collapsed using the two small arrows at the top-right of the panel. When expanded, you can see the features of the panel and when collapsed, you only see the panel name and icon. To toggle between the two modes, simply click the two arrows on the top-right of the panel or panel group (marked *A* in *Figure 1.13*).

7. If you are working with panels in collapsed mode, simply click on the panel name and it will temporarily expand to allow you to use the panel. When finished, you can then click on the panel name again to collapse the panel. This can be an efficient way to work in InDesign as it allows you to have a long list of panels available on the right-hand side of the screen and simply open any of them quickly with a single click. You can see an example of this in *Figure 1.14*.

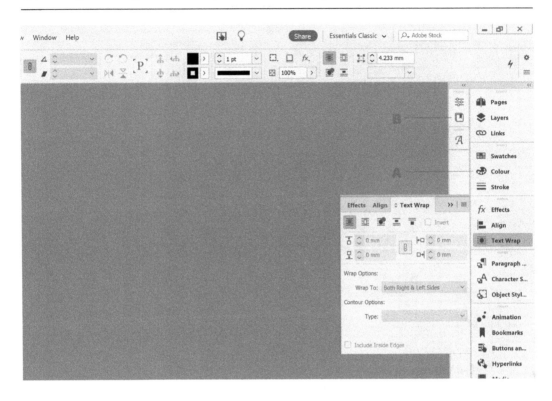

Figure 1.14: A docked panel expanded in InDesign

8. Finally, in addition to having panels either expanded or collapsed, it is worth mentioning that when panels are collapsed, you can choose whether to show the whole panel name with the icon (example marked *A* in *Figure 1.14*) or just the icon alone (example marked *B* in *Figure 1.14*). To do this simply hold your mouse over the left-hand edge of the panel and drag left or right, in order to show more or less of the label. This might be useful if you have a couple of panels that you want available quickly, but you don't want them to take up much space.

Customizing and reordering menus

In this recipe, we will explore ways to customize **menus** in InDesign, including hiding items in the menus, highlighting items in the menus, and even sorting menus alphabetically to make finding items easier.

If you are new to InDesign, it can be especially useful to highlight menu items or quickly sort menus alphabetically in order to find what you are looking for. In general, I would advise against hiding menu items, as it is very easy to forget that you have done this as the months go by and then one day, you might need that option, which can't now be found. Having said that, other people may hide items that you need to access, so it is good to know how and where to do this.

Getting ready

To complete this recipe, simply open InDesign on your system; there is no need to create a document at this stage, which is something we will run through in the *Creating a new document* recipe. If you have the home screen enabled still, look at the *Changing the interface preferences* recipe for details on how to disable this and access the main interface.

How to do it...

To customize and reorder the InDesign menus, follow these steps:

1. In the **Edit** menu, go to the bottom of the menu and you will see an option for **Menus** (if you are on a smaller screen, you may have to scroll a bit to see this). Click this option and it will bring up the **Menu Customization panel**, as seen in *Figure 1.15*:

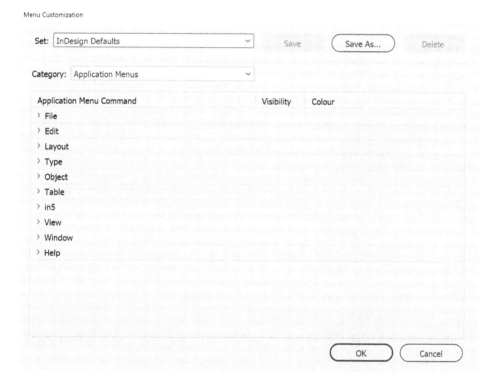

Figure 1.15: The Menu Customization panel in InDesign

In the panel, you can choose to customize either **Application Menus** (across the top in InDesign) or **Content** and **Panel Menus** (within each individual panel) using the **Category** drop-down option in the panel.

2. If you choose **Application Menus**, you will see a column for **Application Menu Command** and the top item listed is **File** with a small arrow on its left. Click this arrow to expand the list and see all the options in the menu, as shown in *Figure 1.16*.

Figure 1.16: Customizing the File menu in InDesign

3. Alongside the **Application Menu Command** column, you will notice that there are two more columns for **Visibility** and **Color**:

    •   **Visibility** allows you to hide menu items, which, as a general rule, is probably not a good idea as you may need them in the future

    •   **Color** allows you to give menu items a background color, which can help them stand out and make them easier to find

    In this example, we will hide the **Check In…** menu item by clicking the eye next to it in the **Visibility** column. We will then set the **Save As…** menu item to have a red background, by choosing **Red** from the dropdown under the **Color** column:

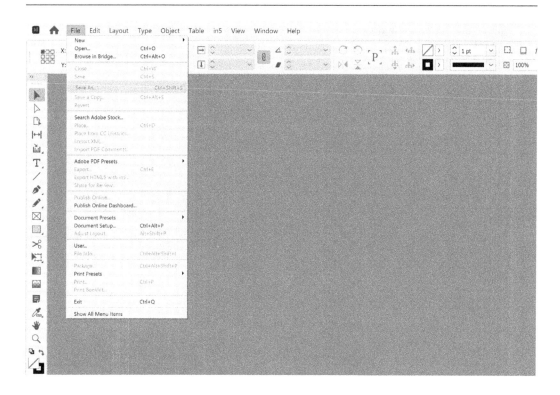

Figure 1.17: Menu customization panel showing menu item hidden and with color applied

4. If we now save these changes by clicking **OK** on the dialog box, we can open up the **File** menu and see that the **Save As…** option has a red background making it stand out, and the **Check In…** option, which was above it previously, has now been removed (as shown in *Figure 1.17*).

5. We are now going to select **Edit** and then **Menus** again, and go back to the **Menu Customization** dialog box. Here, we will set the **Check In…** option back to visible and set **Save As…** back to **None** under the **Color** column.

6. One final trick with the InDesign menus that can be worth being aware of is the ability to sort menus alphabetically when you click on them. The process is very simple: just click any of the menus while already holding down *Ctrl + Alt + Shift* (for PC)/*Cmd + Option + Shift* (for Mac). In *Figure 1.18*, you can see an example of the **Object** menu as it normally looks (on the left), and how it looks when you hold down these modifier keys while clicking on it (on the right).

Figure 1.18: Object menu with and without Ctrl + Alt + Shift (PC)/Cmd + Option + Shift (Mac) keys

Creating, resetting, applying, and deleting workspaces

Workspaces can be a useful time saver for organizing your InDesign desktop and more quickly accessing a wide range of InDesign features. They allow you to save the position of panels within the InDesign interface, as well as specify whether menu items are hidden or highlighted in a specific color.

Using workspaces allows you to have the panels and menu options that you need immediately available when you are working on specific types of documents. For example, you could have a wide range of interactive panels that are all ready to use when you are working on interactive documents, but then have different panels available when working on print documents, all by simply switching workspaces.

In this recipe, we will look at how you can create, reset, apply, and delete workspaces in InDesign.

Getting ready

To complete this recipe, simply open InDesign on your system; there is no need to create a document at this stage, which is something we will run through in the *Creating a new document* recipe. If you have the home screen enabled still, look at the *Changing the interface preferences* recipe for details on how to disable this and access the main interface.

How to do it...

To create, delete, and use InDesign workspaces, follow these steps:

1. The first step in creating a workspace is to position the panels exactly how you would like them to appear (see the *Opening and repositioning panels* recipe) and to make any edits to the menus that you wish to make – for example, by hiding menu items or giving them a background color (see the *Customizing and reordering menus* recipe).

2. Once you have done this, the layout can then be saved as a workspace. To save your workspace, go to the **Window** menu and select the **Workspace** option. This will display a list of preset workspaces that come with InDesign; below these, you will see an option for **New Workspace**, which you should select now.

3. The **New Workspace dialog box** will now be visible for creating a new workspace, as seen in *Figure 1.19*. This includes options to include **Panel Locations** and **Menu Customization**. Tick the boxes you wish to include here and give the workspace a name (I have called mine **MyTestWorkspace**). Then click **OK**.

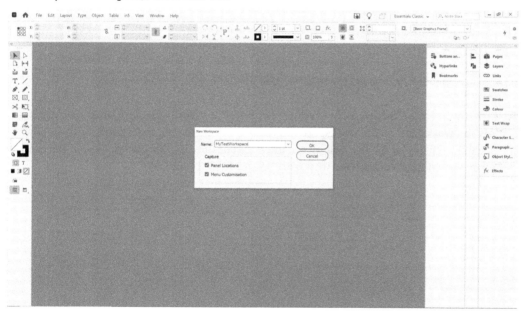

Figure 1.19: New Workspace dialog box

When you created a new workspace and saved it, InDesign automatically applied it as well. As a result, if you now look at the top-right of the screen, you will see the workspace name showing there, with a small drop-down arrow next to it (marked *A* in *Figure 1.20*). This drop-down box is a useful shortcut for quickly switching between workspaces, as well as for things such as resetting your workspaces.

4. With your new workspace created, you can now move panels around, open new panels, edit menus, and generally make a mess of your InDesign layout, as shown in *Figure 1.20*.

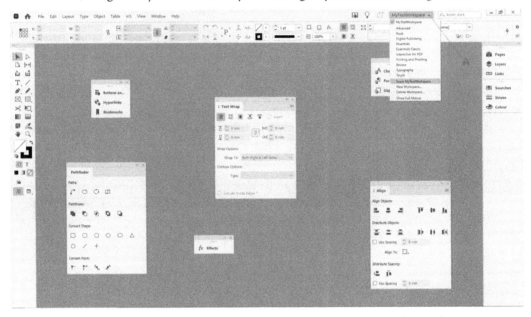

Figure 1.20: Example of workspace after things have been moved around

5. All you need to do to reset everything is go to the **Window** menu, then select **Reset MyTestWorkspace** under **Workspace** (this can also be done even faster from the drop-down menu just mentioned). This will set the interface back to exactly how it looked at the point when you originally created the workspace, as shown in *Figure 1.21*.

Figure 1.21: Example of workspace after it is reset

6. If you wish to switch to a different workspace, simply use the dropdown and click on the name of a workspace to switch to it. When you do this, you will see the layout of panels and any menu customizations change to those set in the workspace you clicked.

7. Finally, you might have created a number of workspaces that you now no longer require and may wish to delete some of them. You can do this from the drop-down menu next to the workspace name. When you click **Delete Workspace**, you will be presented with a dialog box, as shown in *Figure 1.22*, asking which workspace you wish to delete. Select the workspace you want and then click **OK** to delete it.

Figure 1.22: Dialog box when deleting a workspace

Creating a new document

In this recipe, we are going to look at creating your first document from scratch. We will run through the **New Document settings** involved and ensure that your document is set up properly depending on the different types of documents you are creating.

By the end of this recipe, you will be able to set up new documents properly for print or digital use, while ensuring errors aren't introduced that will cause problems at a later stage.

Getting ready

To complete this recipe, simply open InDesign on your system. If you have the home screen enabled still, look at the *Changing the interface preferences* recipe for details on how to disable it and access the main interface.

How to do it...

To create a new document in InDesign, follow these steps:

1. To start a new document, go to the **File** menu and select **New**. Here, you will see three options: **Document**, **Book**, and **Library**. To create a standard InDesign document, you should choose the **Document** option.

    This will bring up the **New Document dialog box**, which can be seen in *Figure 1.23*.

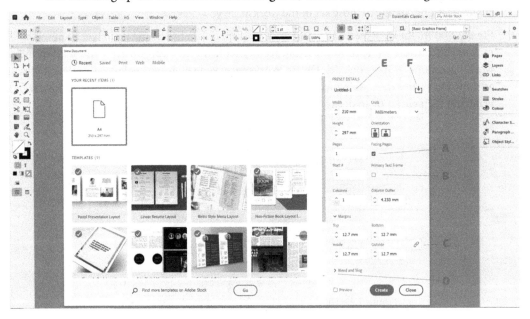

Figure 1.23: The New Document dialog box in InDesign

Adobe includes a number of free templates with InDesign and these can be seen under the **TEMPLATES** section. At the bottom of the dialog box, you can also search for more paid templates on the Adobe Stock site; doing a search here will open your browser and take you to the Adobe Stock website where you can purchase additional templates. In this instance, we are looking to create our own new documents from scratch, so we don't need this.

2. Across the top of the dialog box, you will see five options, as follows:

    *   **Recent** – Your recently used items

    *   **Saved** – Blank custom document presets that you have saved

    *   **Print** – Document presets designed for print use

    *   **Web** – Document presets designed for web use

    *   **Mobile** – Document presets designed for mobile devices

    As you switch between **Print**, **Web**, and **Mobile**, you will notice that not only do the templates and presets shown beneath change but also the settings on the right-hand side of the panel change too.

> **Note**
>
> If you plan on outputting your document for print, you should start with a **Print** preset as this will automatically ensure your document settings are optimized for print. If you plan on using the document for screen use only, then you can choose from the **Web** or **Mobile** options, which are optimized for this type of output.

You should consider that the preset you choose will vary in different regions; I live in the UK so will select the **A4 Blank** preset here, but if you are in North America, for example, you may want to choose **Letter** instead.

3. Having done so, we are now going to focus on the settings on the right-hand side of the dialog box. As you can see, we start out with the **Width** and **Height** settings and **Units** of measurement. As I chose the A4 preset, these have defaulted to the standard A4 size of 210 mm x 297 mm.

4. Below the **Units** dropdown, you will see an **Orientation** option, where you can choose **Landscape** or **Portrait**, in effect swapping the width and height values around. We will leave this set to the default option of **Portrait**.

5. In the **Pages** section, we can enter the number of pages we would like to start with. Don't worry about getting this wrong as you can easily add and remove pages later. In this instance, we are going to set this to **12** pages.

6. Immediately below the **Pages** option, you will see a **Start** option, which specifies which page number the document starts on; we will leave this set to **1**, and in most cases, that is what you will want.

7.   To the right of the **Pages** option, you will see a **Facing Pages** checkbox (marked *A* in *Figure 1.23*). If you select this, InDesign will lay out your documents with left and right pages next to each other, in what are called double-page spreads. You can see this on the right in *Figure 1.24*. This can be useful when laying out multi-page documents for print, as it makes the process of positioning items across two pages much simpler.

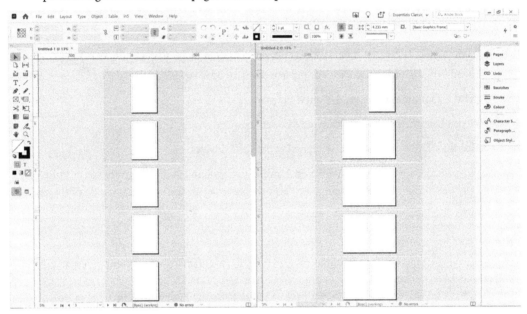

Figure 1.24: Facing Pages is enabled on the right-hand document but not on the left

> **Note**
>
> It's worth noting that if you have the **Start** option set to an even number and then enable **Facing Pages**, your document will start with a double-page spread rather than a standalone first page, as shown in *Figure 1.24*.

If **Facing Pages** is not selected at all, the pages will all appear below each other in one long column, as shown on the left in *Figure 1.24*. This is more common for digital documents that won't be printed. In this instance, we will select **Facing Pages**.

8.   The next option is the **Primary Text Frame** option (marked *B* in *Figure 1.23*), which allows you to have a large text frame automatically included on every page. In many cases, you will want that to remain disabled, as you will be creating your own frames on the pages; however, there are exceptions where it can be useful. In this instance, we will leave it turned off.

9. Moving down, we see the **Columns** and **Column Gutter** settings. These allow you to have column guides included on every page, which can be useful if you are creating a multi-column layout. A column gutter is the spacing between the columns. You can see an example of a page created with a three-column layout in *Figure 1.25*. If you don't require multiple columns, just leave the **Columns** value set to **1**, which is what we will do here.

Figure 1.25: A page created with a 3-column layout and a 4.233 mm column gutter

10. If we scroll down a bit in the dialog box, you will see that the next item is **Margins**. These can all be set to the same value, which is the default behavior; however, if you click the small link icon to the right (marked C in *Figure 1.23*), the values can then be changed independently. The margin is the area between the margin guide (marked A in *Figure 1.26*) and the edge of the page. While it is possible to enter content into the margin, it is generally good practice to avoid doing so, as it can make your design look too busy, impact legibility, and, potentially, even risk content being trimmed off during the printing process. We will leave these set to the default setting.

11. Finally, moving down from **Margin**, you will see the options for **Bleed** and **Slug**. These may be collapsed, in which case simply click the small arrow (marked D in *Figure 1.23*) next to the words **Bleed** and **Slug** to see them. The bleed is the area around the outside of your document, which is used in print to ensure your colors and images go right to the edge of the page. If all goes well, the bleed is cut off and thrown away at the end of the printing process, but if there is any slight misalignment during the printing process, the bleed ensures you won't get a strip of white down the document edge without any ink on it. Typical bleed settings for hand-held print documents vary from 3 mm to 5 mm, but ask your printer what bleed they would like, to be safe.

12. The slug is the area outside of the page where printer information can be included if required, such as the title or date of output or even contact details for any problems. Many jobs won't need a slug, and you should check with your printer on their requirements, but if it is required, this is where you can enable that area. In this instance, we will leave it disabled.

13. Having now entered all of the information, you can save this as a preset for future use if you wish. This can be done at the top of the dialog box by giving it a name right below where it says **Preset Details** (marked *E* in *Figure 1.23*) and then clicking the downward arrow (marked *F* in *Figure 1.23*) in order to save this as a preset. This will then show up under the **Saved** section next time.

14. If you are now ready to create your new document, simply click the **Create** button at the bottom and you should see your new document in the main InDesign window. In *Figure 1.26*, you can see the bleed showing up in red (*B* in *Figure 1.26*), the margin guide can be seen in magenta (*A* in *Figure 1.26*), and the slug is seen at the bottom in blue (*C* in *Figure 1.26*).

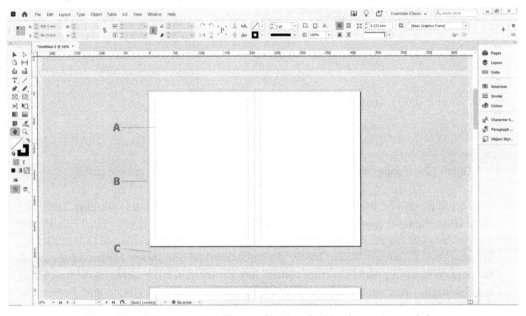

Figure 1.26: A document in InDesign showing the bleed, margins, and slug

---

Tip

When changing number values in Adobe products (e.g., margin settings), you can also do calculations in fields that contain numbers, or after clicking into the box, simply use the up and down arrows on the keyboard, either with or without the *Shift* key, to change numbers.

Navigating the document

When working on your document, it is essential to be able to navigate between **pages**, not to mention add new pages or delete existing pages.

In this recipe, we will look at how to move around using the **Pages** panel, deleting pages individually or together, and adding new pages at a precise point in your document.

Getting ready

To complete this recipe, simply open InDesign on your system and open a new document with 12 pages, as shown in the *Creating a new document* recipe.

How to do it...

To learn how to navigate your documents in InDesign, follow these steps:

1. Let's start by opening up the **Pages** panel. This is typically found docked on the right-hand side, but if you don't see it there, you can find it in the **Window** menu. On the **Pages** panel, you will see the pages that make up the document, as shown in *Figure 1.27*.

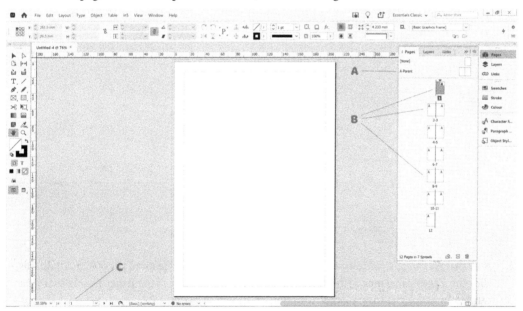

Figure 1.27: The Pages panel in InDesign

2. The **Pages** panel is split in two: **Parents** at the top (marked *A* in *Figure 1.27*) with the pages below (marked *B* in *Figure 1.27*). Parents are a way of rapidly applying content to multiple pages, and we will look at these in *Chapter 6, Creating and Applying Parent Pages*; for now, though, we are going to focus on **Pages**.

3. To navigate to a specific page, you simply need to double-click the **Pages** icon in the **Pages** panel. This will take you straight to the page, which you can confirm by looking at the bottom-left of the screen, where you will see the page number of the page you are currently on (marked *C* in *Figure 1.27*). This can also be used to switch to a different page as an alternative to double-clicking in the **Pages** panel, as can be seen in *Figure 1.28*:

Figure 1.28: Changing pages from the popup

4. Now that we can navigate around the document, we will add some more pages to it. To do this, click the **Pages** panel menu (the three little lines at the top right of the **Pages** panel); there you can see and click the **Insert Pages…** option, as shown in *Figure 1.29*.

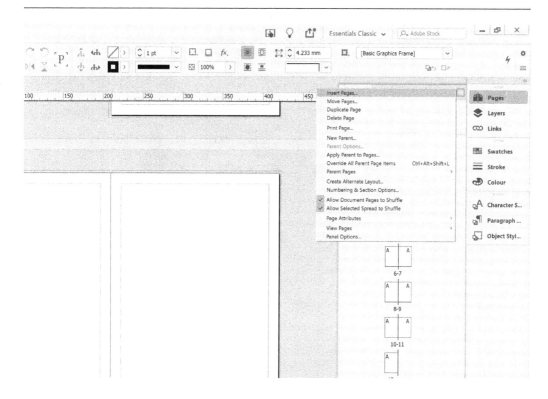

Figure 1.29: The Pages panel menu options

Another option for adding pages is to right-click in the **Pages** panel to the side of the existing pages, and you will see the **Insert Pages…** option. In both cases, you will then be shown the **Insert Pages** dialog box, as shown in *Figure 1.30*.

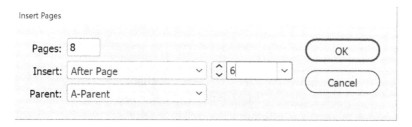

Figure 1.30: The Insert Pages dialog box

5.   In the **Insert pages** dialog box, which can be seen in *Figure 1.30*, you can choose the number of pages to insert (in this case, **8**), where you want to insert them relative to other pages (in this case, **After Page 6**), and whether you want to apply a parent page. Once you have chosen the relevant settings, simply click **OK** and your pages will have been added to the document.

6. If you wish to delete pages, simply select the pages you wish to delete within the **Pages** panel and click the waste bin icon at the bottom-right of the panel.

7. If you wish to select a whole run of pages, you can hold down the *Shift* key and click two pages in the **Pages** panel; then, InDesign will select the two pages that you clicked as well as all the pages in between. In *Figure 1.31*, pages 7 through 14 have been selected using this method.

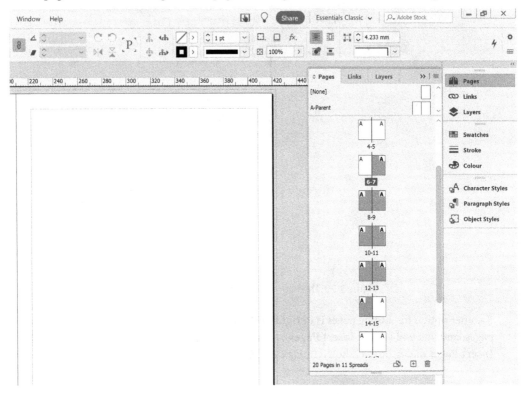

Figure 1.31: Selecting pages 7 to 14 in the Pages panel with Shift

8. If you wish to select a variety of pages scattered throughout the document, you can use the *Ctrl (PC)/Cmd (Mac)* shortcut to select multiple different pages at once. This can be seen in *Figure 1.32*, where pages 7, 10, 12, and 15 have all been selected.

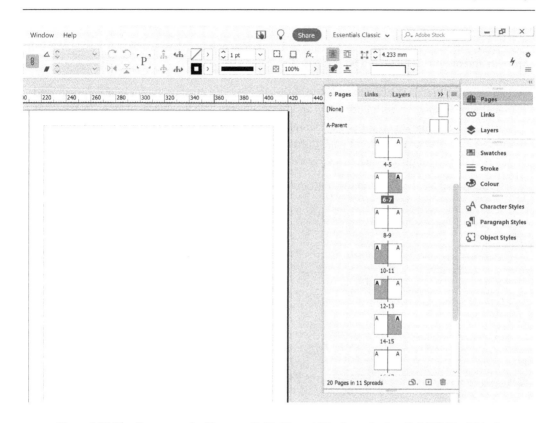

Figure 1.32: The Pages panel with pages 7, 10, 12, and 15 selected using Ctrl (PC)/Cmd (Mac)

Zooming in InDesign

Sometimes, it's useful to be able to **zoom in** and get a closer look at your work in InDesign, as it can make life easier when aligning things, checking spelling, and completing a multitude of other common tasks. In other cases, it might be more helpful to **zoom out** and get a good overall view of your document.

In this recipe, we are going to look at how to zoom in and out in your document, snap the document to fit the screen size you are working on, and simply zoom straight to 100% size.

Getting ready

To complete this recipe, simply open InDesign on your system and open a new document with 12 pages, as shown in the *Creating a new document* recipe.

How to do it...

To zoom in and out precisely within your document, follow these steps:

1. We are going to start this recipe with one of the simplest and most useful tricks in InDesign and one that also works in both Photoshop and Illustrator too. Whatever part of your document is currently being shown on the screen, simply double-click the hand tool icon on the left-hand side and it will snap the current page to **fit the screen**. This is great if you have been zooming in and want to simply go back to seeing the whole page.

    The hand tool can be found at the bottom of the toolbar and is marked *A* in *Figure 1.33*.

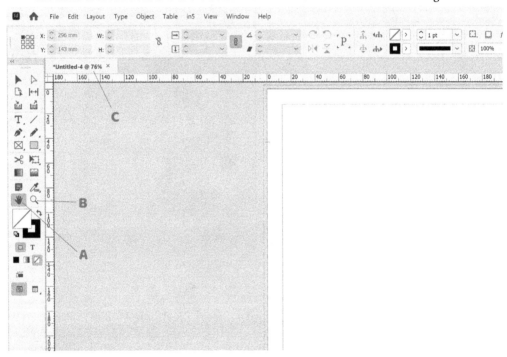

Figure 1.33: The InDesign toolbar with the hand tool (A) and zoom tool (B) near the bottom

2. If you ever want to know how far in you have zoomed, all you need to do is look at the document's tab, which is found just below the menus at the top of the document. In *Figure 1.33*, you can see that this document is called **Untitled-4** and is zoomed at **76%** (marked *C* in *Figure 1.33*).

3. To zoom in further into this document, we are now going to use the **zoom tool**, which is marked *B* in *Figure 1.33*. The zoom tool can work in multiple ways. If you click on the document with it, you will find it zooms you in closer with each click using predefined increments. For example, if you are currently zoomed at 100%, clicking once will zoom to 125%, clicking again will zoom to 150%, and so on. This will continue until you reach the maximum zoom of 4,000%.

4. To zoom out, you can use the zoom tool again, but this time, hold down the *Alt* (PC)/*Option* (Mac) key, and each click will zoom you out incrementally in a reversal of the previous behavior. As we saw in *step 1*, however, it is often just quicker to double-click the hand tool and instantly snap the document to fit the screen.

5. Another way of zooming with the zoom tool is to click and drag a box around the area you wish to zoom in on. When you let go of the mouse button, it will automatically resize the view to fit that area.

   Additionally, it is worth mentioning that your standard operating system shortcuts to zoom will also work, such as the *Ctrl* (PC)/*Cmd* (Mac) key together with the + or – keys.

6. One final trick when zooming is the ability to reposition the document slightly. For example, you may have zoomed on a specific area and accidentally zoomed slightly to one side of where you wanted to be. The hand tool can be easily used to reposition your documents, by just clicking on the document with the hand tool and dragging on the screen to reposition it.

Using the baseline and document grids

Aligning items accurately is a useful thing to be able to do when laying out documents. It not only makes your documents look more professional but it allows you to ensure a degree of consistency across your documents, which, in turn, reinforces your brand identity.

The document grid and baseline grids can be useful tools in doing this and, in this recipe, we will look at how to enable these grids, customize them to your specific requirements, and align content to the grids.

In terms of the **baseline grid**, this is a bit like the lines on traditional lined writing paper and is a useful tool for ensuring consistency with your vertical text spacing throughout the document. The **document grid**, on the other hand, is more useful for aligning objects consistently, such as frames.

Getting ready

To complete this recipe, simply open InDesign on your system and open a new document with 12 pages, as shown in the *Creating a new document* recipe.

How to do it...

To start working with the baseline grid and document grid in InDesign, follow these steps:

1. To enable the baseline grid, go to the **View** menu and select **Show Baseline Grid** under **Grids and Guides**. Depending on the baseline grid preferences, you may not immediately see anything, so our first step should be to amend these preferences. To open the preferences, simply use the keyboard shortcut *Ctrl + K* (PC)/*Cmd + K* (Mac), then click **Grids** on the left-hand side of the panel.

The **Baseline Grid preferences** (shown in *Figure 1.34*) are at the top of the **Grids** section.

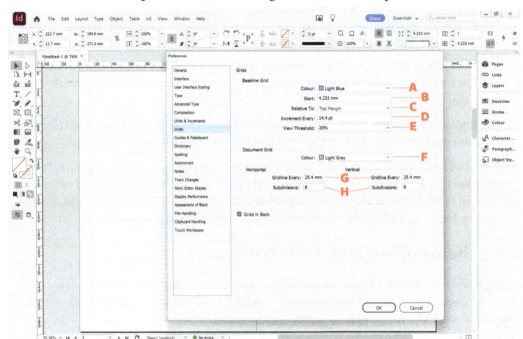

Figure 1.34: Document with baseline grid visible and grid preferences open

In terms of what these settings represent, this can be broken down as follows:

- **Color** (*A* in *Figure 1.34*) – The color that the baseline grid appears in on the document; in our case, we have used **Light Blue**.

- **Start** (*B* in *Figure 1.34*) and **Relative To** (*C* in *Figure 1.34*) – These work together, for example, by letting you start the grid 12 pt from the top margin. In this case, **12 pt** would be the **Start** value and **Top Margin** would be the **Relative To** value (see the note re: units of measurement changing from **pt** to **mm** in the preferences).

- **Increment Every** (*D* in *Figure 1.34*) – How frequently the grid lines repeat; in this case, every 14.4 pt.

- **View Threshold** (*E* in *Figure 1.34*) – The zoom point below which the grid shows on the screen; here, ours is **20%**.

> **Tip**
>
> A useful approach can be to set the **Increment Every** value to reflect your standard body copy leading size and have the **Start Relative to** value set to the same value and relative to the top margin.

> **Note**
>
> You might notice in *Figure 1.34* that the **Start** value is showing in mm and not in pt. This will depend on your **Units and Increments** preferences; if they are set to mm, you can still enter the value as 12 pt, but it will automatically be converted to mm.

2. Place a text frame on the page (as shown in *Chapter 2, Creating Text Frames and Adding Placeholder Text*) and highlight the text. At the bottom of the **Paragraph** panel, which can be found in the **Window** menu under **Type and Tables**, use the right-hand icon (marked *A* in *Figure 1.35*) to align to the baseline. Upon clicking this, you will find all the text vertically realigns, as needed, to sit neatly on the baseline grid that you created.

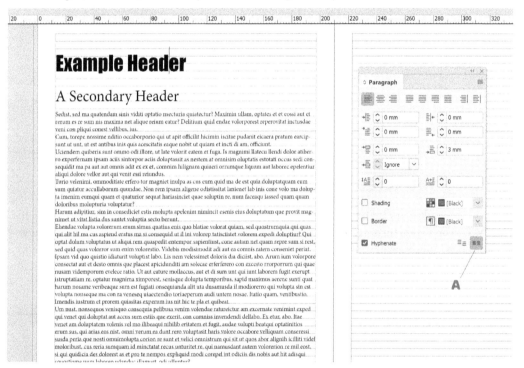

Figure 1.35: Text aligned to the baseline – the Align to baseline
button is in the Paragraph panel and marked A

3. Having looked at the baseline grid and how that can be used to ensure consistency with your vertical text alignment, let's now take a look at the document grid, which can be used to ensure your frames are lined up consistently throughout the document. To enable **Document Grid**, simply go to the **View** menu and select **Show Document Grid** under **Grids and Guides**.

4. As with the **Baseline Grid** settings, the **Document Grid settings** can also be changed in the preferences under **Grids**. Here you can adjust the following settings:

    - **Color** (*F* in *Figure 1.34*) – The color of the gridlines. We won't change this setting.

    - **Gridline Every** (*G* in *Figure 1.34*) – The distance between primary gridlines. We will set this to **25.4 mm**.

    - **Subdivisions** (*H* in *Figure 1.34*) – The number of secondary-level gridlines between the primary gridlines. We will set this to **8**.

5. Finally, to make maximum use of the document grid, you will want to enable the **Snap to Document Grid** option, which can be found in the **View** menu under **Grids and Guides**. Enabling this ensures that as you are moving objects around on your document, InDesign will attempt to automatically line them up with gridlines that you drag them close to.

> Tip
>
> If you feel items are snapping to gridlines either too soon or too late, open the **Preferences** panel (*Ctrl + K* for PC/*Cmd + K* for Mac), then under **Guides and Pasteboard**, change the value for **Snap** to **Zone** found in the **Guide Options** section.

Changing the screen mode

When you are working in InDesign, there are a number of different **screen modes** you can use to control what you see on the screen. For example, when you are laying out documents, you want to see frame edges, guides, and grids as it makes the process easier. Sometimes, though, you want to take a step back and hide all of these and get a better feel for how your final document will look, and switching modes can help you achieve this in a single click.

In this recipe, we are going to look at how to change the screen mode in order to ensure you work as efficiently as possible.

Getting ready

To complete this recipe, simply open InDesign on your system and open a new document with 12 pages, as shown in the *Creating a new document* recipe. It is also beneficial to add two or three text frames to the page, as shown in *Chapter 2, Working with Text in InDesign*.

How to do it…

To understand and move between the different screen modes in InDesign, follow these steps:

1. The standard mode you should be working in is the **Normal** mode, and this will allow you to see everything on the page with the exception of hidden items. Normal mode is enabled using the button at the bottom of the toolbar (marked *A* in *Figure 1.36*). This means you will see the edges of all your frames, guides, or grids that are on the page, as well as the bleed and slug areas.

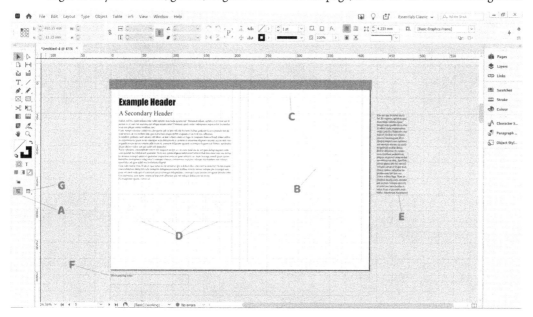

Figure 1.36: The view when working in Normal mode

You will also be able to see any items on the pasteboard next to your document; this can be seen in *Figure 1.36* where you can see grids (marked *B*), guides (*C*), frames (*D*), items on the pasteboard (*E*), and content in the slug area (*F*).

2. If you want to get a better idea of how your document will look when finished, switch from Normal mode to **Preview** mode, which can be chosen by clicking and holding the mouse button down on the button marked as *G* in *Figure 1.36*. The Preview mode hides all of these different indicators with the exception of any items that are selected.

In *Figure 1.37*, you can see the same document as in *Figure 1.36* but viewed in Preview mode. In this instance, only the right-hand frame of the middle row of four frames has been left selected, hence the edge of the frame can be seen still.

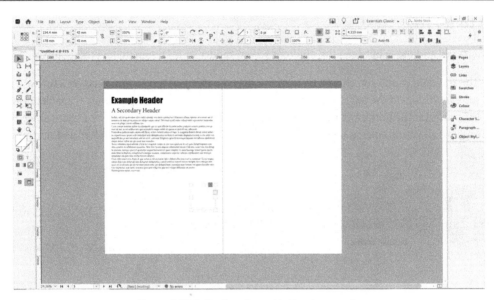

Figure 1.37: InDesign viewed in Preview mode

3. Grouped in with Preview mode, three other modes can be accessed by holding down the left mouse button (or by using the right mouse button) when clicking on the Preview mode button (marked *G* in *Figure 1.36*). The options are as follows:

    - **Bleed** – Similar to Preview mode but you can also see the bleed area and anything in it (this can be seen in *Figure 1.38*).

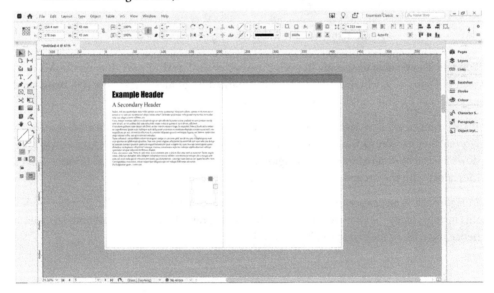

Figure 1.38: InDesign Preview in bleed mode

- **Slug** – This is like the preview mode but also includes the slug area.

- **Presentation** – This can be used to display your InDesign document in a similar fashion to a slide presentation, hiding all the guides, frames edges, and so on, and fitting your document to the screen (this can be seen in *Figure 1.39*). To exit **Presentation** mode, simply hit the *Esc* key on the keyboard.

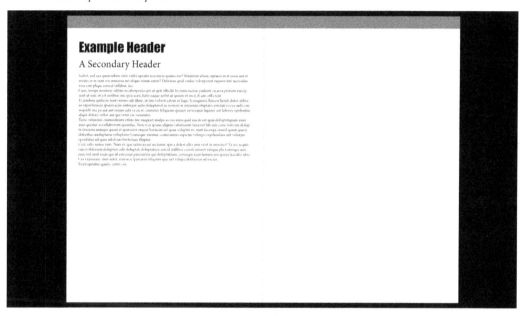

Figure 1.39: InDesign in Presentation mode

Tip
It can be tempting to work in Preview mode but try to avoid this temptation. While Preview mode looks more like your final document, you won't see any frame edges, guides, or other indicators and, as such, it can be easy to miss something while working on the document. Always work in Normal mode.

Enabling and changing rulers

Whether you are working with single pages or spreads (a single unified area made up of multiple pages), **Rulers** can be an incredibly useful tool for ensuring consistency in your designs and helping you position things accurately.

In this recipe, we are going to take a look at rulers and how to enable and disable them. We will learn to change the **units of measurement** that are used, control whether they run across each page individually or right across the entire spread, and even reset the origin point that the ruler starts measuring from.

Getting ready

To complete this recipe, simply open InDesign on your system and open a new document with 12 pages, as shown in the *Creating a new document* recipe.

You will also need to ensure the rulers are enabled; this can be done from the **View** menu, where you will see an option for **Show Rulers**. If the option says **Hide Rulers**, it means the rulers are already enabled.

How to do it...

To learn how to work with the rulers in InDesign, follow these steps:

1. When you are working with the rulers, it is useful to be able to use a unit of measurement that corresponds to your brand guidelines or to other measurements you plan to use. For example, if the brand guidelines have sizes in mm, it is unhelpful if the rulers are in inches. One option for changing the units of measurement is to do so through the InDesign preferences where the setting can be found under the **Units and Increments** section. This is under the **Edit** menu on a PC or the **InDesign** menu on a Mac.

2. A faster way to change this, however, is to simply right-click on the ruler and choose the units of measurement you wish to use. This can be done on both the vertical and horizontal ruler, and the changes made here will then be reflected in the preferences. Alternatively, you can just right-click on the point where the rulers join (marked *A* in *Figure 1.40*) to change both rulers together. You can see the options that appear when you right-click on the rulers in *Figure 1.40*.

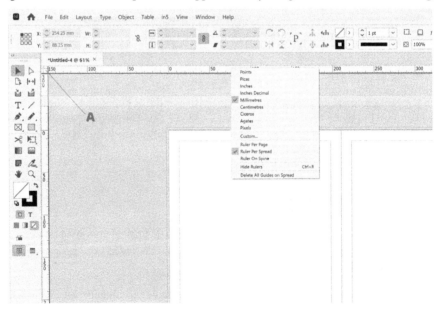

Figure 1.40: The options available when right-clicking on the rulers

3. Other useful options found when right-clicking on the rulers are as follows:

    *   **Ruler Per Page** – Ensures the starting point for the ruler is the top-left corner of each page, making it easy to count out from the side of each page

    *   **Ruler Per Spread** – Gives you a single ruler across the whole spread, so when working with facing pages, it will carry on counting across onto the right-hand page without restarting

    *   **Ruler On Spine** – Causes the counting to be done from the spine of the document, with positive numbers going right and negative numbers going left

    Which of these you use will depend on your particular documents; however, I often find **Ruler Per Page** can be handy for ensuring the distances on my right-hand pages mirror my left-hand pages.

4. One final useful trick when working with rulers is the ability to set the origin point of the ruler to a specific place. For example, you may want to count from the edge of a certain object on the page. To do this, simply click in the top-left corner of the rulers where the vertical and horizontal rulers meet (marked as *A* in *Figure 1.40*), and drag to the point on the document that you wish to count from. This will move the origin point to that place and the numbering on the vertical and horizontal rulers will adjust accordingly, and zero will be in line with the point you chose.

    To reset the origin point back to the top left of the page, simply double click on the point where the rulers join (marked *A* in *Figure 1.40*).

Applying and deleting guides

Guides are a great way to place items in precise positions on your page, ensuring that you maintain a consistent look and feel throughout your document, and if stipulated, can fully comply with your brand guidelines.

In this recipe, we will look at how to manually apply ruler guides to pages or spreads and adjust them, delete guides that are no longer needed, apply multiple guides at preset distances, enable snapping to guides and adjust the settings for this, and even add column guides on page setup.

Getting ready

To complete this recipe, simply open InDesign on your system and open a new document with 12 pages, as shown in the *Creating a new document* recipe.

How to do it...

To apply, delete, and snap to guides in InDesign, follow these steps:

1. **Ruler guides** can easily be applied to either a regular page or a parent page (the latter being useful for consistency across multiple pages). To insert a **vertical ruler guide**, simply click on the ruler on the left-hand side of the document and drag it onto the page where you would like the guide to be. If you don't see the rulers (marked *A* in *Figure 1.41*), simply click *Ctrl + R* (PC)/*Cmd + R* (Mac).

2. To fine-tune the positioning of the guide, click on it with the **Selection** tool and you can then adjust the numeric value of its position on the control panel at the top-left, as shown by item *B* in *Figure 1.41*.

Figure 1.41: InDesign document with rulers and a guide showing

3. To insert a **horizontal ruler guide**, simply drag down from the top ruler. If you drag onto a page, the guide will be across that page; however, if you are working with facing pages, dragging down onto the pasteboard at the side of the document will result in a guide that runs across the whole spread rather than only one page on the spread.

4. One final option here is to create a vertical and horizontal guide at the same time. This can be done by clicking on the corner where the vertical and horizontal rulers connect, and dragging onto the document, all while holding down the *Ctrl* (PC)/*Cmd* (Mac) key. If you do this without holding down the *Ctrl/Cmd* modifier key, bear in mind you are resetting the origin point for the rulers, as shown in the *Enabling and changing rulers* recipe, rather than creating guides.

5. If you have guides that you no longer wish to use on the document, simply select them with the **Selection** tool and hit *Delete* on the keyboard.

6. Having created individual guides manually, let's now look at creating multiple guides with a set distance between them. Under the **Layout** menu, select **Create Guides**, which is near the top of the menu. You will then see a dialog box where you can select the number of rows and columns, together with the gutter setting for the spacing between the rows and columns. You can also choose whether the guides are to fit the page or within the margins. In *Figure 1.42*, we can see a grid being created with 3 columns, 3 rows, a 5 mm gutter, and set to fit within the margins.

Figure 1.42: A document with a 3-column, 3-row grid being created

7. An alternative to ruler guides would be to use **column guides**. These can be created when you are starting a new document, in the **New Document** dialog box, but can also be created on existing pages. To do this, simply select the pages you wish the columns to apply to in the **Pages** panel, and then under the **Layout** menu, select **Margins and Columns**. This can be especially useful if you are working with multi-column layouts, as it offers a quick and easy way of generating guides in precise columns.

8.   Whether you are using ruler or column guides, you will almost certainly want to align your page content to the guides. In order to make this easier, simply go to the **View** menu, and under **Grids and Guides**, ensure that you have **Snap to Guides** ticked. With this turned on, you will find that as you are either creating or moving objects around on the page, they will jump into line with the guides when they come within 4 px of the guide. While 4 px is the **default snap zone**, you can alter this value to anything from 1 px to 36 px, but for most people, leaving this at 4 px will be the best option.

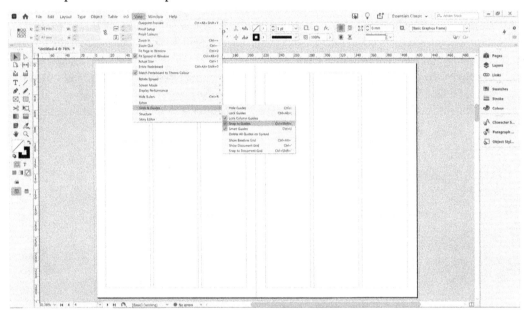

Figure 1.43: InDesign View menu showing Snap to Guides and Smart Guides options

9.   While enabling the **Snap to Guides** functionality, you may have also noticed an option for **Smart Guides** in the **View** menu under **Grids and Guides**. Turning this on will enable a set of intuitive auto guides that pop up and help you in aligning with other objects on the page. For example, when you drag a frame under another frame, you will notice green lines now appearing to tell you the left-hand edges, centers, or right-hand edges are lined up. You will also see magenta-colored pop-up guides now appearing when elements of your frame are in line with the horizontal or vertical center of the page. In *Figure 1.44*, you can see the smart guides showing that the left-hand side of the lower frame is now in line with the left-hand side of the upper frame while dragging the lower frame across the page.

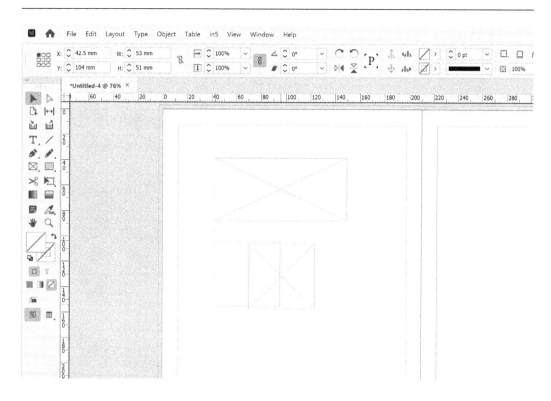

Figure 1.44: Smart guide showing left edges are perfectly aligned

2

Working with Text in InDesign

In this chapter, we will look at working with text in InDesign. You will learn how to create text frames in InDesign and use the built-in placeholder text, before going on to adjust the character formatting. We will change the font face and size, alter line spacing, and apply features such as superscript and subscript, as well as apply and customize underlines and strikethroughs.

We will then go on to apply paragraph formatting options, which—as the name suggests—apply to whole paragraphs of text, including aligning text within the frame, applying space after paragraphs, using drop caps, and even applying shading and borders to individual paragraphs.

Later in the chapter, we will go into using glyphs and special characters, which can come in useful for things such as accessing international characters, and then we will take a look at bulleted and numbered lists. Finally, we will look at threading multiple text frames together into a single story.

When you are laying out pages in InDesign, accurate formatting of your text is vital. It's an area that sometimes gets rushed, but done properly, it can ensure the document is easy to read, help to reinforce your brand identity, and assist in communicating information in ways that make it easier to consume.

The recipes we will cover in this chapter are listed here:

- Creating text frames and adding placeholder text
- Inserting special characters
- Working with glyphs
- Adjusting character formatting
- Applying superscript and subscript
- Using and formatting underlines and strikethroughs
- Applying a baseline shift

- Making paragraph formatting changes
- Applying shading and borders to paragraphs
- Working with bullets and numbering
- Threading text frames
- Using text frame options

Technical requirements

To complete this chapter, you will need a PC or Mac, with a copy of Adobe InDesign installed. An active internet connection is also recommended, as without it some features will not work. You should be comfortable navigating the InDesign interface as covered in *Chapter 1*—being able to open and close panels, for example.

Creating text frames and adding placeholder text

When you work within InDesign, everything sits inside a frame. In this recipe, we will look at how to create **text frames** in InDesign for including type within your documents. You will learn how to add **placeholder text** (sometimes known as **lorem ipsum** text), in order to give you some dummy content to work on.

We will then look at how to reposition your text frames, as well as how to resize the frames independently of the text and together with the text.

Getting ready

In order to complete this recipe, simply open InDesign on your system and create a new document with 12 pages, as shown in the *Creating a new document* recipe in *Chapter 1*.

How to do it...

In order to create text frames, add placeholder text, and then reposition and resize your text frames, follow these steps:

1. Select the **Type** tool from the toolbar, marked as *A* in *Figure 2.1*.
2. With the **Type** tool selected, simply click and drag (while holding the mousing button down) to create a rectangular shape on the page, at whatever size you stipulate. If you wish to create a perfect square rather than a rectangle, simply hold down the *Shift* key at the same time, and let go of the mouse before releasing the *Shift* key:

Figure 2.1: The InDesign toolbar

> **Tip**
>
> If you hold down the space bar during the frame creation process while still holding down the mouse button, you can temporarily move the mouse to reposition the frame. If you then release the space bar, you can continue creating your frame again.

3. When you create a new text frame, the cursor can be seen blinking at the top left of the frame, and if you type on the keyboard, you will see the text appear in the frame; however, we want to generate placeholder text automatically. To automatically generate placeholder text in the frame, either go to the **Type** menu and select **Fill with Placeholder Text** or you can right-click on the text frame with the mouse and select **Fill with Placeholder text** from the pop-up menu that appears.

4. Having created a text frame and added placeholder text you may now wish to reposition the text frame within your document. To do this, you will need to select the **Selection** tool, marked as B in *Figure 2.1*. Using this tool, you can now click on the text frame and drag it around within the document to the place you want it. In this instance, we will drag it so that the text frame touches the top and left margins, as shown in *Figure 2.2*:

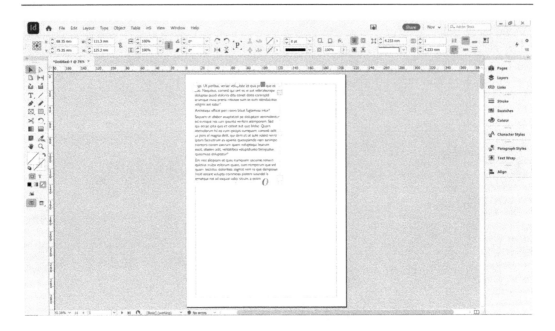

Figure 2.2: Repositioning a text frame so that it is aligned with the top and left margins

5.   Having repositioned the frame so that it aligns with the top and left margins, we will now resize
     it so that it also aligns with the bottom and right margins. To resize a text frame, select the frame
     with the **Selection** tool, and then move the cursor to hover over the bottom right-hand corner
     of the frame. As you do this, you should see the cursor change to two little arrows (shown by
     A in *Figure 2.3*). When you see the two little arrows, click and hold down the mouse button,
     then drag the corner of the frame down to align it with the bottom and right-hand margins
     before releasing the mouse button.

     While we have resized the object from the bottom-right corner, it is worth noting that you can
     resize objects in this way from any of the corners of the object, as well as from halfway through
     the four sides of the object:

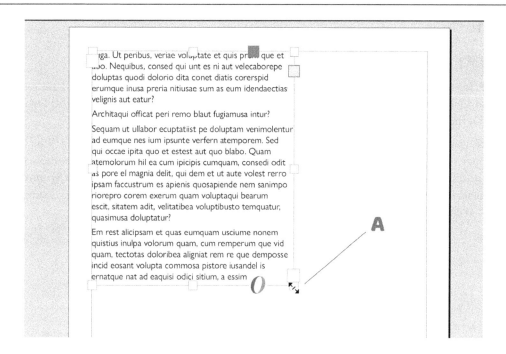

Figure 2.3: A text frame selected and ready to be resized

Inserting special characters

Occasionally, you might want to quickly insert characters such as copyright symbols or trademark symbols, which can't always be done easily through the keyboard. **Special characters** are a way of achieving this quickly and easily; in this recipe, we will show you how.

Getting ready

In order to complete this recipe, simply open InDesign on your system and create a new document with 12 pages, as shown in the *Creating a new document* recipe in *Chapter 1*. You will also need to add a text frame containing some text, as shown in the previous *Creating text frames and adding placeholder text* recipe.

How to do it...

In order to insert special characters, follow these steps:

1. Place the cursor where you want to apply the special character within your text. I am going to apply a registered trademark symbol after the name of the *Highlander* company, so I would put the cursor immediately after the company name.

2. Now, go to the **Type** menu and navigate to the **Insert Special Character** option. This will open another menu, where you should select **Symbols**, which in turn expands to show you the different symbol options, as shown in *Figure 2.4*. Click **Registered Trademark Symbol** to generate a registered trademark symbol within the text (subject to the current font containing that character within it):

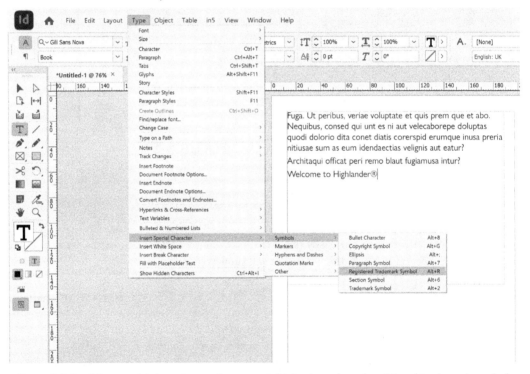

Figure 2.4: Applying special characters such as copyright, trademark, and registered trademark symbols

> **Note**
>
> Special characters also come in useful for generating page numbering, as shown in the *Generating page numbers in parent pages* recipe, which can be found in *Chapter 6*, and when creating story jumps, the recipe for which can be found in *Chapter 9*.

Working with glyphs

Glyphs are the individual symbols that together make up the content of a font face. They generally represent a single character (although can sometimes represent more than one character—for example, with ligatures), and the InDesign **Glyphs** panel gives you a useful window through which to both see and access characters that you may not typically find on your keyboard.

One common use of glyphs I encounter is for accessing **international character sets**—for example, when writing people's names that contain characters you generally won't find on a standard British or North American keyboard.

In this recipe, we will look at adding glyphs to your text frames as well as creating reusable glyph sets, which make it quick and easy to find the glyphs you commonly use when you are working.

Getting ready

In order to complete this recipe, simply open InDesign on your system and create a new document with 12 pages, as shown in the *Creating a new document* recipe in *Chapter 1*. You will also need to create a text frame containing some text, as shown in the *Creating text frames and adding placeholder text* recipe.

How to do it...

In order to use glyphs in your content, follow these steps:

1. Start by opening the **Glyphs** panel, which can be found under the **Window** menu under the **Type and Tables** section.

2. The **Glyphs** panel is where you can see all the glyphs within the fonts that you have installed. Here, you can switch to different fonts (marked as *A* in *Figure 2.5*), and then choose to show the entire font or a particular subset from the dropdown (marked as *B* in *Figure 2.5*) such as math symbols or currency symbols.

    It is worth noting that if you are trying to find a specific glyph, you can also search by name, Unicode value, or character/glyph ID using the search bar (marked as *C* in *Figure 2.5*):

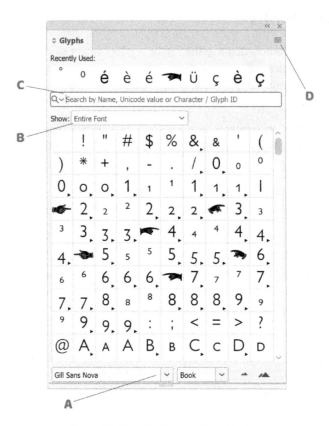

Figure 2.5: The Glyphs panel in InDesign

3. With our cursor in the place where we would like to insert our glyph, double-click on a glyph within the **Glyphs** panel, and it will be inserted at that position.

4. This allows us to easily insert a single glyph, but you might want to reuse a small group of glyphs on a regular basis, so let's have a look now at how to do that using glyph sets.

5. A **glyph set** is a reusable collection of glyphs, and it can be a good time saver when it comes to finding and using glyphs. To create a glyph set, click the **Glyphs** panel menu icon (marked as *D* in *Figure 2.5*) to open the **Glyphs** panel menu, and then select **New Glyph Set**. A small pop-up box will appear for creating your new glyph set; here, you can give your set a name and control how new glyphs will be added to the set, with the options being:

    • **Insert at Front**: Adds them at the top of the glyph set

    • **Append at End**: Adds them at the end of the glyph set

    • **Unicode Order**: Inserts them in the order they appear within the font

6. With our glyph set created, we now need to add some glyphs to it. To do this, simply find a glyph you like within the panel and right-click on it with the mouse. You will see a pop-up menu appear (marked as *A* in *Figure 2.6*) containing an **Add to Glyph Set** option, and you can then choose the glyph set you created earlier. Add a few glyphs to your glyph set, such as *é*, *ç*, or *è*, or, if you prefer, choose others:

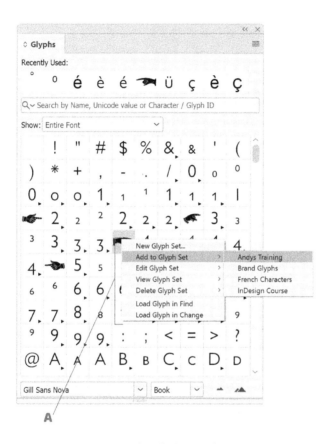

Figure 2.6: The Glyphs panel menu

7. If you are unable to right-click with the mouse, you can always select a glyph and then add it to the glyph set from the panel menu, marked as *D* in *Figure 2.5*.

8. Having created a glyph set and added some glyphs to it, we now need to view the glyph set rather than the whole font. This can be done from the dropdown marked as *B* in *Figure 2.5*. To view just the glyphs in your glyph set, scroll to the top of the list in the dropdown and choose your glyph set. To then go back to viewing the whole font—for example, to add more glyphs to the set—select **Entire Font**.

9. If you decide you want to delete a glyph set, just go to the panel menu and select **Delete Glyph Set**, then the name of the glyph set you wish to delete:

Figure 2.7: Glyphs panel docked for quick and easy access

> **Tip**
>
> I find keeping the **Glyphs** panel docked on the right as a small icon (shown in *Figure 2.7*) can be a quick and easy way to access it without taking up much space at all. Just one click on the icon expands it, and another click hides it again. For more details, see the *Opening and repositioning panels* recipe in *Chapter 1*.

Adjusting character formatting

Once you have some text on the page, it is important to know how to format it. In this recipe, you will learn how to change the **font face**, adjust the font size, and alter the spacing between lines (known as leading), as well as change the spacing between characters (known as kerning and tracking).

We will also learn a few hidden tricks in InDesign when it comes to changing numbers, some of which work in other Creative Cloud tools.

Getting ready

In order to complete this recipe, simply open InDesign on your system and create a new document with 12 pages, as shown in the *Creating a new document* recipe in *Chapter 1*. You will also need to add a text frame containing some placeholder text, as shown in the *Creating text frames and adding placeholder text* recipe.

How to do it...

In order to format your text using a variety of character formatting options, follow these steps:

1. Using the **Type** tool, click and drag to select some text within your text frame. With this text selected, look at the **Control** panel, shown as item *A* in *Figure 2.8*. If you don't see the **Control** panel at all, you can open it by clicking **Control** in the **Window** menu:

Figure 2.8: The InDesign interface showing the Control panel

The InDesign **Control** panel has two views, **Character** and **Paragraph**, and you can toggle between these using either of the two small icons marked as *B* in *Figure 2.8*. Switch to **Character** view now so that the top icon is highlighted, as seen in *Figure 2.8*.

2. Next, we will click the arrow next to the current font family marked as *A* in *Figure 2.9*. This will bring up the font options, where you can choose an alternative font family from a scrollable list. Depending on the font files installed, you may be able to expand the font family using the small arrow next to the font family name (marked as *B* in *Figure 2.9*). This will allow you to access variations of some fonts, such as **Regular**, **Bold**, or **Italic**. Select the font you wish to use now:

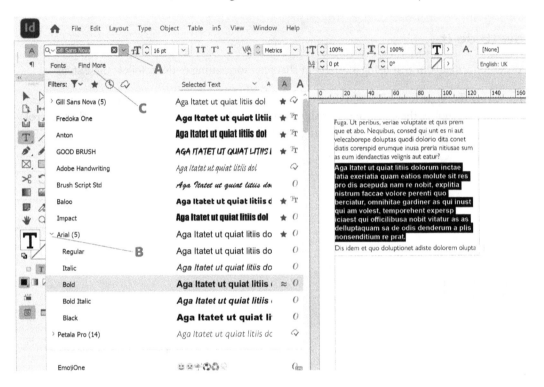

Figure 2.9: The font selection dropdown in InDesign

3. If you can't see the name of the font you want, you can always search for it in the Adobe **Fonts** library. This is a library of over 2,500 font families, which you can access as part of your InDesign subscription. To do this, click the **Find More** tab (marked as *C* in *Figure 2.9*) and you will see a list of **Adobe fonts**. To use one of these, click the cloud icon to the right of the font name, marked as *A* in *Figure 2.10*. When you click back on the **Fonts** tab, the font you activated should show up (occasionally, it can take a few seconds to synchronize):

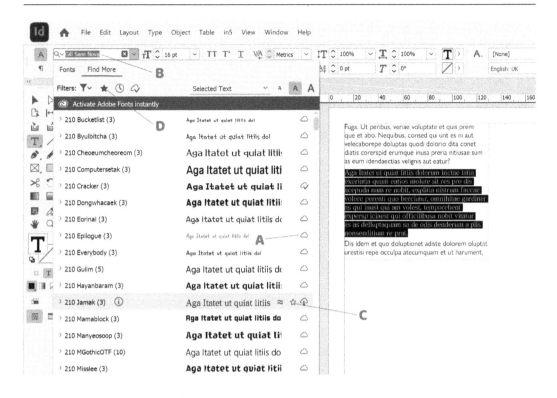

Figure 2.10: Find More fonts dialog

4. You can also search for a font by name; simply start typing the name in the search bar (marked as *B* in *Figure 2.10*), and all fonts with that text in the name will be listed.

> **Note**
>
> If you want to add your own font files to InDesign, you can copy the files into the **Fonts** folder in the InDesign installation directory, and they will show up when you restart InDesign.

5. If you work with a limited number of fonts (for example, to comply with brand guidelines), you might prefer to only see those fonts when opening the font selection dropdown. To do this, you can mark fonts as favorites by clicking the star icon, which shows up to the right of the font name when you hover over a font (marked as *C* in *Figure 2.10*), and then filtering to only show these favorites by clicking the **Filter by favorites** icon (marked as *D* in *Figure 2.10*).

6. Having now chosen the font you want to work with, we can change the **font size**. This can be done by clicking the dropdown for font size (marked as *A* in *Figure 2.11*), which is positioned to the right of the font family dropdown. You can choose from the preset sizes or just type a number straight into the font size box itself. My personal favorite method is clicking the font size

box and then using the up and down keys on the keyboard to adjust the size 1 pt at a time. If you hold down the *Shift* key while using the arrows, it changes the size in 10-pt increments instead:

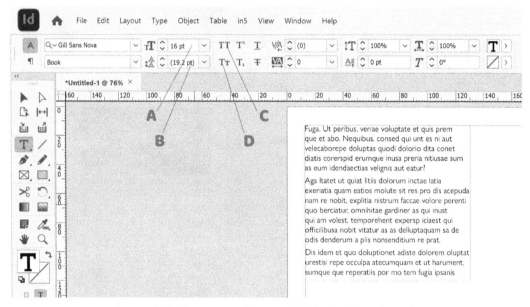

Figure 2.11: Character settings on the InDesign Control panel

---

Tip

When you are working in number boxes in Adobe tools, such as the font size box, many of them let you do sums. For example, typing 2 + 3 and hitting *Return* will set the size to 5 pt. You can use the +, -, *, and / characters for doing plus, minus, multiply, and divide calculations.

---

7.   The next setting we want to adjust is the **Leading** setting, marked as *B* in *Figure 2.11*. **Leading** is the space between the lines in paragraphs; by default, it is set to **Auto**, which means as the font size changes, so does the leading. When set to **Auto**, the leading is always set to 120% of the font size, and this will be a good setting for most of your text. However, in this instance, we want to space the lines out further though, without changing the font size. To do this, just increase the leading value either by selecting a new value from the dropdown or by using any of the other methods for changing numbers that are shown in *step 6*.

8. Having chosen a font face and adjusted the size and leading, we now want to turn the text into **capitals**. You have two **Caps** options available in the **Control** panel:

    •   The first is the **All Caps** button marked as *C* in *Figure 2.11*; this will turn all the selected letters into uppercase letters.

    •   The second option is the **Small Caps** button marked as *D* in *Figure 2.11*.

In this instance, we are going to apply the **All Caps** method to the first three words (marked as *A* in *Figure 2.12*) by selecting them and clicking the **Small Caps** button, then on a new line apply small caps to some text (marked as *B* in *Figure 2.12*), again by selecting it and hitting the **Small Caps** button. Your content should now look something like that shown in *Figure 2.12*:

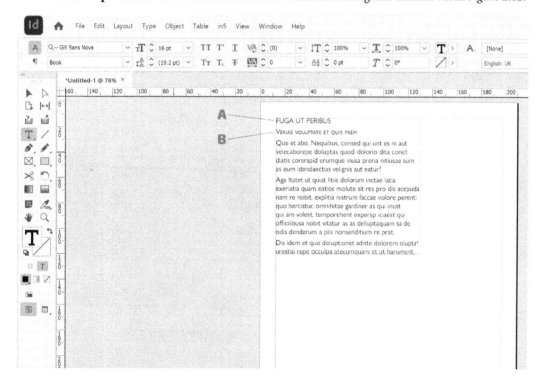

Figure 2.12: Text frame with the first line in all caps, then the second line in small caps

If small caps are available within the font face, InDesign will use these, but if not, InDesign will simulate small caps. You can control what scale InDesign uses for simulating small caps in the **Preferences** panel (*Ctrl* + *K* (PC)/*Cmd* + *K* (Mac)), under **Advanced Type**, marked as *A* in *Figure 2.13*:

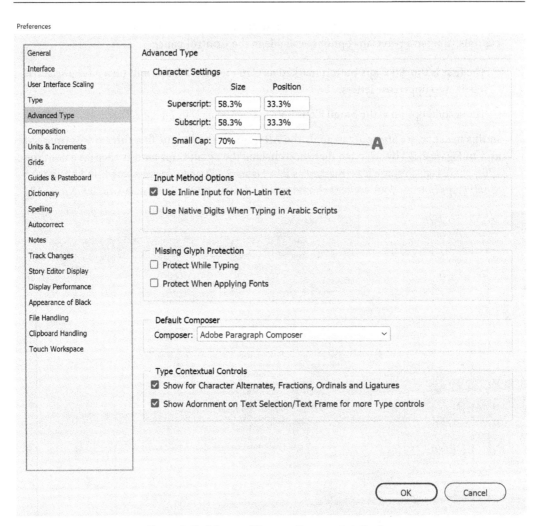

Figure 2.13: Advanced Type preferences in InDesign

9.   Having set the first three lines to **All Caps**, we now want to adjust the spacing between the second and third letters on that line. To do this, we will use the **Kerning** property, which is used to adjust the spacing between two individual characters. Click to place the cursor in between the second and third letters of the first line, then click into the **Kerning** box, marked as *A* in *Figure 2.14*. Use the up and down arrows on the keyboard to increase or decrease the kerning. In our case, we will set the value to **20**.

As with the other number boxes, you can use the *Shift* key to move in larger increments, type numbers directly into the box, or select a value from the dropdown.

> **Note**
>
> In the **Kerning and Tracking** dropdown, you will see options for **Metric** and **Optical**, which are automatic kerning options, based on either the font design (metric) or the character shapes (optical). We are using manual kerning (and tracking) here, which is based on a percentage of the current font size being used.

10. Moving on to the second line, we are now going to set the spacing between the characters for the whole of the second line using **Tracking**. Select the whole line and click into the **Tracking** box, marked as *B* in *Figure 2.14*. Again, use the arrows to adjust the spacing until the second line is extended to the width of the frame, as shown by *C* in *Figure 2.14*:

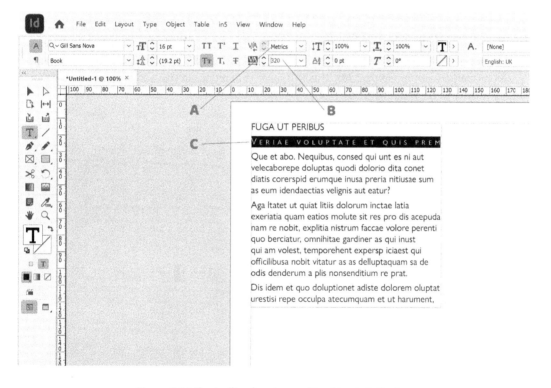

Figure 2.14: Controlling kerning and tracking in InDesign

Applying superscript and subscript

Whether you are adding in a trademark or copyright symbol, putting ordinals on dates, creating chemical formulae, or producing mathematical equations, **Superscript** and **Subscript** can be useful tools to get your text looking the way you want.

Getting ready

In order to complete this recipe, you need a document open containing a text frame that you wish to adjust. If you don't already have this, you can create a new document with 12 pages, as shown in the *Creating a new document* recipe in *Chapter 1*. You can then add a text frame, as shown in the *Creating text frames and adding placeholder text* recipe. Finally, you will need the **Control** panel set to show character formatting rather than paragraph formatting options, as shown in *step 1* of the *Adjusting character formatting* recipe.

How to do it...

In order to use superscript and subscript to fine-tune your text, follow these steps:

1. In your text frame, add the following text: The 1st of January.

2. We are going to start by superscripting **st** in **1st**, so select **st** and then click the **Superscript** icon (marked as *A* in *Figure 2.15)*. This will cause **st** to reduce in size and be positioned higher up relative to the other text:

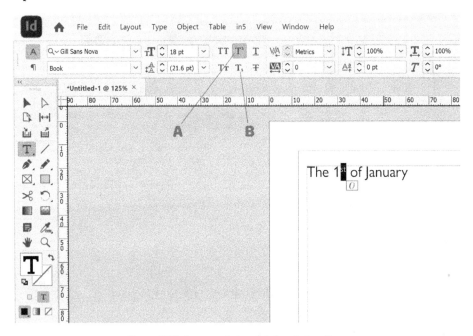

Figure 2.15: Superscript and Subscript options

3. On the next line in the text frame, we will add the following text: **Water is H2O**.

4. Now, select the number **2** in **H2O** and click the **Subscript** button (marked as *B* in *Figure 2.15)* to apply subscript to this, resulting in the number **2** dropping lower down.

Using and formatting underlines and strikethroughs

Underlines and strikethroughs can be a great way to draw attention to content in a paragraph, but why stick to the default formatting? In this recipe, we will show you how to apply **underlines** and **strikethroughs**, and then subsequently change the formatting to match your exact needs. You will even learn a neat little trick using underlines to create a highlighter pen effect.

Getting ready

In order to complete this recipe, simply open InDesign on your system and create a new document with 12 pages, as shown in the *Creating a new document* recipe in *Chapter 1*. You will also need to add a text frame containing some placeholder text, as shown in the *Creating text frames and adding placeholder text* recipe. Finally, you will need the **Control** panel set to show character formatting rather than paragraph formatting options, as shown in *step 1* of the *Adjusting character formatting* recipe.

How to do it...

In order to use and format underlines and strikethroughs on your text, follow these steps:

1. Select the text that you would like to apply your underline to and click the **Underline** button marked as *A* in *Figure 2.16*. The text will now have a thin black line below it, as marked by *B* in *Figure 2.16*:

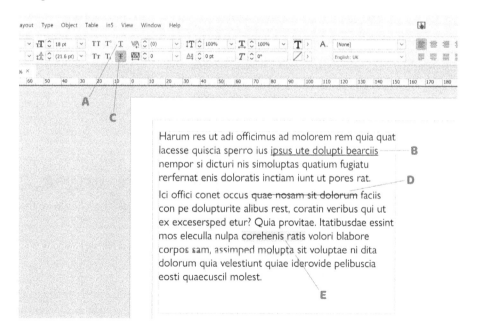

Figure 2.16: Underline and strikethrough options in InDesign

2. We now want to change the formatting of the underline, so with the text still selected, hold down *Alt* (PC) or *Option* (Mac) and click the **Underline** button again. This will bring up the **Underline Options** dialog box (shown in *Figure 2.17*):

Figure 2.17: Underline Options dialog box

3. Before adjusting any settings, make sure to check the **Preview** checkbox within the dialog box, and now you can adjust any of the following settings and see the changes live on the document:

- **Weight**: This determines the thickness of the underline or strikethrough line
- **Type**: Lets you choose from a list of preset underline or strikethrough styles
- **Offset**: A bit like the **Baseline Shift** property (*see the next recipe*), this applies an adjustment to the strikethrough or underline relative to the baseline of the text it is applied to
- **Colour**: The color of the underline or strikethrough
- **Tint**: Increase the lightness of the chosen color by increasing the white content
- **Gap Colour**: If you choose a type that includes gaps, this lets you apply a color to those gaps
- **Gap Tint**: Increase the lightness of the gap color by increasing the white content

In this instance, we will change the **Colour** setting to blue and adjust the **Weight** setting to **2 pt** to make the line a little thicker.

> **Tip**
>
> If you would like to create a highlighter pen effect, simply apply an underline, switch the **Colour** setting to yellow, make the **Offset** value a negative number until the line is vertically in the middle of the text, and then increase the **Weight** value until it is the same height as the text. You can simply adjust the offset to fine-tune the positioning. See the text marked as *E* in *Figure 2.16*.

4. Next, we will apply a strikethrough. Select the text that you would like to apply your strikethrough to and click the **Strikethrough** button (marked as *C* in *Figure 2.16)*. The text will now have a thin black line through the middle of it, as marked by *D* in *Figure 2.16.*

5. We now want to change the formatting of the strikethrough, so with the text still selected, hold down *Alt* (PC) or *Option* (Mac) and click the **Strikethrough** button again, which will bring up the **Strikethrough Options** dialog box, which will look very similar to the **Underline Options** dialog box.

6. Again, you will need to check the **Preview** checkbox in the dialog box to see any changes, and you can then adjust the settings for the strikethrough in the dialog box.

On rare occasions, I come across somebody who, for a variety of reasons, can't *Alt-/Option*-click on the buttons to bring up the **Underline Options** and **Strikethrough Options** dialog boxes. If you encounter this, you can also open the **Options** dialog box from the drop-down menu at the top right of the InDesign program window, as marked by *A* in *Figure 2.18*:

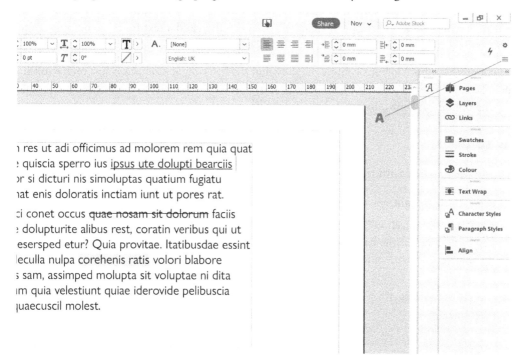

Figure 2.18: Alternative method of accessing strikethrough and underline options

Applying a baseline shift

Sometimes you just want to quickly move a few characters, or even a word or two, up or down relative to the rest of the text. It might be special characters such as copyright or trademark symbols that don't quite sit where you'd like, or maybe your bullets need a bit of tweaking, or it could just be things such as fractions that you'd like to smarten up a bit.

When working in InDesign, your text all sits on an invisible line called the baseline, and this baseline can be moved up and down. Using InDesign's **Baseline Shift** feature, you can easily move the baseline for one or more characters, in effect moving the characters up or down relative to the rest of the text in that frame. In this recipe, we are going to look at how you can achieve this.

Getting ready

In order to complete this recipe, you need a document open containing a text frame that you wish to adjust. If you don't already have this, you can create a new document with 12 pages, as shown in the *Creating a new document* recipe in *Chapter 1*. You can then add a text frame containing some placeholder text, as shown in the *Creating text frames and adding placeholder text* recipe.

Add a copyright symbol to your content, as shown in the *Inserting special characters* recipe in this chapter. You will need the **Control** panel set to show character formatting rather than paragraph formatting options, as shown in *step 1* of the *Adjusting character formatting* recipe.

How to do it...

In order to use **Baseline Shift** to fine-tune your text, follow these steps:

1. Select the copyright symbol that you added to your text.
2. Click into the **Baseline Shift** box (marked as *A* in *Figure 2.19*) and use the up arrow on the keypad to increase the baseline shift value. You will see the copyright symbol is now moving up relative to the rest of the text:

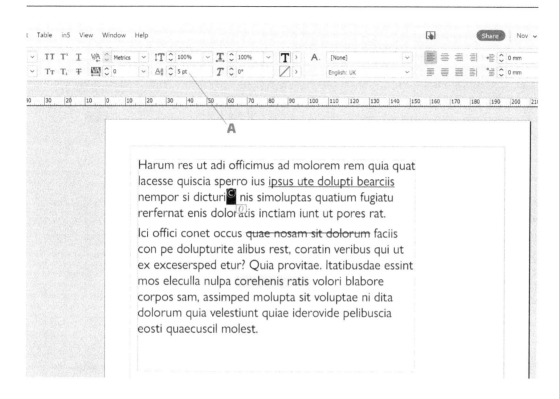

Figure 2.19: Baseline Shift option on the Control panel

Having increased the baseline shift value and pushed the character up relative to the other text, we are now going to reverse this.

3.   When selecting characters that have a baseline shift applied, you must select them on the original line the text was written on, and not the line it is now positioned on (as shown in *Figure 2.20*). Do this now with the text you selected in *step 1* and set the baseline shift back to **0**:

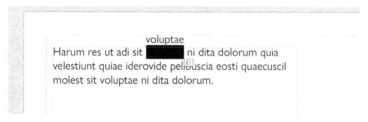

Figure 2.20: Example of text with baseline shift applied and baseline selected

Making paragraph formatting changes

When it comes to working with paragraphs of text in InDesign, there are a number of formatting options that apply to whole paragraphs rather than individual characters. These options allow you to align your text in a particular way, configure spacing between different paragraphs, create interesting effects with drop caps, and even turn hyphenation on and off. In this recipe, we will have a look at applying these paragraph formatting options.

Getting ready

In order to complete this recipe, simply open InDesign on your system and create a new document with 12 pages, as shown in the *Creating a new document* recipe in *Chapter 1*. You will also need to add a text frame large enough to contain a few paragraphs of text, as shown in the *Creating text frames and adding placeholder text* recipe. Finally, you will need the **Control** panel set to show paragraph formatting rather than character formatting options, as shown in *step 1* of the *Adjusting character formatting* recipe.

How to do it...

In order to use the **paragraph formatting options** in InDesign, follow these steps:

1. Select some text in one of the paragraphs within your text frame. You don't need to precisely select the whole paragraph, as the paragraph formatting tools will affect any paragraph that you have selected even a single character within.

2. With your text selected, you should see an option on the left of the **Control** panel to set the **horizontal alignment of the text**. On the top row, you have the option to align the paragraph to the left (*A* in *Figure 2.21*), center (*B* in *Figure 2.21*), or right (*C* in *Figure 2.21*). Alternatively, you can justify your text with the last line aligned left (*D* in *Figure 2.21*), with the last line center-aligned (*E* in *Figure 2.21*), or with all lines together (*F* in *Figure 2.21*). In our case, we will align the text to the left (*A* in *Figure 2.21*):

> **Note**
> **Justify** is when InDesign attempts to align the text to reach both sides of the frame; as a result, there are no ragged edges to the lines, which all line up.

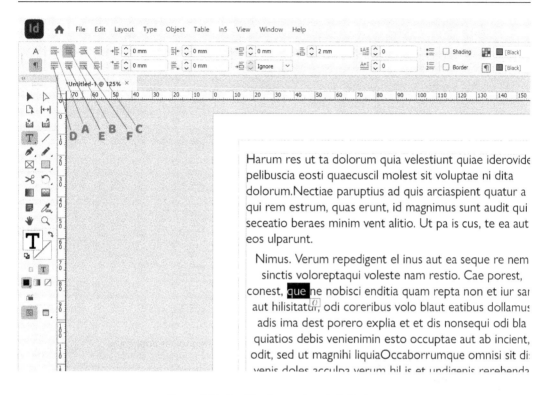

Figure 2.21: Justification options in InDesign

In addition to the preceding options, there are two more justification options that you should be aware of, albeit you may not use them as frequently: one aligns toward the spine (marked as *A* in *Figure 2.22*), and the other aligns away from the spine (marked as *B* in *Figure 2.22*). These become more relevant when you are working on documents with facing pages, such as magazine layouts, where the spine is the black line between the left- and right-hand pages.

In *Figure 2.22*, you can see a document with two text frames, both aligned toward the spine. Note how the alignment behaves the opposite on the left-hand page to the right-hand page:

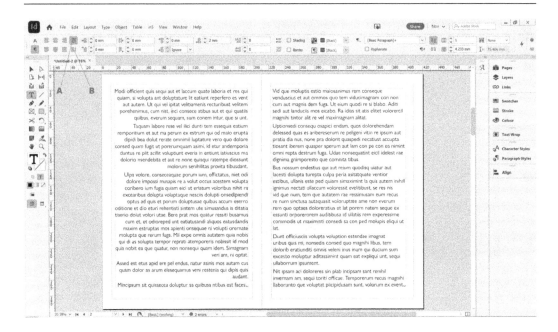

Figure 2.22: An example of two frames with text aligned toward the spine

3. Having aligned our text to the left, we now want to **indent** the second paragraph slightly by 10 mm. To do this, select part of that paragraph and type **10 mm** in the **Left Indent** box (marked as *A* in *Figure 2.23*).

    In addition to the **Left Indent** option, you will see other indent options available here: **First Line Indent** (marked as *B* in *Figure 2.23*), **Right Indent** (marked as *C* in *Figure 2.23*), and **Last Line Right Indent** (marked as *D* in *Figure 2.23*):

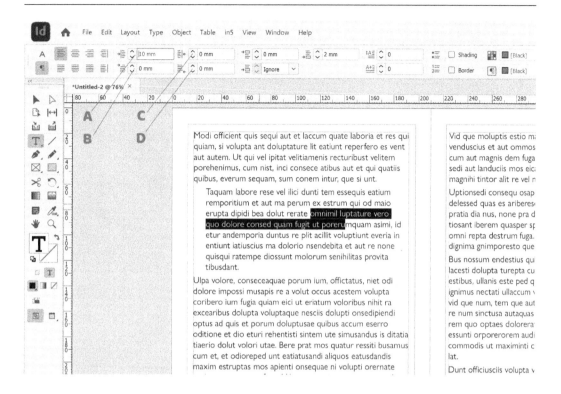

Figure 2.23: Paragraph indent options in InDesign

4. When working with multiple paragraphs of text, putting a little space either after or before your paragraphs can make it easier for the reader, not to mention visually more appealing. To do this, select all your text and apply **3 mm** to the **Space After** option (marked as *A* in *Figure 2.24*). This will add **space after** each paragraph—in this case, 3 mm.

If you prefer to add **space before** each paragraph, simply use the **Space Before** option, marked as *B* in *Figure 2.24*, instead.

In *Figure 2.24*, you can see a text frame on the left-hand page with 3 mm of space applied after each paragraph. On the right-hand page, the exact same text is shown with no space applied after each paragraph, for comparison:

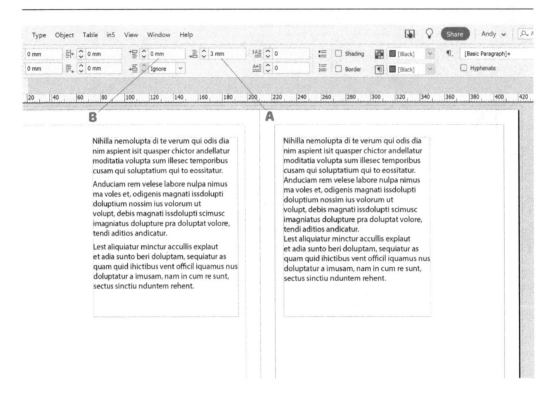

Figure 2.24: Space Before and Space After options in InDesign

5. Having now formatted our text with some space after each paragraph, we want to apply a decorative effect called **drop caps**. Click into the paragraph that you would like to apply drop caps to, and then select the number of letters you would like to use (marked as *A* in *Figure 2.25*) and the number of lines you would like them to drop over (marked as *B* in *Figure 2.25*). In our case, we will drop two letters over three lines, as shown in *Figure 2.25*:

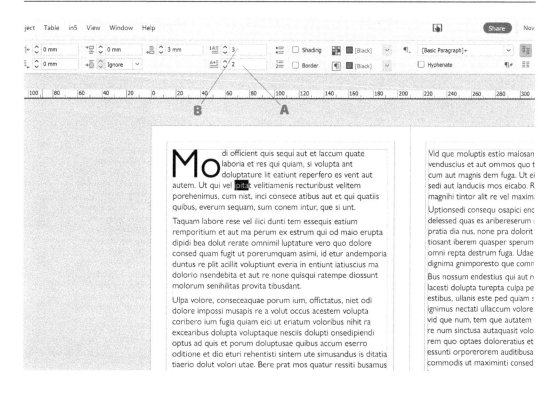

Figure 2.25: Applying drop caps in InDesign

> **Note**
>
> Drop caps have been used for a very long time, with numerous examples dating back as far as the 15th century and even earlier.

6. Having applied our alignment, indents, space after, and drop caps, we want to finish off by controlling hyphenation on the text. **Hyphenation** is when longer words are effectively split in the middle and part of the word pushed onto the next line. In InDesign, you can turn hyphenation off or on by simply selecting your text and then deselecting or selecting the **Hyphenate** checkbox on the **Control** panel (marked as *A* in *Figure 2.26*):

Figure 2.26: Disabling hyphenation in InDesign

Tip

When working on a document in InDesign, switch to the **Type** tool, and with no text selected, disable the **Hyphenation** checkbox (marked as *A* in *Figure 2.26*). You will now find hyphenation is automatically disabled for all new text frames within that document. If you switch to the **Type** tool and deselect the **Hyphenation** checkbox in InDesign when no document is open, it is now disabled by default for every new document you create going forward. This method of setting default properties in InDesign also works for a wide range of other properties, from **Font Face** and **Swatches** to **Paragraph Styles** and **Character Styles**.

Applying shading and borders to paragraphs

A more recent feature in InDesign is the ability to apply shading and borders to paragraphs, and it can be a useful option for everything from creating cut-out coupon effects to simply highlighting a single paragraph of text within your story. In this recipe, we will look at how to apply borders and shading, as well as how to customize the settings to ensure you can make the most of the feature.

Getting ready

In order to complete this recipe, simply open InDesign on your system and create a new document with 12 pages, as shown in the *Creating a new document* recipe in *Chapter 1*. You will also need to add a text frame large enough to contain a few paragraphs of text, as shown in the *Creating text frames and adding placeholder text* recipe. Finally, you will need the **Control** panel set to show paragraph formatting rather than character formatting options, as shown in *step 1* of the *Adjusting character formatting* recipe.

How to do it...

In order to use the **paragraph shading** and **borders** options in InDesign, follow these steps:

1. Select some text within one of your paragraphs. Then, in the **Control** panel, check the **Shading** box, marked as *A* in *Figure 2.27*:

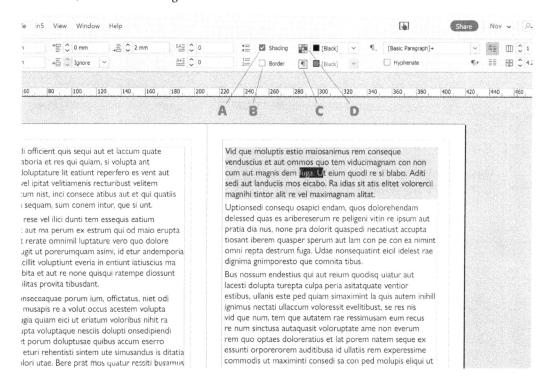

Figure 2.27: Paragraph shading and border options on the Control panel

2. By default, the shading is applied as a shade of gray, but let's customize this. With the paragraph still selected, simply hold *Alt* (PC) or *Option* (Mac) down and click on the small icon to the right of the word **Shading** on the **Control** panel (marked as *D* in *Figure 2.27*). This will bring up the **Paragraph Borders and Shading** dialog box shown in *Figure 2.28*.

There are a range of options here that may be of interest (if you want to see changes happen as you make them, remember to enable the **Preview** checkbox, found at the bottom of the shading options dialog box):

- **Colour**: Sets the color for the shading. We will set this to **Cyan**.

- **Tint**: Allows you to lighten the color by increasing the white content. We will set this to 20%.

- **Corner Size and Shape**: Lets you change the shape of the corner and set the size for each corner. To change corners individually, click the small link symbol (marked as *A* in *Figure 2.28*); to change them all together again, click the link symbol again. Set them to **0**.

- **Offsets**: This allows you to push the shading out beyond the edge of the text. You can either change the sides individually or all together, by clicking the link symbol in the middle of the **Offsets** group, just as we did previously with the **Corner Size and Shape** options. Change these to 2 mm.

- To the right of the offsets are options for **Top Edge**, **Bottom Edge**, and **Width**. These allow you to fine-tune what the shading is being applied relative to. We won't adjust these at this time.

- The **Clip To Frame** option allows you to prevent shading from extending beyond the edge of the frame. We will enable this here.

- **Do not Print or Export** does exactly what it says, preventing the shading from being printed or included when you export documents:

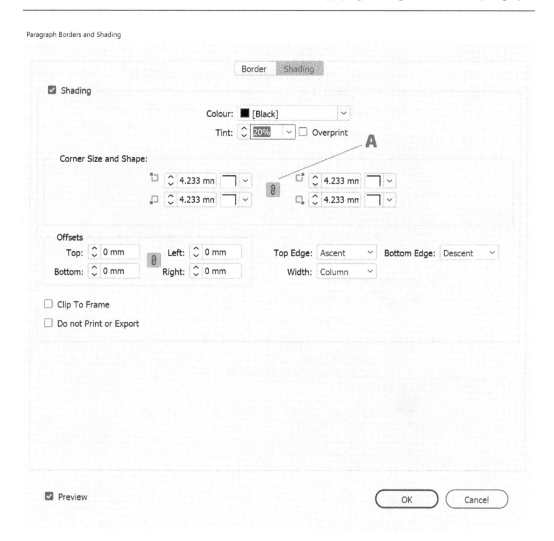

Figure 2.28: Paragraph shading options in InDesign

Note

If you can't edit the settings by *Alt* (PC) or *Option* (Mac) and clicking on the icon, you can also access these from the drop-down menu at the top right of the InDesign interface, as shown previously at the end of the *Using and formatting underlines and strikethroughs* recipe.

3. Having applied your shading if you wish to disable it, simply uncheck the shading checkbox. In this instance, we will do this in order to look at borders more clearly.

4.   Next, select part of a paragraph and click the **Border** button on the **Control** panel (marked as B in *Figure 2.27*. This will apply a thin 1 pt black border around the selected paragraph.

5.   Next, we want to customize our paragraph border, so hold down the *Alt* (PC) or *Option* (Mac) key and click the icon to the right of the word **Border** on the **Control** panel (marked as C in *Figure 2.27*). This will bring up the paragraph border options, which can be seen in *Figure 2.29*:

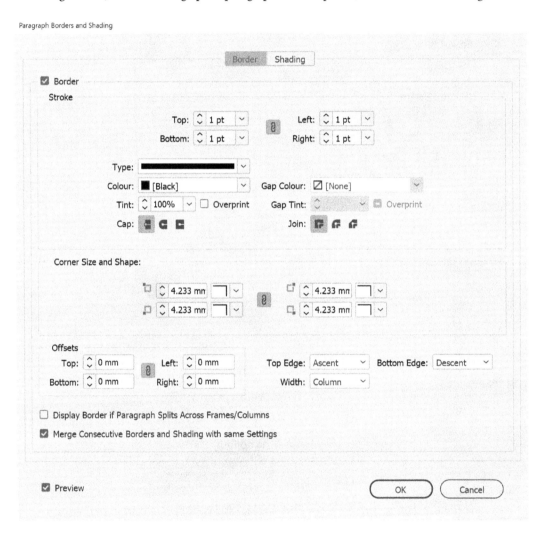

Figure 2.29: Paragraph Border and Shading options

The border options are more extensive than the shading options, and in addition to the properties listed in *step 2* also include the following options:

- **Top**, **Bottom**, **Left**, **Right**: These let you control the stroke width on the different sides. As with the **Corner Size and Shape** options in *step 2*, the link icon allows you to control whether all 4 numbers change together or individually. We will set this to **4 pt**.

- **Type**: Lets you choose the type of border from a range of preset border types. We will choose **Dashed (3 and 2)**.

- **Gap Color** and **Gap Tint**: If you have applied a border type with gaps, such as a dashed line, these properties allow you to set a color and tint (lightness) for the gap. We will leave this unchanged.

- **Cap**: This property allows you to control the look of the dash ends. We will select **Rounded**.

- **Join**: Allows you to control the look of the corners where the sides join. We will choose **Rounded**.

The final two options toward the bottom of the dialog box are:

- **Display Border if Paragraph Splits Across Frames/Columns**: Turning this on will result in frames that split across multiple frames or columns having a border on all four sides. If it is off, the border will not be shown at the point where the frame splits.

- **Merge Consecutive Borders and Shading with same Settings**: If this is selected border and shading effects will be merged together, where consecutive paragraphs have the exact same border and shading settings. An example of this can be seen in *Figure 2.30*:

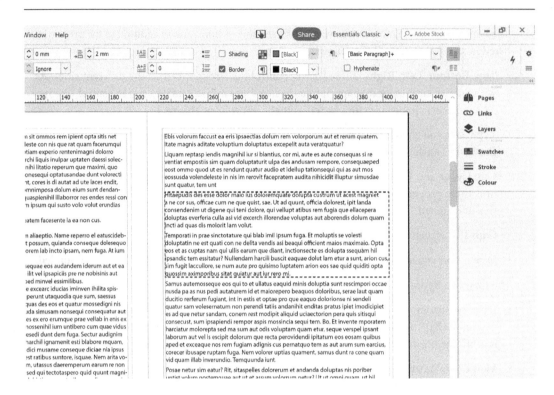

Figure 2.30: Paragraph borders merged across two paragraphs

Working with bullets and numbering

Using bulleted and numbered lists can be a great way to organize your content and present it in a way that is often easier to interpret and understand. As an added benefit, it often results in a cleaner and less crowded layout that is aesthetically more pleasing.

In this section, we are going to look at how to apply **bullet points** and **numbering** to your content. We will look at customizing the formatting of these lists, creating **custom bullet points**, switching to different numbered list types, fine-tuning the positioning of the bullets and numbers, restarting and continuing numbering, and even converting a numbered list into editable numbers.

Getting ready

In order to complete this recipe, simply open InDesign on your system and create a new document with 12 pages, as shown in the *Creating a new document* recipe in *Chapter 1*. During this exercise, you will also need to be able to create text frames and add placeholder text, as shown in the *Creating text frames and adding placeholder text* recipe.

How to do it...

In order to use bulleted and numbered lists, follow these steps:

1. Start by creating a text frame and typing in some content that we can use for our lists. I have typed a list of fruit, as shown in *Figure 2.31*:

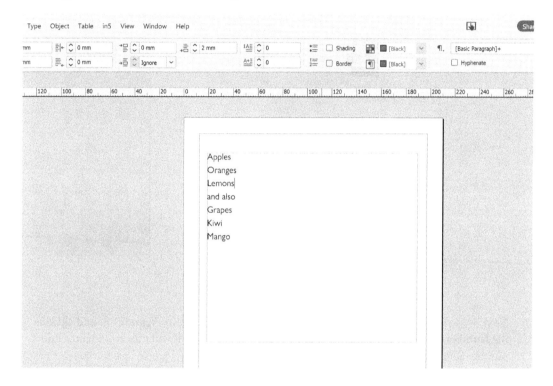

Figure 2.31: Text ready to be converted into lists

2. Next, select the first three lines of text and click on the **Bulleted list** icon, marked as *A* in *Figure 2.32*. If you don't see the list icons, just make sure you are looking at the paragraph formatting options and not the character formatting options (switching between the two is covered in the *Adjusting character formatting* recipe from the first chapter).

   You will see these items are now indented, and a bullet point is added in front of each item (as marked by *B* in *Figure 2.32*):

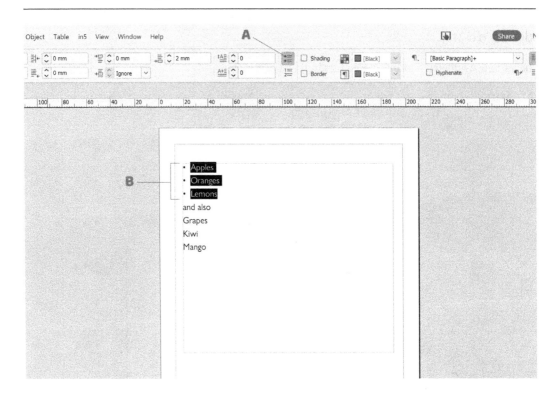

Figure 2.32: Bullets applied in InDesign

3. Next, we will select the last three lines of the text (marked as *A* in *Figure 2.33*) and click on the **Numbered list** icon (marked as *B* in *Figure 2.33*). These items will now be indented and a number added in front of each of the selected items:

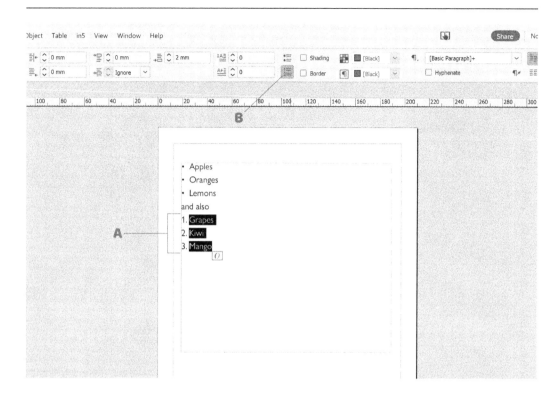

Figure 2.33: Numbered list applied in InDesign

4. The bullets and numbers that are generated pick up basic formatting such as font face or size from the first character of the paragraph they are applied to, but this can be customized. To do this, select the text that has the bullets applied (in this case, the first three lines), and while holding down the *Alt* (PC)/*Option* (Mac) key, click once again on the **Bulleted list** icon. This will bring up the **Bullets and Numbering** dialog box (shown in *Figure 2.34*), showing the bulleted list formatting options:

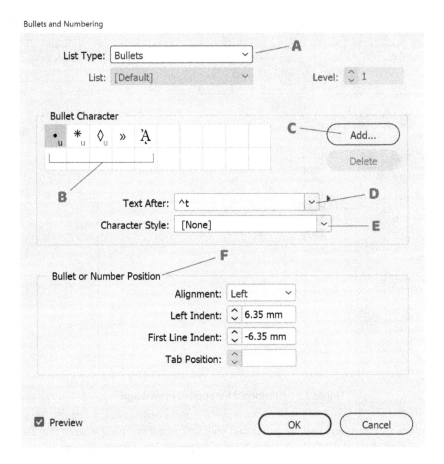

Figure 2.34: Bullets and Numbering dialog box showing bulleted list options

Let's review the options:

> **Note**
>
> If you wish to see changes live on the page as you make them, remember to check the **Preview** checkbox at the bottom of the dialog box.

- **List Type** (*A* in *Figure 2.34*): This will default to **Bullets** as that's what we have applied here, but it can be changed to either **Numbers** or **None** if you wish to change the list type. We will leave it set at **Bullets**.

- **Bullet Character** (*B* in *Figure 2.34*): Here, you can quickly choose from previously used bullet characters. We will ignore this on this occasion as we haven't previously used bullets.

- **Add** (*C* in *Figure 2.34*): Click to use characters from your fonts as bullets.

When clicked, an **Add Bullets** popup appears (shown in *Figure 2.35*), and you can select characters from any of your fonts. You can change the font family (marked as *A* in *Figure 2.35*), and I would recommend checking the **Remember Font with Bullet** checkbox (marked as *B* in *Figure 2.35*) to ensure the bullet character isn't affected if you change the font face used for the bullet items. When you have chosen a character, click **OK** (marked as *C* in *Figure 2.35*) to add that character and close the box, or click **Add** (marked as *D* in *Figure 2.35*) if you would like to continue selecting additional characters before closing the box:

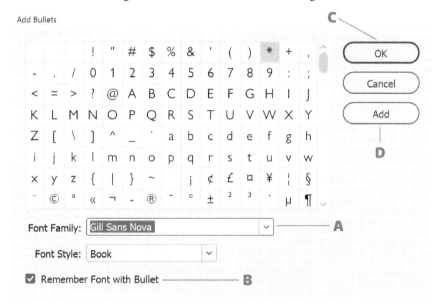

Figure 2.35: Add Bullets dialog box

- **Text After** (*D* back in *Figure 2.34*): Lets you control what comes immediately after the bullet points, which by default is a tab character, but you can change this if you wish. We will leave this unchanged.

- **Character Style** (*E* in *Figure 2.34*): Allows you to apply a character style to your bullets (these are covered in *Chapter 8, Formatting with Paragraph and Character Styles*). We will leave this unchanged too.

Finally, under the **Bullet or Number Position** section (*F* in *Figure 2.34*), you can fine-tune the bullet position. We won't adjust these settings in this instance, but they include the following:

- **Alignment**: Allows you to align the bullets to the left, center, or right of the bullet area.

- **Left Indent**: Controls how far the bullets are indented from the left.

- **First Line Indent**: Allows you to adjust the indent on the first line. If you have a single bullet point that contains multiple lines of text, it can be useful to increase the left indent value and also reduce the first line indent value so that the bullet character itself isn't directly in line with the subsequent lines of text.

- **Tab Position**: Adjusts the space between the bullets and the content of the list.

5. Having formatted the bulleted list, we can now format the numbered list. Select the last three lines that we applied the numbered list to in *step 3*, and while holding down the *Alt* (PC)/*Option* (Mac) key, click once again on the **Numbered List Icon** (marked as *B* in *Figure 2.33*). This will bring up the **Bullets and Numbering** dialog box seen in *Figure 2.36*, this time showing the numbered list options:

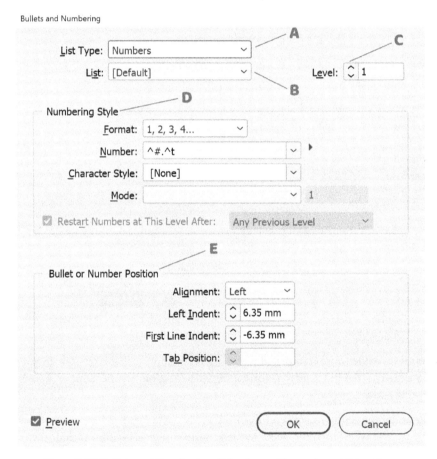

Figure 2.36: Bullets and Numbering dialog box with numbered list options

The dialog box now contains the following options:

- **List Type** (*A* in *Figure 2.36*): As seen in the previous step, except this will now default to **Numbers**; we will leave this unchanged.

- **List** (*B* in *Figure 2.36*): Allows you to create a defined list that can be identified by name to distinguish it from other lists. This can be useful for continuing numbering across multiple stories or across documents within a book. We will leave this set to [**Default**].

- **Level** (*C* in *Figure 2.36*): Lists can have multiple levels. Enabling this feature gives you more advanced control over the continuation and restarting of numbering at different levels (see the *Note* information box at the end of this recipe).

- Under the **Numbering Style** section (*D* in *Figure 2.36*), you will see settings for the following:

  - **Format**: Select from a range of predefined numbering types, including numbers, letters, Roman numerals, and more.

  - **Number**: Here, you can customize the appearance of the number. We will leave this set to the default setting.

  - **Character Style**: Allows you to apply a character style to your list (these are covered in *Chapter 8*, *Formatting with Paragraph and Character Styles*). We will leave this set to [**None**].

  - **Mode**: Allows you to either continue your numbering or restart at a defined number. We won't change this setting.

- The **Bullet or Number Position** options (*E* in *Figure 2.36*) are all exactly the same as discussed previously in *step 4*, and there is no need to change these in this instance.

Having created both numbered and bulleted lists, we will next look at how to replace the bulleted list with numbers, which continue across both parts of the list.

6. Select the text that was previously formatted with bullets and click the **Numbered List** icon (marked as *B* in *Figure 2.33*). While this changes it into a numbered list, the numbers have reset back to 1 for the second part of the list (as shown in *Figure 2.37*):

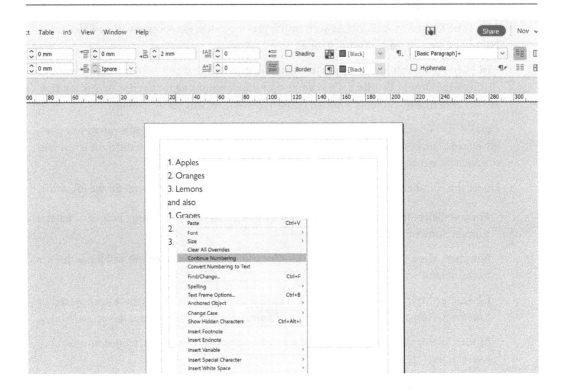

Figure 2.37: Numbered list with numbering restarting

In order to have the numbering continue from the previous part of the list, place the cursor on the first line of the second part of the list then right-click, bringing up the options shown in *Figure 2.37*. The fifth option listed is **Continue Numbering**, and you should select this. If you change your mind and wish to have the numbering restart at 1 here, simply repeat this process, and you will find the option that previously said **Continue Numbering** now says **Restart Numbering** instead, as the numbering is already being continued.

> **Note**
>
> The **Continue Numbering** and **Restart Numbering** options can also be accessed through the **Type** menu under **Bulleted and Numbered Lists**.

There's more...

For more advanced customization of lists, including working with multi-level lists, please see the following article: `https://www.highlander.co.uk/blog/advanced-lists-in-indesign`.

Threading text frames

In some documents, you might only require a few lines of text—for example, with single-page flyers—but there are many other documents where you have many pages of content such as magazines, books, large reports, tender documents, and so on. In such documents, it can be really useful to thread your text frames together into a single story. This enables all the frames in the story to function as one, allowing text to flow from one frame to another seamlessly as though it were in a single frame.

In this recipe, we are going to learn how to **thread text frames** together, view text threads to check the order of flow, add frames to a story, remove frames from a story without losing the text, and change the flow of the story, as well as thread text using the semi-auto and auto flow modifiers.

Getting ready

In order to complete this recipe, simply open InDesign on your system and create a new document with 12 pages and facing pages enabled, as shown in the *Creating a new document* recipe in *Chapter 1*. Facing pages are not required for threading text frames, but they will make it easier for us to demonstrate how text threads can run across multiple pages. During this exercise, you will also need to be able to create text frames and add placeholder text, as shown in the *Creating text frames and adding placeholder text* recipe.

How to do it...

In order to work with text threading in InDesign, follow these steps:

1. Scroll down to a double-page spread, and on the left-hand page, create a text frame that fills the page, then fill it with placeholder text. Now, make the frame shorter by dragging up from the handle at the bottom of the frame (marked as *A* in *Figure 2.38*) to roughly the halfway point, and you will notice there is a small box at the bottom right of the frame that turns red (marked as *B* in *Figure 2.38*). This is the out port for the frame; when it goes red, it means you have what is called **overset text**. Overset text is text that still exists; it hasn't been deleted, but it isn't visible because there is no space currently available to display it within the text frame at its current size.

2. Next, add a new text frame at the top of the right-hand page in which we can continue our story. Switch to the **Selection** tool and select the text frame we created in *step 1*. Now, click once on the out port for that frame (marked as *B* in *Figure 2.38*), which happens to be red as we currently have overset text, and you will notice the cursor changes at this point. Move your cursor over to the right-hand page and click into the new frame you just created at the top of the right-hand page:

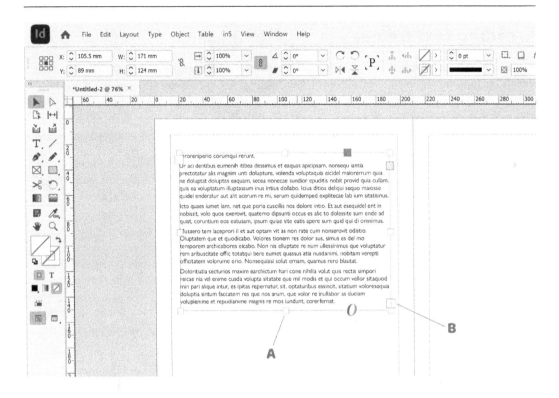

Figure 2.38: Text frame with overset text before threading

> **Note**
>
> When threading text frames, be sure to just click once on the out port, then click into the new frame. I often see people try to click and drag the out port across onto the new frame, which doesn't work.

I am using facing pages (as shown in the *Creating a new document* recipe in *Chapter 1*) in order to make this easier to show here, but that isn't necessary for this to work. You could just as easily thread 2 frames together that are 20 or 30 pages apart.

3. Having done this, you will see the text that was previously overset now appears over in the second frame, but you may not immediately see the actual text threads (a line between the two frames, marked as *A* in *Figure 2.39*). Go to the **View** menu, and toward the bottom, you will see a flyout menu called **Extras**. Within this menu, select **Show Text Threads**. If the option here says **Hide Text Threads**, it means they are already enabled and you don't need to select it:

Figure 2.39: Two frames threaded with Show Text Threads enabled

If you don't immediately see the threads, one reason might be you don't have any of the frames in the story selected. Simply switch to the **Selection** tool and click on one of the frames, and you should then see the threads.

If you *still* aren't seeing the threads, one other reason for this could be you are working in **Preview** mode rather than **Normal** mode, in which case you should switch to **Normal** mode (which is what you should generally use when working), as shown in the *Change the screen mode* recipe in *Chapter 1*.

4. Having added an existing frame to the story, we would now like to create a third frame as part of the story, as shown in *Figure 2.40*. Switch to the **Selection** tool and select the top-right frame that we created in *step 2*. Now, click once on the out port, which may or may not be red, and then click and drag on the document exactly where you would like the new frame to be created. This new frame will be automatically included in the story:

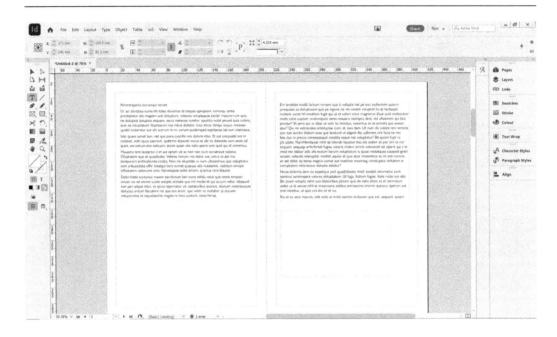

Figure 2.40: Adding a new frame at the end of a story

5. Having threaded together three frames, create a fourth frame below the first frame on the left-hand page.

6. We now want to insert this frame into the middle of the story, and it makes the most sense to do so after the top-left frame but before the right-hand frames in this instance. This would result in the story flowing down the left-hand page before then continuing down the right-hand page.

   To insert the new frame into the middle of the story, select the frame that you would like to insert it after—in this case, the frame at the top of our left-hand page—and click the out port of that frame (marked as *B* in *Figure 2.38*). Your cursor will now change, and you should click into the new frame, which will cause InDesign to insert the frame at that point in the story, continuing the rest of the story afterward.

   In *Figure 2.41*, I have added the bottom-left frame to the story, causing the threads to update and include the bottom-left frame in the middle of the story:

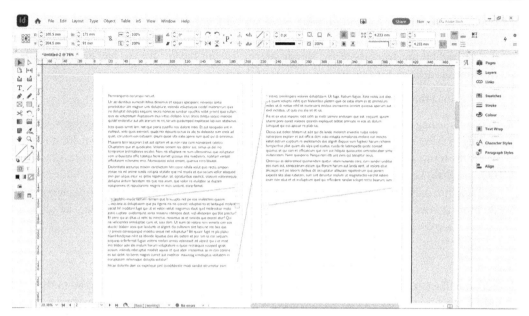

Figure 2.41: Inserting a text frame into the middle of an existing story

7. Having now threaded four frames over two pages, we might decide we would like the second page to be an independent story from the first page. To achieve this, we need to first break the thread at the end of page 1. To do this, select the last frame you want in the first story, and then double-click the out port of that frame. This breaks the threading at that point, with any text beyond that being brought into that second frame as overset text.

8. You now have a story on page 1 with two frames, and a second story on page 2 with two frames; however, all the text is currently in the first story, with nothing in the second. To correct this, we will place the cursor at the end of the first story, and on the keyboard hit *Ctrl* (PC)/*Cmd* (Mac) + *Shift* + *End*. This is a useful shortcut that selects all text from that point through to the end of the story, including overset text. Having selected the text, you can select **Cut** from the **Edit** menu to cut it out, and then click into the new story and select **Paste** from the **Edit** menu to copy the text into the new frames.

In order to reverse this, let's now thread our second and third frames back together by clicking the out port in frame 2 and clicking into frame 3.

Advanced quick tip

Would you like to remove a single frame from a story and have it retain its own text, while automatically reflowing the other frames? If so, go to the **Window** menu, and under **Utilities** open the **Scripts** panel. In the **Scripts** panel, expand the **Application** section, then expand the **Samples** section, followed by the **JavaScript** section. Select the frame you want to separate out and now double-click the BreakFrame.jsx extension listed in the panel. Job done.

9. One thing you might want to do when working with stories is completely remove a single frame from a thread while retaining its content within the story. In this case, we will remove the top-right frame from the story. Simply select it and hit *Delete*, and you will find that while the frame is deleted, the text remains as part of the story.

    Having done this, let's now delete all but the first frame.

10. When threading frames, sometimes you might want to thread multiple frames together without having to select each frame and click on the out port to individually thread them. To do this, select the frame and click the out port ready to thread your text. Now, hold down the *Alt* (PC)/*Option* (Mac) key while creating your new frame. When you let go of the mouse button, you will find not only has the text threaded into the new frame, but you can carry straight on and do more frames, and as long as you keep holding down the *Alt* (PC)/*Option* (Mac) key, it will let you keep creating new frames, all of which are threaded.

> **Tip**
>
> Would you like to unthread a whole story? Simply select a frame in the story and go to the **Window** menu, then under **Utilities**, open the **Scripts** panel. In the **Scripts** panel, expand the **Application** section, then expand the **Samples** section, followed by the **JavaScript** section. Select a frame in the story, and now double-click the `SplitStory.jsx` extension listed in the panel.

Using text frame options

The text frame options can be a useful feature when working with text in InDesign. You can use them to format your text into multiple columns within a frame, apply **inset spacing** around the edge of a frame, **align your text vertically** within a frame, and lots more.

In this recipe, we will look at some of the more useful features of this dialog box, along with some practical examples of how these are applied.

Getting ready

In order to complete this recipe, simply open InDesign on your system and create a new document with 12 pages, as shown in the *Creating a new document* recipe in *Chapter 1*. During this exercise, you will need to be able to create text frames and add placeholder text, as shown in the *Creating text frames and adding placeholder text* recipe.

How to do it...

In order to use **text frame options**, follow these steps:

1. Let's start by adding a large text frame and filling it with placeholder text. Select the frame, then under the **Object** menu, choose **Text Frame Options**. You can also access the feature by right-clicking on the text frame and then choosing **Text Frame Options**. This will bring up the **Text Frame Options** dialog box, as seen in *Figure 2.42*:

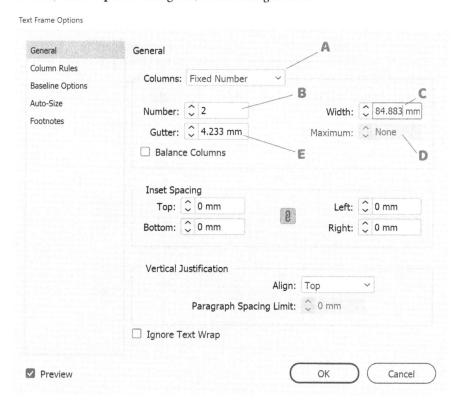

Figure 2.42: Text Frame Options dialog box

2. In the **Columns** dropdown (marked as *A* in *Figure 2.42*), you have a choice of three options:

   - **Fixed Number**: Lets you decide the number (marked as *B* in *Figure 2.42*) of columns to use

   - **Fixed Width**: Lets you set the width (marked as *C* in *Figure 2.42*) value of columns, and InDesign automatically adjusts the text frame width to compensate

- **Flexible Width**: Allows you to set a maximum width (marked as *D* in *Figure 2.42*) value for your columns, and InDesign will add as many equally sized columns as possible without exceeding this width on each column

There is also a **Gutter** option here (marked as *E* in *Figure 2.42*) that allows you to control the space between the columns (we won't be using this, but it's worth knowing).

In our case, we will choose **Fixed Number** and set the number value to **2**, and then click **OK**. This will result in the text frame having two columns of equal width.

3. Next, we will delete a bit of text from the second column, and you will notice the columns automatically become unbalanced, with the first column being full while the second column is now half empty, as shown in *Figure 2.43*. To resolve this, bring up the **Text Frame** options again, as shown in *step 1*, and click the **Balance Columns** checkbox (marked as *A* in *Figure 2.43*), and InDesign will attempt to balance out the columns to a similar length, as seen in *Figure 2.44*:

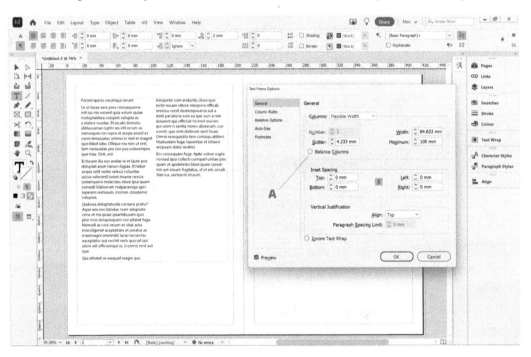

Figure 2.43: Balancing columns in Text Frame Options

4. When working on multiple-column layouts, you might want to add column rules into the gutter separating the columns. In the **Text Frame Options** dialog box, you will see down the left-hand side there are five options to choose from, and with our text frame set to two columns, we will now click on the second of these options, which is **Column Rules** (marked as *A* in *Figure 2.44*), and this will bring up the **Column Rules** options.

Column rules are decorative dividing lines that can be inserted between the columns, and if you choose to use these, you can format them to the style you prefer. You can turn column rules on and off with the checkbox at the top of the dialog box (marked as *B* in *Figure 2.44*):

Figure 2.44: The Column Rules options within the Text Frame Options dialog box

The settings available when creating column rules will include the following:

- **Rule Length |Start** and **End**: How far from the top and bottom of the column the rule starts and ends (marked as *C* in *Figure 2.44*)

- **Horizontal position | Offset**: Allows you to move the column rule from left to right in relation to the column gap (marked as *D* in *Figure 2.44*)

- **Stroke Weight**: How thick the column rule is going to be (marked as *E* in *Figure 2.44*)

- **Type:** The type of line used for the column rule; you can choose here from a range of decorative presets (marked as *F* in *Figure 2.44*)

- **Colour**: Lets you set the color of the line (marked as *G* in *Figure 2.44*)

- **Tint**: Lets you adjust the lightness of the color by changing the white content (marked as *H* in *Figure 2.44*)

- The **Overprint** box is for creating effects within print and can be left disabled when creating standard column rules

In our case, we will leave the column rules with all default settings except for **Type**, which we will change to a **Dashed (3 and 2)** line.

5. Another useful feature of the **Text Frame Options** feature is the inset spacing. Let's create another small text frame, but this time give the frame a background color. To do this, simply select the frame with the **Selection** tool, and then click the **Fill** box on the **Control** panel (marked as *A* in *Figure 2.45*) and change the **Colour** value to **Cyan**:

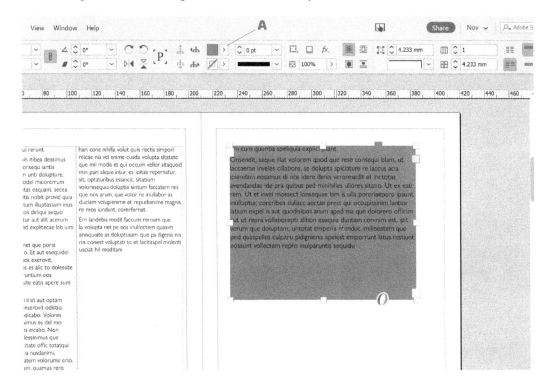

Figure 2.45: Changing the frame fill color

6. Now, right-click on the text frame and open **Text Frame Options** (or, if you prefer, do so from the **Object** menu). In the **General** section, you will see an **Inset Spacing** option with entry boxes for **Top**, **Bottom**, **Left**, and **Right**. All four are linked by default, so changing one will change the others. If you wish to unlink them, you can click the small link symbol (marked as *A* in *Figure 2.46*); in this instance, we won't do so. We will increase the indent value (marked as *B* in *Figure 2.46*) to 6 mm, and you should now have an area of padding around the edge of your frame (marked as *C* in *Figure 2.46*).

If you don't see the changes immediately, just check that the **Preview** checkbox is checked (marked as *D* in *Figure 2.46*):

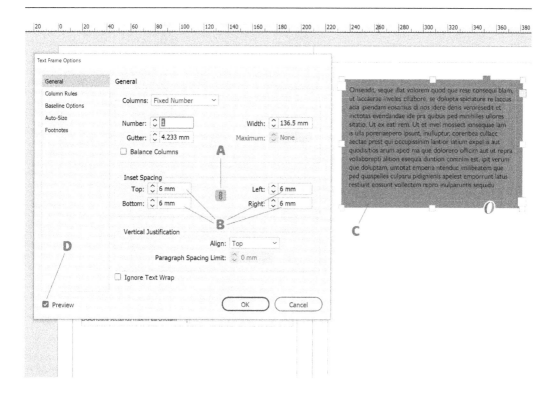

Figure 2.46: Changing inset spacing in Text Frame Options

See also

In this chapter, we have looked at working with text in InDesign; however, if you are regularly formatting text, I would strongly advise learning to use paragraph and character styles as this will save you a significant amount of time. They are covered in *Chapter 9, Formatting with Paragraph and Character Styles.*

3
Creating and Using Tables

In this chapter, we will learn how to create a blank table that can be used to display a wide range of data. We will learn how to generate a new table from existing text, select and reorder rows and columns, insert and delete rows and columns, and create alternating strokes and fills. As this chapter progresses, we will merge and split cells, convert a body row into a header row, and even include images within our tables.

Before continuing, it is worth noting that tables won't perform calculations in the same way as traditional spreadsheet software – they are very much a design feature. That said, they can be a powerful way to communicate often complex content in a way that is easy to interpret and understand.

The recipes we will cover in this chapter are as follows:

- Inserting and creating tables
- Converting text into tables
- Adjusting Table Setup
- Selecting and moving rows and columns
- Inserting and deleting rows and columns
- Creating alternating strokes and fills
- Merging, unmerging, and splitting cells
- Converting a row into a header or footer and setting repeating options
- Including images in tables
- Adjusting cell options

Technical requirements

To complete this chapter, you will need a PC or Mac, with a copy of Adobe InDesign installed.

In particular, for the *Including images in tables* recipe, an active internet connection is needed.

Inserting and creating tables

Tables can be a useful feature in your designs for presenting content in a way that is very quick and easy to interpret, allowing readers to analyze and compare data easily. In this recipe, we are going to look at both adding a blank table to an existing text frame, as well as how to create a table straight on the page within a dedicated frame. You will choose this frame depending on whether your table is free-standing or mixed in with the document's existing text.

Getting ready

To complete this recipe, simply open InDesign on your system and create a new document with 12 pages, as shown in the *Creating a new document* recipe in *Chapter 1, Customizing the InDesign Interface and New Document Settings*.

How to do it...

To create new tables within your document, follow these steps:

1. First, create a blank text frame within your document, as shown in the *Creating text frames and adding placeholder text* recipe in *Chapter 2*. Now, put your cursor inside the text frame by clicking on it with the **Type** tool.

    Where you position the cursor will control where the table is generated, so bear this in mind if you are working with text frames that already contain existing text and are planning to insert a table into the middle of the text.

2. Next, go to the **Table** menu and choose **Insert Table**; this will bring up the **Insert Table** dialog box, as shown in *Figure 3.1*. If this option says **Create Table**, it means you haven't positioned your cursor within the text frame:

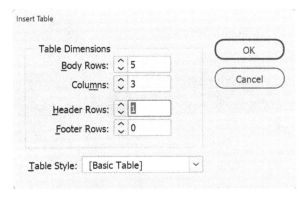

Figure 3.1: The Insert Table dialog box

The **Insert Table** dialog box contains the following options:

- **Body Rows**: This is the number of rows in your table. In our case, we will set this to **5**.

- **Columns**: This is the number of columns in your table. We will set this to **3**.

- **Header Rows**: These are a special type of row that contain several useful properties that aren't available with **Body Rows**; for example, **Header Rows** can be set to repeat automatically across columns, frames, or pages. Additionally, it is ignored for formatting purposes when alternating fills and strokes are applied to a table. We will set the value to **1** here.

- **Footer Rows**: These are similar to **Header Rows** except they are positioned at the bottom of the table. We will set this to **0** as we are not including any **Footer Rows** here.

- **Table Style**: At a more advanced level, you can create reusable table styles that control the formatting of your tables. We will just leave this set to the default value, **Basic Table**.

Having set the properties, you can now click **OK** to generate your table.

3. Having generated a table within an existing text frame, we would now like to create a table without first generating a text frame. To do this, we must first deselect the existing table and frame with the *Ctrl* (Windows)/*Cmd* (Mac) + *Shift* + *A* shortcut command.

4. Now, go to the **Table** menu; you will notice that the first option has been renamed **Create Table**. Select this option; you will see the **Create Table** dialog box. This is the same as the **Insert Table** dialog box shown in *Figure 3.1*, except it says **Create Table**.

5. Set the following settings for your table:

   - **Body Rows**: 4

   - **Columns**: 3

   - **Header Rows**: 1

   - **Footer Rows**: 0

   - **Table Style**: **Basic Table**

6. Now that you've chosen your settings, click **OK** and then drag with your mouse exactly to where you would like your table frame to be created. InDesign will now create a frame and automatically insert your new table into it, sized to fill the frame.

Converting text into tables

Sometimes, you might already have the text that you want to include in a table, and it can make more sense to simply generate a table straight from the text. In this recipe, we will take a look at doing this with the **Convert Text to Table** feature, and the options that you will encounter when using this handy feature.

Getting started

To complete this recipe, simply open InDesign on your system and create a new document with 12 pages, as shown in the *Creating a new document* recipe in *Chapter 1*. You will also need to add a text frame, as shown in the *Creating text frames and adding placeholder text* recipe in *Chapter 2*, though there is no need to insert placeholder text into the frame here.

How to do it...

To convert text into a table within your document, follow these steps:

1. Create a blank text frame on your document.

2. Now, when converting text into a frame, you are effectively telling InDesign to recognize a particular character as a column or row separator. This is usually the comma, tab, or paragraph return, although other characters can be used too.

    With that in mind, type the following sample content into the text frame:

    ```
    Name,Age,Telephone
    Bob,55,0800 123 4567
    Wendy,21,0800 156 0777
    Melissa,33,0345 123 456
    Sami,44,0345 987 654
    ```

    After each line, make sure you hit the *Return/Enter* key to include a paragraph return (as opposed to a line break).

3. Highlight the text, and then, in the **Table** menu, select **Convert Text to Table**. This will bring up the **Convert Text to Table** dialog box, as shown in *Figure 3.2*:

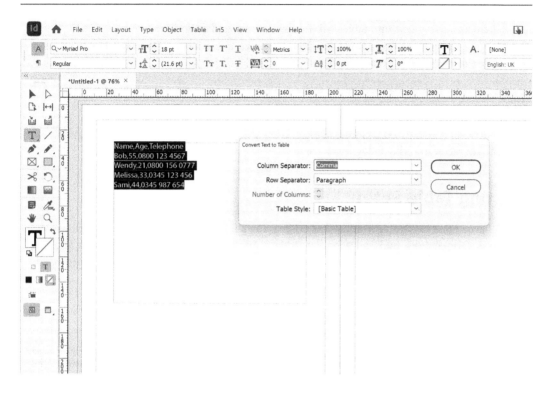

Figure 3.2: The Convert Text to Table dialog box

4. The **Convert Text to Table** dialog box contains the following options:

    *   **Column Seperator**: This is where you can choose the character that is being used to separate the columns. In our case, we will set this to **Comma**.

    *   **Row Separator**: This is where you can choose the character that is being used to separate the rows. In our case, we will set this to **Paragraph** since we have used paragraph returns at the end of each row.

    *   **Number of Columns**: This can be left blank unless you have used the same character to separate both columns and rows. In such a case, you can specify how many columns to use in this box, effectively overriding the column separator value.

    *   **Table Style**: This box lets you select a predefined table style. Table styles are more advanced features that allow you to save and reuse styling across more than one table.

    Once you have chosen these options, click **OK**; your table will be generated with the content automatically inserted into the different cells.

When converting text into tables, all the rows are created as body rows automatically. If you wish you can convert **Body Rows** into **Header Rows**, take a look at the technique shown later in the *Converting a row into a header or footer and setting repeating options* recipe.

> **Note**
>
> You don't have to use commas, paragraphs, or tabs to separate your rows and columns. Most other characters can be used and instead of choosing them from the dropdown, you can simply type the character into the dialog box instead.

Adjusting Table Setup

Once you have a table, being able to adjust it is crucial. The **Table Setup option** in InDesign allows you to alter **Table Dimensions**, make adjustments to the **Table Border** property, change **Table Spacing** by inserting space before or after the table, and even fine-tune the **Stroke Drawing Order** property.

Getting started

To complete this recipe, simply open InDesign on your system and create a new document with 12 pages, as shown in the *Creating a new document* recipe in *Chapter 1*. Create a text frame and type My new Table then hit return twice and type Another bit of info. Now position the cursor on the empty line between the two lines of text and insert a table as shown in the *Inserting and creating tables* recipe.

How to do it...

To make adjustments to tables within your document, follow these steps:

1. Using the **Type** tool, click inside your table. Now, go to the **Table** menu and expand the **Table Options** fly-out menu. Click the first option, which is **Table Setup**.

> **Note**
>
> If you don't see changes happening to your table as you make them, in the **Table Setup** options dialog box, check that the **Preview** checkbox is checked.

2. The first section in **Table Setup** is **General Dimensions** (marked *A* in *Figure 3.3*). Here, you will see the following sections, which will contain existing settings based on the currently selected table:

   • **Body Rows:** This shows the total number of body rows. Increasing or decreasing this number will add or remove rows from the bottom of your table. Increase the current number here by **1**.

- **Header Rows**: This shows the total number of header rows. Increasing or decreasing this number will add or remove header rows from the top of your table. We will set this to **1**.

- **Columns**: This shows the total number of columns in the table. Increasing or decreasing this number will add or remove columns to/from the right-hand side of the table. We will set this to **3**.

- **Footer Rows**: This shows the total number of footer rows in the table. Increasing or decreasing this number will add or remove footer rows at the bottom of the table. We will set this to **0**.

Having confirmed these **General Dimensions**, next, we will move on to the **Table Border** options. If you don't see the extra row that we added, it may be within overset text, which is indicated by a red box at the bottom right of the text frame. If so, resize the frame, as shown in the *Creating text frames and adding placeholder text* recipe in *Chapter 2*:

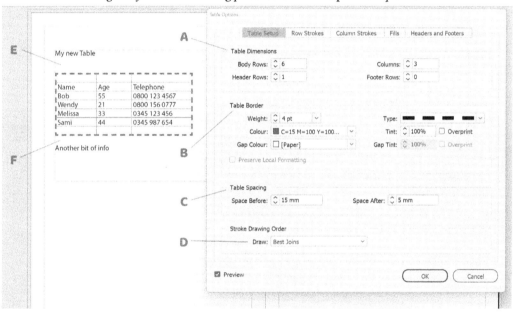

Figure 3.3: The Table Setup dialog box

3. Next, we will adjust the **Table Border** options (marked *B* in *Figure 3.3*). This section allows us to control the look of the table border around the outside of the table:

- **Weight**: The width of the border around the table. A larger number will result in a thicker border. We will set this to **4 pt**.

- **Type**: Allows you to choose from a list of preset border styles. We will choose **Dashed (3 and 2)**.

- **Color**: The color of the border. We will set this to **Red**.

- **Tint**: Used to lighten the color by increasing the white content. We won't change this.

- **Gap Color**: Used to change the color of the gaps. We won't change this.

- **Gap Tint**: Used to lighten the color of the gaps by increasing the white content. We won't change this either.

- The **Preserve Local Formatting** checkbox at the bottom of the dialog box will result in any local edits made to the table cells overriding **Table Setup Options**. If this is disabled, **Table Setup Options** will take priority. We will disable this.

- You will notice there are also two checkboxes called **Overprint** next to **Tint** and **Gap Tint**. Leave these unchecked.

What is overprinting?

Overprinting is a technique whereby colors are printed on top of existing colors, causing the two to merge and form a third color. This is as opposed to the default knockout behavior, whereby the color on top overwrites everything behind it (assuming no transparency is being used). For example, yellow printed on top of blue with overprint disabled would result in yellow, while yellow printed on top of blue with overprint enabled would result in green.

---

4.   We are now going to look at the **Table Spacing** settings (marked *C* in *Figure 3.3*). Here, you will see the options for **Space Before** and **Space After**. When the table is positioned in a frame with other text, this allows you to put additional space before and after the table. We will adjust this to put **15 mm** of **Space Before** (see *E* in *Figure 3.3*) and **5 mm** of **Space After** (see *F* in *Figure 3.3*).

If the table is at the start of a blank frame that contains no other text, you won't see any change.

5.   The final option in the **Table Setup** dialog box is **Stroke Drawing Order** (marked *D* in *Figure 3.3*). As its name suggests, this controls the order in which the lines are drawn and how they are joined. In the drop-down menu, you have the following options:

- **Best Joins**: Row strokes will be positioned on top, where different colors are used for row strokes and column strokes. In addition, some strokes will be joined up when rows and column strokes cross over. We will select this option.

- **Row Strokes in Front**: When this is selected, row strokes will always be positioned in front of column strokes.

- **Column Strokes in Front**: When this is selected, column strokes will always be positioned in front of row strokes.

- **InDesign 2.0 Compatibility**: When selected, row strokes will appear in front. However, with some stroke types, the crossing points will be connected only where strokes cross in a T shape.

6. Now that we've confirmed all our settings, we just need to click **OK** to apply them to the selected table. Your table should now look like the table on the left in *Figure 3.3*.

Selecting and moving rows and columns

When working with tables, you will want to select rows or columns so that you can format them or maybe even reposition them within the table. In this recipe, we will look at how to select one or multiple rows, select one or multiple columns, and then reposition rows and columns within the table, moving them up and down or side to side.

Getting started

To complete this recipe, simply open InDesign on your system and create a new document with 12 pages, as shown in the *Creating a new document* recipe in *Chapter 1*. You will also need to create a new frame containing a table, as shown in the *Inserting and creating tables* recipe.

How to do it...

To select and move rows and columns within your table, follow these steps:

1. With the **Type** tool selected, click inside your table. Now, move your cursor to the left of the table. As you move it past the edge of the table, you will notice that your cursor changes into an arrow pointing toward the right (marked *A* in *Figure 3.4*). If you click now, you will select that row; in our case, we will select the second row in the table:

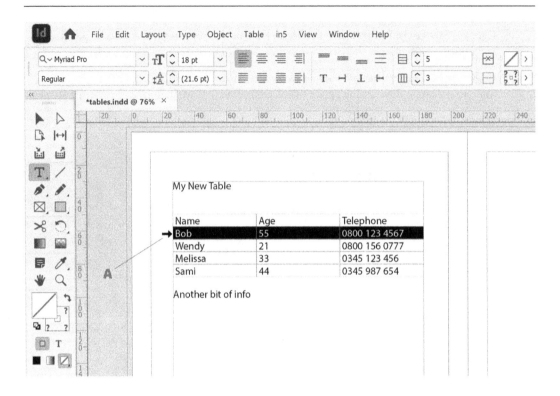

Figure 3.4: Selecting rows in a table

2.   Having selected a row, move your mouse over the middle of the selected row; you will see that the cursor changes to look a bit like a hamburger menu icon (marked *A* in *Figure 3.5*). Click and hold down the mouse button, then drag the row up or down to reposition it:

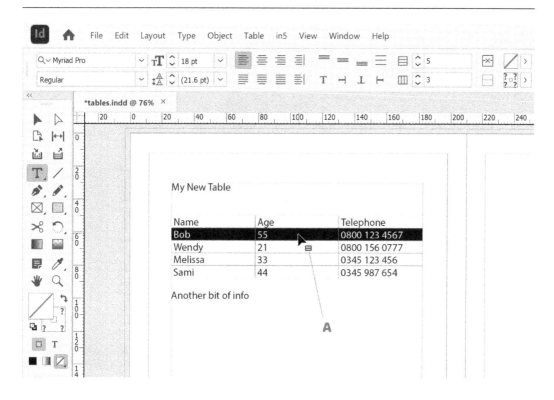

Figure 3.5: Moving a row within your table

3. Having moved a row within our table, let's do the same with a column. Hold your mouse just above the top of the table; you will see the cursor turn into an arrow pointing down (marked *A* in *Figure 3.6*), much as it did with rows in *step 1*. Now, select the second column in your table:

> **Note**
>
> In addition to selecting rows and columns this way, you can also select cells, rows, columns, or the entire table from the right mouse menu. To do this, click into a cell and then right-click in the same place to bring up the right-click menu. Here, you will see a **Select** option listed, under which you can choose **Cell**, **Row**, **Column**, or **Table**.

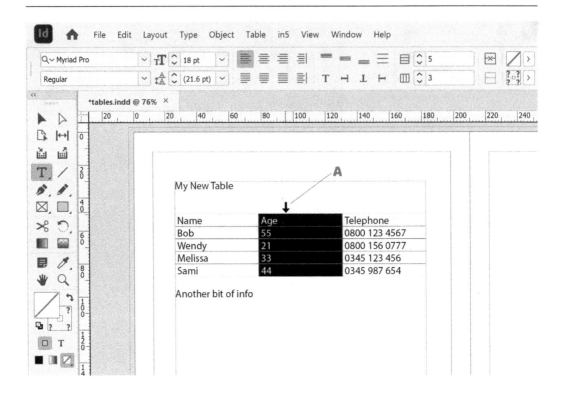

Figure 3.6: Selecting a column in a table

4. With the second column selected, move your mouse over the middle of the selected column; you will see that, once again, the cursor changes to look a bit like a hamburger menu icon. Click and hold down the mouse button, then drag the column to the right within the table to reposition it.

> **Tip**
>
> If you wish to select multiple rows or columns, simply repeat what you did in *step 1* or *step 3*, but this time, hold down the mouse button and move the mouse up and down the rows or left and right across the columns to select more than one.

Inserting and deleting rows and columns

When working in tables, you will often need to add additional rows or columns to your table or delete existing rows and columns. In this recipe, we will look at the options available for doing this.

Getting started

To complete this recipe, simply open InDesign on your system and create a new document with 12 pages, as shown in the *Creating a new document* recipe in *Chapter 1*. You will also need to create a new frame containing a table, as shown in the *Inserting and creating tables* recipe.

How to do it...

To insert and delete rows and columns within your table, follow these steps:

1. Let's start by adding rows to our table. Using the **Type** tool, position your cursor within a row that you would like to insert more rows in, either above or below. Now, click on the **Table** menu; then, under the **Insert** section, click on the **Row...** option (marked *A* in *Figure 3.7*). This will open the **Insert Row dialog box**:

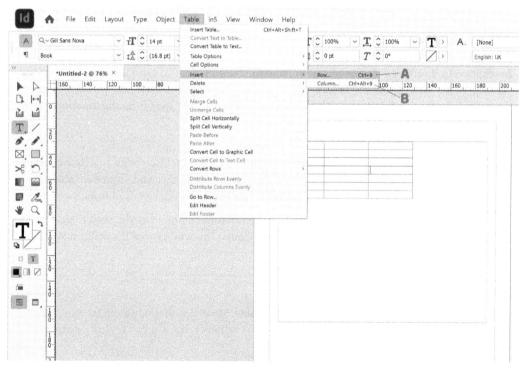

Figure 3.7· Inserting rows from the menu

2. In the **Insert Row** dialog box, select how many rows you wish to insert and whether you want to insert them above or below the row the cursor is currently placed in. In our case, we will insert **2** rows above the current row.

3. Next, we want to insert a column. Position your cursor in a cell within the table; then, from the **Table** menu, under the **Insert** section, click on the **Column…** option (marked *B* in *Figure 3.7*). This will bring up the **Insert Column dialog box**. We can now choose how many columns we wish to insert and whether these will be **Left** or **Right** of the column currently containing the cursor. We will insert **1** new column to the right, as shown in *Figure 3.8*:

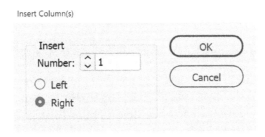

Figure 3.8: The Insert Column(s) dialog box

> **Tip**
> In addition to inserting columns and rows from the table menu, you can also do so by right-clicking on the table; under the **Insert** option, you will see **Row** and **Column**. This brings up the same dialog box as the menu method. This method can also be used to access the selection and deletion operations.

4. Having inserted some new rows and columns into our table, we now want to delete columns and rows from the table. Click into the third row down in your table and, from the **Table** menu, under **Delete**, select **Row**. You will see that the row has now been removed from the table.

5. We can delete columns in the same way. Simply click on a column that you wish to delete and, from the **Table** menu, under **Delete**, select **Columns**. You will see that the column is deleted from your table immediately.

> **Note**
> In InDesign, it is possible to have a table inside a table. Simply click inside a cell in your table and, from the **Table** menu, choose **Insert Table**. Your new table will be created within the selected cell.

Creating alternating strokes and fills

Tables in InDesign are simply a design feature and can't do sums or calculations in the way tools such as Excel can. However, the ability to create alternating patterns with your fills, row strokes, and column strokes allows you to present complex information in ways that make it far more intuitive and easier to understand.

In this recipe, we will look at applying alternating patterns to fills and strokes, including adjusting the patterns, changing colors, and skipping rows and columns.

Getting started

To complete this recipe, simply open InDesign on your system and create a new document with 12 pages, as shown in the *Creating a new document* recipe in *Chapter 1*. You will also need to create a new frame containing a table, as shown in the *Inserting and creating tables* recipe.

How to do it...

To apply **alternating fills and stokes** to your table, follow these steps:

1. Click anywhere in the table with the **Type** tool. Then, from the **Tables** menu, go to **Table Options** and choose **Alternating Fills**, as seen in *Figure 3.9*:

Figure 3.9: The Fills dialog box

2. To activate the panel, you need to first choose an **Alternating Pattern** from the dropdown (marked *A* in *Figure 3.9*). These are presets that control what settings are initially entered in the **Alternating** section (marked *B* in *Figure 3.9*), and include the following:

    - **None**: This disables the **Alternating Pattern** feature
    - **Every Other Row**: The color will alternate on every row (our chosen setting)
    - **Every Second Row**: The color will alternate every two rows
    - **Every Third Row**: The color will alternate every three rows
    - **Custom Row**: This allows a custom pattern, such as two rows in blue followed by four in red
    - **Every Other Column**: The color will alternate on every column
    - **Every Second Column**: The color will alternate every two columns
    - **Every Third Column**: The color will alternate every three columns
    - **Custom Column**: Allows a custom pattern, such as two columns in blue followed by four in red

3. Having chosen **Every Other Row** as the alternating pattern, we now need to tell InDesign what colors to use. In the **Alternating** section, you will notice that the **First** and **Next** options (marked *A* and *B* in *Figure 3.10*) are both set to **1** automatically since we chose **Every Other Row**. Below these, we can see the section where we can set the two colors to be used. On the left, we will choose **Cyan** and set **Tint** to **20%**, while on the right, we will choose **Magenta** and again set **Tint** to **20%**, as seen in *Figure 3.10*.

    If you don't see the changes live on the table, just make sure the **Preview** checkbox is ticked (marked *C* in *Figure 3.10*):

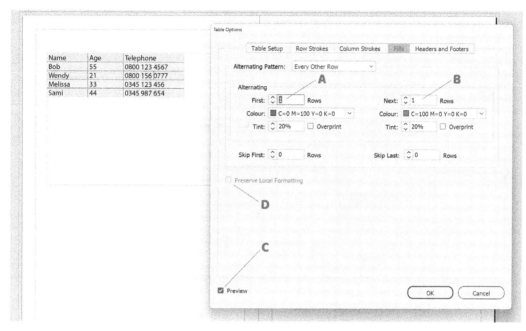

Figure 3.10: Configuring alternating fills on a table

4. If you wish, you can tell **Alternating Pattern** to skip several rows at the start or end using the **Skip First** or **Skip Last** option. We won't use these on this occasion. You may also notice a checkbox for **Preserve Local Formatting** (marked *D* in *Figure 3.10*), which is grayed out in *Figure 3.10*. Ticking this means any local formatting that's applied to cells will be used instead of the alternating pattern for those cells. If this is unchecked, the alternating pattern will override local formatting. If this is grayed out, this means you have no local formatting applied to cells.

5. To apply the changes we have made to the alternating fills, simply click **OK** at the bottom of the dialog box.

    Next, we will apply alternating patterns to the strokes (the lines between the rows and columns).

6. Click anywhere in the table with the **Type** tool, and then, from the **Tables** menu, go to **Table Options** and choose **Row Strokes**. This will bring up the alternating **Row Strokes** dialog box, as seen in *Figure 3.11*:

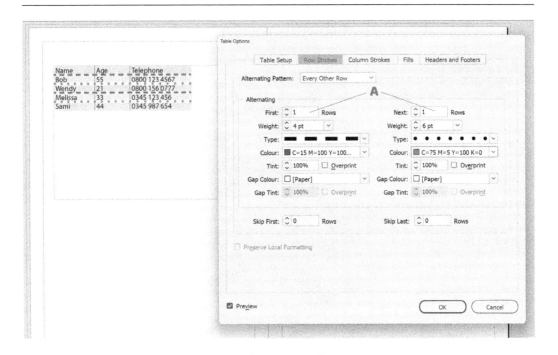

Figure 3.11: The alternating Row Strokes dialog box

7. As with the alternating fills, the first step here is to choose an alternating pattern preset for the row strokes from the **Alternating Pattern** dropdown. There are several options:

    • **None**: No alternating pattern is applied

    • **Every Other Row**: The stroke will alternate on every row (our chosen option)

    • **Every Second Row**: The stroke will alternate every second row

    • **Every Third Row**: The stroke will alternate every third row

    • **Custom Row**: This allows a custom pattern such as two rows with blue strokes followed by four with red strokes

    We have chosen the **Every Other Row** preset so that the **First** and **Next** boxes (marked *A* in *Figure 3.11*) are both set to **1** automatically.

8. Next, we want to define the alternating pattern settings for the row strokes. We have the following options for both the first and second part of the pattern (as shown in *Figure 3.11*):

    • **Weight**: The thickness of the stroke. We have set these to **4pt** and **6pt**.

    • **Type**: You can choose from a range of preset stroke types. Here, we have chosen **Dashed (3 and 2)** and **Dotted** as our two types.

- **Color**: You can choose the color from your existing color swatches. If you wish to create more color swatches, check out *Chapter 7, Working with Color and Gradients*. Here, we will choose **Red** and **Green**.

- **Tint**: Used to increase the white content of the color. We will set this to 100% on both colors.

- **Gap Color**: If you are working with a **Type** that includes gaps, this allows you to set its color so that it isn't just blank. We will leave this blank.

- **Gap Tint**: If you set a **Gap Color**, you can set its tint.

You can also choose to **Skip First** or **Skip Last** rows at the bottom of the dialog box, just as we discussed in *step 4*. The **Preserve Formatting** checkbox allows you to either override or preserve local formatting, which was also discussed in *step 4*.

Finally, we are going to set some **Alternating Column Strokes**. We still have the dialog box open, so we will just click the tab for **Alternating Column Stokes**.

9. **Alternating Column Strokes** works exactly like **Alternating Row Strokes**, with the only difference being they run vertically on the lines between the columns as opposed to horizontally on the lines between rows. With this in mind, set the following settings:

- **Alternating Pattern**: **Every Other Column**

- **First** and **Next**: **1**

- **Weight**: **4 pt** and **6 pt**

- **Type**: **Triple** and **Wavy**

- **Color**: **Navy** and **Red**

- **Tint**: **100%**

If you have used the same settings, your table should now look like the one in *Figure 3.12*. While it isn't the most beautiful table ever created, hopefully, it gives you a good overview of the alternating features that are available when creating tables:

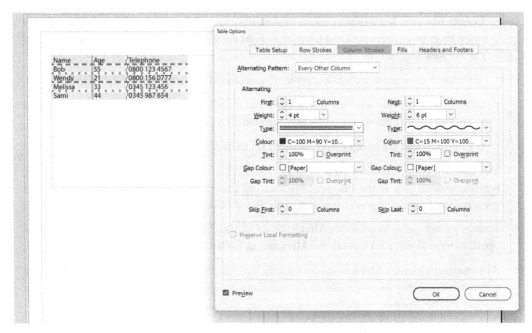

Figure 3.12: The final table with the Column Strokes dialog box open

Merging, unmerging, and splitting cells

When working with tables, it is quite common to have cells that run across more than one row or column or are split into two cells to present information in the most effective way possible. In this recipe, we are going to look at how to split, merge, and unmerge cells within InDesign, giving you the exact layout you need.

Getting started

To complete this recipe, simply open InDesign on your system and create a new document with 12 pages, as shown in the *Creating a new document* recipe in *Chapter 1*. You will also need to create a new frame containing a table, as shown in the *Inserting and creating tables* recipe.

How to do it...

To merge, unmerge, and split cells, follow these steps:

1. With the **Type** tool, click inside one cell and drag your mouse into the next cell, then release the mouse button. In our case, we will select two cells, one above the other, as shown in *Figure 3.13*:

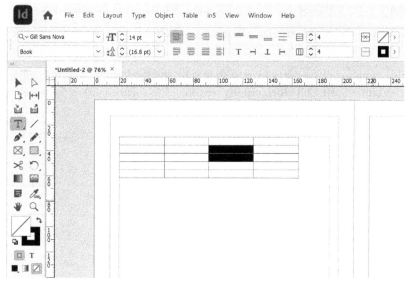

Figure 3.13: Two cells in the table selected

2. With the two cells selected, click on the **Table** menu and select **Merge Cells** (marked *A* in *Figure 3.14*). This will immediately merge the two cells; any content that existed will appear in the merged cell:

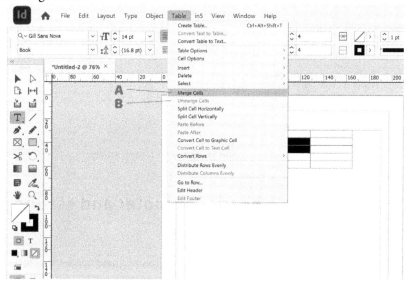

Figure 3.14: The Merge Cells option in the menu

3. Cells that have been merged this way can easily be unmerged. Simply click back into the merged cell and, from the **Table** menu, select **Unmerge Cells** (marked B in *Figure 3.14*). Any content will remain in the cell closest to the top left and will not be split into different cells.

    Note that if you click inside regular cells that haven't already been merged with other cells, the option to **Unmerge Cells** won't be active. You can, however, split a regular cell.

4. To do this, simply click on the cell you wish to split, and then, from the **Table** menu, select the option for either **Split Cell Horizontally** (marked A in *Figure 3.15*) or **Split Cell Vertically** (marked B in *Figure 3.15*).

    You can see an example of how this looks in *Figure 3.15*, with the cells marked C being split vertically and the cells marked D being split horizontally:

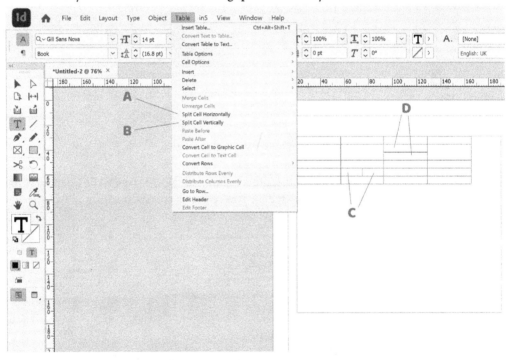

Figure 3.15: Splitting cells vertically and horizontally

Converting a row into a header or footer and setting repeating options

A useful feature when using tables in InDesign is the ability to designate header and footer rows. If your table continues across multiple frames, columns, or pages, this can be especially helpful as it allows you to have the header or footer repeat in each new frame, column, or page. Header and footer rows can also be useful when it comes to styling your content since they are not included when you apply alternating fills.

In the *Inserting and creating tables* recipe, we learned how to create header and footer rows as part of the new table creation process. In this recipe, we will learn how to create the header and footer within an existing table.

Getting started

To complete this recipe, simply open InDesign on your system and create a new document with 12 pages, as shown in the *Creating a new document* recipe in *Chapter 1*. You will also need to create a new frame containing a table, as shown in the *Inserting and creating tables* recipe.

How to do it...

To convert a row into a header or footer and set repeating options, follow these steps:

1. To select the top row of your table, switch to the **Type** tool, and then hold your cursor slightly to the left of the top row of the table. When the cursor changes into an arrow, as shown in *Figure 3.16*, click to select the row:

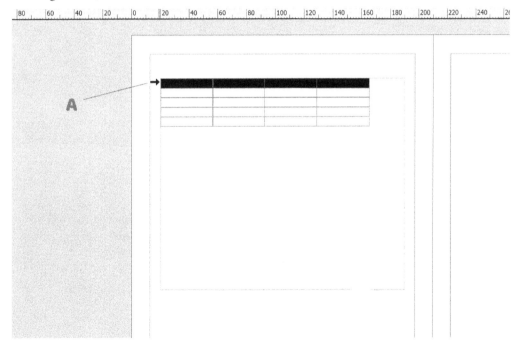

Figure 3.16: Selecting a whole row in a table

2.   Now, we want to convert the regular body row into a header row. Select the **Table** menu; then, under **Convert Rows**, select **To Header** (marked *A* in *Figure 3.17*):

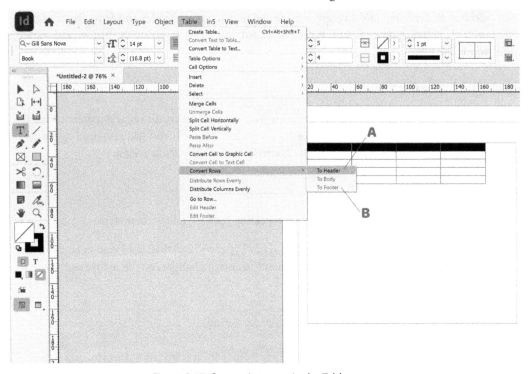

Figure 3.17: Converting rows in the Table menu

3.   Next, we will convert the bottom row into a footer row. Select the bottom row by holding your cursor to the left of the row. When you see the cursor turn into an arrow again, click to select the row.

4.   To convert the regular body row into a footer row, select the **Table** menu and, under **Convert Rows**, select **To Footer** (marked *B* in *Figure 3.17*).

5.   Now, in the **Table** menu, under **Table Options**, select **Headers** and **Footers**. This will bring up the **Table Options dialog box**, which contains the **Headers and Footers settings**, as seen in *Figure 3.18*:

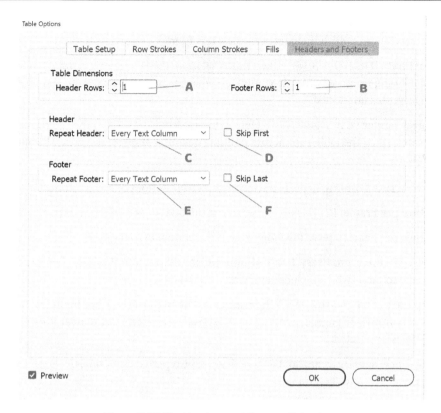

Figure 3.18: The Headers and Footers dialog box

The **Headers and Footers** section contains the following options:

- **Header Rows** (*A* in *Figure 3.18*): Choose how many header rows you would like. We set this to **1** row in *step 2*, so we don't need to change this.

- **Footer Rows** (*B* in *Figure 3.18*): Choose how many footer rows you would like. We set this to **1** row in *step 4*, so we don't need to change this.

- **Repeat Header** (*C* in *Figure 3.18*): Here, you can decide how often the header row will be repeated when the table runs across multiple columns, frames, or pages. The options are as follows:

  - **Every Text Column**: Repeats the header row at the top of every column

  - **Once per Frame**: Repeats the header row at the top of every frame

  - **Once per Page**: Repeats the header row at the top of every page

We will leave this set to **Every Text Column**, which will result in the header being repeated in every new column (which includes every new text frame).

- **Skip First** (*D* in *Figure 3.18*): When this is selected, the header row is not included in the first column, frame, or page, depending on what has been selected in **Repeat Header**. We will leave this unselected.

- **Repeat Footer** (*E* in *Figure 3.18*): Here, you can decide how often the footer row will be repeated when the table runs across multiple columns, frames, or pages. The options are as follows:

  - **Every Text Column**: Repeats the footer row at the bottom of every column

  - **Once per Frame**: Repeats the footer row at the bottom of every frame

  - **Once per Page**: Repeats the footer row at the bottom of every page

We will leave this set to **Every Text Column**, which will result in the footer being repeated in every new column (which includes every new text frame).

- **Skip Last** (*F* in *Figure 3.18*): When selected, the footer row is not included in the last column, frame, or page, depending on what has been selected in **Repeat Footer**. We will leave this unselected.

Our table now has header and footer rows that will be repeated every time the table is threaded into a new column (or text frame).

There's more...

At a more advanced level, table header and footer rows can even have a cell style applied from within reusable table styles. You can find out more about this here: `https://www.highlander.co.uk/blog/using-table-and-cell-styles`.

Including images in tables

In more recent years, Adobe has made it easier to include graphics within tables. This can be useful in several scenarios, such as if you use small icons and symbols to identify content in your tables. InDesign does this by effectively converting the cell into a **graphic cell** and inserting a graphic into it, which results in additional settings specific to the graphic being made available for that cell.

In this recipe, we will look at including images in our table cells, and how we can customize how these images to fit within the graphic cell.

Getting started

To complete this recipe, simply open InDesign on your system and create a new document with 12 pages, as shown in the *Creating a new document* recipe in *Chapter 1*. You will also need to create a new frame containing a table, as shown in the *Inserting and creating tables* recipe. An active internet connection is needed to complete *step 3* of this recipe.

How to do it...

To include images in your tables, follow these steps:

1. With the **Type** tool, click inside the cell that you want to contain the image.

2. Then, from the **File** menu, click on the **Place** option (this can also be accessed with the *Ctrl* (Windows)/*Command* (Mac) + *D* shortcut), select an image, and click **Open**. InDesign will place the image (within its own frame) into the selected cell. It will also automatically set the fitting options so that **AutoFit** is enabled, **Fill Frame Proportionally** is enabled, and **Align From** is set to **Center**.

   If the cell containing the image is subsequently resized, you will also find that the image is also proportionally resized at the same time.

3. If you use **CC Libraries**, you will want to place an image from there into the table. Open the **CC Libraries** panel, click on an image in one of your libraries, and drag it into your chosen cell in the table. Again, it will automatically set the fitting options so that **AutoFit** is enabled, **Fill Frame Proportionally** is enabled, and **Align From** is set to **Center**.

> Note
>
> We will learn more about CC Libraries in *Chapter 11*, *Using and Collaborating with CC Libraries*.

4. Having placed an image into the cell, you may want to add a crop value to one or all sides of the image. Click on the image with the **Selection** tool and, from the **Object** menu, under **Fitting**, select **Frame Fitting Options**. This will bring up the **Frame Fitting Options** dialog box, where you will see the **Crop Amount** options (marked *A* in *Figure 3.19*):

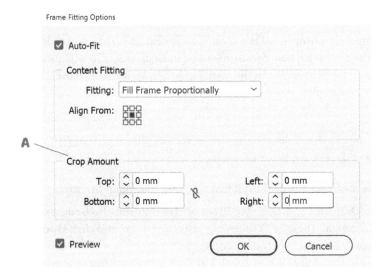

Figure 3.19: The Frame Fitting Options dialog box

Adjusting the crop settings here will result in the size of the image changing and the areas outside of the cell being cropped off.

There's more...

In the next recipe, *Adjusting cell options*, *step 2* covers specific properties for **Graphic Cells** and is worth a read.

Adjusting cell options

While formatting a whole table with alternating fills and strokes is very useful, sometimes, you might just want to alter the formatting of a specific individual cell. This could be by adjusting inset spacing, fine-tuning the strokes or fills for that individual cell, or altering the width or height of the cell. In this recipe, we are going to run through the cell options that allow you to do this, and use them to fine-tune our table.

Getting started

To complete this recipe, simply open InDesign on your system and create a new document with 12 pages, as shown in the *Creating a new document* recipe in *Chapter 1*. You will also need to create a new frame containing a table, as shown in the *Inserting and creating tables* recipe.

How to do it...

To adjust the **cell options** for a specific cell in your table, follow these steps:

1. Using the **Type** tool, select a cell containing text within your table. If you are struggling to do this manually with your mouse, you can click into the cell with the **Type** tool; then, from the **Table** menu, under **Select**, choose **Cell**. Alternatively, you can click into the cell with the **Type** tool and then right-click with your mouse and use the **Select** option in the pop-up menu. With the cell selected, go back into the **Table** menu and, under **Cell Options**, choose **Text**.

    This will bring up the **Cell Options** dialog box, which contains five sections. The first tab in the **Cell Options** dialog box is **Text Options**, as shown in *Figure 3.20*:

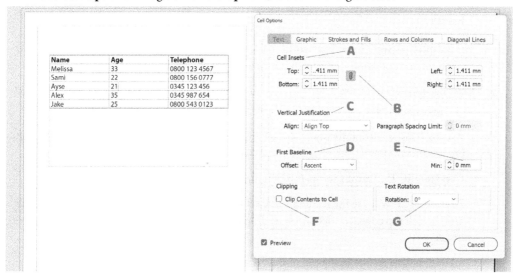

Figure 3.20: Customizing Text in the Cell Options dialog box

This tab contains several options:

- **Cell Insets** (*A* in *Figure 3.20*): Allows you to adjust the inset spacing between the cell content and the edge of the cell. By default, all four sides are changed together. However, if you only wish to change the value for one side, simply click the link icon (*B* in *Figure 3.20*) to allow this. We will leave this set to the default settings.

> **Note**
> If you have set a value for **Cell Insets**, this will need to be taken into account when you're adjusting the following settings as it will add additional space between the content and the cell edge.

- **Vertical Justification** (*C* in *Figure 3.20*): Here, you can control the alignment of your cell content relative to the cell with the following options:

  - **Align Top**: Your text will align to the top of the cell

  - **Align Center**: Your text will align to the center of the cell (we will choose this)

  - **Align Bottom**: Your text will align to the bottom of the cell

  - **Justify Vertically**: Multiple lines of text will spread out to fill the cell

- **Paragraph Spacing Limit**: This works in conjunction with **Justify Vertically**, allowing you to set a maximum amount of spacing to be used between paragraphs.

- **First Baseline** (*D* in *Figure 3.20*): This lets you control where the baseline for the first line of text is positioned relative to the top of the cell. The dropdown here offers the following options:

  - **Ascent**: This results in the top of the "d" character being below the top of the cell (we will choose this option).

  - **Cap Height**: This results in the top of uppercase letters reaching the top of the cell.

  - **Leading**: This will use the leading value set for the text as the space between the baseline and the cell top edge. For details on leading, see the *Adjusting character formatting* recipe in *Chapter 2*.

  - **x Height**: This results in the top of the "x" character being below the top of the cell.

  - **Fixed**: This allows you to specify the distance of the baseline from the top edge of the cell by setting a value in the **Min** field (*E* in *Figure 3.20*). If nothing is set, the baseline will be in line with the top of the cell.

- **Min** (*E* in *Figure 3.20*): Allows you to set a minimum value to be used for **First Baseline**. This means that if the option chosen for **First Baseline** results in a value that is lower than the **Min** value, the **Min** value will be used instead. We will leave this set to **0 mm**.

- **Clipping**: We will tick the **Clip Contents to Cell** option (*F* in *Figure 3.20*), which will ensure the contents of the cell do not extend beyond the edge of the cell.

- **Text Rotation**: Here, you can set a value for **Rotation** (*G* in *Figure 3.20*), with the options being **0**, **90**, **180**, and **270** degrees. This will rotate the text relative to the cell. We will set it to **0**.

Now click **OK** to save and apply your changes.

2. Select a cell containing an image, then go to the **Table** menu, and under **Cell Options**, choose **Graphic**. This section specifically works in conjunction with graphic cells, which we discussed in the previous recipe, *Including images in tables*.

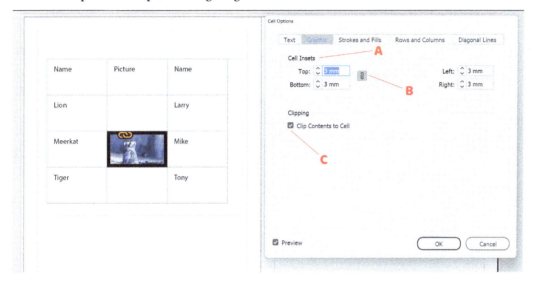

Figure 3.21: Customizing the Graphic options in the Cell Options dialog box

The options here are fairly minimal:

*   **Inset Spacing** (*A* in *Figure 3.21*): This allows you to adjust the inset spacing between the graphic and the edge of the cell. By default, all four sides are changed together. However, if you only wish to change the value for one side, simply click the link (*B* in *Figure 3.21*) to allow this. We will set the inset spacing to **3 mm** for all sides.

*   **Clipping**: Here, you can **Clip Content to Cell** by ticking the respective box (*C* in *Figure 3.21*). This will ensure the content of the cell does not extend beyond the edge of the cell. We will select this.

3. The third tab in the **Cell Options** dialog is **Strokes and Fills** and is where you can customize the stokes or fills for specific cells. This section can be applied to one or multiple cells; some of the settings are designed for selecting multiple cells, as mentioned shortly. So, select a block of four cells, as seen in *Figure 3.22*:

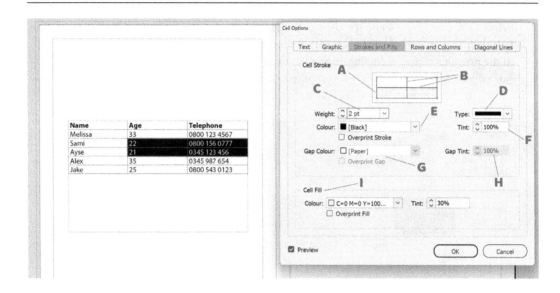

Figure 3.22: Customizing Strokes and Fills in the Cell Options dialog box

Now, let's look at the options in this section:

- **Cell Stroke**: Here, you can format the stroke for the cells. The stroke you are going to be changing is identified in blue (*A* in *Figure 3.22*); any strokes not being edited are marked in gray (*B* in *Figure 3.22*). To select or deselect specific strokes, simply click on the blue or gray lines here within the **Cell Options** dialog box. *Figure 3.23* shows four examples of cell stroke selection:

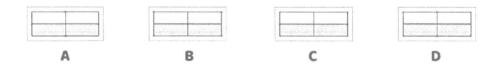

Figure 3.23: Examples of cell stroke selection

Let's look at each option:

- *A*: Multiple cells have been selected and the row and column strokes that pass between the selected cells are selected for editing, while the strokes around the outer edge of the selected cells are not selected for editing

- *B*: Multiple cells have been selected and the strokes around the outer edge of the selected cells are going to be edited, while the strokes that run between the selected cells are not selected for editing

- *C*: Only the row strokes (lines between the rows) of the selected cells will be edited, while the column strokes (lines between the columns) will not

- *D*: Only the column strokes (lines between the columns) of the selected cells will be edited, while the row strokes (lines between the rows) will not

We will select the strokes around the outside of the selection, as shown by *B* in *Figure 3.23*.

Additional settings within the **Cell Stroke** section include the following:

- **Weight** (*C* in *Figure 3.22*): Alters the thickness of the stroke. We will set this to **2 pt** here.

- **Type** (*D* in *Figure 3.22*): Allows you to choose from a range of preset stroke types. Here, we will choose **Solid**.

- **Color** (*E* in *Figure 3.22*): Allows you to choose the color of the cell from your existing color swatches. If you wish to create more color swatches, check out *Chapter 7, Working with Colors and Gradients*. Here, we will choose **Cyan**.

- **Tint** (*F* in *Figure 3.22*): Increases the white content of the color. We will set this to **100%** here.

- **Gap Colour** (*G* in *Figure 3.22*): If you are working with a type that includes gaps, this allows you to set the gap color so that it isn't just transparent. We have chosen a solid stroke, so this is not relevant.

- **Gap Tint**: (*H* in *Figure 3.22*): If you set **Gap Color**, you can set the tint for it.

> **Note**
>
> For more details on the **Overprint Stroke** and **Overprint Fill** options found here, please see the *Note* on overprinting, which can be found in the *Adjusting Table Setup* recipe.

- **Cell Fill** (*I* on *Figure 3.22*): Here, you can format the fill color for the cells by setting the **Color** and **Tint** options for the **Cell Fill** option. We will set this to **Yellow** with a 30% tint.

4.   Now, select the header row in your table and click the **Rows and Columns** tab in the **Cell Options** dialog box:

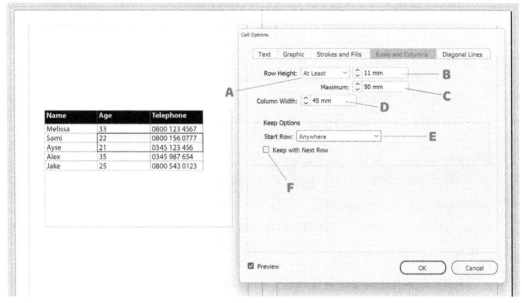

Figure 3.24: The Rows and Columns settings in the Cell Options dialog box

Here, you will find the following settings:

- **Row Height** (*A* in *Figure 3.24*): You can set this to either of the following options:

  - **Exactly**: This allows you to enter an exact value in the number box (marked *B* in *Figure 3.24*) for the row height

  - **At Least**: This allows you to set a minimum value in the number box (marked *B* in *Figure 3.24*) for the row height

  The same number box (marked *B* in *Figure 3.24*) is used for both of the **Row Height** options. So, we will set **Row Height** to **At Least** with a value of **11 mm**.

- **Maximum** (*C* in *Figure 3.24*): This lets you set a maximum height for the rows selected. The height of the selected rows won't go larger than this value, and any surplus text will become overset. We will set this to **50 mm**.

- **Column Width** (*D* in *Figure 3.24*): This lets you set a precise value for the selected columns. I have set this to **5 mm** but depending on the amount of content you have in the cells, you may decide to do more or less.

- **Start Row** (*E* in *Figure 3.24*): This option allows you to control a row's behavior concerning the location of the table within the document and force it to appear in a specific location. The following options are available:

  - **Anywhere**: The selected row can appear anywhere (we will choose this option)

  - **In Next Text Column**: The selected row will always appear in the next text column to the previous row

  - **In Next Frame**: The selected row will always appear in the next frame to the previous row

  - **On Next Page**: The selected row will always appear on the next page from the previous row

  - **On Next Odd Page**: The selected row will always appear on the next odd page from the previous row

  - **On Next Even Page**: The selected row will always appear on the next even page from the previous row

- **Keep with Next Row** (*F* in *Figure 3.24*): This option will ensure this row stays immediately above the previous row. It's worth noting that this option is overridden by the **Start Row** option. We will leave this unchecked.

5. The final section in the **Cell Options** dialog is **Diagonal Lines**, as shown in *Figure 3.25*:

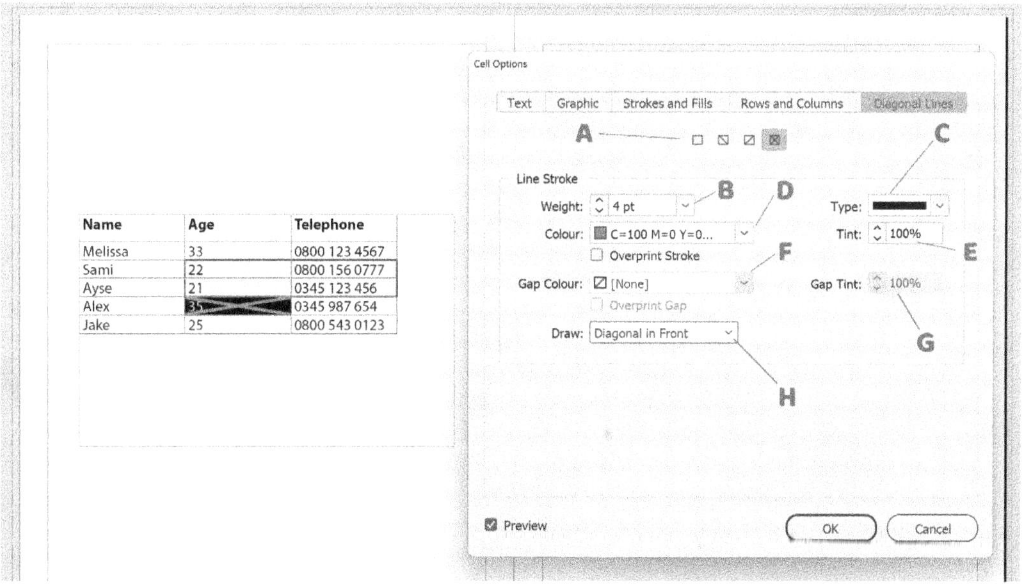

Figure 3.25: The Diagonal Lines settings in the Cell Options dialog box

The four icons (marked *A* in *Figure 3.25*) allow you to draw diagonal lines either in front or behind the content in the cell. Click on one of the icons to choose the pattern for the lines (we will choose the icon on the far right). Then, you can set the properties as follows:

- **Weight** (*B* in *Figure 3.25*): Alters the thickness of the lines. We have set this to **4 pt**.

- **Type** (*C* in *Figure 3.25*): Choose from a range of preset stroke types. Here, we have chosen **Solid**.

- **Color** (*D* in *Figure 3.25*): Choose a color from your existing color swatches. We have chosen **Cyan** here.

- **Tint** (*E* in *Figure 3.25*): Increases the white content of the color. We have set this to **100%**.

- **Gap Color** (*F* in *Figure 3.25*): If you are working with a type that includes gaps, this allows you to set the gap color so that it isn't just blank. We will leave this blank.

- **Gap Tint** (*G* in *Figure 3.25*): If you set a gap color, you can set the tint for it here.

- **Draw** (*H* in *Figure 3.25*): This allows you to control whether you draw the cell's **Content in Front** of the diagonal or **Diagonal in Front** of the cell's content.

4

Using the InDesign Frame Tools

When it comes to content in InDesign, everything sits inside a frame. These frames can contain a wide range of content, including other INDD files, along with PDF, PSD, TIFF, EPS, JPG, DOCX, XLS, RTF, DOC, XLSX, TXT, SVG, MP4, MP3, GIF, and OAM files. This is something people don't always realize, especially when some tools and processes, such as placing an image on a page (covered in *Chapter 5*), can seamlessly create a frame without you even realizing it.

In this chapter, we will learn how to create frames using the **Rectangle Frame**, **Ellipse Frame**, and **Polygon Frame** tools, as well as how to rotate, skew, align, and resize frames afterward. We will also look at how to use smart guides with frames, customize frame corners, insert a QR code into a frame, and finish off by using the **Pathfinder** tool to merge multiple frames together into a single compound frame.

These are the recipes we will cover in this chapter:

- Creating rectangle and elliptical frames
- Creating polygon frames
- Rotating and skewing rectangle frames
- Resizing frames
- Aligning frames with the Align panel
- Using smart guides with frames
- Customizing corners on frames
- Merging frames with the Pathfinder tool
- Generating a QR code in a frame

Technical requirements

To complete this chapter, you will need a PC or Mac, with a copy of Adobe InDesign installed. An active internet connection is also recommended because without it, some features will not work.

Creating rectangle and elliptical frames

In this recipe, we will learn how to use the **Rectangle Frame tool** or the **Ellipse Frame tool** to create frames, adjust the positioning of frames on the fly during the creation process, and even create multiple identical frames with a simple shortcut trick.

The steps shown can be completed with either the **Rectangle Frame** tool or the **Ellipse Frame** tool and work exactly the same in both cases, with the only difference being the shape of the resulting frame. For this specific recipe, I will complete the steps using the **Rectangle Frame** tool.

Getting ready

In order to complete this recipe, simply open InDesign on your system and create a new document with 12 pages, as shown in the *Creating a new document* recipe in *Chapter 1*.

How to do it...

In order to create rectangle frames or elliptical frames on your document, follow these steps:

1. Select the **Rectangle Frame** tool from the **Tools** panel (marked as *A* in *Figure 4.1*). This option can be found in the same group as the **Ellipse Frame** tool and **Polygon Frame** tool, so if you are currently set to one of those tools, switch to the **Rectangle Frame** tool using the methods described in the following *Note* box.

> **Note**
>
> Sometimes similar tools are grouped together in the **Tools** panel in order to save space. You can tell when this is the case as the bottom-right corner of the **Tools** icon will have a small triangle in it (marked as *B* in *Figure 4.1*). To switch to other tools in the same group, you can either right-click on the icon or, if you prefer, left-click on the icon and hold down the mouse button, which will result in a list of the tools appearing that you can choose from. Alternatively, you can click on the icon while holding down the *Alt* (PC)/*Option* (Mac) buttons on the keyboard, which will cause the next tool in the group to be selected each time you click.

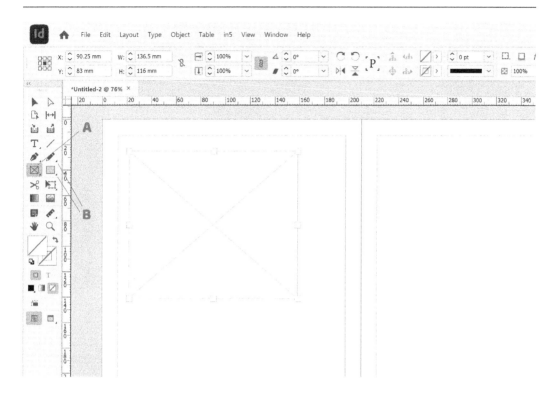

Figure 4.1: Creating a rectangle frame in InDesign

2.   With the **Rectangle Frame** tool, click on the page, hold down your mouse, and drag your cursor to set the size of your frame. Then, while still holding down the mouse button, hold the spacebar too, and you can reposition the frame you are creating. If you want to ensure that your frames are an exact square shape rather than a rectangular shape (or a circle rather than an ellipse, in the case of the **Ellipse Frame** tool), hold down the *Shift* key while creating the frame and keep it held down until you have let go of the mouse. Now, let go of the mouse button, and your new frame will be visible on the page with a large cross in the middle of it (as shown in *Figure 4.1*), indicating it is a graphic frame.

Having created a single rectangle frame on the page, we now want to move to the next page and create multiple rectangle frames at once.

3.   With the **Rectangle Frame** tool still selected, click on the page with the mouse (as we did in *step 2*) and drag, but this time don't let go of the mouse; we are going to keep the mouse button held down now until the end of *step 4*. So, with the mouse button still held down, click the right arrow on the keyboard twice, and this will split the frame into three separate frames of equal dimensions, positioned in a line next to each other. Every time you click the right arrow it will add another frame, whereas every time you click the left arrow it will remove a frame.

4. Having created three identical frames side by side, we now want to create more frames in a vertical direction to give us a grid of nine frames (*A* in *Figure 4.2*):

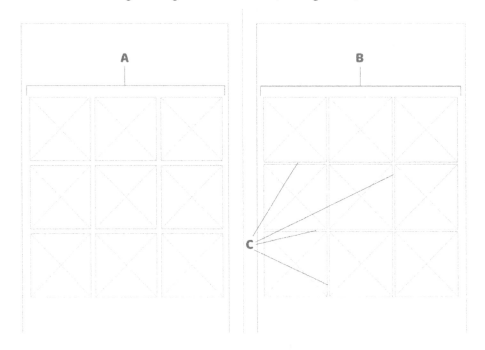

Figure 4.2: A grid of frames in InDesign

Still holding down the mouse button, click the up arrow twice on the keyboard, and you should now see the frames further split, giving a grid of three rows and three columns, containing a total of nine frames. (Clicking on the down arrow would remove rows, but we don't need to do that.) You can now let go of the mouse.

5. Having created a grid of identically sized frames, we now want to create a second grid of frames that has exactly 2 mm of space between each of the frames in the grid (*B* in *Figure 4.2*). To do this, go to the **Layout** menu and select **Margins and Columns**. Then, in the **Margins and Columns** dialog box, change the **Gutter** value to **2 mm** and click **OK**.

Now, create a grid of nine frames like before, but this time you will see the spacing between the frames is exactly 2 mm (marked as *C* in *Figure 4.2*). If you were using the **Ellipse Frame** tool, the distance from the edge of one ellipse to the edge of the next ellipse would be 2 mm.

6. Having used the **Rectangle Frame** tool to create a number of frames, we are now going to use the **Ellipse Frame** tool to create an elliptical frame with a very precise width and height of 50 mm x 75 mm. In order to do this, switch to the **Ellipse Frame** tool and then click once anywhere on the page. You will now see the **Ellipse dialog box** (*Figure 4.3*):

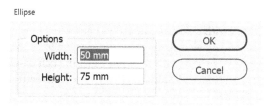

Figure 4.3: Ellipse dialog box

Enter **50 mm** into the **Height** box and **75 mm** into the **Width** box, then click **OK**. An ellipse frame will now appear on the page (marked as *A* in *Figure 4.4*), and the top and left edges of the frame will be aligned to the exact point you clicked, which in my case was where the top and left margins join. This technique works just the same with the **Rectangle Frame** tool:

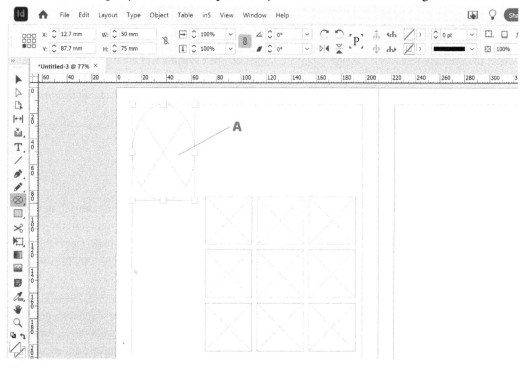

Figure 4.4: Ellipse frame aligned to the top and left margins

> **Warning**
>
> If you have set up your pages with column guides, you need to be aware that changing the gutter value as shown in *step 5* will also change the gutter value for your column guides (the space between the columns) on the currently selected page. In such cases, after creating your grid of frames, you will need to reset this value back to its previous setting in order to reverse the change to the column guides.

Creating polygon frames

In this recipe, we will learn how to use the **Polygon Frame tool** to create a range of different shaped frames, creating multiple shapes at once and changing the actual shapes themselves during the creation process.

Getting ready

In order to complete this recipe, simply open InDesign on your system and create a new document with 12 pages, as shown in the *Creating a new document* recipe in *Chapter 1*. You will also need to know how to create new frames on your pages, as shown in the *Creating rectangle or elliptical frames* recipe just covered.

How to do it...

In order to create polygon frames on your document, follow these steps:

1. Switch to the **Polygon Frame** tool, click on the page, hold down your mouse, and drag your cursor in order to create a polygon frame. Without releasing the mouse button, hold down the spacebar and move your mouse around to reposition the frame within the page, then let go of the spacebar again to continue resizing your frame with the mouse. Once you have positioned the frame at the size and position you want, let go of the mouse.

2. Next, we will repeat *step 1*, but this time don't release the mouse button at the end. Instead, click twice on the right arrow and once on the up arrow on the keyboard, and you will have a grid of six polygon frames (*A* in *Figure 4.5*). We want to ensure they are all sized with the width and height in proportion, so hold down the *Shift* key and then release the mouse button, ensuring the width and height are the same:

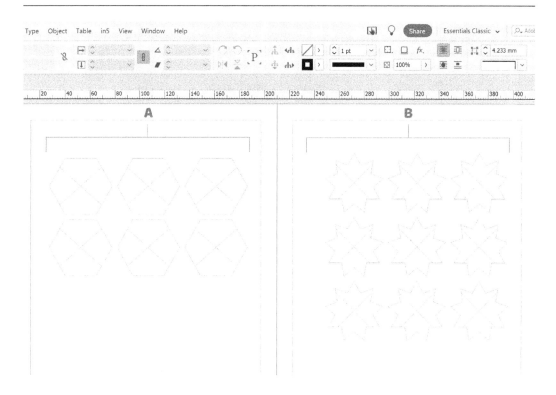

Figure 4.5: The Polygon Frame tool

> **Tip**
>
> While the **Gridify** feature shown here in *step 2* is a fast way to create multiple frames of the same size, it's also worth mentioning that you can quickly duplicate an existing frame by simply clicking on it with the **Selection** tool, holding down the *Alt* (PC)/*Option* (Mac) key and dragging it onto a different part of the page, remembering to release the mouse button before releasing the *Alt* (PC)/*Option* (Mac) key.

When working with the **Polygon Frame** tool, there is a useful shortcut that doesn't exist with the other frame tools, which we will take a look at in the next step.

3. With the **Polygon Frame** tool, create a frame on the page. Keeping the mouse button held down (we won't release it until *step 5*), press the spacebar once, then click the up arrow three times to add more sides to the polygon shape. (Pressing the down arrow will remove the sides, but we don't need to do this here.)

4. Still holding down the mouse button, next click the right arrow five times to increase the inset, leaving us with a small star shape, like those commonly used on price promo boxes. (Pressing the left arrow would reduce the inset, but we don't want to do this.)

5. Still holding down the mouse button, now press the spacebar once, and you will find that the arrows now once again allow you to create multiple frames, as seen previously in *step 2*. Press the up arrow twice and the right arrow twice to create a grid of nine stars (*B* in *Figure 4.5*), then release the mouse button to finish creating the frames.

    In effect, every time you press the spacebar it switches the functionality of the arrows between creating multiple frames and changing the actual shape. Don't forget in addition to this behavior holding down the spacebar also lets you reposition your frames while you are still creating them.

6. Finally, if you would like to create a polygon frame with very specific dimensions, simply click once on the page at the point you would like the top and left edges of the frame to be in line with, and this will bring up the **Polygon** dialog box:

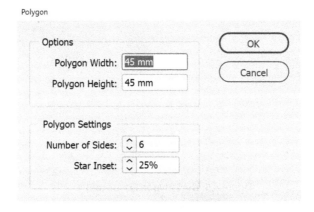

Figure 4.6: Polygon dialog box

In this dialog box, you can set the following four settings:

- **Polygon Width**: This is the width of the polygon, which we will set to **45 mm**.

- **Polygon Height**: This is the height of the polygon, which we will also set to **45 mm**.

- **Number of Sides**: This is either the number of sides on a polygon or the number of points on the star if you set a star inset. We will set this to **6**.

- **Star Inset**: This is the distance between the outer points of the star and its center, and is measured as a percentage. We will set this to **25%**.

Rotating and skewing rectangle frames

In this recipe, we will learn how to adjust your frames by both skewing and rotating them. We will be looking at rotating frames manually, using preset rotations, and rotating by precise amounts. We will also be looking at changing the reference point for the rotation using preset reference points, as well as setting completely custom reference points for rotation.

We are going to be working with rectangle frames, where the results of rotation tend to be more visibly obvious when compared to rotating a circle, for example. However, these techniques can all be applied to ellipse and polygon frames as well.

Getting ready

In order to complete this recipe, simply open InDesign on your system and create a new document with 12 pages, as shown in the *Creating a new document* recipe in *Chapter 1*. You will also need to know how to create new frames on your pages, as shown in the *Creating rectangle or elliptical frames* recipe found earlier in this chapter.

How to do it...

In order to skew and rotate rectangle frames in your document, follow these steps:

1. The first way to skew a frame is to change the **Shear X Angle** value in the **Control** panel. With your frame selected, you can either type a value into the box (marked as *A* in *Figure 4.7*), use the small arrows to increase or decrease the value (marked as *B* in *Figure 4.7*), or simply choose from the preset values by clicking the drop-down arrow to the right (marked as *C* in *Figure 4.7*). We will apply a **25°** shear to the *X* angle on our frame:

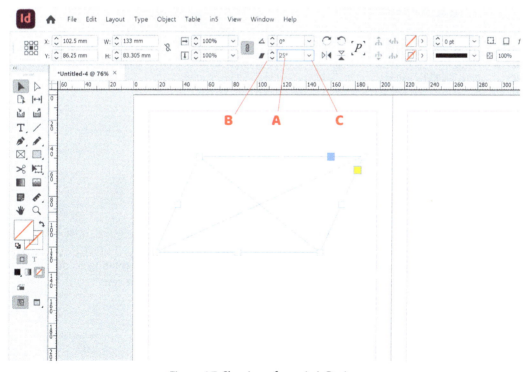

Figure 4.7: Skewing a frame in InDesign

> **Note**
>
> If you are working with a frame that already contains content and you wish to **skew** only the content, simply select the content with the **Direct Selection** tool and then apply the skew. Alternatively, if you wish to skew only the frame and not the content, apply the skew as normal then direct select the content and set the skew back to **0** for the content, leaving the frame skewed.

2. Now, let's look at rotating the frame manually. Create another rectangle frame and select it with the **Selection** tool. Hold the mouse just outside a corner of the frame, and you will see the cursor change (shown as *A* in *Figure 4.8*); at this point, you can click and drag to rotate the frame around its center. If you hold down the *Shift* key too, this will result in the frame rotating in 45° increments; we will rotate our frame 45° clockwise:

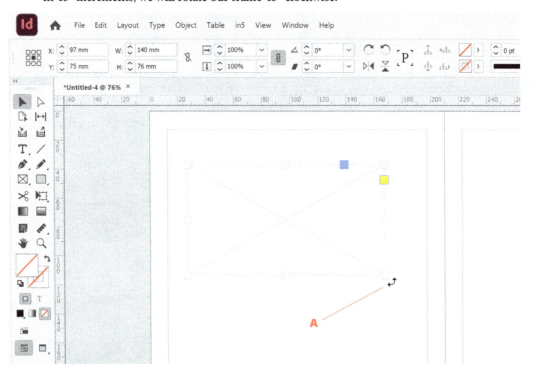

Figure 4.8: Rotating a frame freehand

While rotating manually like this is quick and easy, it isn't very good for rotating accurately by precise amounts, and also the rotation is always done around the frame center, which might not be what you need. Let's try a different method.

3. On the next page, create a rectangle frame and select it—this time, we will rotate it by a precise value. On the very left of the **Control** panel, you will see a small grid of nine squares (marked as *A* in *Figure 4.9*). This is where you can set the reference point on the frame, around which the rotation will take place. We will click on the bottom-left square to set that as the reference point, meaning any rotation applied will be done around that corner of the frame:

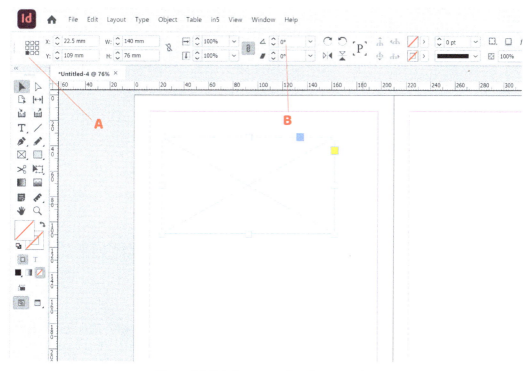

Figure 4.9: Rotating around a reference point

4. With the reference point set, we will now adjust the rotation value to **-35°** in the **Rotation Angle** entry box (marked as *B* in *Figure 4.9*).

   You may also notice that as you change this to **-35°**, the small grid we used in *step 3* to set the reference point also rotates, mirroring the frame's rotation.

5. Next, we are going to create a new rectangle frame and with a single click rotate it by 90° either clockwise or anti-clockwise. Once created, simply select your frame and click on the **Rotate 90° clockwise** (marked as *A* in *Figure 4.10*) or the **Rotate 90° anticlockwise** (marked as *B* in *Figure 4.10*) buttons. In our case, we will choose **Rotate 90° clockwise**.

   It is worth noting that the reference point for the rotation is again based on the grid of nine squares shown in *step 3*:

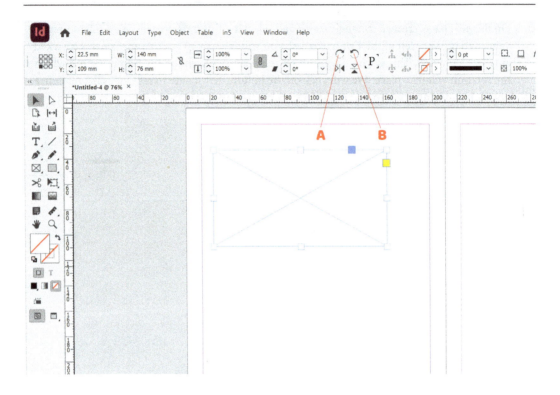

Figure 4.10: Rotating by 90° clockwise or anti-clockwise

All of the methods shown so far for rotating frames are both quick and useful, but occasionally you might want to rotate the frame around a very precise point on the page. This is where the **Rotate tool** can come in useful.

6.   Create a new rectangle frame and switch to the **Rotate** tool. Then, click a point anywhere on the page you would like to set as the reference point for your rotation. Now, click on the frame, and while dragging the mouse, you will see the frame rotates around the reference point (marked as *A* in *Figure 4.11*):

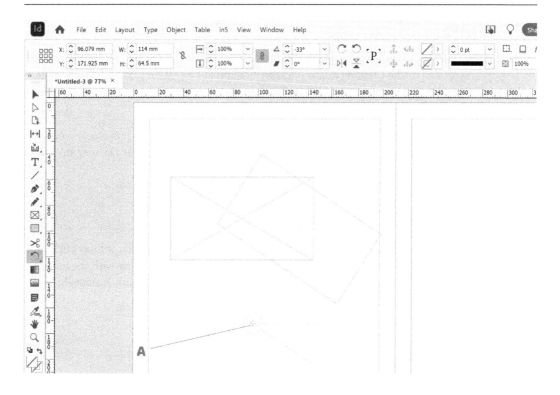

Figure 4.11: Using the Rotate tool to set a reference point

It is worth noting this method for setting a reference point can also be used in conjunction with the rotation methods covered in *step 4* and *step 5* as well.

7. Finally, one nice little trick with the **Rotate** tool—if you hold down the *Alt* (PC)/*Option* (Mac) key while you click to set a custom reference point, it will set the reference point and at the same time bring up the **Rotate** dialog box, which allows you to set a specific angle value for the rotation.

Resizing frames

In this recipe, we will learn how to resize frames in InDesign, doing so freehand, resizing to precise width and height values, and doing so by exact percentages. We will also look at useful shortcuts for resizing your content proportionally along with the frame and auto-resizing the frame to display all overset text.

Getting ready

In order to complete this recipe, simply open InDesign on your system and create a new document with 12 pages, as shown in the *Creating a new document* recipe in *Chapter 1*. You will also need to know how to create new frames on your pages, as shown in the *Creating rectangle or elliptical frames* recipe found earlier in this chapter.

This recipe will also involve resizing a frame containing an image; if you haven't previously worked with images in InDesign, this is covered in *Chapter 5, Working with Images in Your Documents*.

How to do it...

In order to resize your frames in InDesign, follow these steps:

1. Create a rectangle frame on the page and switch to the **Selection** tool. Then, simply click on any of the frame adjustment handles (marked as *A* in *Figure 4.12*) and drag with the mouse held down. Holding down the *Shift* key while doing this will ensure the width and height stay in proportion to each other, ensuring the frame doesn't become stretched:

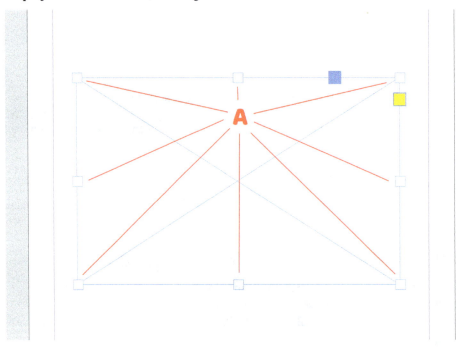

Figure 4.12: Resizing handles on frames

2. Resizing manually can be very quick and easy, but in this instance, we actually want to resize the frame to an exact size. With this in mind, select the frame with the **Selection** tool, and on the **Control** panel, you will see options to set the **Width** value (marked as *A* in *Figure 4.13*) or **Height** value (marked as *B* in *Figure 4.13*). To use the default unit of measurement (which is millimeters here), just type in a number for the width and a number for the height; in our case, we will type **130 mm** for the width and **80 mm** for the height.

> **Note**
>
> If you prefer to use different increments, just type the value in with an abbreviation after it, such as **5 in** or **65 mm**, and InDesign will convert it into the current default unit of measurement (which can be set in the InDesign preferences). Options available include **in** (inches), **mm** (millimeters), **cm** (centimeters), **p** (picas), **px** (pixels), **c** (ciceros), and **ag** (agates).

If you want to ensure the width and height stay in proportion to each other, simply click the **Constrain proportions for width and height** icon, marked as *C* in *Figure 4.13*, which will ensure if one value is changed, the other is proportionally adjusted as well. You'll know if the icon has been enabled because the line through the icon will disappear:

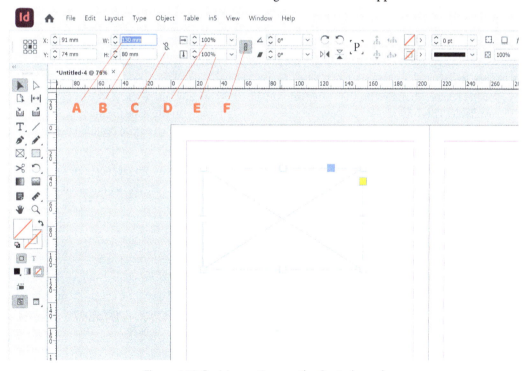

Figure 4.13: Resizing options on the Control panel

> **Note**
>
> It is worth noting that when resizing frames using the **Width** and **Height** fields, the frame will be pinned to the reference point you have set (marked as *A* in *Figure 4.9*) as it resizes.

3. In addition to resizing based on units of measurement, you can also resize something to a percentage of its current width, height, or both. To do this, simply enter the percentage of the current width into the **Scale X Percentage** box (marked as *D* in *Figure 4.13*) or height into the **Scale Y Percentage** box (marked as *E* in *Figure 4.13*). We will set **Scale X Percentage** to **90%**.

    If you wish to scale both *X* and *Y* values proportionally, ensure the **Constrain proportions for scaling** option is enabled (marked as *F* in *Figure 4.13*); again, the line through the icon will disappear when enabled.

4. Create a text frame and fill it with placeholder text (covered in the *Chapter 2* recipe, *Creating text frames and adding placeholder text*). Resize the text frame as shown in *step 1*, but this time hold down *Ctrl* (PC)/*Cmd* (Mac) as well as the *Shift* key while resizing; this will ensure the type is resized proportionally together with the frame.

    Now, resize the frame to make it smaller without holding down the *Ctrl* (PC)/*Cmd* (Mac) key, and you will see the text remains the same size while the frame gets smaller. This results in a small red mark at the bottom right of the frame identifying that there is now overset text on the frame (as explained in the *Chapter 2* recipe, *Threading text frames*).

5. One useful trick in InDesign is if a text frame has overset text, you can double-click on one of the resizing handles on the frame and it will automatically resize the frame to fit the text available. This only works, however, if there is enough room on the page for the new frame to fit. If there isn't sufficient room on the page, nothing will change when you double-click on the resizing handles. Try this now with the overset text frame.

6. Also, when working with frames that contain an object such as an image, you can resize the object proportionally together with its frame by holding down *Ctrl* (PC)/*Cmd* (Mac) + *Shift* and clicking on the frame's adjustment handles and dragging them.

Aligning frames with the Align panel

In this recipe, we will look at how to align your frames. You will learn how to align frames relative to a specific key object, the margins, the page, or the whole spread. We will also look at how to distribute your frames based on a particular edge, and wrap up by looking at how to apply precise spacing between your frames using the **Distribute Spacing** option.

Getting ready

In order to complete this recipe, simply open InDesign on your system and create a new document with 12 pages, as shown in the *Creating a new document* recipe in *Chapter 1*. You will also need to know how to create new frames on your pages, as shown in the *Creating rectangle or elliptical frames* recipe found earlier in this chapter.

How to do it...

In order to align and distribute frames within your document, follow these steps:

1. To begin with, we will create three frames and position them fairly randomly so that one is at the top left of the page, one toward the bottom right, and one somewhere in the center.

2. With the frames selected, navigate to the **Window** menu, then under **Object & Layout**, open the **Align** panel:

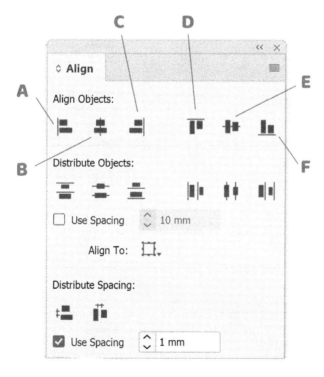

Figure 4.14: Align Objects options in the Align panel

In the **Align** panel, we want to align the frames vertically; there are three options to choose from, as follows:

- **Align left edges** (*A* in *Figure 4.14*): This aligns the left edges of the selected frames

- **Align horizontal centers** (*B* in *Figure 4.14*): This aligns the horizontal centers of the frames

- **Align right edges** (*C* in *Figure 4.14*): This aligns the right edges of the frames

By default, InDesign will use the leftmost frame as the key object when you align the left edges, the rightmost frame as the key object when you align the right edges, and the middle point between the left and right frames when you align the horizontal centers.

In our case, we will align the left edges, as shown in *Figure 4.15*:

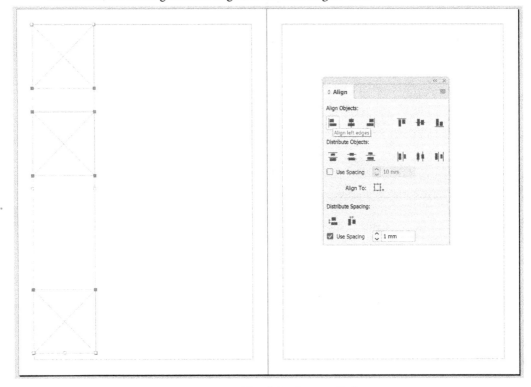

Figure 4.15: Align left edges applied

3. Repeat *step 1*, and this time we are going to align the frames horizontally. Looking back at *Figure 4.14*, we can use:

- **Align top edges** (*D* in *Figure 4.14*): This aligns the top edges of the selected frames

- **Align vertical centers** (*E* in *Figure 4.14*): This aligns the vertical centers of the frames

- **Align bottom edges** (*F* in *Figure 4.14*): This aligns the bottom edges of the selected frames

By default, InDesign will use the topmost frame as the key object when you align the top edges, the bottom frame as the key object when you align the bottom edges, and the middle point between the top and bottom frames when you align the vertical centers.

In our case, we will align the vertical centers, as shown in *Figure 4.16*:

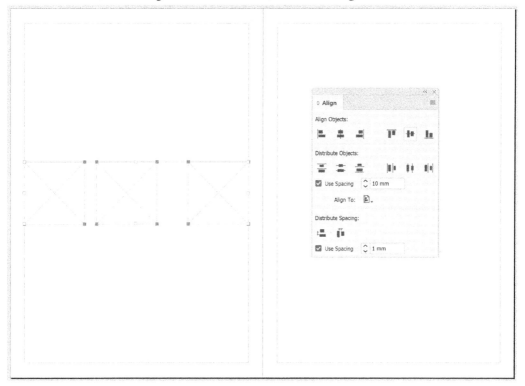

Figure 4.16: Align vertical centres applied

When aligning objects in InDesign, you will often want to align them to a specific object you select, known as the **key object**; we will look at that next.

4. Once again, on the next page, create three frames, scatter them randomly around the page, then select them. This time, we want to specifically align the frames vertically in line with the middle frame, which we need to set as the key object. With all the frames selected, simply click a second time on the object you want to use as the key object for the alignment, and you will notice the frame edge becomes more prominent, as you can see in *Figure 4.17*. If we now click the **Align left edges** option (marked as *A* back in *Figure 4.14*), you will see that it has aligned the left edges, but this time based on the key object:

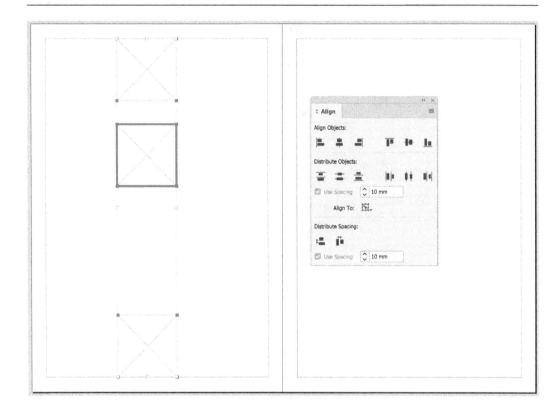

Figure 4.17: Setting a key object during alignment

It's worth noting that once you have selected a key object, you can either click on it again to stop it from being the key object or click on another of the selected objects to make that the key object instead.

5. Having set **Align left edges** with the second frame down selected as the key object, you may well find that the frames are not an equal distance apart. In order to resolve this, we can again select the frames and choose from three options, which are:

    - **Distribute top edges** (*A* in *Figure 4.18*): This spaces the top edges of the frames an equal distance apart

    - **Distribute vertical centres** (*B* in *Figure 4.18*): This spaces the middle of the frames an equal distance apart

    - **Distribute bottom edges** (*C* in *Figure 4.18*): This spaces the bottom edges of the frames an equal distance apart

    In our case, we will choose **Distribute vertical centres**.

In this example, the three options would all have a similar effect as the frames are all sized equally, but if they were of different sizes, choosing **Distribute top edges** would have a different effect from choosing **Distribute vertical centres**, for example:

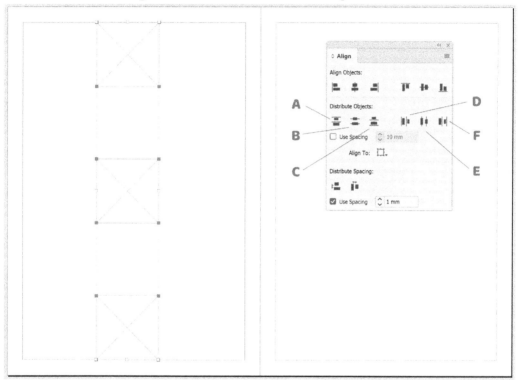

Figure 4.18: Distribute Objects options in the Align panel

6. Let's now go back to the horizontally aligned frames that we created in *step 3* (and that we can see in *Figure 4.16*). We now want to ensure these frames are also spaced evenly, and we have three options to help us, as follows:

*   **Distribute left edges** (*D* in *Figure 4.18*): This spaces the left edges of the frames an equal distance apart

*   **Distribute horizontal centres** (*E* in *Figure 4.18*): This spaces the middle of the frames an equal distance apart

*   **Distribute right edges** (*F* in *Figure 4.18*): This spaces the right edges of the frames an equal distance apart

In our case, we will choose **Distribute horizontal centres**, giving us a neat row of frames, all evenly spaced:

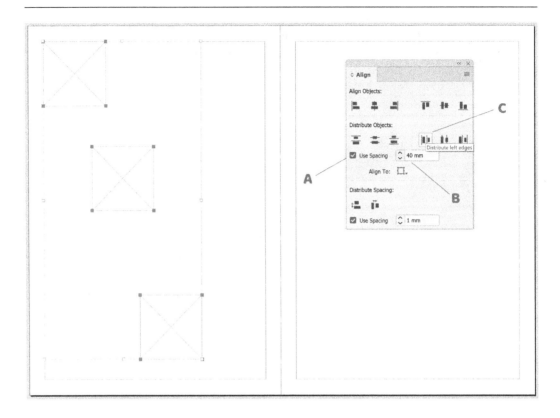

Figure 4.19: Distributing objects using spacing

7. Having looked at positioning frames relative to each other, we now want to look at how you can position frames based on a spacing value we choose. On a new page, create three frames, select them, then choose **Align left edges**.

    Having done this, we now want to position our frames at 40 mm intervals from left to right. So, select all the frames and then check **Use Spacing** (marked as A in *Figure 4.19*) and set the value to **40 mm** (marked as B in *Figure 4.19*). Now, click the **Distribute left edges** icon (marked as C in *Figure 4.19*). The frames should now be positioned so that each of the left edges is exactly 40 mm from the left edge of the previous frame.

8. While spacing edges a set distance from each other can be very useful, sometimes you want to position the frames with an exact spacing between them. This is particularly useful if the frames are different sizes, in which case distributing left edges (which we did in the last step) would result in the frames having a different spacing between them. Let's see how we can make each frame have a space of exactly 20 mm between itself and the next frame:

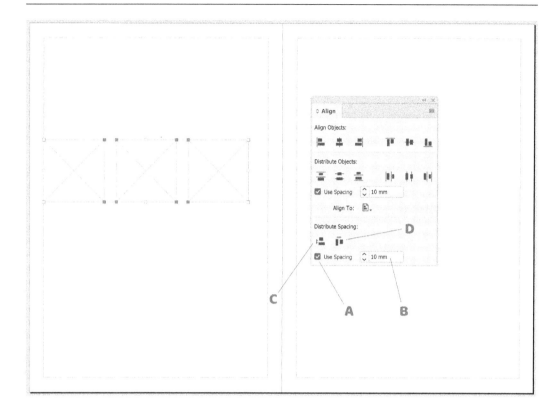

Figure 4.20: Distribute Spacing options in the Align panel

Create three frames on a new page and set the **Align vertical centres** option. Now, select all the frames and check the **Use Spacing** box (marked as *A* in *Figure 4.20*), and set the spacing value (marked as *B* in *Figure 4.20*) to **10 mm**. You have two options for distributing spacing, which are:

- **Distribute vertical space** (*C* in *Figure 4.20*): This positions the frames vertically so that they are the specified distance apart

- **Distribute horizontal space** (*D* in *Figure 4.20*): This positions the frames horizontally so that they are the specified distance apart

In our case, we will choose **Distribute horizontal space**, as seen in *Figure 4.20*.

> **Note**
>
> It is worth noting that when frames are of a similar size, **Distribute Spacing** and **Distribute Objects** may appear to do the same thing. However, the more the frame sizes differ, the more the different behavior of the two features becomes obvious.

9. Finally, we want to look at aligning to the margins, page, or spread rather than to other frames. On the next page, create three frames, scatter them randomly around the page, then select them. Then, in the **Align** panel, click the **Align To** dropdown (marked as *A* in *Figure 4.21*), and you will see the following five options:

    - **Align to Selection**: This will align relative to the selected objects
    - **Align to Key Object**: This will align relative to the chosen key object
    - **Align to Margins**: This will align relative to the margins
    - **Align to Page**: This will align relative to the page
    - **Align to Spread**: This will align relative to the spread

    In our case, we will select **Align to Margins**, then click the **Align Left Edges** option. The left edges of each frame will now be positioned in line with the left margin, as shown in *Figure 4.21*:

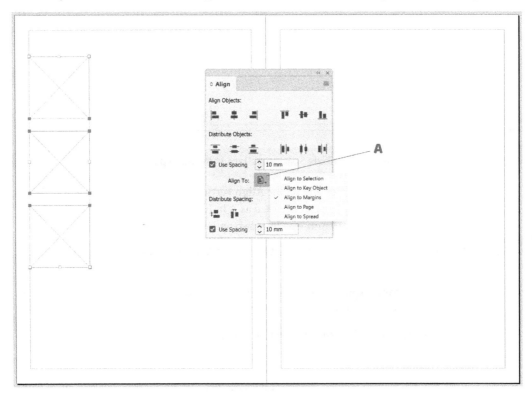

Figure 4.21: Align To dropdown in the Align panel

Using smart guides with frames

In this recipe, we will look at using **smart guides** with your frames, and how they can be a useful tool for quickly and consistently aligning items both to other items and the page, as well as ensuring consistent sizing of objects.

Getting ready

In order to complete this recipe, simply open InDesign on your system and create a new document with 12 pages, as shown in the *Creating a new document* recipe in *Chapter 1*. You will also need to know how to create new frames on your pages, as shown in the *Creating rectangle or elliptical frames* recipe found earlier in this chapter.

How to do it...

In order to use smart guides with your frames, follow these steps:

1. To turn smart guides on, go to the **View** menu, and under **Grids and Guides**, you will find the **Smart Guides options**. Check the box to enable them.

2. Having enabled the smart guides, we now want to check their configuration. Go to the **Edit** menu (PC)/**InDesign** menu (Mac), then under **Preferences**, select **Guides & Pasteboard**. Here, under the **Smart Guide Options** section, you will find the following checkboxes:

    *   **Align to Object Centre** (*A* in *Figure 4.22*): This allows items to align to the center of other objects

    *   **Align to Object Edges** (*B* in *Figure 4.22*): This allows items to align to the edges of other objects

    *   **Smart Dimensions** (*C* in *Figure 4.22*): Enabling this will allow you to get onscreen visual hints when doing things such as resizing or creating objects

    *   **Smart Spacing** (*D* in *Figure 4.22*): Enabling this will allow you to get onscreen visual hints when the spacing between different objects is consistent

    Ensure all four of these options are enabled as they are all useful:

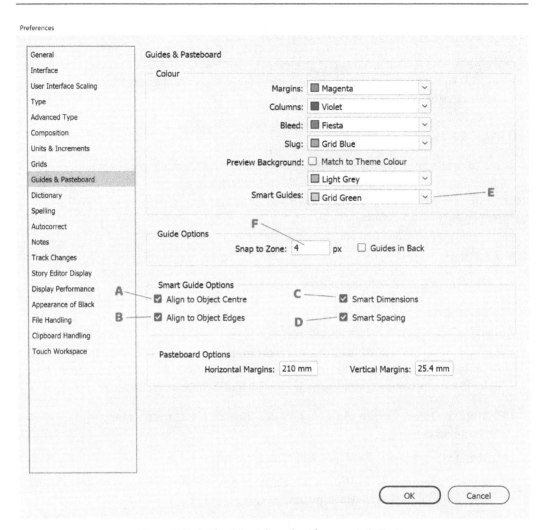

Figure 4.22: Guides & Pasteboard preferences in InDesign

3. Still in the **Guides & Pasteboard** tab, under the **Colour** section, you will see a **Smart Guides** option (*E* in *Figure 4.22*), which is set to **Grid Green** by default. This is the color used for the smart guides, and it doesn't normally need to be changed. Occasionally, though, you might have a conflict with the colors used in your document, so it might be necessary. We will leave this set to **Grid Green** in this instance.

4. One final **Smart Guides** option is **Snap to Zone** (*F* in *Figure 4.22*). This controls how close two objects need to be before they snap into line with each other. By default, it is set to **4 px**, which means if you drag a frame so that the edge is within 4 px of another frame, it will snap into line with it. As a general rule, I would recommend leaving the **Snap to Zone** set to **4 px** (which we will do here), but it is possible to increase it as high as 36 px should the need arise.

Once you're finished with the preferences, click **OK**. Having set the preferences for the smart guides, let's now take a look at using smart guides on the page.

Note

Smart guides only work on items that are in the current page view. Also, it is worth noting that the **Snap to Zone** option mentioned in *step 4* also affects snapping to regular guides on your pages, as shown in the *Chapter 1* recipe, *Applying and deleting guides*.

---

5. Now, switch to the **Rectangle Frame** tool and move your mouse around the page (without clicking). If you look closely, you will notice that the cursor changes slightly, indicating that you are over the horizontal and vertical centers of the page. When you are over the vertical center of the page, click and drag to create a frame that is in line with the vertical center.

6. Still with the **Rectangle Frame** tool, create a small frame sized at **60 mm x 40 mm**, followed by a second frame alongside it, sized at **20 mm x 100 mm**. Next, click below these to start creating a third frame, keeping the mouse button held down. As you drag the mouse, you should see green lines appear across the bottom and sides of the other frames. In *Figure 4.23*, the green lines down the side (*A*) and bottom (*B*) of the bottom frame indicate that the frame is the same height as the top-left frame (*C*) and the same width as the top-right frame (*D*). When the lines on your frame indicate it is the same height as the top-left frame and the same width as the top-right frame, release the mouse button to create the new frame:

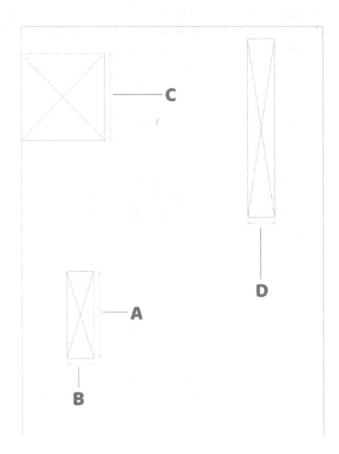

Figure 4.23: Smart Dimensions indicating frames are the same height/width

Having created a third frame that is the same width as the top-right frame, I have now decided I actually want it to be the same width as the top-left frame. Additionally, I want it to be positioned horizontally in line with the top-left frame. Let's look next at how smart guides help with this.

7. Switch to the **Selection** tool and select the bottom frame. Now, resize the frame using the adjustment handle on the right-hand side of the frame. As you start to make the frame bigger, you will find that when it becomes the exact same width as the top-left frame, the green lines (marked as *B* and *D* in *Figure 4.23*) once again reappear below the frames, except this time the line marked as *D* in *Figure 4.23* is now showing below the top-left frame, not the top-right frame.

8. Now we have the bottom frame the same width and height as the top-left frame, we are going to position it exactly beneath the top-left frame. To do this, click on it with the **Selection** tool and drag the frame across until it is under the top-right frame. You should now see the smart guides (marked as *A* in *Figure 4.24*), showing that the edges and center of both frames are directly in line with each other:

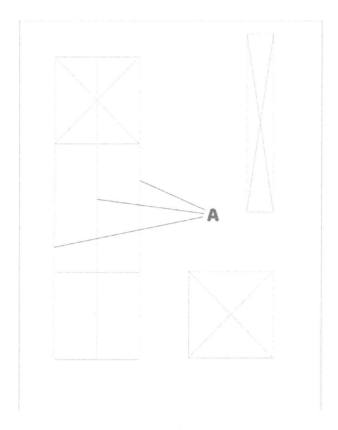

Figure 4.24: Smart guides helping to align frames

Customizing corners on frames

In this recipe, we will look at how to customize the corners on your frames, create rounded corners on one or all corners, adjust the size of the corners all together or individually, and apply different **corner options** to one or all corners using the **Live Corners** capability in InDesign.

Getting ready

In order to complete this recipe, simply open InDesign on your system and create a new document with 12 pages, as shown in the *Creating a new document* recipe in *Chapter 1*. You will also need to know how to create new frames on your pages, as shown in the *Creating rectangle or elliptical frames* recipe found earlier in this chapter.

How to do it...

In order to customize the corners on your frames, follow these steps:

1. Create a rectangle frame on your page, then select it with the **Selection** tool. You should now see a small yellow square near the top right of the frame (marked as *A* in *Figure 4.25*):

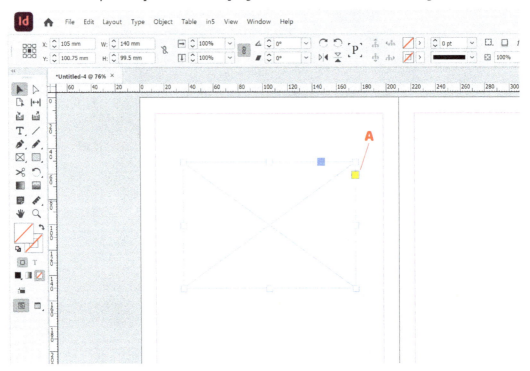

Figure 4.25: Rectangle frame showing the Edit Corners option

2. Then, with the **Selection** tool, click on the square to activate the **Live Corners** functionality. The square disappears to be replaced by a yellow diamond on each corner of the frame (marked as *A* in *Figure 4.26*); these are the live corner adjustment handles:

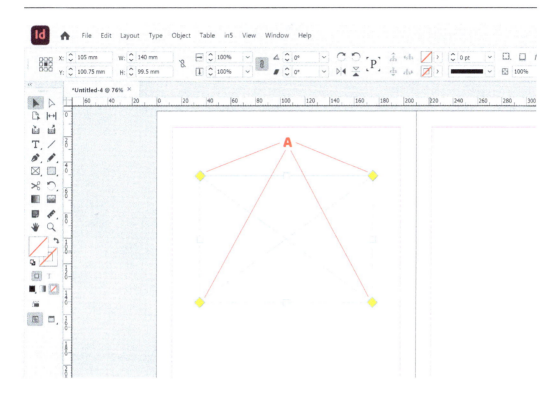

Figure 4.26: Live corner adjustment handles on a frame

3. In order to round all four corners, click on any one of the live corner adjustment handles and drag it horizontally toward the center of the frame, as shown in *Figure 4.27*. How far you drag it will dictate how rounded the corner is; the closer to the center you drag it, the more rounded the corner:

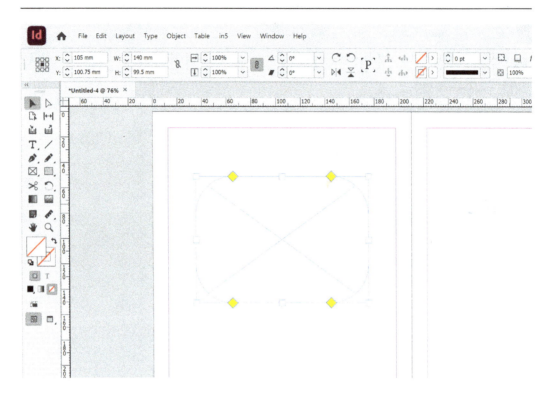

Figure 4.27: Adjusting live corners on a frame

4. Having rounded all four corners, we now want to return the top-right and bottom-left-hand corners to their original square shape. To localize a live corner adjustment to only a single corner, simply hold down the *Shift* key while making the adjustment. Do this with the top-right live corner, dragging it back horizontally to the right side of the frame. Do the same on the bottom-left live corner, dragging it back toward the left of the frame. Your corners will now look like those shown in *Figure 4.28*:

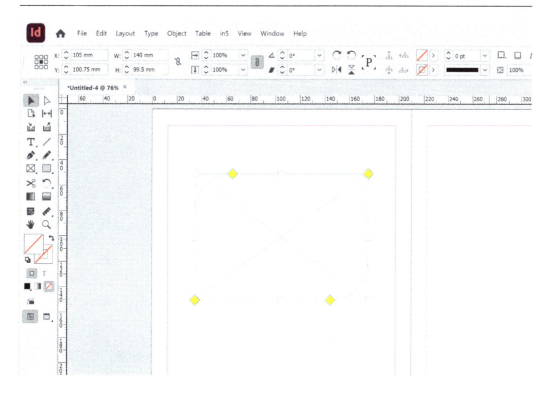

Figure 4.28: Adjusting live corners individually

5. At present, the two rounded corners are the same corner shape, but next, we would like to change the bottom-right corner to a different shape from the top-left one. Holding down the *Alt* (PC)/*Option* (Mac) + *Shift* keys, click on the bottom-right live corner four times until you get to the inverse rounded corner, marked as *A* in *Figure 4.29*:

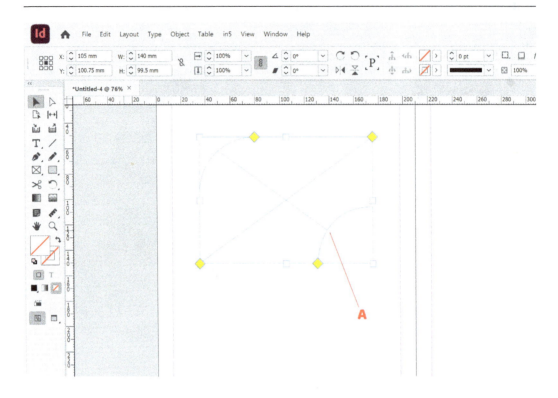

Figure 4.29: Adjusting one corner shape with Live Corners

You will notice each time you click the yellow diamond, the live corner changes to the next corner shape, going through six different shapes until eventually going back to the start again. Doing so without the *Shift* key held down will change all four corner shapes at the same time. The six corner shape options available are:

- **None**: No corner shape
- **Fancy**: A more elaborate corner shape
- **Bevel**: A beveled corner shape
- **Inset**: An inset on the corner
- **Inverse Rounded**: Corners are rounded in toward the center
- **Rounded**: Corners are rounded out

> **Note**
>
> It is worth noting that **None** is classed as one of the corner shapes when cycling through the corner shapes. Despite the square appearance of this, you can still continue to *Alt* (PC)/*Option* (Mac) and click on the diamond (with or without the *Shift* key) to continue on to the next shape.

While the **Live Corners** feature can be a nice quick easy way to change corners, sometimes you simply want to set precise corner values—for example, as dictated by brand guidelines.

6. To do this, let's create a new frame and select it with the **Selection** tool. Then, go to the **Object** menu and select **Corner Options** to open the **Corner Options** dialog box (as shown in *Figure 4.30*). Make sure to check the **Preview** checkbox (marked as *A* in *Figure 4.30*) so that you can see changes to the frame live:

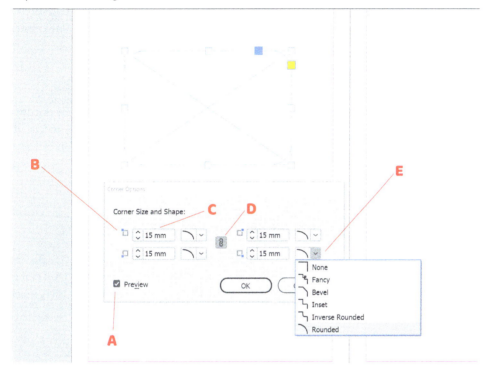

Figure 4.30: Corner Options dialog box

The **Corner Options** dialog box contains visual indicators to let you see which specific corner you are changing (marked as *B* in *Figure 4.30*), and you can change the size of the corners by typing a value in the number boxes by the corners (marked as *C* in *Figure 4.30*). If you wish to change all four corners together, click the link icon (marked as *D* in *Figure 4.30*) so that it no longer has a line through it. In our case, we will do this to set all four corners to **15 mm**.

We are also going to change the shape of all four corners by clicking one of the shape dropdowns (marked as *E* in *Figure 4.30*) and selecting **Rounded Corner**. The other options available include **None**, **Fancy**, **Bevel**, **Inset**, and **Inverse Rounded**, as seen in *step 5*. If you wish to use different shapes on different corners, simply disable the link (marked as *D* in *Figure 4.30*) that makes all settings the same.

Merging frames with the Pathfinder tool

When you are working in InDesign, sometimes you want to use a frame that's not a square, an ellipse, or a polygon. You might just want a differently shaped frame. Many people don't realize it, but InDesign's frames are actually just vector shapes, and as such, you can use the **Pathfinder** tool on them in the same way you use it when working with vector shapes in Adobe Illustrator.

The **Pathfinder** tool lets you combine frames together, punch holes in one frame using another, create shapes from overlapping areas, and much more. In this recipe, we will take a look at some common uses of the **Pathfinder** tool for creating interesting frame shapes.

Getting ready

In order to complete this recipe, simply open InDesign on your system and create a new document with 12 pages, as shown in the *Creating a new document* recipe in *Chapter 1*. You will also need to know how to create new frames on your pages, as shown in the *Creating rectangle or elliptical frames* recipe found earlier in this chapter.

How to do it...

In order to use the **Pathfinder** tool in InDesign, follow these steps:

1. First, create a rectangle frame, then create an elliptical frame that overlaps the rectangle frame (like *A* in *Figure 4.31*). Now, select both frames with the **Selection** tool, go to the **Object** menu under **Pathfinder**, and click **Add**. The two frames will now be merged together, forming a single frame that can be used like any other frame (similar to *B* in *Figure 4.31*):

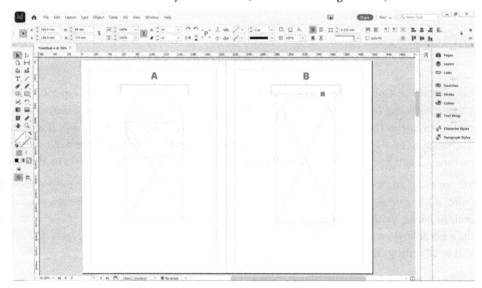

Figure 4.31: Adding two frames together with the Pathfinder tool

Having merged together two frames to form a single frame, we now want to merge together multiple frames to form a compound frame.

> **Note**
>
> Think of a compound path as a container that allows the individual paths to all function as one—for example, for the purposes of containing content.

2. Create a grid of 8 frames vertically x 10 frames horizontally with a **Gutter** setting of **2 mm**, as shown by *A* in *Figure 4.32* and covered in the *Creating Rectangle and elliptical frames* recipe earlier in this chapter. Now, with all the frames selected, go to the **Object** menu, and under **Pathfinder**, select **Add**. The frames have now been combined into a **compound path** (*B* in *Figure 4.32*), and as a result, you will see a single large *X* across the whole compound path as opposed to the individual X in each individual frame, which we saw before applying the **Pathfinder** tool:

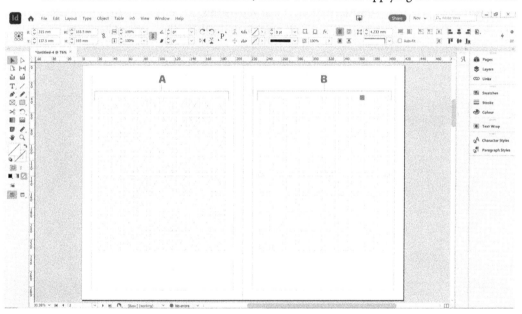

Figure 4.32: A compound path in InDesign

We could now place an image into this, for example (covered in *Chapter 5*), and it would be displayed right across the compound frame.

Note

If you are unsure whether your path is a compound path, simply open the **Layers** panel and check beneath the relevant layer—it should be named **Compound path**.

It is also possible to reverse a compound path should you wish. To do this, select the compound path, and then in the **Object** menu, under **Paths**, select **Release Compound Path**. This splits the compound path back into the original paths. If you do this having already added content, such as an image, the content will be placed into one of the resulting paths, with the rest being left blank.

Having used the **Pathfinder** tool to merge frames together, we now want to look at how we can use it to subtract an area from a frame.

3. Create a rectangle frame on your page and then create an elliptical frame on top of this, as shown by *A* in *Figure 4.33*. Now, with both frames selected, go to the **Object** menu, then under **Pathfinder**, select the **Subtract** option. When you do this, InDesign uses the top objects to cut holes in the back object, leaving you with a single frame that will function like any other frame (as shown by *B* in *Figure 4.33*):

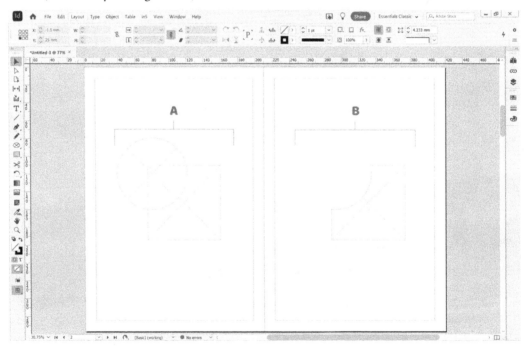

Figure 4.33: Subtracting an object with the Pathfinder tool

Having subtracted one frame from another, let's take a look next at intersecting frames.

4. Add an elliptical frame to your page and then create a second elliptical frame overlapping it, as shown by *A* in *Figure 4.34*. With the two frames selected, go to the **Object** menu, and under **Pathfinder**, select the **Intersect** option. **Intersect** will create a frame from the areas that overlap and delete everything else, as shown by *B* in *Figure 4.34*:

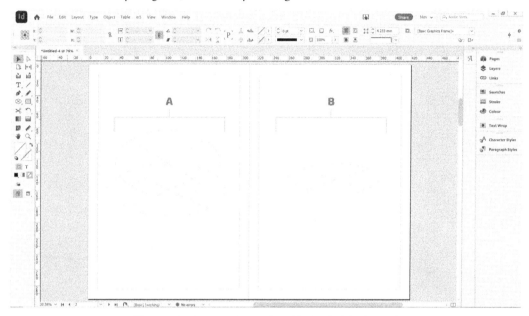

Figure 4.34: Intersecting paths with the Pathfinder tool

5. The final **Pathfinder** tool option we will use is **Minus Back**. Create a rectangle frame first, and then on top of this, create a polygon frame, as shown by *A* in *Figure 4.35*. Select both frames, then in the **Object** menu, under **Pathfinder**, select the **Minus Back** option. Areas of the polygon shape that overlap with the rectangle frame (which is at the back) will now be removed, leaving the remaining areas, as shown by *B* in *Figure 4.35*.

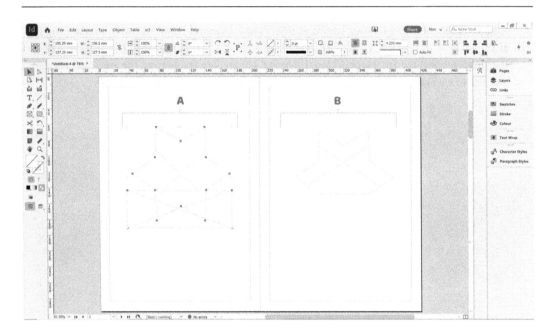

Figure 4.35: Minus Back option in the Pathfinder tool

Generating a QR code in a frame

QR codes are effectively a type of barcode that can be scanned by most modern mobile devices and can convey a variety of useful information. The most common use of QR codes is to provide a quick way of linking to online information, with users being able to point their mobile phone at a QR code on a poster, flyer, or sign, and a website will be opened up on the user's device.

Despite QR codes being easy to generate in InDesign, I still come across many users that are unaware of this feature and are using third-party apps and online resources to create their QR codes instead. In this recipe, we will look at how to create a QR code, the different types of QR codes available, and even how to customize the color of your QR code. In the next chapter, we will then look at placing external content such as images into your frames.

Getting ready

In order to complete this recipe, simply open InDesign on your system and create a new document with 12 pages, as shown in the *Creating a new document* recipe in *Chapter 1*. You will also need to know how to create new frames on your pages, as shown in the *Creating rectangle or elliptical frames* recipe found earlier in this chapter.

How to do it...

In order to generate QR codes in InDesign, follow these steps:

1. Create a square frame on your page using the **Rectangle Frame** tool. Then, with the frame selected, go to the **Object** menu and select **Generate QR Code**. This will bring up the **Generate QR Code** dialog box. There are two sections to the box: **Content** (marked as *A* in *Figure 4.36*) and **Colour** (marked as *B* in *Figure 4.36*):

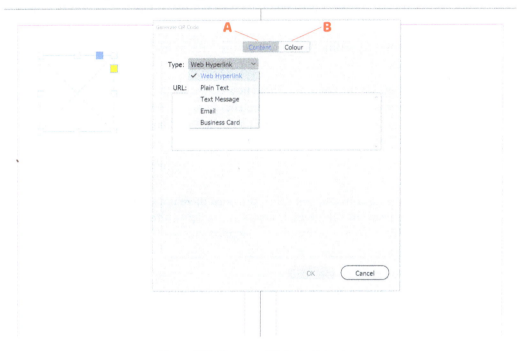

Figure 4.36: Generate QR Code dialog box

2. The first option in the **Content** section is **Type**; here, you can choose the type of QR code you want to create. The options here include the following:

    *   **Web Hyperlinks**: This allows you to enter a website URL. When scanned, users will be given the option to open the web page.

    *   **Plain Text**: This lets you create a plain text message that will be displayed on the user's screen when the code is scanned.

    *   **Text Message**: This lets you enter a telephone number and message. When scanned, it will bring up the relevant SMS messaging app on the mobile device and automatically populate the phone number and message fields, meaning the user just has to click **Send**.

- **Email**: This lets you enter an email *To* address that you would like email messages sent to, a subject for the message, and the actual message content. When a user scans it, their default mail program will automatically create a new email and populate the **To**, **Subject**, and **Message** fields, ready for them to click **Send**.

- **Business Card**: This option lets you enter a broad range of contact information, including **Forename, Surname, Title, Cell Phone Number, Phone Number, Email, URL, Organisation, Address, Town/City, State, Postal Code**, and **Country**. When the user scans the code, they will be prompted to add the record to their mobile phone contacts, complete with all the information.

We will choose **Web Hyperlinks**, and I will set the **URL** to my website: `http://www.highlander.co.uk`.

3. Having set the content for the QR code, we can now customize the color of the QR code using the **Colour** tab. Here, you will see solid color swatches from your swatches panel displayed, and you can choose from these. To create new color swatches, see *Chapter 7, Working with Colors and Gradients*, but for now, we will choose **Cyan**.

> **Note**
>
> QR codes generally work fine in different colors provided there is a strong contrast with the background; they can even contain multiple colors or gradients, although they would need careful testing. InDesign's QR code generator only supports single-color QR codes at this time.

4. Now, click **OK** at the bottom of the dialog box to generate your new QR code.

    Having finished creating the QR code, you might then spot a mistake you wish to edit. In my case, I have just noticed that I entered the URL as *http* and not as *https*, which it should be; let's look at how to edit the QR code.

5. To do this, with the **Selection** tool, select the frame containing the QR code. Then, in the **Object** menu, select the **Edit QR Code...** option. You can also access this option by selecting the object and then right-clicking on it with the mouse, as seen in *Figure 4.37*:

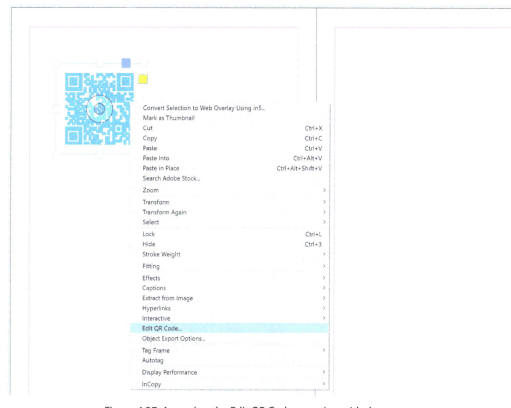

Figure 4.37: Accessing the Edit QR Code… option with the mouse

6. This will bring up the **Edit QR Code** dialog box; it is identical to the **Generate QR Code** dialog box seen in *Figure 4.36* but with a different name at the top. Here, I change the URL from `http://www.highlander.co.uk` to `https://www.highlander.co.uk` and then click **OK** to save the changes.

5

Adding Images to Your Documents

In this chapter, we are going to look at how to work with images in your documents. You will learn how to insert **images**, and then manipulate them independently of the frames that hold them. We will also look at how to resize images, apply a range of fitting options, and understand image resolution and its impact. Later in the chapter, we will look at how missing links can occur in your documents and why and how to fix them, as well as modified links and how to update them. Finally, we will look at the **Text Wrap** feature, learn how to wrap text around your images, and fine-tune this by adjusting the **Offset** and **Wrap To** features.

These are the recipes we will cover in this chapter:

- Placing images into InDesign
- Adjusting images versus frames
- Resizing images
- Applying fitting to images
- Checking the image resolution
- Working with image file links
- Wrapping text around images

Technical requirements

To complete this chapter, you will need a PC or Mac, with a copy of Adobe InDesign installed.

You will also need some images. I have used some of my own images, along with a number of images by photographer Tim Hill, which can be found at `https://pixabay.com/users/timhill-5727184/`.

Placing images into InDesign

In this recipe, you will learn how to place images into InDesign. We will add individual images into a frame, learn how to add an image without a pre-existing frame, and even look at bringing in multiple images all at once.

Getting ready

In order to complete this recipe, simply open InDesign on your system and create a new document with 12 pages, as shown in the *Creating a new document* recipe from *Chapter 1*. You should be comfortable creating both single and multiple frames on your page, as covered in *Chapter 4, Using the Frame Tools in InDesign*.

How to do it...

In order to place images into your document, follow these steps:

1. Using the **Elliptical Frame** tool, create an elliptical frame on your page. Then, with the frame still selected, go to the **File** menu and select **Place** (or press *Ctrl* (PC)/*Cmd* (Mac) + *D*) to bring up the **Place dialog box**, as seen in *Figure 5.1*:

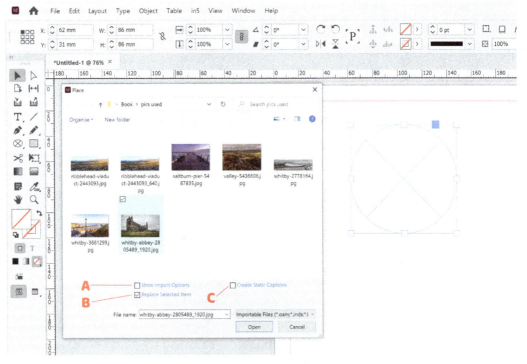

Figure 5.1: Placing an image into a frame in InDesign

Here, you can navigate through the folders on your computer and choose the image you want to insert. There are also a number of checkboxes at the bottom of the dialog box:

- **Show Import Options** (*A*): This brings up more advanced import options that we won't be using in this recipe. We will leave this unselected.

- **Replace Selected Item** (*B*): This will cause the image to automatically replace any existing content in the selected frame. We will leave this selected.

- **Create Static Captions** (*C*): This will automatically generate a static caption based on the current caption settings. We will leave this unchecked here but will look at captions in the *Using metadata for captions* recipe in *Chapter 6*.

To finish placing your image in the frame, simply select **Open**.

2. While the image is now showing in the frame, you will probably find that it doesn't fit especially well by default. We will explore this in more detail in the *Applying fitting to images* recipe, but for now, with the frame still selected, apply the *Ctrl + Alt + X* (PC)/ *Cmd + Option + X* (Mac) keyboard shortcut. This will cause the image to fit into the frame using InDesign's **Content-Aware Fit** option.

3. Having placed an image into an existing frame, we now want to place an image on the page without first creating a frame. With no frame selected, go to **File**, then **Place** (alternatively, you can press *Ctrl* (PC)/*Cmd* (Mac) + *D*). Select an image and click **Open**. Now, click on the page, and while holding down the mouse button, drag it to the size you want the image. When you let go of the mouse, InDesign will create a frame at that size and place the image into it, automatically resizing it to fit into the frame.

    It is worth noting that if you simply click once on the page instead of dragging, InDesign will automatically place the image on the page in a frame at 100% scale.

4. Having placed individual images onto the page, we now want to place four images at once. Create a grid of four frames on the page, then go to the **Edit** menu and click **Deselect All** to deselect all of the frames. Next, go to **Place**, but this time select four images at the same time by holding down the *Ctrl* (PC) *Cmd* (Mac) key. Then, click **Open**.

    You will notice the cursor has a thumbnail of the first image, similar to when we placed a single image, only this time it also has a small number *4* in brackets in the top left of this thumbnail (the location is marked as *A* in *Figure 5.2*; however, as the number can be quite small, it will likely be clearer on your screen). This shows the total number of images selected. Using the left and right arrow keys on your keyboard, you can cycle through the images, and the thumbnail will change to reflect the currently selected image:

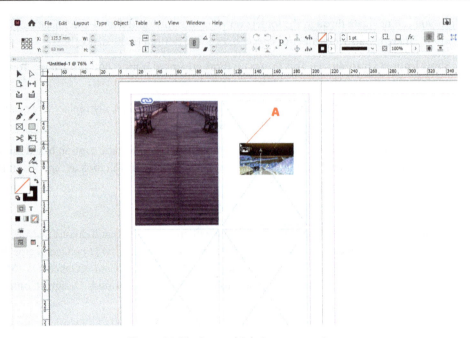

Figure 5.2: Placing multiple images at a time

When you find the right image, click into the frame you would like to place it in, and then continue with the next image until all four images have been placed, as seen in *Figure 5.3*:

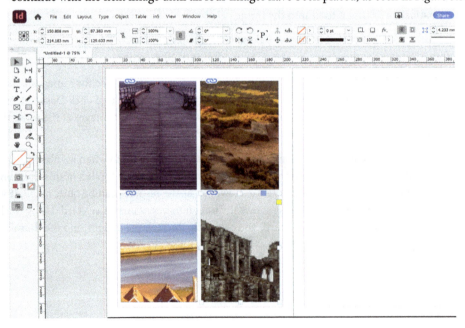

Figure 5.3: Images placed into four separate frames

> **Warning**
>
> As a rule of thumb, it is bad practice to use copy and paste to bring images into your InDesign documents. Doing so means you will have no link back to the original file, so you cannot update it, and you might lose your images if the InDesign document becomes corrupt. Additionally, the operating system clipboard that is used during copy/paste actions may alter the image, causing a low-resolution preview image to be inserted instead of the higher-quality original file.

Adjusting images versus frames

In this recipe, we are going to look at the difference between the image and the frame it sits in. We will be using the **Selection** and **Direct Selection** tools on your images, as well as enabling and working with the **Content Grabber** feature.

Getting ready

In order to complete this recipe, simply open InDesign on your system and create a new document with 12 pages, as shown in the *Creating a new document* recipe in *Chapter 1*. You should be comfortable adding images to your document, as shown in the previous recipe, *Placing Images into InDesign*.

How to do it...

In order to adjust the images and their frames within your document, follow these steps:

1. Create a rectangle frame in the middle of your document. Then, with the frame selected, go to **File** then **Place**, and insert an image into the frame.

    You now have a frame on the page containing an image—at this point, it's important to understand that these are two separate entities, in much the same way that a painting hanging in an art gallery is separate from the frame that it is mounted in.

2. If we want to now move the picture around within the InDesign page, we can simply use the **Selection** tool to click anywhere on the image (except the small circle in the middle, which is marked as C in *Figure 5.4*) and drag it to where we want it. This will move both the frame and the image that sits within it.

3. Now, we would like to reposition the image *within* its frame, but without moving the actual frame. This time, we will use the **Direct Selection** tool—when you click on the image, you will see a brown border appear (marked as A in *Figure 5.4*). This represents the border of the image as opposed to the frame that contains it. You can now drag the image around within its frame to reposition it within the frame. It should be noted that any areas of the image that sit outside of the frame will not be visible in the finished document. When you are done moving the image inside its frame, you can click on the gray pasteboard area (marked as B in *Figure 5.4*) to the side of the document to deselect everything:

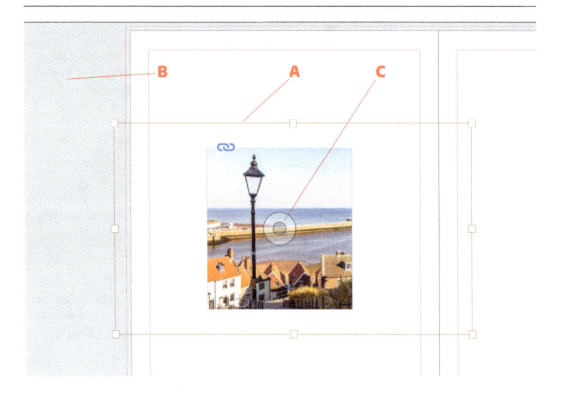

Figure 5.4: Direct selection of an image within its frame

> **Note**
>
> The frame border color is dictated by the color of the layer that the frame is being created on in the **Layers** panel and can be set to any color. We are just used to seeing it as blue as this is Layer 1's default color.

4. Switching between the **Selection** and **Direct Selection** tools is one way to switch between moving a frame and an image together or just an image by itself. There is, however, a faster way by using a feature called the **Content Grabber**. Before using it, we need to enable it. To do so, go to the **View** menu, and under **Extras**, click on **Show Content Grabber** (if the option says **Hide Content Grabber**, it's already enabled).

5. With the **Content Grabber** feature now enabled, we can move both the image and frame together or just the image by itself all using the **Selection** tool, without the need to switch to the **Direct Selection** tool. To move the image and frame together, simply repeat what we did in *step 2*; however, to move only the image without moving the frame, you can now click on the **Content Grabber** feature (marked as *C* in *Figure 5.4*) with the **Selection** tool and drag. If you need to move both together again, just make sure to click on the pasteboard before again moving both, as shown in *step 2*.

6. Finally, it is worth mentioning that the ability to select either an image by itself or an image and a frame together can be combined with other features such as **Skew** and **Rotate** (shown in the *Chapter 4* recipe *Rotating and skewing rectangle frames*). With this in mind, select the image by itself with the **Content Grabber** feature and then apply a 15-degree skew (marked as *A* in *Figure 5.5*), and you will notice that it only affects the image, not the frame, as shown in *Figure 5.5*:

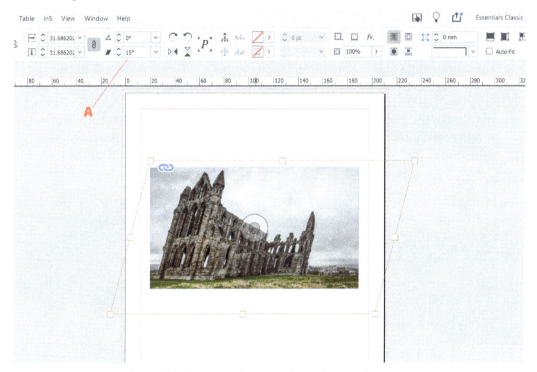

Figure 5.5: A skew applied to the image but not the frame

Resizing images

In this recipe, we are going to look at a number of ways to resize your images, both manually using the mouse together with shortcut keys and also numerically using the **Properties** panel or, if you prefer, the **Control** panel, where the same resizing options can also be found.

It is important to note that resizing your images on the page will also affect the effective resolution of the image, so if you are not already comfortable with resolution and its impact, I would recommend the *Checking the image resolution* recipe later in this chapter. In that recipe, we will resize and apply fitting to images, and look more closely at the impact this has on the resolution.

Getting ready

In order to complete this recipe, simply open InDesign on your system and create a new document with 12 pages, as shown in the *Creating a new document* recipe in *Chapter 1*. You should be comfortable adding images to your document, as shown in the *Placing images into InDesign* recipe earlier in this chapter.

How to do it...

In order to resize the images within your document, follow these steps:

1. Place an image into your document, then select the frame and image with the **Selection** tool. To resize the image and frame together proportionally, hold down *Ctrl + Shift* (PC)/*Cmd + Shift* (Mac), and then click on the corner of the image frame (marked as *A* in *Figure 5.6*) and drag. The *Ctrl* (PC)/*Cmd* (Mac) key will ensure the image is resized along with the frame, while the *Shift* key will ensure that the width and height are kept in proportion. Make sure to let go of the mouse button before releasing the keyboard keys, and your image will then be resized:

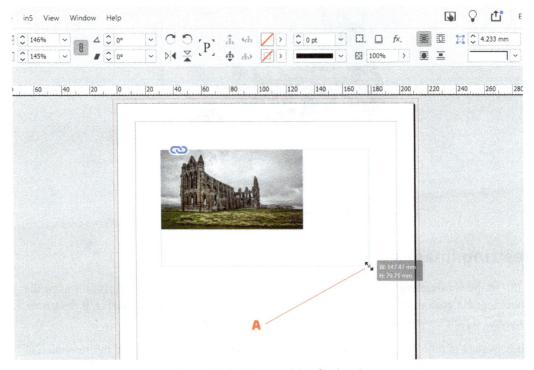

Figure 5.6: Resizing an object freehand

2. If you wish to deliberately stretch the image, repeat *step 1*, but this time without holding down *Shift*. When you release the mouse, the image will be resized, but the width and height will no longer be in proportion and the image will appear stretched.

Having resized images freehand, let's take a look next at resizing numerically.

3. Place an image into your document and select the whole object with the **Selection** tool. Now, go to the **Window** menu and click **Properties** to open the **Properties** panel.

    The **Properties panel** is a context-sensitive panel that offers up a range of options relevant to the current task or tool you are working with. As we currently have a frame containing an image selected, the **Properties** panel gives us options for transforming the selected object, as well as adjusting the appearance, wrapping text, and setting fitting options:

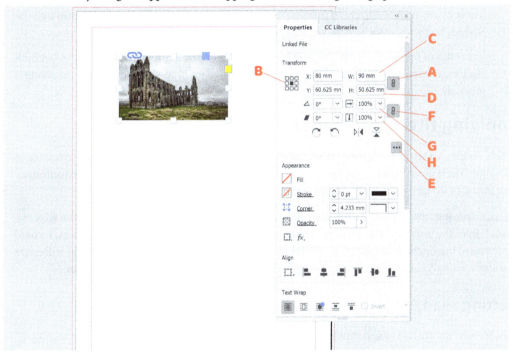

Figure 5.7: The Properties panel in InDesign

4. First, let's adjust the width and height of the frame proportionally so that the image is cropped slightly. To do this, enable the **Constrain proportions for width and height** button (marked as *A* in *Figure 5.7*). We also want to set a reference point for resizing the frame—for example, does the frame expand/contract from the top left or from the center? This is set using the **Reference Point** grid (*B* in *Figure 5.7*), where we have set it to the center of the frame. Now, you can reduce the value of either the **Width** or **Height** property (*C* and *D* in *Figure 5.7*), and whichever value you change, the other value will also automatically change proportionally. In my case, I have set the width to **90 mm** and it has therefore automatically reduced the height to **50.625 mm**, keeping the width-to-height ratio the same.

5. Having reduced the size of the frame to crop the image slightly, I now want to scale the entire object. At this stage, if you don't see the icons marked as *F*, *G*, and *H* in *Figure 5.7*, it means you have some of the **Transform** options hidden in the panel. To show these options, just click the **More options** icon, marked as *E* in *Figure 5.7*.

6. Now, with the object still selected, click the **Constrain Proportions for Scaling** icon (*F* in *Figure 5.7*) and then enter a value in either the **Scale X** (*G* in *Figure 5.7*) or **Scale Y** (*H* in *Figure 5.7*) box. These boxes work on percentages by default, so entering **110%** would increase the size of the object to 110% of its current size. In my case, I want to increase the size of the whole object proportionally so that it is 120 mm wide, though, so I will type **120 mm** into the **Scale X** box and hit the *Return* key.

The result of this would be the original image is still cropped slightly, as seen in *step 4*, but both the image frame and its contents have now been scaled up proportionally so that the frame is precisely 120 mm wide.

Applying fitting to images

In this recipe, we are going to look at fitting as it applies to images and their respective frames in InDesign. There are a variety of options that, when used correctly, can simplify and even automate your fitting of images within their respective frames in InDesign.

As with resizing images, it is worth noting that the fitting of images will also impact the effective resolution of the image, so if you are not already comfortable with resolution and its impact, I would recommend the *Checking the image resolution* recipe later in this chapter. In that recipe, we will resize and apply fitting to images, and look more closely at the impact this has on the resolution.

Getting ready

In order to complete this recipe, simply open InDesign on your system and create a new document with 12 pages, as shown in the *Creating a new document* recipe in *Chapter 1*. You should be comfortable adding images to your document, as shown in the *Placing images into InDesign* recipe earlier in this chapter.

How to do it...

In order to adjust the fitting of images within your document, follow these steps:

1. First, create a rectangle frame on the page, and then place an image into it. Unless you happen to have created a frame exactly the same size and dimension as the image, you should find either some of the image is outside the frame area (shown by *A* in *Figure 5.8*) or the image is smaller than the frame, leaving white space around the edges (shown by *B* in *Figure 5.8*):

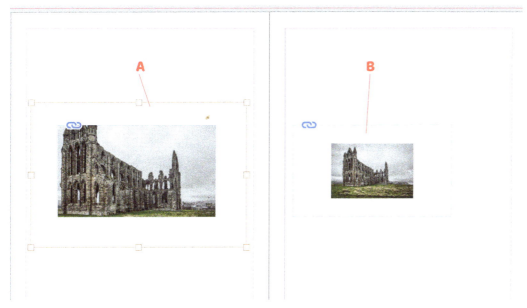

Figure 5.8: Examples of images without fitting applied in InDesign

2. Deselect everything by clicking on the pasteboard to the side of the document, and then, using the **Selection** tool, click on the object containing the image to select it. Now, right-click on the object, then under **Fitting** you will see the following **frame fitting options** to choose from:

- **Fill Frame Proportionally**: This will resize the image while keeping the width and height in proportion, to completely fill the frame. Typically, your frame and image will have different proportions, and as a result, this will cause some of the image to be cropped outside of the frame.

- **Fit Content Proportionally**: This will resize the image while keeping the width and height in proportion so that all of the image is visible within the frame. Again, your frame and image will likely have different proportions, but this time, the result of that will be some of the frame will be left empty, either at the top and bottom or at the sides. This is sometimes referred to as letterboxing or pillarboxing, terms that come from the video production industry.

- **Content-Aware Fit**: This will automatically fit your image to the frame proportionally but does so based on the image content, unlike **Fill Frame Proportionally**. As a result, if there is a fairly clear and obvious subject within the image, it will attempt to display that area within the frame.

- **Fit Frame to Content**: This resizes a frame to fit the image, altering the width and height of the frame to match that of the image.

- **Fit Content to Frame**: This resizes the image to fit the frame, altering the width and height to that of the frame, and can result in stretching of the image.

- **Centre Content**: This will simply center your image within the frame, leaving the size of both the frame and the image unchanged.

- **Clear Frame Fitting Options**: This will clear any previously applied fitting settings.

- **Frame Fitting Options**: This will open the **Frame Fitting Options** dialog box, which we will look at shortly.

In our case, we will choose **Fill Frame Proportionally**.

> **Note**
>
> In addition to accessing the fitting options by right-clicking on the image, you can also access the settings through the **Object** menu, where they can be found under **Fitting**.

3. Now, let's undo the **Fill Frame Proportionally** fitting option. To do this simply, right-click on the object, and under **Fitting** select **Clear Frame Fitting Options**.

4. With our fitting cleared, we will now right-click on the object and, under **Fitting**, select **Frame Fitting Options**. This will bring up the **Frame Fitting Options** dialog box seen in *Figure 5.9*. In here, we will check the box for **Auto-Fit** (*A* in *Figure 5.9*), which will both automatically switch the **Fitting** option (*B* in *Figure 5.9*) to **Fill Frame Proportionally** and cause the content to now resize automatically as the frame resizes:

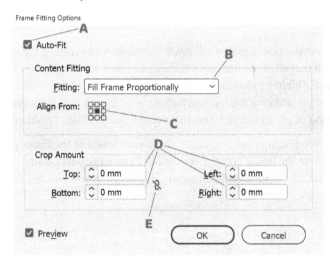

Figure 5.9: Frame Fitting Options dialog box in InDesign

Other settings available in the **Frame Fitting Options** dialog box include:

- **Reference Point** (*C* in *Figure 5.9*): This allows you to set a reference point, which is the point from which any changes originate when applying both fitting and cropping settings.

- **Crop Amount** (*D* in *Figure 5.9*): This allows you to control how much of the image is cropped—for example, if you set all four sides to **25 mm**, then 25 mm of the image will be cropped off on each side. It is worth bearing in mind that the fitting options chosen can impact this, so if you choose **Fit Proportionally to Frame** and then subsequently set a crop amount on only one side, it will crop more than one side in order to keep the fitting proportional. If you wish to crop all four sides to the same value, just click the **Make all settings the same** icon (marked as *E* in *Figure 5.9*) to ensure all four sides crop by the same amount.

5. Let's take a look at how we can use some of InDesign's newer content-aware technology to fit our images. Create another frame and place an image into it. Then, with the object selected, open the **Properties** panel:

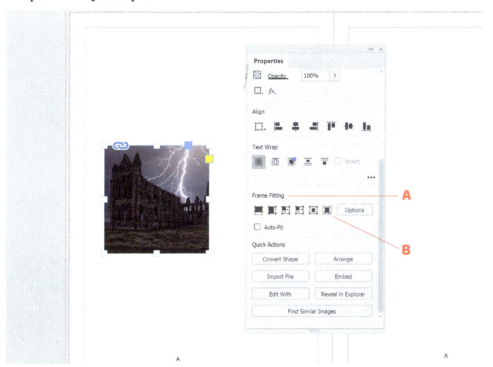

Figure 5.10: Fitting via the InDesign Properties panel

In the **Properties** panel, you should see the **Frame Fitting** section (marked as *A* in *Figure 5.10*); the options here are the same as those available via a right-click, as described in *step 2*. We will select **Content-Aware Fit**, which is the last icon (marked as *B* in *Figure 5.10*).

Content-Aware Fit uses **Adobe Sensei**, Adobe's **artificial intelligence** (**AI**) and **machine learning** (**ML**) technology, to analyze your image and apply fitting in a way that displays the most relevant part of the image. With this in mind, you might prefer to make it the default behavior when placing new images into InDesign.

If so, open the **Preferences** panel using *Ctrl + K* (PC)/ *Cmd + K* (Mac). Within the **General** section of the panel, you will see an option named **Make Content-Aware Fit the Default Frame Fitting Option**. If you check this box (marked as *A* in *Figure 5.11*) and then click **OK**, all new images placed into your documents will now automatically have **Content-Aware Fit** applied to them by default:

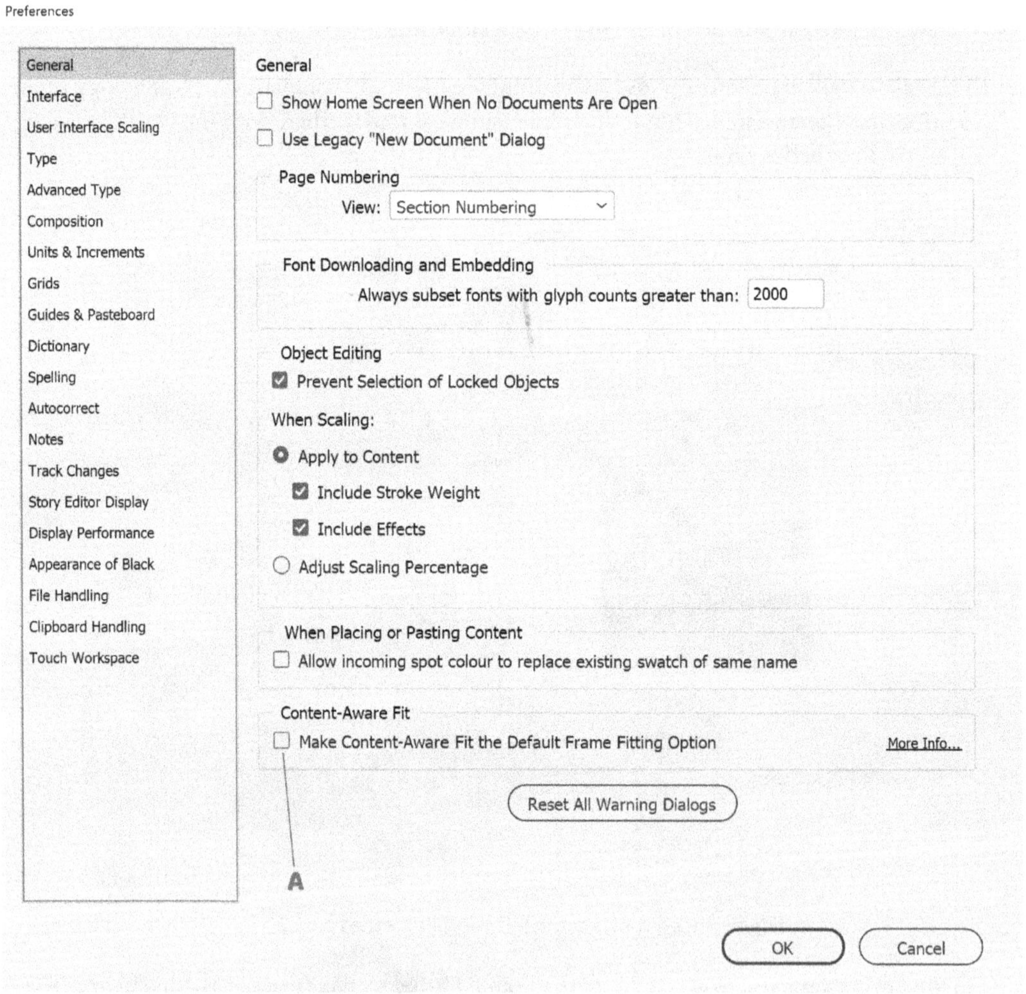

Preferences

General	**General**
Interface	☐ Show Home Screen When No Documents Are Open
User Interface Scaling	☐ Use Legacy "New Document" Dialog
Type	Page Numbering
Advanced Type	View: Section Numbering ⌄
Composition	
Units & Increments	Font Downloading and Embedding
Grids	Always subset fonts with glyph counts greater than: 2000
Guides & Pasteboard	
Dictionary	Object Editing
Spelling	☑ Prevent Selection of Locked Objects
Autocorrect	When Scaling:
Notes	● Apply to Content
Track Changes	☑ Include Stroke Weight
Story Editor Display	☑ Include Effects
Display Performance	○ Adjust Scaling Percentage
Appearance of Black	
File Handling	When Placing or Pasting Content
Clipboard Handling	☐ Allow incoming spot colour to replace existing swatch of same name
Touch Workspace	
	Content-Aware Fit
	☐ Make Content-Aware Fit the Default Frame Fitting Option More Info...
	(Reset All Warning Dialogs)

A

(OK)   (Cancel)

Figure 5.11: Making Content-Aware Fit the default option in the properties

Checking the image resolution

When working with images, there are two distinct types of images.

One type is called **vector images**, and they are made up of many individual points (called anchor points) that are connected by mathematically calculated lines (called paths), which can be either straight or curved. Vector images are constructed a bit like a child's dot-to-dot drawing, and no matter how big you make them, the paths between these anchor points simply get recalculated, meaning they can be scaled infinitely to any size you wish. In effect, they have no resolution, and for this reason, they are commonly used in the design of logos, packaging, fashion, and other areas where such scalability is a factor. For example, the same vector logo could be used on your business cards and also your 50-foot-long building sign with no impact on the quality. Common vector file formats include AI and SVG files.

The other type of image is a **raster image**, and these images are made up of millions of individual pixels of color. Anything produced by a camera would be a raster image, and the level of detail in such files is described as the **resolution**. The resolution is typically measured by the number of pixels found in a straight line, both horizontally and vertically across 1 inch of your image. As your images will normally contain square pixels, the number should be the same in both directions. So, for example, a 300-**pixels-per-inch** (**PPI**) image would have 300 pixels in a 1-inch straight line horizontally and the same number vertically. This means each square inch of your image would contain 90,000 pixels (that is, 300 x 300).

It is worth also noting that while resolution is typically measured by the number of PPI, you may also hear people refer to **dots per inch** (**DPI**). PPI refers to the square pixels on a screen, while DPI refers to the dots of ink used in the printing process. These terms are often used interchangeably, and while they are referring to different things, we can think of them as being the same for the purpose of working in InDesign. As a result, if your printer requires that all your images are 300 DPI, you can equate that to an effective resolution of 300 PPI when working in InDesign.

In this recipe, we are going to look at the resolution of raster images in InDesign and discuss actual PPI versus effective PPI, along with how fitting and resizing impact your effective resolution.

Getting ready

In order to complete this recipe, simply open InDesign on your system and create a new document with 12 pages, as shown in the *Creating a new document* recipe in *Chapter 1*. You should be comfortable adding images to your document, as shown in the *Placing images into InDesign* recipe. You should also be comfortable resizing your images and using fitting, as shown in the *Resizing images* and *Applying fitting to images* recipes in this chapter.

How to do it...

To check and understand the resolution of your images within your document, follow these steps:

1. Start by creating a frame on the page and placing an image into it. Then, with the frame selected, open the **Links panel**, where you will see the selected image (marked as *A* in *Figure 5.12*), with the page number the image is found on shown alongside it (marked as *B* in *Figure 5.12*). Because the image is selected, we are also able to see a variety of information about it in the links panel. If you are unable to see the **Link Info** area, you can click the small arrow (marked as *C* in *Figure 5.12*) to expand that section.

    Of particular interest in the **Link Info** area is the following:

    - **Actual PPI** (marked as *D* in *Figure 5.12*): This is the resolution of the image when it is sized at its original size—that is, 100%. In this case, this is **300**.

    - **Effective PPI** (marked as *E* in *Figure 5.12*): This is the resolution of the image at the size it is currently scaled to in InDesign. In this example, the image is being displayed in InDesign at a much smaller size than its original size, but it still has exactly the same number of pixels in the image. As a result, they are being squeezed into a smaller area, and the effective resolution is currently **1110**.

    - **Dimensions** (marked as *F* in *Figure 5.12*): This is the width and height of the image in pixels, which in this case is **6000** pixels by **4000** pixels.

    - **Scale** (marked as *G* in *Figure 5.12*): This is the percentage of the original size at which the image is now being displayed within InDesign. In this case, it is currently set to **27%** of the original size:

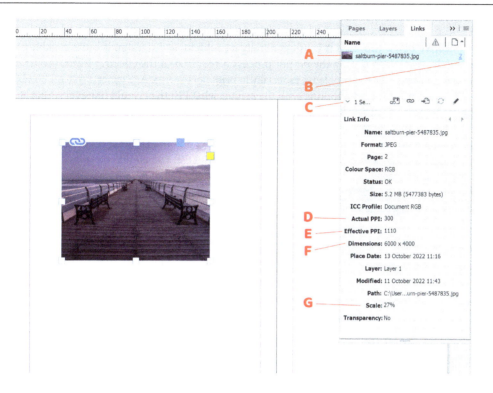

Figure 5.12: The InDesign Links panel

As you resize an image and make it larger, the effective resolution reduces and the pixels get bigger (so, fewer PPI); if you make it smaller, the pixels get smaller (so, more PPI), and the effective resolution increases. In effect, the number of pixels in the image stays the same, and resizing the image just resizes those pixels.

> **Note**
>
> While we are using the **Links** panel with its default settings, it is worth noting that these settings can be customized, allowing you to hide or show different properties within the panel. This is done from the **Links** panel menu by selecting **Panel Options**.

This effective resolution dictates whether an image can be successfully resized, as if the effective PPI becomes too small, the quality will look poor. With handheld print documents, you will typically want to aim for an effective resolution of around 300 PPI as this looks good when viewed at arm's length; for something like a window poster, you can aim for a lower resolution as people are looking at it from further away.

In my case, the image currently has an effective resolution of **1110** PPI, which means we are able to use it at a larger size, while still keeping the resolution above **300** PPI.

Note

If the effective PPI is too high it is not generally a problem, as InDesign is quite capable of reducing the resolution during the output process if required. If the effective PPI is too low, however, it can cause serious problems, especially in print documents. As a general rule of thumb, I would always recommend checking with the printer what PPI they would like everything at. For handheld print documents such as brochures, this will often be 300 PPI, while larger format print such as exhibition stands and advertising boards would often be at a lower resolution. In terms of screen documents, the decision often comes down to the fact that higher resolution means bigger files, so while it is tempting to aim for 300 DPI, you could end up with a huge document. Screen resolutions range from 72 PPI to over 400 PPI, but with today's technology, aiming for around 144 PPI can give you a nice compromise where the document looks fairly good without being huge in size.

2. Resize the image proportionally so that it reaches the bleed line at the top and left of the document and the spine in between the two pages that make up the spread (as seen in *Figure 5.13*). Resizing the image like this doesn't make any difference to the actual PPI or the dimensions as they were determined when the image was created and will only be changed if the image is edited in something such as Photoshop.

    As a result of resizing the image, the **Effective PPI** value (marked as *A* in *Figure 5.13*) has been reduced to **618** and the **Scale** value has now increased to **48.6%** (marked as *B* in *Figure 5.13*):

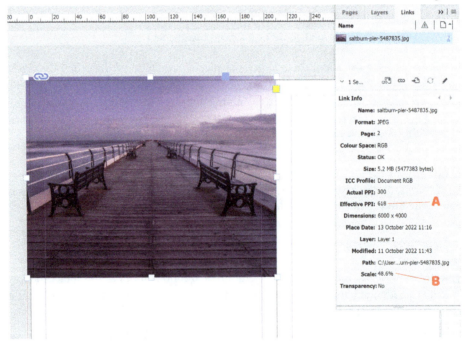

Figure 5.13: Impact of resizing on Effective PPI and Scale values

Having looked at how resizing your image affects the effective resolution, we are now going to take a look at how fitting affects things.

3. Next, create a new frame and place an image into it. I am going to use an image with a landscape orientation, as this will better demonstrate the impact of the different fitting options being applied on the resolution.

In the example shown in *Figure 5.14*, the image has no fitting applied yet. As a result, we can see both the **Effective PPI** and the **Actual PPI** values show as **300** PPI, due to the image being its original size still. It is also worth mentioning that the **Links** panel shows the image we used earlier in this recipe (marked as *A* in *Figure 5.14*), as well as the new image (marked as *B* in *Figure 5.14*). All of the images contained in a document are shown in the **Links** panel, and as a result, you might want to drag the dividing bar (marked as *C* in *Figure 5.14*) up or down a bit to show more images:

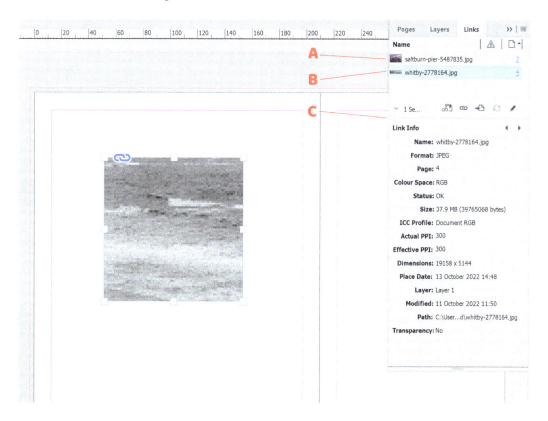

Figure 5.14: Image placed in InDesign with no fitting applied

> **Note**
>
> If you are planning to print a document with images, it is important to ensure they are the right resolution. It may look fine on your screen, but that doesn't mean it will look good when printed, and it is important to check the effective resolution either manually via the **Links** panel (shown in *Figure 5.14*) or via preflighting (covered later, in the *Chapter 13, Preflighting and Output*). There are various reasons for this, not least being the fact that screens contain technology such as anti-aliasing, which improves poor images, while paper doesn't.

4. Having placed the image into InDesign at its original size, we now want to apply some fitting settings to it. Right-click on the image, and under **Fitting**, select **Fill Frame Proportionally**. If you now look at the **Links** panel, you will notice the **Effective PPI** value has changed; in the case of my image, this now shows as **1281** (*A* in *Figure 5.15*), while the **Actual PPI** value still shows as **300** (*B* in *Figure 5.15*). The **Scale** value is showing as **23.4%**:

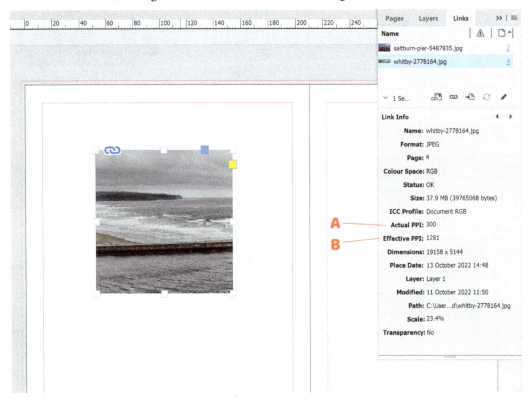

Figure 5.15: Effective resolution after applying Fill Frame Proportionally

5. Having filled the frame proportionally, let's now change that by right-clicking, and again under **Fitting**, selecting **Fit Content Proportionally**. You will notice the **Effective PPI** value is now far higher at **4771** (*A* in *Figure 5.16*), and the **Scale** value is right down at **6.3%** (*B* in *Figure 5.16*):

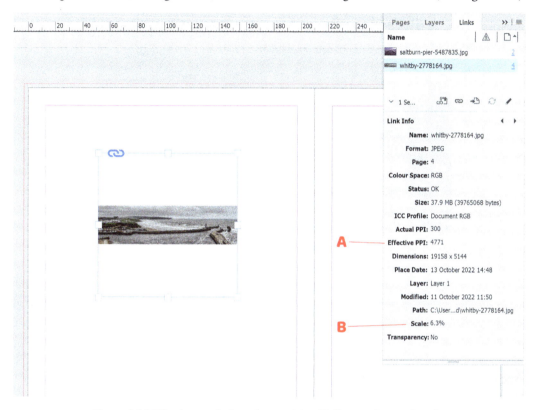

Figure 5.16: Effective resolution after applying Fit Content Proportionally

6. Finally, on fitting, it is worth looking at the impact of non-proportional scaling on resolution. Right-click on the same image, and from the **Fitting** options, select **Fit Content to Frame**. When you now look at the **Links** panel, you will see that while the **Actual PPI** value remains at **300**, the **Effective PPI** value now contains two numbers—in this case, **4771 x 1281** (*A* in *Figure 5.17*). This is down to the fact that the scaling was not proportional, and it has in effect stretched the image, leaving every inch horizontally containing 4,771 pixels while every inch vertically only contains 1,281 pixels. The displayed pixels are now effectively no longer square, but tall thin rectangles. Additionally, the **Scale** value has also changed and is showing as **6.3% x 23.4%** (*B* in *Figure 5.17*):

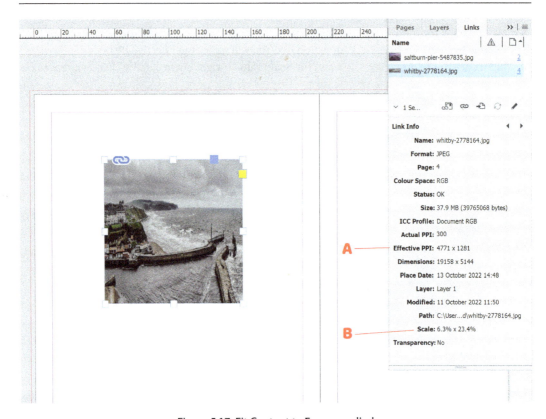

Figure 5.17: Fit Content to Frame applied

By default, InDesign displays images using **Typical Display**, which uses a low-resolution proxy image that is good enough for you to identify and adjust images while still allowing the machine to run smoothly. In effect, the quality you are seeing on the screen isn't what will output. In some cases, you may want to change these **Display Performance** settings, as they are called, and in the next step, we will look at doing this.

7. To change the **display performance settings** for all images, go to the **View** menu and select **Display Performance**, or for individual images go to the **Object** menu under **Display Performance**. There are three options available, as follows:

    *   **Fast Display** (example *A* in *Figure 5.18*): This mode replace the images with a gray box and can be useful for quickly scrolling through many pages—for example, when proofing your text

    *   **Typical Display** (example *B* in *Figure 5.18*): This mode uses a low-resolution proxy image instead of the original and is the default mode unless this is changed in the preferences

    *   **High Quality Display** (example *C* in *Figure 5.18*): This is a high-resolution version of the image and a better reflection of the actual quality of the image, although on slower machines this can cause performance issues

By default, InDesign displays images using **Typical Display**, and in our case, this is what we want, so there is no need to change these settings:

Figure 5.18: Display Performance examples in InDesign

While you can change the **Display Performance** settings, it is worth bearing in mind that it makes no difference whatsoever to the document you output from InDesign. For example, the three images seen in *Figure 5.18* would all look identical when output to a PDF.

Working with image file links

When you place an image into InDesign, the original image actually remains a separate file and is not copied into the InDesign document. Instead, InDesign creates a link to the image file and then creates a low-resolution proxy version of the image for display within InDesign. It is important these links remain intact as **missing links** or **modified links** can cause significant problems for your documents.

In this recipe, we are going to look at embedding images, unembedding images, fixing missing links, and updating modified links.

Getting ready

In order to complete this recipe, simply open InDesign on your system and create a new document with 12 pages, as shown in the *Creating a new document* recipe in *Chapter 1*. You should be comfortable adding images to your document, as shown earlier in the *Placing images into InDesign* recipe.

You will also need to be able to rename files and folders using your system file manager, and *step 5* will also require you to be able to make a simple edit of your image using Adobe Photoshop (an equivalent tool can be used, but the example here uses this particular tool). As some steps in this recipe involve editing your images, you might also want to take a backup copy of your images before starting.

How to do it...

In order to work with embedded images and fix missing or modified image links in your document, follow these steps:

1. Create a frame and place an image into it, then open the **Link** panel and select the image. In the **Link** panel, click the **Panel** menu icon (marked as *A* in *Figure 5.19*) and select the **Embed Link** option. You will now see the embedded link icon appear (marked as *B* in *Figure 5.19*), which identifies that a copy of the image is now embedded into the InDesign document and will be saved as part of it. The original image is still where it was, but it is now no longer being used by InDesign:

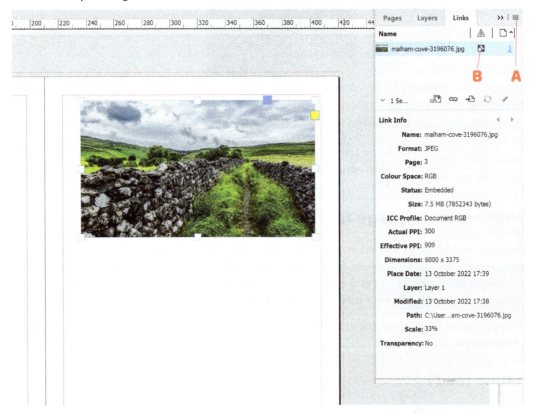

Figure 5.19: Embedding an image into an InDesign document

In general, it is better to not embed all of your images, for the simple reason that it can result in very large InDesign files that can become slow to respond and, depending on your machine, even cause InDesign to crash. Having said that, it makes sense in some scenarios—for example, if it is a text-heavy document and the only image being used is your logo.

Having embedded our image, let's now reverse this by unembedding it.

> **Note**
>
> The embed and unembed options can also be accessed by right-clicking on the image's name within the **Links** panel.

2.   With the image still selected, click the **Links** panel menu and select **Unembed Link**. You will see a small pop-up box (shown in *Figure 5.20*) asking whether you want to link to the original file or whether you'd prefer InDesign to create a copy of the image in a new folder. If you know where the original image file is and want to link to it, click **Yes**. If you no longer have the original image or don't know where it is, click **No**, and InDesign will then create a new folder and put a copy of the image into it for you. In our case, we still have the original file and haven't moved it, so I will click **Yes**, and InDesign will once again link to it, deleting the embedded version from within the InDesign file:

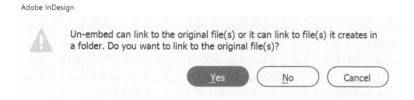

Figure 5.20: Unembed option in InDesign

Now that the image is once again linked rather than embedded, you will notice the **Embedded** icon has disappeared, and in addition, the link symbol has now reappeared on the frame of the image (marked as *A* in *Figure 5.21*), denoting that this is a linked file:

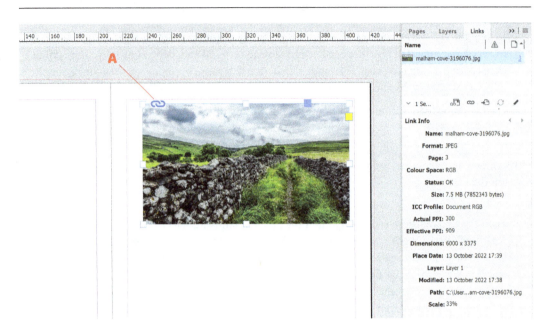

Figure 5.21: Linked image in InDesign

3. A common problem people encounter is linked files being moved, renamed, or deleted, often by other people when they use shared drives. When this happens, InDesign can no longer find the linked file and shows this as a missing link. You can very easily simulate this by just using your operating system file manager to rename your image file or the name of the folder it sits in. Do this now with the image you have placed in your document.

    Having renamed the file or folder, you should now see the missing link icon in InDesign, both on the image itself (marked as *A* in *Figure 5.22*) and in the **Links** panel (marked as *B* in *Figure 5.22*):

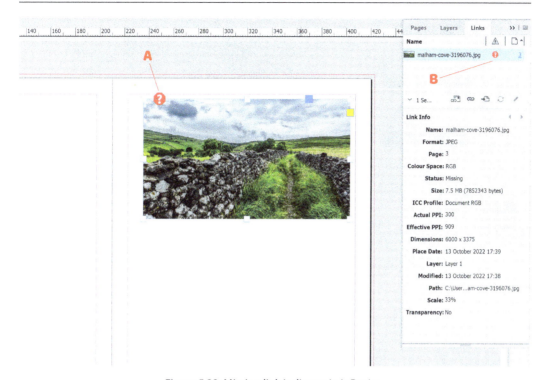

Figure 5.22: Missing link indicator in InDesign

If you hover your mouse over the missing link icon, it tells you how to fix the missing link. This involves either clicking on the missing link icon on the image or double-clicking on the icon in the **Links** panel and simply selecting the correct image before clicking **Open**. This will recreate the link to this new image:

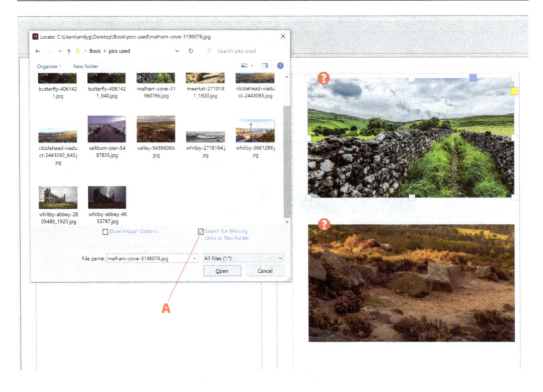

Figure 5.23: Search for Missing Links in This Folder option

When fixing missing links, it is worth noting the checkbox for **Search for Missing Links in This Folder**. This is useful in a scenario where a folder containing multiple images was moved or renamed, and checking it will result in InDesign re-linking all of the images in that folder at the same time, saving you the frustration of having to do each image individually.

> **Note**
>
> Missing links is one of the more common causes of problems in printed documents. It can result in the images within a printed document being very poor quality, due to InDesign being unable to find the image files during output and instead using the low-resolution proxy image generated within InDesign.

Having ensured all our links are not missing, we are now going to look at how InDesign handles images in your document that are edited in another program.

4. Place a new image into your document and open the **Links** panel. Select the image in the **Links** panel and click the **Edit Original** icon (*A* in *Figure 5.24*). This will open up the image in whichever program your operating system associates that particular file type with:

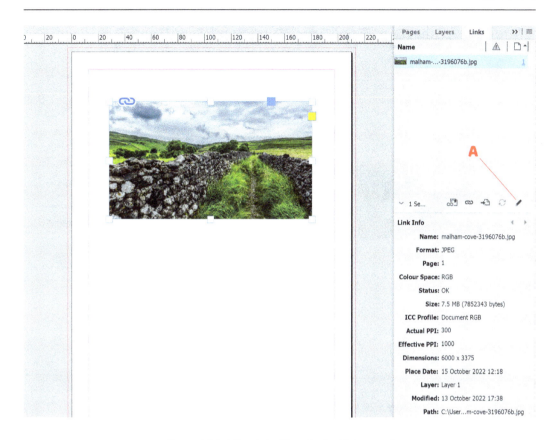

Figure 5.24: Edit original icon in the Links panel

While the **Edit Original** icon is a fast way to quickly open your image for editing in another program, sometimes the program that's opened isn't what you wanted. For example, it might open it in the operating system picture viewer instead of Adobe Photoshop. If this happens, you have two options:

- Option one is to change the default program for that file type within your operating system. Doing so means every time you click the **Edit Original** icon in the future, your computer will then open the image in the program you have chosen. This might be a good idea if you are planning to do this regularly.

- Option two is to select the image in the **Links** panel and then click on the **Links** panel menu (*A* in *Figure 5.25*), where you will see an **Edit With** option. If you have Adobe Photoshop installed, it should show up here (*B* in *Figure 5.25*), but if not, you can select **Other** (*C* in *Figure 5.25*) and choose whichever image editing application you have installed. In my case, I am going to open the image in Adobe Photoshop:

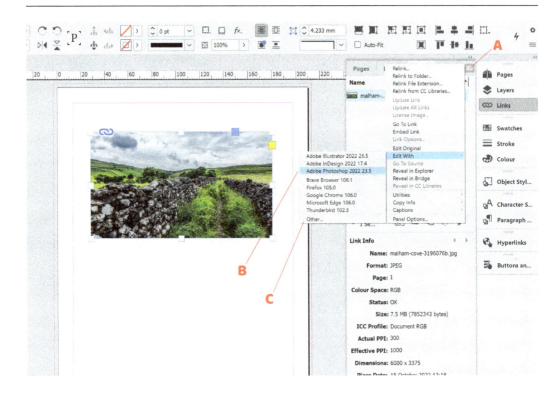

Figure 5.25: Image editing options in the Links panel

5.   Having opened the image in Adobe Photoshop, we are now going to make a very simple change in Photoshop by applying a filter to the image. If you are using a different image editor or prefer to make a different adjustment, please do so and then advance to *step 6*.

In Photoshop, click the **Filters** menu then select **Neural Filters…** (marked as *A* in *Figure 5.26*):

Figure 5.26: Making a simple edit in Photoshop

In the **Neural Filters** panel, enable **Style Transfer** by clicking the button to enable it (marked as *A* in *Figure 5.27*). Now, click one of the images under **Artist Styles** on the right; I will choose the second one (marked as *B* in *Figure 5.27*). It will take Photoshop a minute or so to process the changes, and you will see the image refresh when it has finished. The output option should be set to **Current Layer** (marked as *C* in *Figure 5.27*), at which point you can click **OK** (marked as *D* in *Figure 5.27*):

Figure 5.27: Applying a neural filter destructively in Photoshop

Having made our changes in Photoshop, we will now go to the **File** menu and hit **Save**. In the Photoshop **Save** dialog box, I will use the default settings, which have the **Quality** value as **Maximum** and the **Format Options** setting set to **Baseline ("Standard")**:

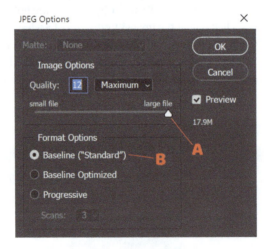

Figure 5.28: Photoshop Save dialog box

> **Note**
>
> When working in Photoshop, I would normally use a non-destructive workflow, which includes using smart objects when working with neural filters. This is so that I can easily return to edit the work later in a layered file such as a PSD file. In this instance, however, I have made a destructive edit to the current layer in order to keep things as simple as possible for those who have never opened Photoshop before.

Having made a simple Photoshop edit here, let's return to InDesign.

6. When we return to InDesign, you should now see the **Modified Link** icon both on the image (marked as *A* in *Figure 5.29*) and in the **Links** panel (marked as *B* in *Figure 5.29*). To update InDesign so that it is using the latest version of the image, you just need to click once to update this icon on the image or double-click the icon in the **Links** panel to update it. If you have updated a number of images and wish to update all the modified links, that can be done by pressing *Alt* (PC)/*Option* (Mac) and clicking on the **Update Link** icon in the **Links** panel (marked as *C* in *Figure 5.29*):

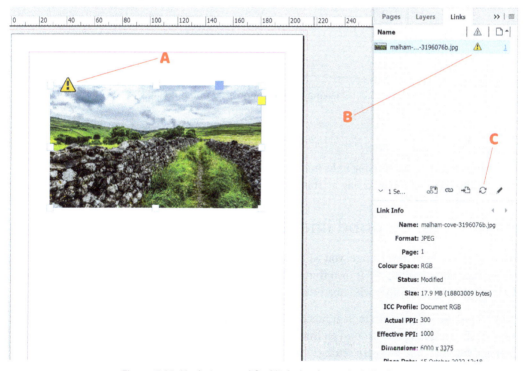

Figure 5.29: Updating modified links back over in InDesign

Having updated the modified link in InDesign, we should now see the image with the neural filter applied to it, as shown in *Figure 5.30*:

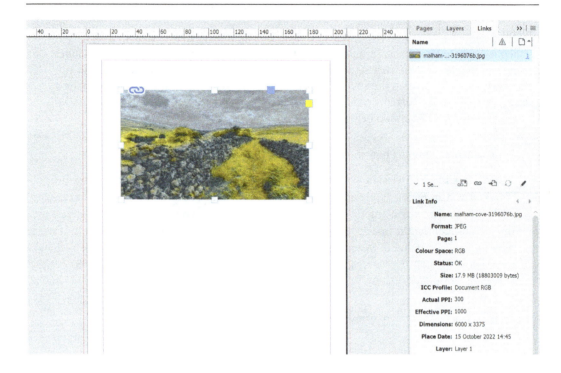

Figure 5.30: Final image in InDesign after updating links

See also

We have touched on fixing missing links in this recipe; however, it is worth checking your document for all missing links before exporting it. This is covered in *Chapter 13, Preflighting and Outputting*.

Wrapping text around images

When you are working in InDesign, you will often have text on a page as well as images, and they are each separate objects within their own frames. If you place these in the same area of the page, they will simply overlap each other with one sitting right on top of the other, and this can be unhelpful.

In this recipe, we are going to look at positioning your items above each other in the layer stack, automatically wrapping text around an image, and adjusting the settings for the text wrap to add offsets and fine-tune the **Wrap To** settings.

Getting ready

In order to complete this recipe, simply open InDesign on your system and create a new document with 12 pages, as shown in the *Creating a new document* recipe in *Chapter 1*. You should be comfortable adding images into your document, as shown earlier in the *Placing images into InDesign* recipe, as well as adding text, which was covered in the *Creating text frames and adding placeholder text* recipe found in *Chapter 2*.

How to do it…

In order to use text wrap within your documents, follow these steps:

1. Add an image to your page and position it in the center, then create a large text frame on top of the image and fill it with placeholder text, as shown in *Figure 5.31*:

Figure 5.31: Image with text sitting on top in InDesign

The image is currently positioned behind the text, and this can be seen both on the page and in the **Layers panel**, where the image (marked as *A* in *Figure 5.31*) is positioned below the text (marked as *B* in *Figure 5.31*). When you look at items in the **Layers** panel, their position there reflects their position on the page. So, within the page, items will show up in front of those that are below them in the **Layers** panel, and behind those that are above them in the **Layers** panel. If you do not see the individual items in the **Layers** panel, it might just be that the layer needs to be expanded by clicking the small arrow to the left of the layer name (marked as *C* in *Figure 5.31*).

Note

When working in the **Layers** panel, you can click the icons in line with the relevant objects to hide them (marked as *D* in *Figure 5.31*), lock them (marked as *E* in *Figure 5.31*), or select them (marked as *F* in *Figure 5.31*) if needed.

---

2. In our case, we would like the image to be positioned on top of the text so that we can more easily reposition and adjust it on the page. Within the **Layers** panel, we can click on the image and drag it above the text item, in order to reposition it in front of the text frame.

    It is worth noting that the repositioning of objects in front or behind one another can also be done by right-clicking on a selected object with the **Selection** tool and going down to **Arrange**, where you will see options such as **Bring Forward** or **Send Backward**.

    With the image object positioned on top of the text, we can now select it and move it around more easily, but if you do so, you will notice the text doesn't change, and this is because it is simply being hidden by the image and not interacting with it in any way. What we really want is for the text to interact with the image object and wrap around it.

3. Go to the **Window** menu and select **Text Wrap**, which will open the **Text Wrap** panel. Now, select the image object using the **Selection** tool, and in the **Text Wrap** panel, click the **Wrap to Bounding Box** icon (marked as *A* in *Figure 5.32*). You should now see the text wrap around the image object, and if you move the image object around on the page, you should see the text adjust to wrap around it:

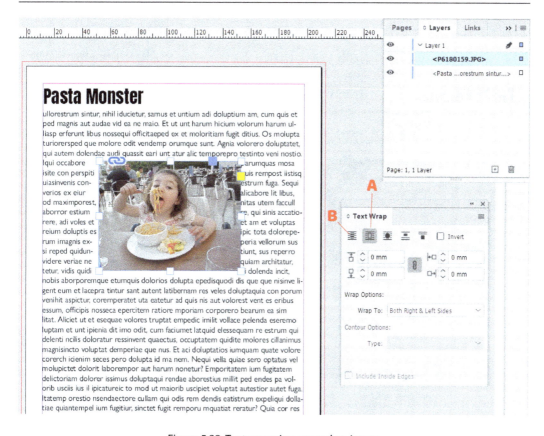

Figure 5.32: Text wrapping around an image

If you wish to disable the text wrap, just select the image object again, and in the **Text Wrap** panel, click the **No Text Wrap** icon (marked as *B* in *Figure 5.32*).

Having wrapped text around the image, we now want to adjust the space around the outside edge of the image.

4. The space between the edge of the image and the text is known as the offset, and it can be adjusted in the **Text Wrap** panel. To adjust the **offset** on all four sides, first select the image object and then check the **Make all settings the same** icon (marked as *A* in *Figure 5.33*) is enabled and has no line through it. Now, adjust the offset value in any of the four boxes (marked as *B* in *Figure 5.33*). In our case, we will increase the value to **5 mm**, and you will now see the offset spacing around the edge of the image (marked as *C* in *Figure 5.33*):

Figure 5.33: Adjusting the offset for Text Wrap

Having set the offset and with the image selected, click the drop-down box for the **Wrap To** options (marked as *A* in *Figure 5.34*), and you will see there are six options in total, as follows:

- **Right Side**: This will wrap text around the right-hand side of the image, leaving the area of the text frame to the left of the image empty

- **Left Side**: This will wrap text around the left-hand side of the image, leaving the area of the text frame to the right of the image empty

- **Both Right and Left Sides**: This will wrap text around both sides of the image

- **Side Towards Spine**: This will wrap text around the side of the image closest to the spine

- **Side Away from Spine**: This will wrap text around the side of the image farthest from the spine

- **Largest Area**: This will wrap text around the side of the image where the text frame is widest, leaving the narrower side empty

We will choose **Both Right and Left Sides** for our image:

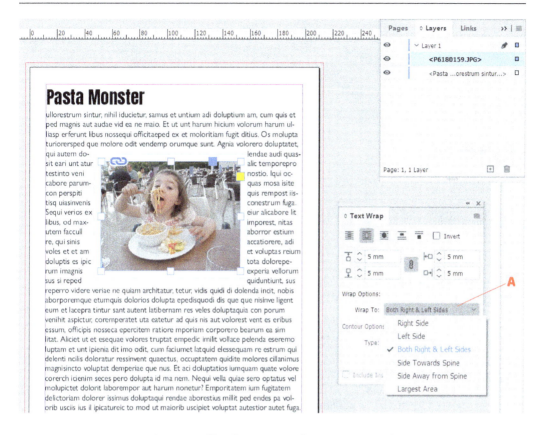

Figure 5.34: Wrap To options in the Text Wrap panel

Having enabled text wrap on the image, we are now going to position a small text frame on top of the image containing a caption.

5. Create a small text frame on the pasteboard area to one side of your page, and enter your caption text in it. If you wish, you can give the frame a fill color in order to make the text stand out. To do this, simply select the frame with the **Selection** tool and change the fill color on the **Control** panel above (marked as *A* in *Figure 5.35*). Now, using the **Selection** tool, drag the text frame and position it on top of the image:

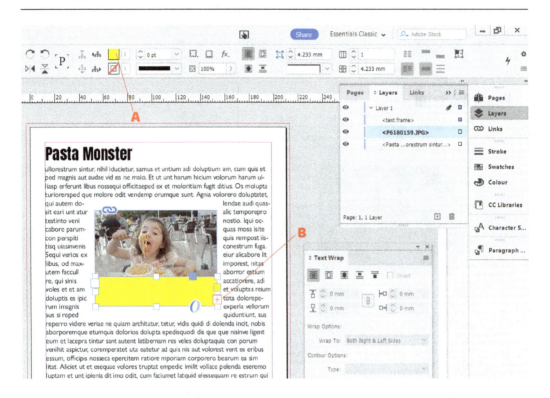

Figure 5.35: Text frame positioned on top of the image with text wrap applied

Because we previously enabled **Text Wrap** on the image, we have in effect given it a specific instruction to not allow text on top of the image. The result of this is that when we try to position the caption on top of the image, the text is pushed out of the frame and into overset text (marked as *B* in *Figure 5.35*) due to the **Text Wrap** setting on the image.

6. In order to override the **Text Wrap** settings on this text frame, select the frame with the **Selection** tool and open the **Text Frame Options** setting under the **Object** menu. In the **Text Frame Options** dialog box, you will see a checkbox for **Ignore Text Wrap** (marked *A* in *Figure 5.36*), which you should select, then click **OK** to close the dialog box. You should now see the text on top of the image, which in turn still has text wrap enabled, as shown in *Figure 5.36*:

Figure 5.36: Ignore Text Wrap in the Text Frame Options dialog box

There's more...

In this recipe, we have covered the basics of **Text Wrap**, but there are a number of more advanced options available, including the **Wrap around Object Shape** feature, which is based on Adobe Sensei, Adobe's AI and ML technology. These additional options are covered in the *Wrapping text around objects in an image* recipe, which we will look at in the next chapter.

6
Taking Images Further

In this chapter, we'll look at some more advanced techniques when it comes to working with images in InDesign. You will learn how to wrap text automatically around the subject of an image rather than the rectangular frame, as well as create an **alpha channel** in Photoshop and then wrap text around it within InDesign. We also will create a simple layered PSD file within Photoshop, and then look at how to hide and show those layers while working within InDesign.

Later in this chapter, you will use metadata, which has been added to the image in either Photoshop or Bridge, to automatically generate captions for the image in InDesign. And finally, we will look at anchoring an image's position to a specific place within the text, ensuring it moves as the text moves.

The recipes we will cover in this chapter are as follows:

- Wrapping text around objects in an image
- Hiding and showing image layers in InDesign
- Using metadata for captions
- Anchoring an image's position to text
- Hiding areas of an image with an alpha channel

Technical requirements

To complete this chapter, you will need a PC or Mac, with a copy of Adobe InDesign installed.

You will also need to have and be familiar with Adobe Photoshop, as well as have some images to use. I have used some of my own images in this chapter, along with several images by photographer Tim Hill, which can be downloaded for free at https://pixabay.com/users/timhill-5727184/.

Wrapping text around objects in an image

While wrapping around the rectangular frame of an image is often all you need, it's nice to be able to take text wrapping a bit further.

In this recipe, we will look at the recently updated **Wrap around Object Shape** feature, which is powered by Adobe Sensei, Adobe's own AI and machine learning technology. This allows you to wrap text around a prominent subject in an image in just a few clicks. We will also take a look at how to create alpha channels from a Photoshop selection and then use this back over in InDesign to wrap text around that area. Additionally, we will look at fine-tuning our text wrap boundary, as well as adjusting the inset spacing, to get the result that we want.

Getting ready

To complete this recipe, simply open InDesign on your system and create a new document with 12 pages, as shown in the *Creating a new document* recipe in *Chapter 1*. You should be comfortable adding images to your document, as shown in the *Placing images in InDesign* recipe in *Chapter 5*, as well as adding text, as covered in the *Creating text frames and adding placeholder text* recipe in *Chapter 2*.

You should also be comfortable with the basics of Photoshop, including creating selections and saving PSD files from within Photoshop. Plus, if you wish to adjust the boundary contour, as shown in *step 7*, then knowledge of editing vector shapes using tools such as the **Pen** tool, which is most commonly used in Adobe Illustrator, will be required.

How to do it...

To wrap text around objects in your images, follow these steps:

1. Find an image that has a reasonably prominent subject and place it on your page. Then, create a text frame that overlaps the image, as shown in *Figure 6.1*:

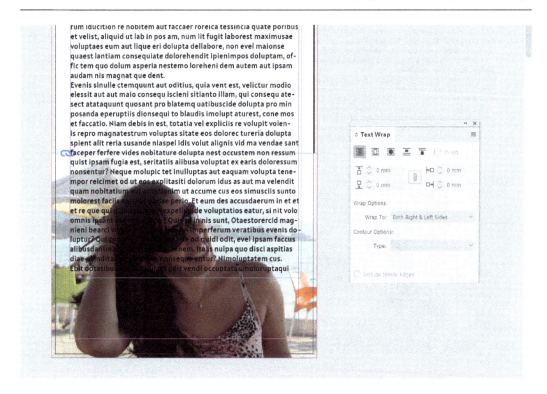

Figure 6.1: Image with text positioned on top of it in InDesign

2. With the image selected, go to the **Window** menu and click **Text Wrap** to open the **Text Wrap** panel. When you select the **Wrap Around Object Shape** icon (marked *A* in *Figure 6.2*), you will notice that the text wraps around the rectangular image:

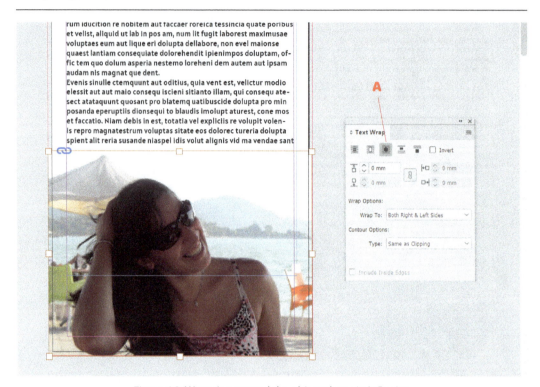

Figure 6.2: Wrapping around the object shape in InDesign

3.   To wrap the text around the subject, open the **Type** drop-down menu and choose **Select subject** (marked *A* in *Figure 6.3*). You should then see the image wrap around the actual subject of the image, as seen in *Figure 6.3*:

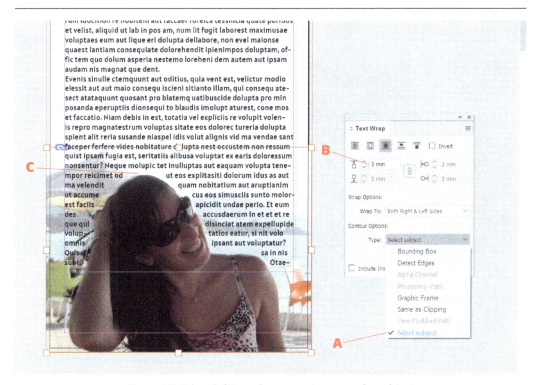

Figure 6.3: Select Subject when wrapping around an object

Having done this, we now want to add a little space between the image and the text. This can be done by adding **3mm** to **Offset** (marked *B* in *Figure 6.3*). You should see a small area of space (marked *C* in *Figure 6.3*) between the text and the image's subject.

The AI behind this generally does a very good job of selecting the subject, but occasionally, it will struggle with an image, typically when there isn't an obvious subject in the image. In such cases, you might want to clearly identify the subject yourself manually, which we will look at next.

4. Move to Adobe Photoshop and open an image that you would like to apply text wrap to when working on your InDesign document. Then, select the area of the image that you wish to be able to wrap text around in InDesign, and save that selection using the **Save Selection** option (marked *A* in *Figure 6.4*). If you look in the Photoshop **Channels** panel once you have done this, you will notice a new alpha channel (marked *B* in *Figure 6.4*):

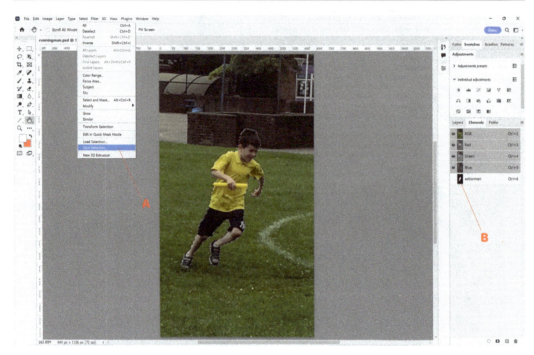

Figure 6.4: Creating an alpha channel in Photoshop

Alpha channels are only supported in a small number of file formats, including **PSD** (Photoshop's native document format). They are not supported in many other image formats, including **JPG**. As such, we will now go to the **File** menu, select **Save As**, and then save the file as the **Photoshop (*.PSD;*.PSDD;*.PSDT)** type.

> **Note**
>
> In addition to wrapping text around an alpha channel, InDesign will also allow you to wrap around **Photoshop Path**. In terms of InDesign, the two work in the same way, with the user simply choosing **Photoshop Path** instead of **Alpha Channel** in the **Text Wrap** panel. In this recipe, I have chosen to demonstrate this using **Alpha Channel** as those who are less experienced with Photoshop will potentially find it both easier and quicker to work with.

5. Back over in InDesign, we will now place the image in our document, remembering to turn off **Show import option** (this option is persistent, so it will be automatically enabled if you have used it before). Next, we will place a large text frame on the page and fill it with placeholder text. In my case, I have set the font color to white (as seen in *Figure 6.5*) since the image is quite dark:

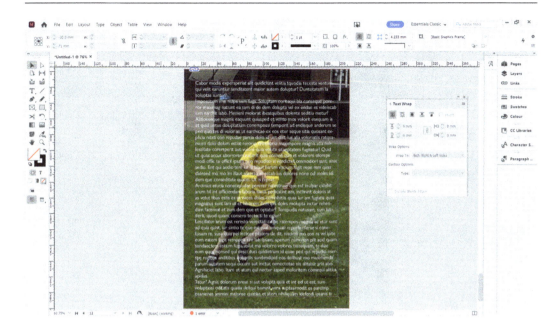

Figure 6.5: Image with text on top before wrapping around the channel

6. Select the image object. Then, in the **Text Wrap** panel, select **Wrap around object shape** (marked *A* in *Figure 6.6*). Now, under **Contour Options**, from the **Type** drop-down menu, choose **Alpha Channel** (marked *B* in *Figure 6.6*).

    You will notice that a new dropdown appears immediately below this (marked *C* in *Figure 6.6*), where you can choose the name of the alpha channel you created. If there are multiple alpha channels, they will appear here.

    Finally, we will increase the offset spacing (marked *D* in *Figure 6.6*) to **3mm** to push the text away from the edge of the alpha channel slightly:

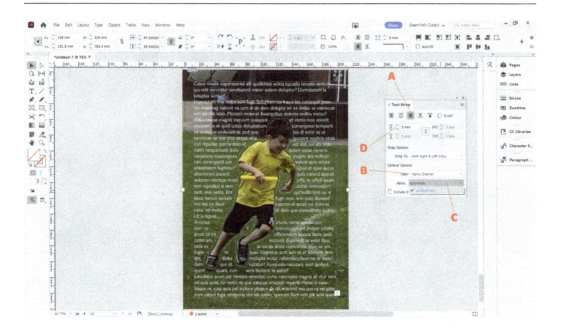

Figure 6.6: Image with text wrapped around an alpha channel

Having applied the wrapping around the alpha channel, you might encounter cases where there are areas that need to be manually adjusted. Typically, these are things that you maybe didn't notice when creating the alpha channel back in Photoshop but now pose a problem. In this instance, I have noticed that the letter "t" has appeared between the legs in the image. This is because, in our original Photoshop selection, this area wasn't selected. The knock-on effect of this is that InDesign is now trying to wrap text into this area. So, let's resolve this problem.

7. If you zoom in on the area where the problem exists, you will notice that the boundary is a vector path containing anchor points. If you click on one of these anchor points with the **Direct Selection** tool and move it even slightly, you will see that it changes from an alpha channel to **User-Modified Path** in the **Text Wrap** panel (marked *A* in *Figure 6.7*):

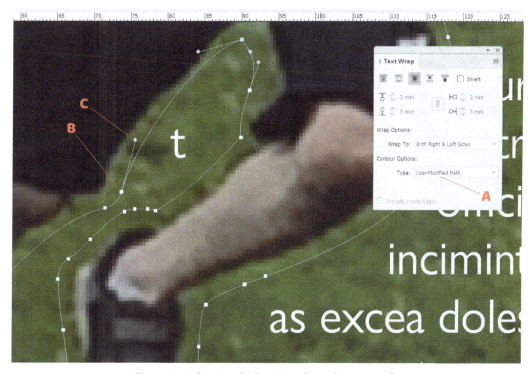

Figure 6.7: Adjusting the Text Wrap boundary manually

The vector paths here can be edited in the same way as you would edit a vector in Illustrator. InDesign allows you to move and adjust the anchor points (marked *B* in *Figure 6.7*) and handles (marked *C* in *Figure 6.7*) with the **Direct Selection** tool and the **Convert Direction Point tool**. Additionally, you can delete anchor points with the **Delete Anchor Point** tool, add additional anchor points with the **Add Anchor Point** tool, or if you prefer, use the **Pen** tool to do both.

8. In my case, I will use the **Delete Anchor Point** tool to remove seven of the anchor points by clicking on them. Each time you remove an anchor point, the remaining anchor points on either side of it will connect directly to each other:

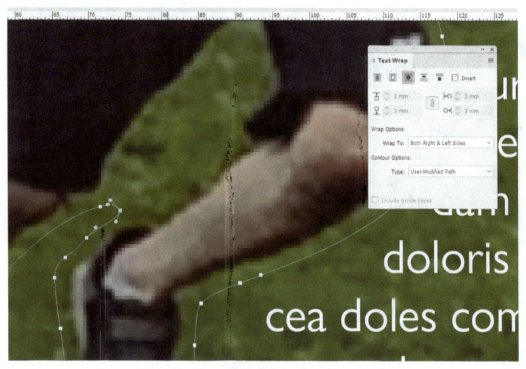

Figure 6.8: User-Modified Path is being used for text wrap after editing

As a result, the **User-Modified Path** now connects lower down (as seen in *Figure 6.8*), preventing any text from appearing higher up where the letter "t" used to be.

Hiding and showing image layers in InDesign

When you work with professional image editing tools such as Photoshop, you work with layers. This has several benefits, with the main one being that it allows you to edit and adjust items independently of each other.

Only certain file types support layers, though, and if you save your files in formats such as JPG or PNG, they will be flattened. This means that all the layers will be merged into a single layer and you will lose all the benefits of working with multi-layered files.

By saving your files in the native Photoshop PSD format, not only are all the layers retained but you can access them from within InDesign, allowing you to hide and show layers without the need to return to Photoshop every time.

In this recipe, we are going look at how to enable and disable layers in InDesign, both as you import the file initially, and also later on while working within the document.

Getting ready

To complete this recipe, simply open InDesign on your system and create a new document with 12 pages, as shown in the *Creating a new document* recipe in *Chapter 1*. You should be also comfortable adding images to your document, as shown in the *Placing images in InDesign* recipe in *Chapter 5*.

You should also be comfortable creating basic selections, working with layers, and saving PSD files within Photoshop.

How to do it...

To hide and show image layers within your document, follow these steps:

1. We will start in Photoshop, where we will open an image that we want to edit. With the image open, select an area of the image where you wish to change its color. Then, in the **Window** menu, click **Adjustments** to open the **Adjustments** panel.

    In the **Adjustments** panel, we will click on the **Hue/Saturation** adjustment icon (marked *A* in *Figure 6.9*), which will automatically create a new adjustment layer in the **Layers** panel (marked *B* in *Figure 6.9*), as well as open up the **Properties** panel, where you can change the settings for the adjustment. Within the **Properties** panel, drag the **Hue** slider (marked *C* in *Figure 6.9*) toward the right; you will notice that the color of the selected area changes:

Figure 6.9: Creating a Hue/Saturation adjustment layer in Photoshop

When you created the original adjustment layer, it automatically created a black-and-white mask on that layer (marked *D* in *Figure 6.9*), to control which areas of the image are affected by the **Hue/Saturation** adjustment. Next, we are going to create a second adjustment layer that affects the same areas of the image as the first. The mask will help us do this quickly.

2. To create a selection from this existing mask, simply hold down the *Ctrl* (Windows)/*Cmd* (Mac) key and click directly on the mask (marked *D* in *Figure 6.9*) in the **Layers** panel. Again, click the **Hue/Saturation** adjustment icon in the **Adjustments** panel to create a second adjustment layer (marked *A* in *Figure 6.10*) but this time, in the **Properties** panel, drag the **Hue** slider to the left:

Figure 6.10: Adding a second adjustment layer in Photoshop

With two separate color adjustments made to the image, we will now save it as a PSD file by going to the **File** menu, selecting **Save As**, and saving the file as a PSD file.

3. Now, let's go back to our InDesign document and, from the **File** menu, select **Place**. Choose the PSD file we just saved from Photoshop and tick the **Show import options** box before clicking **Open**.

The **Show Import Options dialog box** will open. Because you have multiple layers in the PSD file, it will default automatically to show the **Layers** tab (*A* in *Figure 6.11*). Here, you can hide and show the layers within the image, using the small eye icon next to each layer. We will hide the middle layer (*B* in *Figure 6.11*) by clicking the eye so that it disappears, and then click **OK**:

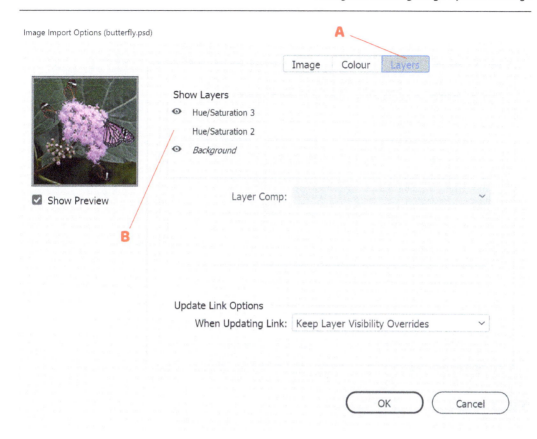

Figure 6.11: The Show Import Options dialog box

We should now see the image on our page. However, since the middle layer is disabled, you will see the original image with the top adjustment layer applied to it.

Having placed the image onto the page, we have now realized that the wrong adjustment layer has been enabled; in the next step, we will look at how to switch to the other color adjustment layer instead.

4. To do this, select the image object with the **Selection** tool; then, in the **Object** menu, click **Object Layer Options**. This will open the **Object Layer Options** dialog box (it looks quite similar to the **Layers** tab of the **Import Options** dialog box). Here, you can hide the first layer (marked *A* in *Figure 6.12*) and show the second layer (marked *B* in *Figure 6.13*) instead:

Figure 6.12: The Object Layer Options dialog box

If you have the **Preview** tick box checked (marked *C* in *Figure 6.12*), you should see the changes live on your screen immediately. Now, click **OK** to apply the changes.

Using metadata for captions

Image files can contain a variety of hidden data within them, which is known as **metadata**. This metadata can include details on the content creator, the location and date where the photo was taken, a description of the image, details on the camera used, and much more.

One nice feature of InDesign is that it allows you to use this metadata to generate **captions** for your images. This could be useful when working with documents that contain lots of images, where the designer may not be familiar with the contents of the images.

In this recipe, we will look at how to use this metadata to automatically generate captions for our images and how we can update these captions when the metadata is changed.

Getting ready

To complete this recipe, simply open InDesign on your system and create a new document with 12 pages, as shown in the *Creating a new document* recipe in *Chapter 1*. You should also be comfortable adding images to your document, as shown in the *Placing images in InDesign* recipe in *Chapter 5*.

We will also be using Adobe Photoshop to edit the metadata within an image.

How to do it...

To use metadata to automatically generate captions for your images, follow these steps:

1. To generate captions from metadata, first, we need to ensure we have some metadata to use within our images. Start by opening an image in Photoshop; then, from the **File** menu, select **File Info**. This will open the **File Info** dialog box, which breaks the metadata down into a variety of sub-sections (marked *A* in *Figure 6.13*). We will just focus on the **Description** field (marked *B* in *Figure 6.13*):

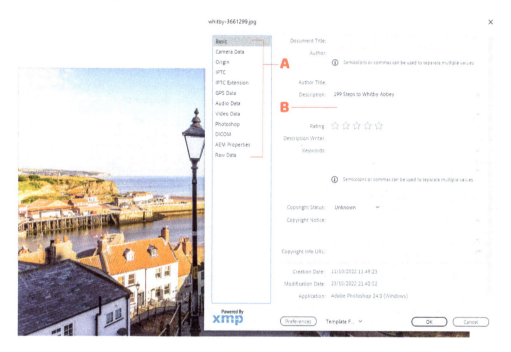

Figure 6.13: The File Info dialog box in Photoshop

In the **Description** field, type a short description of the image that you are using, in my case `199 Steps to Whitby Abbey`, and then click **OK**.

> **Note**
>
> While editing metadata in **Photoshop** makes sense for a single image, as we are doing in this recipe, it is worth noting that **Adobe Bridge** has extensive Metadata editing capabilities. Not only can you make use of metadata templates there, but it offers a far easier interface when it comes to quickly editing the metadata in multiple files.

2. Having edited the metadata in the image, go to the **File** menu, select **Save**, and then close the document.

3. Back over in InDesign, go to the **File** menu and select **Place**, choose your image with the edited metadata, and place it on the page. Now, go to the **Object** menu and, under **Captions**, select **Caption Setup**. This will open the **Caption Setup dialog box**:

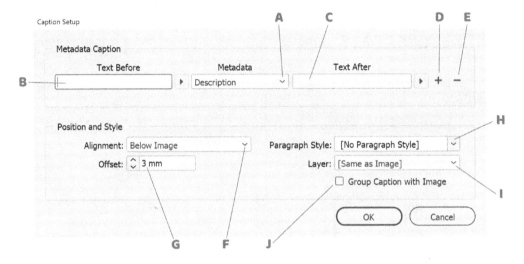

Figure 6.14: The Caption Setup dialog box

Here, you can choose the **Metadata** field you would like to use from the **Metadata** dropdown (*A* in *Figure 6.14*), which in our case is the **Description** field. You can also enter custom text to show before or after your metadata by entering it into the **Text Before** (*B* in *Figure 6.14*) or **Text After** (*C* in *Figure 6.14*) fields. We will leave these two fields blank.

If you wish to use more than one **Metadata** field for your caption, simply click the + icon (*D* in *Figure 6.14*) to add extra rows. If you wish to subsequently remove rows, click the – icon (*E* in *Figure 6.14*). We will just use the one row here.

When setting up your captions, you can also choose an **Alignment** value (*F* in *Figure 6.14*), which controls where the generated caption will be positioned concerning the image. The options are as follows:

- **Below Image**: Positions the caption below the image (we will select this option)

- **Above Image**: Positions the caption above the image

- **Left of Image**: Positions the caption to the left of the image

- **Right of Image**: Positions the caption to the right of the image

The **Alignment** setting works in conjunction with the **Offset** value (*G* in *Figure 6.14*), which stipulates how far from the chosen alignment position the caption will then be offset. We will set this to **3 mm**.

Additional options in the **Caption Setup** dialog box include the following:

- The **Paragraph Styles** dropdown (*H* in *Figure 6.14*), which allows you to apply paragraph styles to your captions (covered in *Chapter 9*, *Formatting with Paragraph and Character Styles*). We won't change this.

- The **Layer** drop-down menu (*I* in *Figure 6.14*), which allows you to select a specific layer for the captions to be generated in. This is useful for hiding and showing all captions at once, by simply hiding and showing a layer that contains all your captions. We won't change this setting now.

- The **Group Caption with Image** tick box (*J* in *Figure 6.14*), which ensures that when you move the image, the related caption is also moved automatically. We will leave this disabled.

Having configured **Caption Setup**, let's look at how we can generate captions.

4. With the image selected, click on the **Object** menu. Under **Captions**, there will be three other options, in addition to **Caption Setup**:

- **Generate Live Caption**: This generates a variable based on the caption settings. In our case, we chose the description field from the metadata, so the **Live Metadata Caption: Description** variable will be generated. In practical terms, what this means is that InDesign is linked to the image and automatically extracts the **Description** metadata, and uses it as a caption.

- **Generate Static Caption**: This creates a static caption based on the caption settings. It is not linked back to the image and can only be modified manually. In effect, InDesign will extract the current text from that **Metadata** field and use it as the caption.

- **Convert to Static Caption**: This allows you to convert **Live Caption** into **Static Caption**, removing the connection from the image and, as a result, preventing any changes to the metadata from affecting the caption text.

> **Note**
>
> When you create live captions, the variables that are created depend on the field chosen; for example, if you chose the **Camera** metadata field, the **Live Metadata Caption: Camera** would be generated. You can see what variable has been chosen by selecting the text frame containing the caption and looking at it in the **Story Editor** area, which can be found under the **Edit** menu. The **Story Editor** area shows the variable's value rather than the content from the **Metadata** field.

In this recipe, we will select **Generate Live Caption**. You should now see the description from the metadata appear below the image as a caption (marked *A* in *Figure 6.15*):

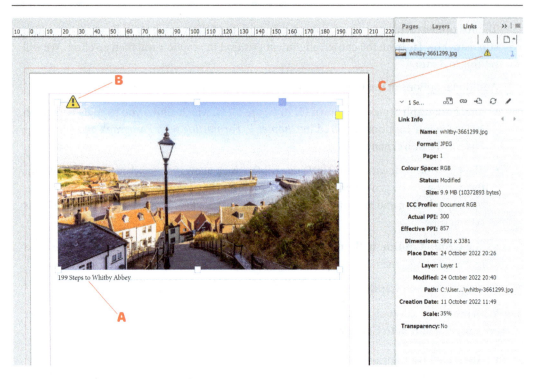

Figure 6.15: A live caption that has been modified

5. Now, let's look at why it's called a live caption. Open the image again in Photoshop, go to the **File** menu, and click **File Info**; you'll see the **File Info** dialog box. Change the **Description** metadata, click **OK**, save the changes, and close the image.

6. Back in InDesign, you will see that the image now has a yellow triangle with an exclamation mark at the top left (marked *B* in *Figure 6.15*). This means that the linked file has been **Modified** since it was placed in InDesign. The same icon can also be seen next to the image in the **Links** panel (marked *C* in *Figure 6.15*). To update the caption, simply select the image, then click once on the icon on the image (or double-click if you are doing it in the **Links** panel); it will immediately update the caption with the latest data.

> **Note**
>
> While live captions can be very useful, there is a risk factor to be aware of: if somebody else edits the image's metadata, you will see the modified link icon automatically. InDesign doesn't differentiate between you making the changes to the image or somebody else. In such a case, if you updated the link, the caption would be updated with whatever data that person modified.

7. Having generated our live caption and updated it, what if we decide that maybe **Static Caption** would be better after all? To convert the live caption into a static caption, simply select the caption text frame with the **Selection** tool. Then, in the **Object** menu, under **Captions**, select **Convert to Static Caption**.

   Having worked on the caption for our first image, we are now going to add a second image, but this time, we'll generate a static caption automatically as we place the image.

8. Open another image in Photoshop. Then, from the **File** menu, select **File Info**. In the **File Info** dialog box, again, we will enter a suitable short description in the **Description** field before clicking **OK**, then saving and closing the image.

   In *step 3*, we set up **Caption Setup Options** to use the **Description** metadata field. As a result, there is no need to do so again here, since we are using the same **Metadata** field.

> **Note**
>
> Be aware of the captions being too long for the text frame as they won't wrap when you use live captions. This is because they are generated from a variable. However, static captions will wrap onto the next line automatically.

9. Back over in InDesign, go to the **File** menu and select **Place**. This time, though, before you click **OK**, select the tick box for **Create Static Caption** (marked *A* in *Figure 6.16*):

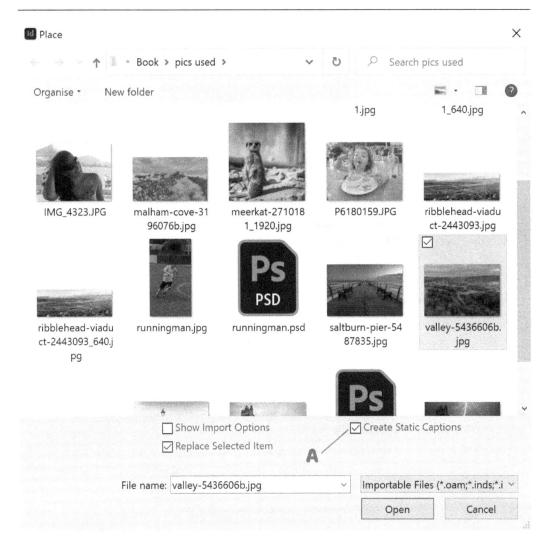

Figure 6.16: Creating a static caption while placing an image

After placing the image, the cursor will change immediately, ready for you to click on the page and drag to create a text frame containing the static caption.

Anchoring an image's position to text

Sometimes, you may want to be able to fix an object's position relative to specific text – this is known as **anchoring**. This can be useful for a variety of scenarios; for example, icons that relate to a specific section of text could be anchored to that text so that they move with it.

In this recipe, we are going to look at anchoring your images relative to your text and learn how to accurately control the positioning of the objects.

Getting ready

To complete this recipe, simply open InDesign on your system and create a new document with 12 pages, as shown in the *Creating a new document* recipe in *Chapter 1*. You should also make sure that you have followed the *Using text frame options* recipe in *Chapter 2*, as well as the *Placing images in InDesign* and *Wrapping text around images* recipes in *Chapter 5*.

How to do it...

To anchor your images to specific text, follow these steps:

1. Create a large text frame on the page, then click within the frame where you would like your image to be positioned relative to the text. Next, from the **File** menu, select **Place**, choose your image, and click **OK**. The image will appear **Inline** within the text. The anchor symbol at the top of the image (marked *A* in *Figure 6.17*) confirms that the image is anchored to the text:

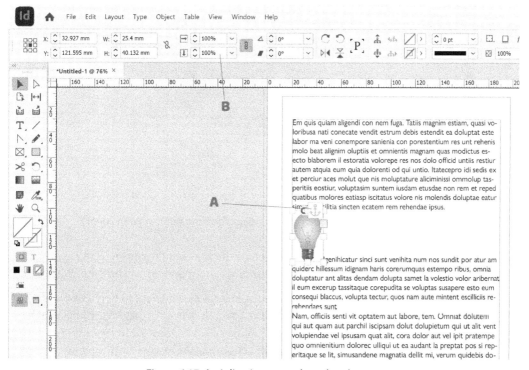

Figure 6.17: An inline image anchored to the text

If you do not see your image, but instead a large white space where the rest of the text previously sat, this means your image was too large for the frame. As the image is still selected, you can easily resize it by reducing the percentage (marked *B* in *Figure 6.17*) via the **Control** panel, which will reduce the width and height percentage proportionally. When the image is small enough, it will automatically appear in the frame. Another alternative would be to resize the image in Photoshop before placing it in InDesign.

Having anchored our image within the text, it is now pushing the text out of place, leaving a large empty gap alongside it. Let's fix that.

2. With the image selected, open the **Text Wrap** panel and select **Wrap Around Bounding Box** (*A* in *Figure 6.18*). Then, go to the **Object** menu and, under **Anchored Object**, select **Options**. This will open the **Anchored Object Options dialog box**:

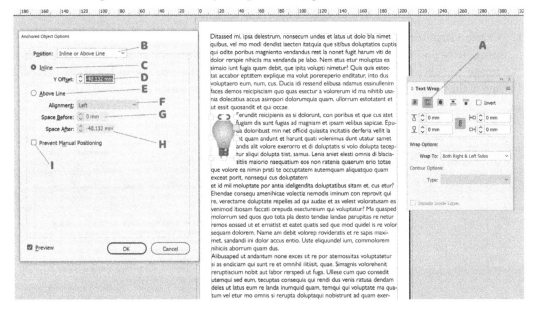

Figure 6.18: The Anchored Object Options dialog box and the Text Wrap panel

3. Within the **Anchored Object Options** dialog box, the **Position** dropdown (*B* in *Figure 6.18*) will default to **Inline or Above Line** and, as a result, various options will become available.

The **Inline** tick box (*C* in *Figure 6.18*) causes the bottom of the image to be aligned with the baseline of the text. In this instance, it will be selected already as we placed the image inline, so we will keep it selected. **Inline** has one sub-option called **Y Offset** (*D* in *Figure 6.18*), which allows you to adjust the position of inline images concerning the baseline by the amount entered. When using negative values, the maximum allowed cannot exceed the height of the image, so we will decrease this number to the maximum negative value allowed.

After the **Inline** options, we have the **Above Line** tick box (*E* in *Figure 6.18*), which results in the image being positioned above the text line to which it is anchored. As we are using the **Inline** option, this won't be selected. However, if you did tick it, you can edit these options:

- **Alignment** (*F* in *Figure 6.18*): Allows you to set the horizontal alignment, as follows:

  - **Left**: Aligns to the left of the text column

  - **Center**: Aligns to the center of the text column

  - **Right**: Aligns to the right of the text column

  - **Towards Spine**: Aligns toward the spine on spreads using facing pages

  - **Away from Spine**: Aligns away from the spine on spreads using facing pages

  - **(Text Alignment)**: Alignment depends on the alignment settings for the paragraph it is anchored to

- **Space Before** (*G* in *Figure 6.18*): Allows you to increase or decrease the space between the image and the bottom of the leading on the previous line

- **Space After** (*H* in *Figure 6.18*): Allows you to increase or decrease the space between the image and the cap height of the first character in the following line of text

- **Prevent Manual Positioning** (*I* in *Figure 6.18*): Prevents you from accidentally manually adjusting the image's position on the page – for example, if you accidentally click and drag an image

> **Note**
>
> With inline images, you can adjust the **Y Offset** value manually by clicking on the image with your mouse and dragging it up and down. With **Above line** images, you can adjust the **Space After** value using this method.

Having set our inline settings, you should see that the white space has now disappeared and the text is flowing into it, as seen in *Figure 6.18*.

Now that we've placed an image anchored inline within the text, we want to anchor the position of a regular image relative to some text.

4. Create a text frame that fills the left-hand side of a blank page, as seen in *Figure 6.19*. Now, place a separate image in a frame to the right of the text frame. This time, we are going to anchor the image so that it moves as the text moves. Select the image; you will notice a blue square (marked *A* in *Figure 6.19*) near the top right of the image:

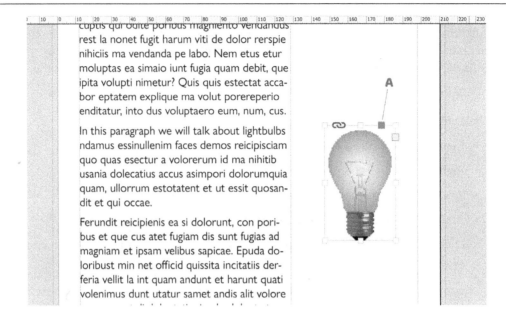

Figure 6.19: Anchoring an image to the text

Click the blue square and drag it to the place in the text where you would like to anchor this image. You will know it has been anchored as the blue square will be replaced with an anchor symbol (labeled *A* in *Figure 6.20*):

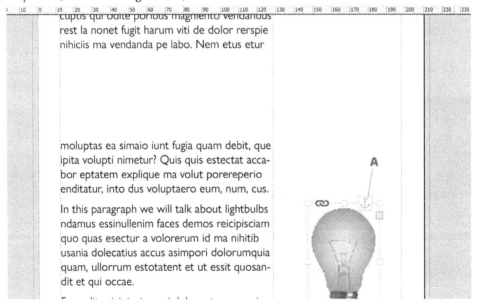

Figure 6.20: Anchored image moving relative to the text

When you add and remove text in the text frame above the area you anchored the image to, you will see that the image now moves up and down on the right, staying in line with the specific text you anchored it to.

5.   Having anchored an image to some text, later, you might want to have it anchored anymore. To do this, simply select the image; then, in the **Object** menu, under **Anchored Objects**, select **Release**. Your image will no longer be anchored to the text.

Hiding areas of an image with an alpha channel

In the *Wrapping text around objects in an image* recipe, we looked at how to add alpha channels to an image in Photoshop, then use them back over in InDesign to wrap text around that area of the image. Sometimes, though, you might just want to hide that whole area of the image and not have it appear in InDesign.

In this recipe, we will look at how to create an alpha channel within an image in Photoshop. Then, back over in InDesign, we will use that alpha channel to hide that part of the image.

Getting ready

To complete this recipe, simply open InDesign on your system and create a new document with 12 pages, as shown in the *Creating a new document* recipe in *Chapter 1*. You should also be comfortable adding images to your document, as shown in the *Placing images in InDesign* recipe in *Chapter 5*.

Additionally, you should be comfortable with the basics of Photoshop, including creating selections and saving PSD files from within Photoshop. Plus, if you wish to adjust the boundary contour, as shown in *step 7*, then knowledge of editing vector shapes using tools such as the **Pen** tool, which is most commonly used in Adobe Illustrator, will be required.

How to do it...

To use an alpha channel to hide an area of your image in InDesign, follow these steps:

1.   In Adobe Photoshop, open an image that you would like to hide part of while working on your InDesign document. In my case, I'll use an image of Whitby Abbey, where I want to hide the sky. Use Photoshop's selection tools to select the area that you want to remain visible, and then go to the **Select** menu and click **Save Selection** (marked *A* in *Figure 6.21*). This will open the **Save Selection** dialog box. In this dialog box, fill out the following fields:

     -   **Document** (*B* in *Figure 6.21*): This is the name of the document that the selection will be saved to. The default name is the current document name; we will leave it set to this.

     -   **Channel** (*C* in *Figure 6.21*): This will default to **New**. We don't need to change this as we are planning to create a new channel as opposed to editing an existing channel.

- **Name** (*D* in *Figure 6.21*): Here, we can give the channel a name that allows us to distinguish it from any other alpha channels that might be present. I will name mine **Whitby Abbey**.

- **Operation** (*E* in *Figure 6.21*): As we selected **New**, under **Channel**, the only option available here is **New Channel**, which is what we want. If we had selected the name of an already existing channel under **Channel**, we would get the options to **Add**, **Subtract**, or **Intersect** with that existing channel.

Having chosen our settings here, click **OK**. Then, from the **File** menu, choose **Save As** and save the image as the **Photoshop Document** type:

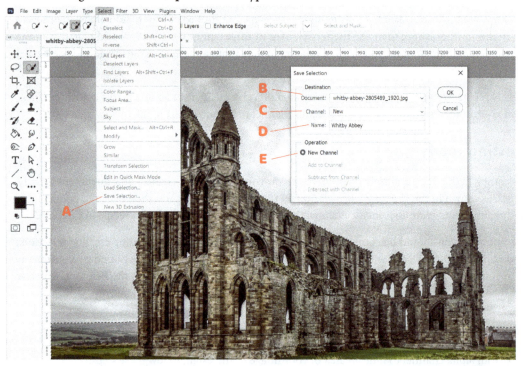

Figure 6.21: The Save Selection dialog box in Photoshop

2. Back over in InDesign, place the PSD file that you just created into your document. With the image selected, go to the **Object** menu and, under **Clipping Path**, select **Options**. This will open the **Clipping Path dialog box**, which contains several options:

- **Type**: (*A* in *Figure 6.22*) Here, you can choose between four options to use for your clipping path, as follows:

- **Detect Edges**: With this option selected, InDesign will attempt to hide the areas of the image that are either lightest or darkest. This can be a quick easy solution when your image contains a clear subject with a white or black background behind it, potentially removing the need to create an alpha channel.

- **Alpha Channels**: This allows you to select an alpha channel that's been created in Photoshop to clearly define the area to show/hide. We are using this method, so we will select this option. Once we've done this, we can choose the name of the alpha channel we wish to use in the **Alpha** dropdown that appears (marked *B* in *Figure 6.22*), below the **Type** box.

- **Photoshop Path**: This option allows you to select a Photoshop path.

- **User Modified Path**: This option will be automatically selected if you have used one of the other methods and subsequently modified the clipping path within InDesign.

- **Threshold**: (*C* in *Figure 6.22*) The **Threshold** slider allows you to extend the areas that are hidden based on the lightness of the pixels. As you move the slider to the right, the path will be expanded to include darker pixels around the edge; the further right it is, the darker the pixels that are included. As you move the slider to the left, the path will be contracted, excluding lighter and lighter pixels the further left you go. In my case, I am going to increase the **Threshold** value to **90**.

- **Tolerance**: (*D* in *Figure 6.22*) The tolerance value dictates how close to the **Threshold** value that pixels around those already included in the path will need to be before they are included/excluded. With this in mind, a high tolerance value will typically result in a smoother path as it increases the range of nearby pixels that are included/excluded in the path, while a lower tolerance value will result in a rougher more precise path with more anchor points. I will increase the **Tolerance** value to **2.2** in this instance.

- **Inset Frame**: (*E* in *Figure 6.22*) This value shrinks the clipping path by a set amount. A positive value will contract the clipping path, while a negative value will expand it. We will leave this unchanged.

- **Invert**: (*F* in *Figure 6.22*) This inverts the path so that visible and invisible areas are reversed. We will leave this deselected.

- **Include Inside Edges**: (*G* in *Figure 6.22*) This setting allows the **Threshold** and **Tolerance** values to affect areas inside the clipping path, provided they have a lightness value within the set range. I will enable this so that InDesign automatically includes the sky behind the abbey windows as part of the hidden areas.

- **Restrict to Frame**: (*H* in *Figure 6.22*) This causes InDesign to ignore any parts of the image outside of the frame when calculating the clipping path. In our case, we can leave this deselected as the frame and the image are the same size, so it is irrelevant.

- **Use High Resolution Image:** (*I* in *Figure 6.22*) This option will result in a more precise clipping path as it uses the original file to calculate the path, whereas disabling it uses the current display performance. In the case of an alpha channel, InDesign will use the alpha channel automatically, in effect enabling this setting:

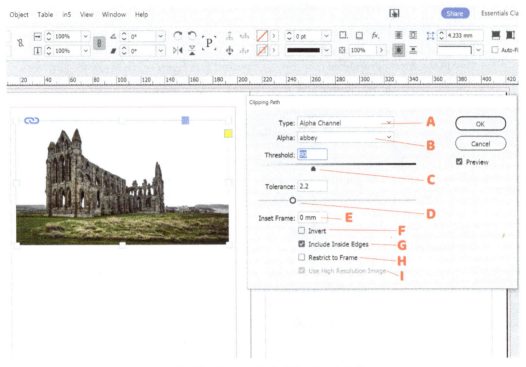

Figure 6.22: The Clipping Path dialog box in InDesign

Having removed the sky by using an alpha channel, it's worth noting that we are still able to wrap text around the alpha channel if we wish to do so.

3. Place a large text frame on the page, on top of the image, then right-click on the text frame. Then, under **Arrange**, choose the **Send to Back** option. Now, select the image object and open the **Text Wrap** panel. In this panel, ensure **Wrap Around Object Shape** is selected (*A* in *Figure 6.23*) and that **Contour Options** is set to **Same as Clipping** (*B* in *Figure 6.23*). I have also added a **1 mm** offset (marked *C* in *Figure 6.23*) to leave a very small gap between the text and the image. These should be the default options when you have already applied a clipping path:

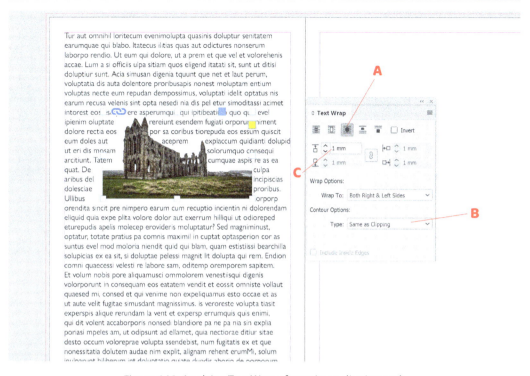

Figure 6.23: Applying Text Wrap after using a clipping path

If you want to look at wrapping text around images in more detail, see the *Wrapping text around images* recipe in *Chapter 5*, as well as the *Wrapping text around objects in an image* recipe from earlier in this chapter, where we looked at the **Text Wrap** options in more detail.

See also

If you would like to learn more about alpha channels, take a look at the following page: `https://www.highlander.co.uk/blog/working-with-alpha-channels`.

7

Creating and Applying Parent Pages

In this chapter, we look at working with **parent pages** in InDesign (formerly known as **master pages**) and how they can be used to rapidly add content to multiple pages.

Parent pages are a special type of page that typically contain recurring elements that can then be applied to multiple other pages. You can think of parent pages as a type of template, although strictly speaking, they are not templates, which, in InDesign terms, refers to a specific type of InDesign document. Parent pages themselves are not included in your final output document, and the content on them is only included as part of a regular page, where the parent page has been applied to that page.

Parent pages can be useful for containing a wide range of design elements including guides, headers, footers, page numbering, repetitive branding elements, and even placeholder content.

In this chapter, we will look at editing content on parent pages, and applying parent pages to regular pages in your document both individually and with multiple pages at a time. You will learn how to import parent pages from other documents, override parent items on a page, detach parent items from the parent page, and manipulate layers so your parent items show in front of your local page items.

We will also look at how to base one parent on another parent allowing it to inherit properties, which can be useful if you want certain items such as guides to appear across multiple parents while remaining easily adjustable in one place.

The recipes we will cover in this chapter are as follows:

- Adding content to a parent page including page numbers
- Applying and removing parent pages
- Creating new parents and inheriting properties
- Creating parents from pages and importing parents

- Overriding and detaching parent items
- Using layers with parents

Technical requirements

To complete this chapter, you will need a PC or Mac, with a copy of Adobe InDesign installed.

You should be comfortable adding content to your documents and formatting it, as shown in *Chapters 1 to 5*.

Adding content to a parent page including page numbers

When a new document is created in InDesign, it will automatically contain an item named **A-Parent** in the **Parents** section at the top of the **Pages** panel. **A-Parent** is your first parent page and, by default, it is empty, but in this recipe, we will look at how to work on your **A-Parent** page and apply content there, including dynamic page numbering.

While we are working specifically on **A-Parent**, it is worth noting that the same techniques for adding content apply to other parent pages as well.

Getting ready

To complete this recipe, simply open InDesign on your system and create a new document with 12 pages, as shown in the *Creating a new document* recipe in *Chapter 1*.

How to do it...

To add content to the **A-Parent** page, follow these steps:

1. From the **Window** menu, open the **Pages** panel, and at the top of the panel, double-click **A-Parent** (marked *A* in *Figure 7.1*). If **A-Parent** is not visible at the top of the **Pages** panel, you can always adjust the size of both the **Parents** section and the entire panel using the adjustment bars, which can be dragged up and down (marked *B* in *Figure 7.1*).

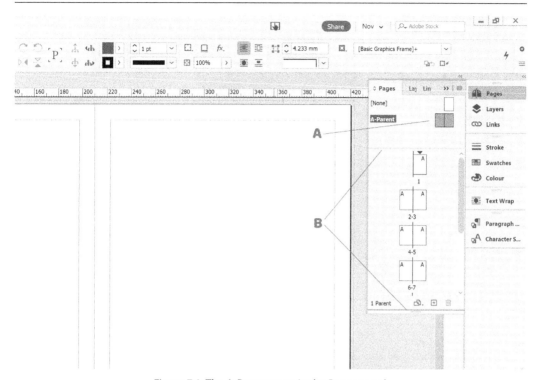

Figure 7.1: The A-Parent page in the Pages panel

You can confirm you are now working on the **A-Parent** page as it will say **A-Parent** at the bottom of InDesign on the left (marked *A* in *Figure 7.2*).

When you are working on a parent page, you will only be able to see that spread and will be unable to scroll up and down to see other parents or pages within the main document area.

Additionally, as this document has **Facing Pages** enabled, **A-Parent** is automatically a double-page spread. As such, pages that have **A-Parent** applied to them will use content from the corresponding side of the **A-Parent**, so left-hand pages in the document will pull content from the left-hand parent page and right-hand pages will pull content from the right-hand parent.

2. On the left-hand page of the **A-Parent** spread, we will now add a header at the top. Using the **Type** tool, create a large text frame and add some text (in my case, `Autumn Collection`), then center the text within the frame and give the frame a background color. I will position this at the top of the page being careful to ensure it doesn't cross the spine (marked *B* in *Figure 7.2*) onto the right-hand parent page.

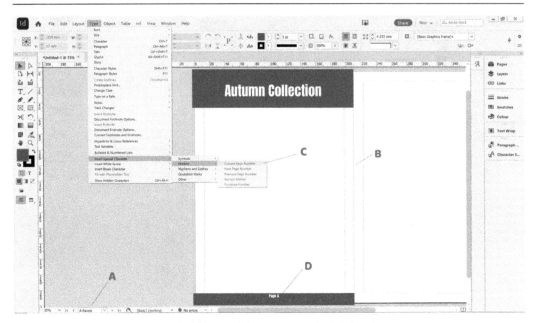

Figure 7.2: A-Parent with content on the left-hand page

Note

When using parent pages with facing pages, make sure objects do not cross the spine accidentally, as they can then be interpreted as being part of the parent page on that side as well. This could result in an item on the left-hand page of a spread also being seen as part of the right-hand page (or vice versa). The consequence of this would be pages that have no parent applied to them suddenly having parent items show up on them, simply because the other page within the same spread has a parent page applied to it.

3. Having given **A-Parent** a header, I want to ensure we have page numbering on the bottom of the pages. I will add a text frame at the bottom of the page and type the word Page and will then add a marker for the current page number.

    To do this, go to the **Type** menu, then **Insert Special Character**, and within the **Markers** section, choose **Current Page Number** (marked C in *Figure 7.2*). This will insert a letter A after the word *Page* (marked D in *Figure 7.2*). This is a dynamic marker for the page number – it shows as A because you are on **A-Parent**; however, it will automatically change to B for **B-Parent**, 2 for **Page 2**, and so on.

> **Note**
>
> When adding the page numbering to a parent, it is important to do so from **Insert Special Character** under the **Type** menu. Do not simply type Page A onto your parent page as this will result in every page the parent is applied to saying **Page A** rather than the relevant page number.

4. Having added the page numbering, I would like the total page count to show up here as well, so it shows, for example, as **Page 2 of 12** instead of just **Page 2**. To do this, click just after the page number marker with the **Type** tool, and type the word of followed by a space. Now, in the **Type** menu, go to **Text Variables** and under **Insert Variable**, choose **Last Page Number** (marked *A* in *Figure 7.3*).

    You will now see the page numbering has changed to show as **Page A of 1** (marked *B* in *Figure 7.3*) but when **A-Parent** is applied to your pages, this will now show as **Page 2 of 12**, for example, on the second page. If the number of pages in the document subsequently changes, so will the value of the **Last Page Number** variable.

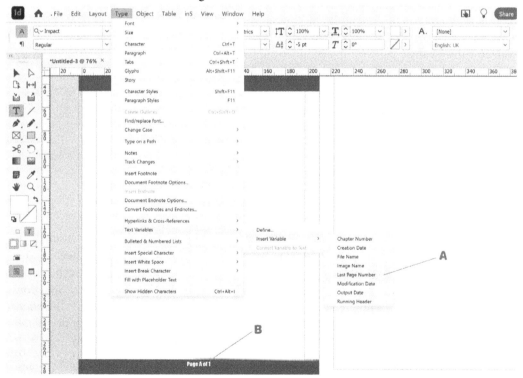

Figure 7.3: Customizing the page numbering on a parent page

Having customized our left-hand **A-Parent**, let's now go back and look at our pages. By default, **A-Parent** is automatically applied to all your document pages, and what you will find is **A-Parent** is now being applied to every left-hand page but not the right-hand pages. This can be seen with a quick glance at the **Pages** panel, where the page thumbnails can be seen containing the new **Autumn Collection** banner and the page numbering on all the left-hand pages but not the right-hand pages, as seen in *Figure 7.4*. You will also notice the small letter *A* on the thumbnails (marked *A* in *Figure 7.4*) telling you which parent page is applied to them; if it was the **B-Parent** page, a letter *B* would be shown there.

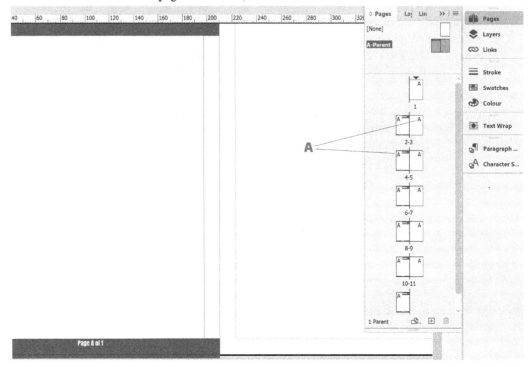

Figure 7.4: Pages panel with thumbnails reflecting the changes made to A-Parent

5. As the **A-Parent** items are only currently on the left-hand page, we need to now ensure they are also on the right-hand page. To do this, we are simply going to duplicate the items across onto the right-hand page. There are various ways to do this but the fastest is to select both text frames on the left-hand page, hold down the *Alt* (PC)/*Option* (Mac) key, and with the **Selection** tool, drag the frames onto the right-hand page. Make sure to hold down the *Alt* (PC)/*Option* (Mac) key until after you have released the mouse button, and also make sure your new items do not cross over the spine onto the left-hand parent page, as explained previously.

When you now look back at the page thumbnails, you should see the **A-Parent** content is now applied to the right-hand pages as well.

See also

You might wish to take page numbering further by having **Page 1** start on the third page in the document and leave the first two pages as the front cover and inside front cover. If so, take a look at `https://www.highlander.co.uk/blog/custom-page-numbering-indesign`.

Applying and removing parent pages

There are a number of different ways to apply parent pages to your pages or remove them. In this recipe, we will look at applying parents to individual pages, applying parents to multiple pages, removing parents from pages, and shortcuts to make it easier to select the exact pages you want while doing this.

Getting ready

To complete this recipe, simply open InDesign on your system and create a new document with 12 pages, as shown in the *Creating a new document* recipe in *Chapter 1*. You should be comfortable adding content to the **A-Parent**, as shown in the previous recipe.

How to do it...

To apply parents to pages and remove them, follow these steps:

1. Our new document contains 12 pages – by default, **A-Parent** is applied to all pages. Let's start by removing **A-Parent** from every page. To do this, click on the thumbnail for page 1 in the **Pages** panel, then hold down the *Shift* key and click the thumbnail for page 12. This should result in all the pages being selected.

2. Having selected all the pages, right-click on any of the page thumbnails in the **Pages** panel and choose the option for **Apply Parent to Pages…** (marked *A* in *Figure 7.5*). This will bring up the **Apply Parent dialog box**, which has two options in it, as follows:

   - **Apply Parent** (*B* in *Figure 7.5*): From the dropdown here, you can choose any of your parent pages or you can choose [**None**], which removes any parents applied. In our case, we will choose [**None**].

   - **To Pages** (*C* in *Figure 7.5*): This will default to **All Pages** as we have already selected every page, so there is no need to alter this. It is worth noting that you can alter the settings here to apply the parent to different pages than those originally selected. For example, `1,3,5` would apply to pages 1, 3, and 5, while `2-6` would apply to pages 2, 3, 4, 5, and 6.

   We can now click **OK**, and **A-Parent** has been removed from all pages.

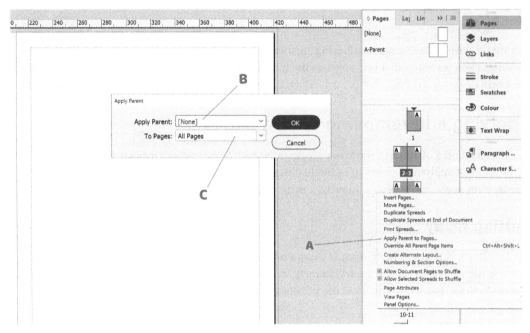

Figure 7.5: Apply Parent to Pages option

3. Having applied [**None**] to all pages, we now want to apply **A-Parent** to the first page. Click on the thumbnail for **A-Parent** in the **Pages** panel and drag it on top of the thumbnail for the first page. You will see **A-Parent** is now applied to the first page.

4. I would now like to also apply **A-Parent** to pages 4 to 10. To do this, click the thumbnail for page 4, then hold down the *Shift* key and click the thumbnail for page 10. You will notice all the pages between 4 and 10 have now been selected.

    I will now click the **Pages** panel menu (marked *A* in *Figure 7.6*) and from here, I can set the option for **Apply Parent to Pages…** (marked *B* in *Figure 7.6*). This will bring up the **Apply Parent** dialog box that we saw in *step 2*. This time, we will choose **A-Parent** from the **Apply Parent** dropdown, and you should also see that the **To Pages** value has defaulted to **4-10**; we can now click **OK** to apply these settings. This is an alternative method of applying parents to pages.

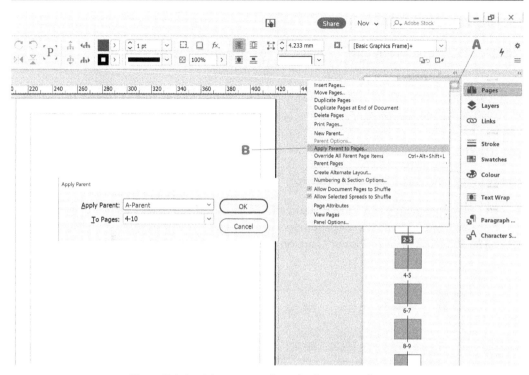

Figure 7.6: Applying parents from the Pages panel menu

5.   Finally, having applied **A-Parent** to pages 4 to 10, I have now decided I would like no parent applied to pages 5, 7, and 9. To select these 3 pages, click on the thumbnail for page 5, then hold down the *Ctrl* (PC)/*Cmd* (Mac) key and click on the thumbnails for pages 7 and 9.

Having selected the three pages, you can now right-click on any of the three selected page thumbnails and choose **Apply Parent to Pages…**. This time, under **Apply Parent**, we will choose the **[None]** option and click **OK**. Now, no parent page is applied to pages 5, 7, and 9.

Creating new parents and inheriting properties

While you won't use parents in some documents and, in others, the **A-Parent** is all you will need, it can be useful to create additional Parents, especially in longer documents such as catalogs or manuals. In this recipe, we will look at how to create more parent pages and how to base a new parent on an existing parent, allowing it to inherit properties from the existing parent page. This can be a useful technique for controlling your guides or page numbering across multiple different parent pages all from one central place.

Getting ready

To complete this recipe, simply open InDesign on your system and create a new document with 12 pages, as shown in the *Creating a new document* recipe in *Chapter 1*.

You should also be comfortable with the previous recipes in this chapter: *Adding content to a parent page including page numbers* and *Applying and removing parent pages*.

How to do it...

To create new parent pages, follow these steps:

1. Our new document has **A-Parent** automatically created within it and applied to every page by default, but we want to create additional parent pages. To do this, click on the **Pages** panel menu and select the **New Parent...** option (marked *A* in *Figure 7.7*).

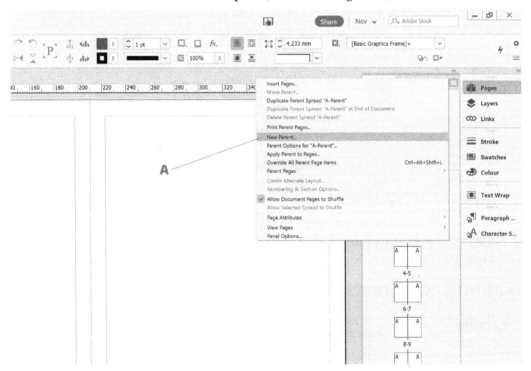

Figure 7.7: New Parent option in the Parent Pages panel

This will bring up the **New Parent dialog box** shown in *Figure 7.8*:

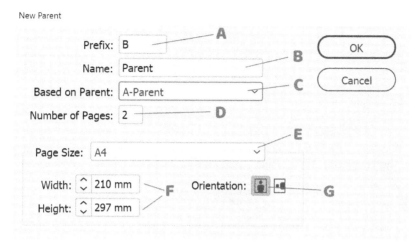

Figure 7.8: New Parent dialog box

Let's look at the options:

- **Prefix** (*A*): This lets you organize your pages alphabetically. As our first parent spread was **A-Parent**, this will automatically set the second one to **B-Parent**.

- **Name** (*B*): If you wish to change this to make specific parent pages easier to identify, you can, but in our case, we will leave this with the name **Parent**.

- **Based on Parent** (*C*): Here you can choose an existing parent to inherit properties from. We will choose **A-Parent** and, as a result, our **B-Parent** page will start out containing everything that is present on **A-Parent**. The **A-Parent** page has in effect become a parent for **B-Parent**. This means that if **A-Parent** subsequently changes, those changes will also be reflected on **B-Parent** and, in turn, any pages it is applied to. If you wish your new parent to be completely independent of other parents, you would set this to **None**.

- **Number of Pages** (*D*): This is the number of pages the parent spread will contain and should be a value from 1 to 10. In our case, we will set this to **2**, as we are working on double-page spreads.

- **Page Size** (*E*): The size of the parent pages to be created. I am working on A4 pages so will set this to **A4**.

- **Width** and **Height** (*F*): These will be set based on the page size chosen, but can be manually altered if you so wish. We will leave them set to the default A4 sizes.

- **Orientation** (*G*): Here you can switch between **Portrait** or **Landscape** orientations. We will leave this set to **Portrait**.

In this document, we aren't going to apply **A-Parent** directly to any pages. Instead, we are going to use it as what is effectively a parent for the other parent pages. This will allow us to use **A-Parent** to control items that will appear on multiple other parent pages, such as guides or page numbering, without having to adjust them separately on each individual parent page.

2. Repeat *step 1* but, this time, the prefix for the new parent page will be **C** instead of **B** – everything else should be the same. Upon completion, the **Pages** panel should then show **[None]** together with three additional parent spreads, **A-Parent**, **B-Parent**, and **C-Parent**, as shown in *Figure 7.9*. **B-Parent** and **C-Parent** (*A* in *Figure 7.9*) will be based on **A-Parent**, which is reflected in the fact that their respective thumbnails contain the letter **A** on them (*B* in *Figure 7.9*).

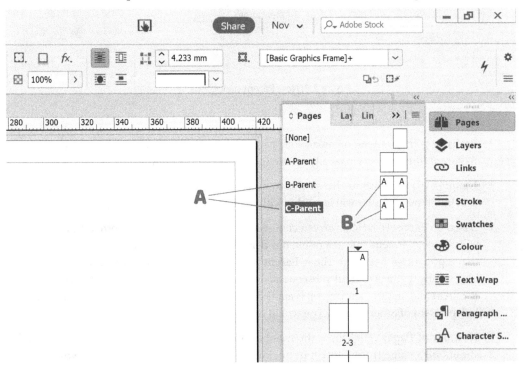

Figure 7.9: Pages panel with A, B, and C Parents showing

3. Double-click **A-Parent** to open it. Let's add some guides to both the left- and right-hand pages. In my case, I am going to put guides 25 mm from the left on each page and 25 mm from the top. Additionally, I will add markers for the current page number at the bottom of the pages.

4. Now switch to **B-Parent**. On **B-Parent**, you will see the guides and page numbering are already there because **B-Parent** is based on **A-Parent**. If you wish to edit these, you can do so on **A-Parent**. Here on **B-Parent**, however, we want to add a title across the top of both pages. I will call it `Summer Selection`.

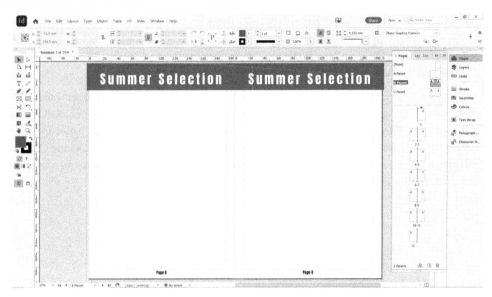

Figure 7.10: B-Parent with inherited guides and numbering and its own banner

5. Having added a banner to **B-Parent**, let's now change to **C-Parent**; again, we can see the guides and page numbering already, as **C-Parent** is based on **A-Parent**. We will again add a banner across the top of the pages, but this time, use a different color as this is going to be applied to a different section of the document. We will call this Autumn Selection:

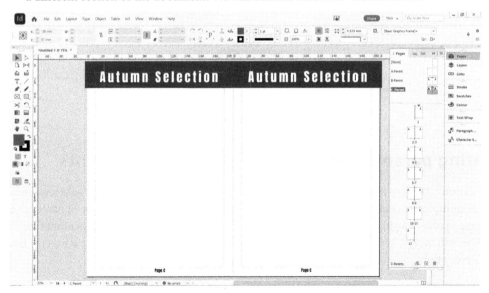

Figure 7.11: C-Parent with its own header and inherited guides and page numbering

6. Having now created our parent pages, let's apply them to some pages. Start by applying [**None**] to all pages, then apply **B-Parent** to pages 2 to 6 and apply **C-Parent** to pages 7 to 11. Now, double-click on page 1 and scroll through your document and you should see the relevant parent pages applied.

7. As one final step, I have decided, after looking at the document, that I no longer want guides or page numbering to appear on the pages using **B-Parent**. In effect, I no longer wish for it to be based on **A-Parent**. To achieve this, right-click on **B-Parent** in the **Pages** panel and select **Parent Options for "B Parent"**, and under **Based On**, set it to [**None**] before clicking **OK**. This will automatically remove all the guides and page numbering from **B-Parent** and all pages it is applied to, as shown in *Figure 7.12*.

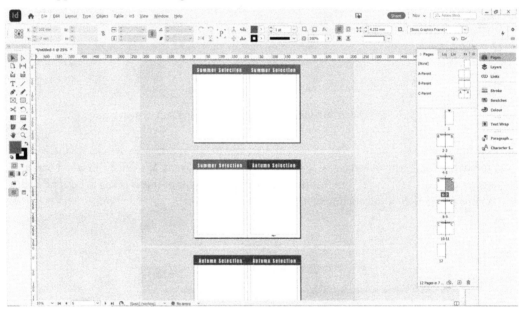

Figure 7.12: B and C Parents applied to pages

Creating parents from pages and importing parents

When working with parent pages, you might want to turn existing pages into parents so you can reuse them on multiple pages and maintain elements in one central place, or even make use of parent pages you created previously in other documents by importing them into your current document. In this recipe, we will look at how to do both of these, saving you from having to create new parents from scratch every time.

Getting ready

To complete this recipe, simply open InDesign on your system and create a new document with 12 pages, as shown in the *Creating a new document* recipe in *Chapter 1*.

How to do it...

To create new parents from an existing page or import parent pages, follow these steps:

1. As this is a brand-new document, let's start by adding some content. Go to the first double-page spread (pages 2 and 3) and add a title at the top of each page, along with any other design elements you want. In my case, I'll include a sidebar, as seen in *Figure 7.13*.

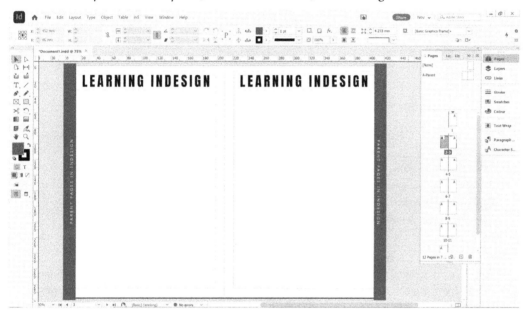

Figure 7.13: Pages 2 and 3 with content added

Having added some content to these two pages, I have now decided it would be good to have the same content on other pages as well and to be able to maintain this easily all in one place. It makes sense, therefore, to create a reusable parent spread from this double-page spread.

2. Select the thumbnails for pages 2 and 3 in the **Pages** panel and then drag them up to the **Parents** section at the top of the **Pages** panel, just below **A-Parent**. When you let go of the mouse button, you should see a new **B-Parent** spread appear immediately below the **A-Parent** spread.

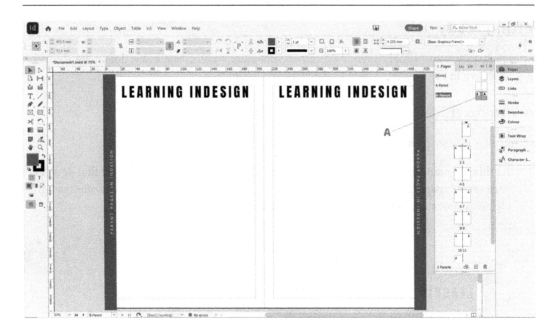

Figure 7.14: New B-Parent created from pages 2 and 3

Since the pages you started from were based on **A-Parent**, this new **B-Parent** is also based on **A-Parent**, and this is reflected in the small **A** icon showing on the **B-Parent** thumbnails in the **Pages** panel (marked *A* in *Figure 7.14*). If the source pages had no parent page applied to them, then the newly generated parent pages would also be based on no parent.

> **Note**
>
> You can also create new parent pages from pages by selecting the relevant pages in the **Pages** panel and then, instead of dragging them, go to the **Pages** panel menu, select **Parent Pages**, and then **Save as Parent**. If working with facing pages, this option is grayed out unless you select a full spread (rather than a single page).

3. Having created a **B-Parent** spread, let's now create a **C-Parent** spread from it. To do this, simply right-click on the name of the **B-Parent** spread in the **Pages** panel and select **Duplicate Parent Spread "B-Parent"**. This will create a **C-Parent** spread that is an exact copy of **B-Parent**. It is worth noting that because **B-Parent** was based on **A-Parent**, **C-Parent** is also based on **A-Parent**.

   Alternatively, you can duplicate the **B-Parent** spread by double-clicking on it to select it and then choosing **Duplicate Parent Spread "B-Parent"** from the **Pages** panel menu.

4. Next, open **C-Parent** by double-clicking on it and make any changes that you wish to make. In my case, I will edit the fill color of the frames to a different color.

   Having done this, we will then save the document to our desktop and call it `Document1.indd` before closing it.

5. Having saved and closed our previous document containing a number of parent pages, we will now create a new document in InDesign with the same dimensions as the previous document – in my case, A4. I want to now use the parent pages from the previous document in my new document. To do so, in the **Pages** panel menu, under **Parent Pages**, select **Load Parent Pages…** (marked *A* in *Figure 7.15*).

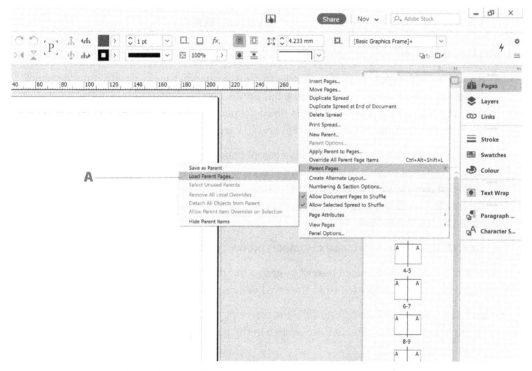

Figure 7.15: Loading parent pages from another document

This will bring up a dialog box allowing you to choose the InDesign document you wish to load pages from. Select the document we previously saved and then click **OK**.

6. You will now see the **Load Parent Page Alert box** (*Figure 7.16*) appear. This box is showing because we are trying to load Parent pages into a document that already contains parent pages with the exact same name. In this instance, our new document has a parent page called **A-Parent**, as does our old document.

Figure 7.16: Load Parent Page Alert

You have three options here, as follows:

- **Replace parent pages**: This will overwrite any existing parent pages with the imported parent pages of the same name. We will choose this option causing **A-Parent** in our new document to be replaced with **A-Parent** from the saved document. As both the old and new A-Parents are blank, it won't matter, and **B-Parent** and **C-Parent** will be imported normally.

- **Rename parent pages**: Where there is a parent page of the same name, this will rename the incoming parent pages to the next incremental number. In this case, our new document has **A-Parent** already, so choosing this option would cause the imported **A**, **B**, and **C-Parents** to become **B**, **C**, and **D-Parents** in this new document. The existing **A-Parent** in this document would be left untouched.

- **Cancel**: This will simply cancel the import process, so no parent pages are imported.

In our case, we chose **Replace parent pages** so the parent pages in our new document are replaced by those we imported from the saved document.

We now have a new document containing all of the parent pages from the previous document, saving us from having to recreate this content from scratch in the new document.

Overriding and detaching parent items

When a parent page is applied to a regular page, the parent page items appear on the regular page, but they are still controlled by the parent page. If they are edited on the parent page, those edits will be reflected on the pages that have the parent applied to them.

Sometimes, you might want to override certain parent item properties locally on an individual page, while still retaining the connection to the parent with respect to other properties. For example, you might have elements on multiple pages that are applied through a parent page, but you would like to change the fill color of a frame on a single page, while still allowing it to reflect any changes to other properties that are made on the parent page, such as the corner options or text frame options.

This is called overriding and, in this recipe, we will look at how to do this. We will also take a look at how you can detach overridden items completely, breaking all links to the parent page and severing the connection.

Getting ready

To complete this recipe, open InDesign on your system and create a new document with 12 pages, as shown in the *Creating a new document* recipe in *Chapter 1*.

In addition to the technical requirements at the start of this chapter, you should be comfortable with the previous recipes in this chapter (*Adding content to a parent page including page numbers* and *Applying and removing parent pages*), as well as the *Applying colors within your document* recipe found in *Chapter 8*.

How to do it

To override or detach parent items, follow these steps:

1. Let's start by creating some content on **A-Parent**. Go to **A-Parent** by double-clicking on it, and add a sidebar down the side of each parent, page numbering at the bottom of the bar, and an image across the top of each page, as seen in *Figure 7.17*.

    Once this is done, apply **A-Parent** to all pages in your document, if it isn't already.

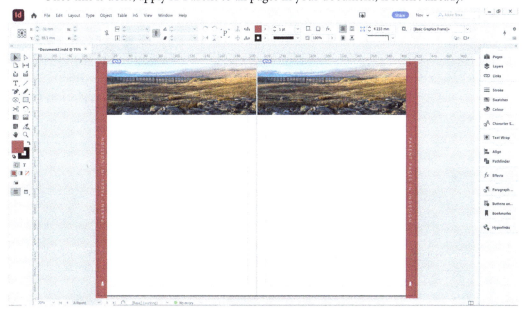

Figure 7.17: A-Parent with initial content applied

2. Next, we will switch to page 2 and override the sidebar on page 2 by holding down *Ctrl* (PC)/ *Cmd* (Mac) + *Shift* and clicking on the sidebar object. This allows us to make local overrides to the object on that page, while still allowing it to inherit the rest of its properties from **A-Parent**. We will change the fill color of the left bar on page 2 to a different color, as seen in *Figure 7.18*.

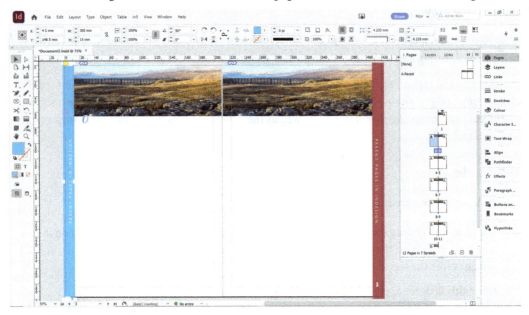

Figure 7.18: A Parent item unlocked locally on a page

3. Having changed the color of the sidebar on page 2, we will now go back to **A-Parent** and apply a thick black dashed stroke to both sidebars on it. Having done this, go back to page 2, and you should see the color is still overridden but the new stroke has now been applied, as seen in *Figure 7.19*.

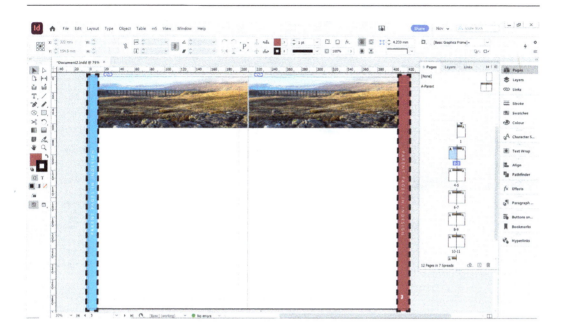

Figure 7.19: The stroke applied on the A-Parent also shows on the overridden object

> **Note**
>
> It is worth noting that only properties of the object are linked back to the parent once objects
> are overridden locally, and not the content itself. If a frame is overridden locally on a page and
> the text itself is edited or the image is changed within the frame on the page, any changes to
> these on the parent won't be passed on to the overridden object on the page, only changes to
> the object properties (not the content) on the parent will be passed through to the page. These
> properties include frame strokes, frame fills, transformations (such as rotating, scaling, shearing,
> or resizing), corner options, text frame options, lock state, transparency, and object effects.

Having applied overrides to an individual object on a page, we now want to apply overrides to
all objects on a specific page, with the exception of page numbering.

4. Go to **A-Parent** and select the two small text frames containing the page numbers, then in the
    Page panel menu, under **Parent Pages**, click on **Allow Parent Item Overrides on Selection**
    (marked *A* in *Figure 7.20*) to disable this option (this option can also be accessed by right-
    clicking on the items with the mouse). This will prevent the page numbering objects from being
    overridden locally on specific pages.

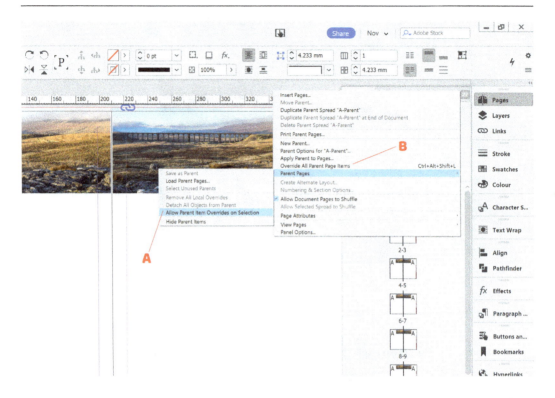

Figure 7.20: Pages panel menu

5. Next, navigate to page 5 of your document by double-clicking the icon for page 5 in the **Pages** panel, then in the **Pages** panel menu, select **Override All Parent Page Items** (marked *B* in *Figure 7.20*) (this option can also be accessed by right-clicking on the page thumbnail in the **Pages** panel with the mouse). This will override all parent items on page 5 except for page numbering, as we have already turned off the ability for page numbering in *step 4*.

> **Note**
>
> If you override a threaded text frame, all frames in that story are overridden, even if they are on a different page in a spread.

6. On page 5, select the image object at the top of the page and go to **File** and **Place** and choose a new image, then click **OK**. We aren't going to alter any other properties of the object so be careful not to accidentally move it or resize it while doing this. Additionally, we will change the color of the sidebar on page 5 to a different color.

You might notice that page numbering has disappeared on page 5. It hasn't actually disappeared; it is simply behind the sidebar. This is because, by default, overridden or local page items are positioned in front of any parent items that are on the same layer. We will look at how to resolve this in the next recipe, *Using layers with parents*.

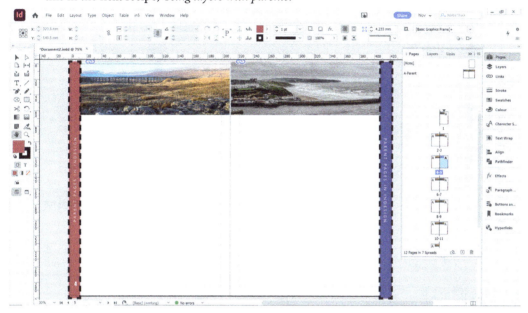

Figure 7.21: Page 5 with the image replaced and the sidebar containing a new fill color

7. Now, return to **A-Parent**, and let's edit the image object on both pages in the **A-Parent** spread by applying an 8 pt solid black stroke to both the image objects and also the sidebars, replacing the existing stroke on the sidebars.

If we now go back to page 5, you will notice the stroke has been passed through to the overridden objects, but the image has not reverted to the original image and the sidebar is still a different color, which is what we wanted to happen.

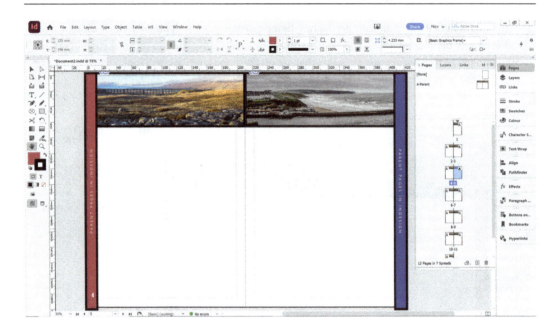

Figure 7.22: Page 5 showing the updated image frame and sidebar

Having looked at ways to override parent objects, you might on some occasions want to completely sever the link to the original parent objects, so no connection is retained.

8. To do this, first unlock the relevant parent object(s) on the page, either by holding down *Ctrl* (PC)/*Cmd* (Mac) + *Shift* and clicking on it or by selecting **Override All Parent Page Items** in the **Pages** panel menu. With the relevant object(s) selected, go to the **Pages** panel menu and, under **Parent Pages**, choose **Detach Selection from Parent** (marked *A* in *Figure 7.23*). If no objects are selected, this will say **Detach All Objects from Parent**, which will detach all overridden objects on the current page.

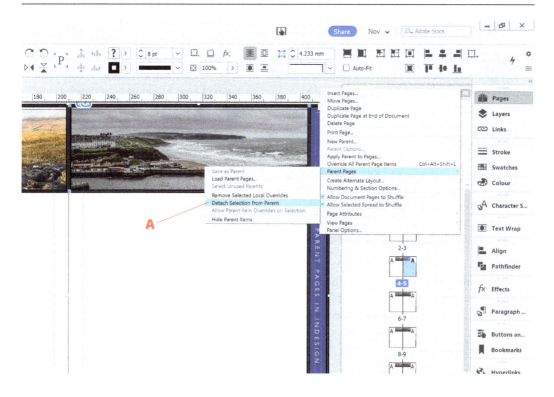

Figure 7.23: Detaching objects from the parent

The link between the parent object and the local object on the page will now be severed completely and the two become totally independent of each other.

> **Note**
>
> One issue with parent page overrides is that there is no easy way to see what items have been overridden, making it hard to tell what has been changed. Hopefully, this will be something addressed in future releases, but for now, if you are using parent overrides, make a note of what properties you override, as you may need to refer to it later.

Using layers with parents

By default, any items you create on a parent page will be on the same layer as your page items, and, by default, the parent items will be positioned behind the local page items. This means local page items will effectively sit on top of your parent items and could hide them. In this recipe, we will look at how to organize your parent items onto a different layer to ensure they will stay on top of page items when you need them to.

Getting ready

To complete this recipe, simply open InDesign on your system and create a new document with 12 pages, as shown in the *Creating a new document* recipe in *Chapter 1*. You should also be comfortable with the previous recipes in this chapter: *Adding content to a parent page including page numbers* and *Applying and removing parent pages*.

How to do it...

To use layers with your parents, follow these steps:

1. In our new document, let's start by adding some content to **A-Parent**. I am going to add a text frame right across the bottom of each page, which has a black fill and contains the page numbering aligned to the outside edge of the page with an 8 mm indent.

    I would also like to apply 50% opacity to the black fill, in order to make it semi-transparent. To do this, select the frame with the **Selection** tool and then open the **Effects** panel (found in the **Window** menu). In the **Effects** panel, click once on the line labeled **Fill** (*A* in *Figure 7.24*) and adjust the **Opacity** value (*B* in *Figure 7.24*) to **50%**.

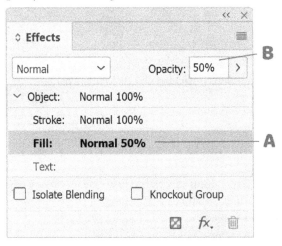

Figure 7.24: Adjust the opacity of the fill with the Effects panel

I will also add ruler guides that are 25 mm from the left and 50 mm and 150 mm from the top on each page, as seen in *Figure 7.25*. Apply **A-Parent** to all pages in your document.

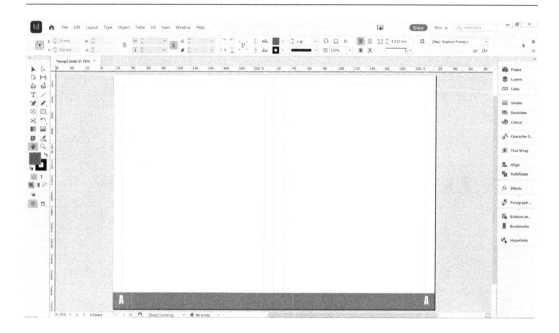

Figure 7.25: Text frame with page numbering added to the A-Parent

2. Next, go to page 2 of your document and add a large image to the bottom-left of the page. Having done this, though, you will notice that the image completely covers the bar with the page numbering that we put on **A-Parent** (shown in *Figure 7.26*). This is because when parent items and page items are on the same layer, the parent items are automatically placed behind the page items.

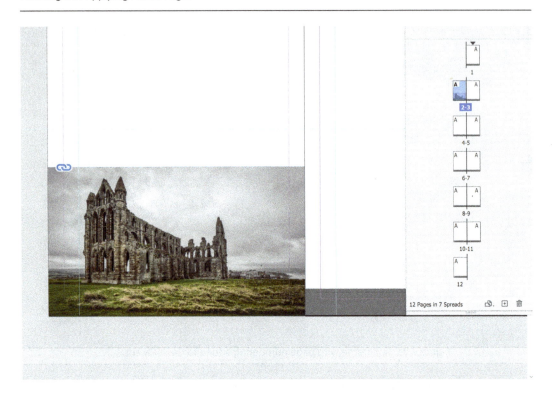

Figure 7.26: Page item covering parent item

3. To fix this, we need to go back to **A-Parent**, open up the **Layers** panel, and you will notice there is only one layer showing. Expand this layer by clicking the small arrow marked *A* in *Figure 7.27* and you will see the individual items that are on **A-Parent**. Open the **Layers** panel menu (marked *B* in *Figure 7.27*) and select **New Layer**.

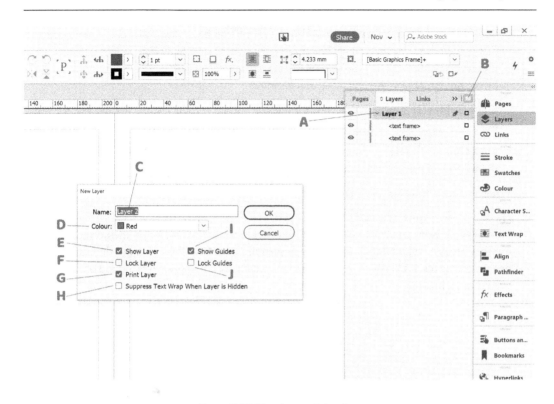

Figure 7.27: New Layer dialog box

This will bring up the **New Layer dialog box**, which contains the following options:

- **Name** (*C*): You can give the layer a custom name, which will show in the **Layers** panel. In our case, we will call it Layer 2.

- **Colour** (*D*): The color not only shows up next to the layer in the **Layers** panel but it is also the color used for the frame edges of any item placed on that layer. We will leave this set to the default color.

- **Show Layer** (*E*): If you wish to create a layer but have it hidden immediately after creation, deselect this. In our case, we will leave this enabled.

- **Lock Layer** (*F*): If you wish to have your new layer automatically locked after creation, select this. In our case, we want to be able to work on the layer so will leave this disabled.

- **Print Layer** (*G*): If you are creating a layer that you potentially do not wish to output to print or PDF, disable this. In our case, we will leave this enabled.

- **Suppress Text Wrap When Layer is Hidden** (*H*): If you hide a layer that contains an object that text on other layers is wrapping around, this will disable text wrap on this object when the layer is hidden, causing the text on other layers to reflow into the area previously occupied by the hidden object. We will leave this disabled.

- **Show Guides** (*I*): Enabling this allows guides on this layer to be visible. In our case, we will leave this enabled.

- **Lock Guides** (*J*): Selecting this locks ruler guides on this layer, preventing you from altering them. We will leave this deselected.

When you have finished, click **OK** to create your new layer.

Having created your new layer, in the **Layers** panel, drag the items that are on **Layer 1** up onto **Layer 2**. Now, go back to page 2 and you should see the parent items, including the page number, are showing on top of the image, as seen in *Figure 7.28* (bear in mind that we set 50% opacity on the black fill, which is why at first glance it may not appear to be on top of the image even though it is):

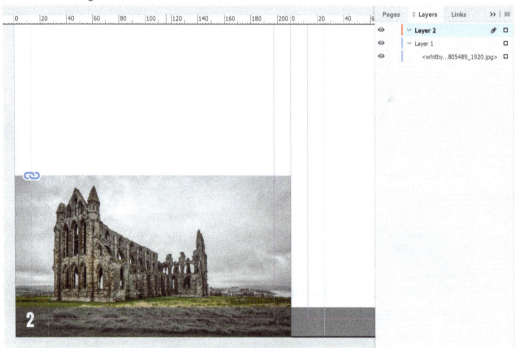

Figure 7.28: Parent items on top of layer items

8
Working with Colors and Gradients

In this chapter, we will learn how to create **color swatches** using CMYK and RGB, as well as discuss options such as spot colors. We will look at creating color swatches from an image, loading and saving swatches using swatch exchange files, creating and saving gradients, and organizing our color swatches using swatch groups. You will learn how to merge two colors, automatically replacing one color with the other anywhere it's used in the document. Finally, we will show you a little trick to allow you to set up default color swatches so that they appear in every new document that you create going forward.

However, before we start creating and using colors, it is important to have a basic understanding of color, including how RGB and CMYK differ, when to use them, as well as where spot colors come into play and what they are.

RGB is an additive color mode that involves combining red, green, and blue light to make up the color you want. The RGB color mode is used by screen devices such as mobile phones, computer screens, TV screens, and tablet devices, which actively push light at you. If you are creating content that will only be viewed on a screen (as opposed to in print), you should be using RGB colors to achieve this.

CMYK, on the other hand, is a subtractive color mode that is created by subtracting cyan, magenta, and yellow from white to create a color and is used by all standard print devices. The K in CMYK refers to the key color (black in modern printing), which is used to strengthen dark colors and improve contrast.

The standard four-color printing process uses CMYK (as opposed to RGB, which is only for screens), so the question isn't so much about which color mode to use, but when. Do you design everything in CMYK from the start, do you design in RGB and then convert it into CMYK at output time, or do you just do everything in RGB and let the printer sort it out (which means they will convert it into CMYK for you)? The reality is it depends a bit on your circumstances and your printer.

If you have specific color values for CMYK in your brand guidelines and are only creating the document for print, it makes sense to create them in CMYK, right from the start. When you output your print-ready PDF at the end, you should see no major color changes.

If you are creating a document for both screen and print use, you might want to work in RGB or even in a mix of RGB and CMYK (yes, that's fine in InDesign) and then just make sure you output the print version correctly using a CMYK color profile. This will ensure that, in the resulting PDF, all your colors have been converted into CMYK, albeit with some possible color shifts in the colors that were originally in RGB. Once this has happened, you will have a print-ready PDF document.

> **Note**
> A **color profile** is a set of specifications that provides a standardized way to represent and communicate colors accurately across different devices and platforms. They help ensure color information is adapted to ensure consistent and accurate color reproduction between devices.

Finally, you might prefer to just do the whole job in RGB and let the printer handle it. This is often quicker for you and most printers will be happy to do this, but you should be aware that some colors will look different after being printed, and the printer is not to blame for this. You have given them a document containing RGB colors that cannot be printed on a CMYK printer, and they have simply printed the nearest possible color to be helpful.

What if you need to reproduce colors exactly in print, or print bright vibrant colors that CMYK just can't handle? That's where **spot colors** come in, with one of the more popular systems being the **Pantone Matching System**. Spot colors are exact match colors that are included in the printing process as additional inks, and they should always produce the same color consistently every time. If you used a single spot color in a job, for example, you would be doing a five-color print run – that is, CMYK plus one spot color. While spot colors can create some great results, it is worth being aware they will add to the cost of a print job, and not every printer will support them.

Now that we are a bit clearer on color, let's look at working with it in InDesign.

The recipes we will cover in this chapter are as follows:

- Creating new color swatches
- Organizing and editing your swatches
- Creating new swatches from an image
- Saving and loading swatches
- Applying colors within your document

- Creating gradients and saving them as swatches

- Merging colors

- Finding colors within your document

- Customizing strokes

- Setting color management settings

Technical requirements

To complete this chapter, you will need a PC or Mac, with a copy of Adobe InDesign installed. You should also be comfortable adding content to your documents and formatting it, as shown in *Chapters 1 to 4.*

Creating new color swatches

When it comes to reproducing color consistently within your InDesign document, the solution is to work with reusable color swatches. These allow you to define a color that can then be reused again and again within the document without you having to remake it every time.

You can create swatches for both CMYK and RGB colors in InDesign, and in this recipe, we will look at creating both within our document. We will also look at a nice little trick to set up default color swatches so that they automatically appear in every new document you create.

Getting ready

To complete this recipe, simply open InDesign on your system and create a new document with 12 pages, as shown in the *Creating a new document* recipe in *Chapter 1.*

How to do it...

To create reusable color swatches in your document, follow these steps:

1. From the **Window** menu, in the **Color** section, click on **Swatches** to open the **Swatches panel** (seen in *Figure 8.1*):

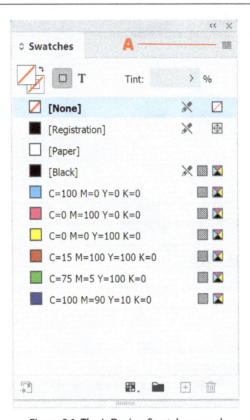

Figure 8.1: The InDesign Swatches panel

By default, you will see the following color swatches:

- **None (transparency)**: This applies transparency to the selected item.

- **Registration**: This is 100% on every color plate in the printing process (see the note).

- **Paper**: This is the color of the paper you will be printing on. By default, this is set to white, but it can be changed to other colors.

- **Black**: This is 100% on the key color (normally, this is black).

- **Cyan**, **Magenta**, and **Yellow**: These three color swatches represent the three primary colors of the CMYK color mode used in printing.

- **Red**, **Green**, and **Blue**: These three color swatches represent the three primary colors of the RGB color mode used by screens.

> **Note**
>
> **Registration** and **Black** are often confused. **Registration** is 100% on all inks (including spot colors) and is only used for printer marks; you should not use **Registration** to apply color to page content within your document. If you wish items in your document to be black, simply use the **Black** color swatch.

2. With the swatches panel open, let's start by creating a new CMYK color swatch. Click the **Swatches** panel menu (*A* in *Figure 8.1*) and select the first option, **New Colour Swatch**; this will bring up the **New Colour Swatch dialog box**:

Figure 8.2: The New Colour Swatch dialog box

There are several settings to choose from here, as follows:

- **Swatch Name** (*A*): By default, this uses the current color value.

- **Name With Colour Value** (*B*): Unticking this box will allow you to edit the swatch name and call it what you wish. In our case, we will untick this and type `My New Color` into the **Swatch Name** field.

- **Colour Type** (*C*): You have the option of **Process** (which we will choose) or **Spot**.

- **Colour Mode** (*D*): Here, you can choose the color mode or matching system you wish to use. In our case, we will choose **CMYK**. If you don't immediately see **CMYK**, remember to scroll up and down.

- **CMYK Sliders** (*E*): As we chose CMYK, we can now see the CMYK sliders to adjust each of the four colors – cyan, magenta, yellow, and black. We will set these values to **0**, **80**, **80**, and **0**, respectively.

- **Add to CC Library** (*F*): This allows you to add color swatches to **CC Library** for sharing or reusing on another machine. We will cover this more in *Chapter 12, Using and Collaborating with CC Libraries*. For now, leave this deselected.

Having selected our settings, click **OK**; the new color swatch will be added at the bottom of the **Swatches** panel (marked *A* in *Figure 8.3*).

Note

If you are looking to create multiple swatches, click **Add** rather than **OK** toward the end of *step 2*; the dialog box will stay open while still adding the new swatch to the swatches panel, allowing you to immediately continue creating another swatch.

You will also notice two small icons to the right of the swatch. The first (*B* in *Figure 8.3*) indicates that the type of color is a process color, while the second (*C* in *Figure 8.3*) indicates that the color mode is CMYK:

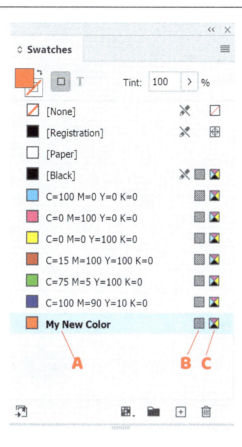

Figure 8.3: New CMYK swatch in the Swatches panel

Having created a new CMYK color swatch, let's create a new RGB color swatch.

3. Once again, go to the **Swatch** panel and select **New Colour Swatch** to bring up the **New Colour Swatch** dialog box. This time, we will choose **Process** for **Color Type** again, but under **Colour Mode**, we will choose **RGB**, which will result in only three sliders being presented for the **Red**, **Green**, and **Blue** values, as shown in *Figure 8.4*. Here, we will set **Red** to **90**, **Green** to **210**, and **Blue** to **50**.

You will notice a new icon appear (marked *A* in *Figure 8.4*). This is called **Out of Gamut Warning** and it tells you that the RGB color swatch you are creating cannot be reproduced in CMYK for print. If you intend to use this document for print at some stage and wish to avoid color differences between the screen and print versions, you would need to select a different color at this stage.

Fortunately, there is an easy fix for this. If you click on the **Out of Gamut Warning** icon, it will automatically change the color values to those of the nearest RGB color that can be reproduced in CMYK. Do this now:

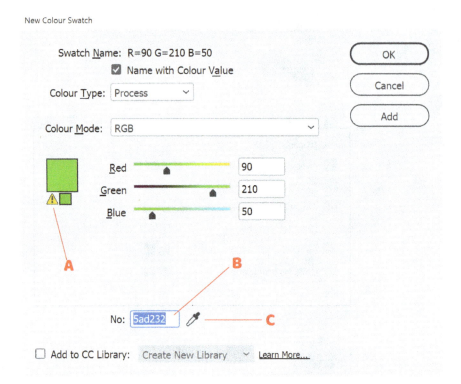

Figure 8.4: The New Colour Swatch box for RGB color

It is also worth noting the **hexadecimal** value (marked *B* in *Figure 8.4*). Hex, as it's known, is a hexadecimal representation of the RGB values of the color; it can be used, for example, in CSS when creating web content.

> **Note**
>
> You will see a small eye dropper icon (marked *C* in *Figure 8.4*). If you click on this and hold down the mouse button, you can drag the dropper over any other item on the screen. When you let go of the mouse button, the **New Colour Swatch** dialog box will display the values of that color.

Having chosen a new RGB color, click **OK** to add the RGB color swatch to the bottom of the swatches panel, as shown in *Figure 8.5*. You will notice that the **Colour Mode** icon (marked *A* in *Figure 8.5*) is different from last time, identifying this as an **RGB** color and not a **CMYK** color instead:

Figure 8.5: The Adobe Swatches panel, including both the RGB and CMYK swatches

> **Note**
> As far as using Pantone colors in Adobe CC goes, the situation has recently changed – from November 2022, only three Pantone books will remain in the **Swatches** panel. Going forward, the Pantone Connect extension for Adobe InDesign will be needed to access Pantone colors from within InDesign. These changes are very recent, and I haven't personally used this extension, which offers both a free and paid version and is available through the Adobe Exchange store.

Organizing and editing your swatches

Sometimes, the smallest things can save you the most time when you are doing them repeatedly. If you are applying colors hundreds of times a day, you can save a lot of time by simply having them ordered properly.

In this recipe, we will explore reordering your colors both manually and from the menus, as well as organizing them into color groups. We will also look at how you can edit swatches so that you can rename them and alter any of the available color values.

Getting ready

To complete this recipe, simply open InDesign on your system and create a new document with 12 pages, as shown in the *Creating a new document* recipe in *Chapter 1*. You should already be comfortable with creating new color swatches, as covered earlier in this chapter.

How to do it...

To organize and edit your color swatches, follow these steps:

1. Start by creating five new **RGB** color swatches in a mix of different colors, leaving the swatch names set to the color values. By default, they will appear at the bottom of your **Swatches** panel, as shown in *Figure 8.6*:

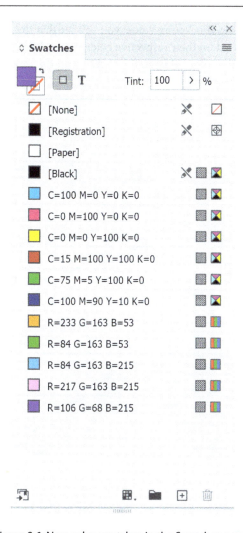

Figure 8.6: New color swatches in the Swatches panel

2.   Next, we are going to sort the new swatches based on their color values. Select the five swatches in the panel, then go to the **Sort** option. Here, you will see these options:

*   **All Swatches by Name**: This will sort all the swatches in the panel based on their name

*   **All Swatches By Colour Value**: This will sort all swatches based on their color values

*   **Selected Swatches by Name**: This will sort the selected swatches in the panel based on their name

*   **Selected Swatches By Colour Value**: This will sort the selected swatches based on their color values

Choose **Selected Swatches By Colour Value**; you will see that the swatches that you selected have been reordered based on their respective color values. You can see this because we left the swatch name set to the color value, so the swatch with the smallest red value is at the top and the largest is at the bottom:

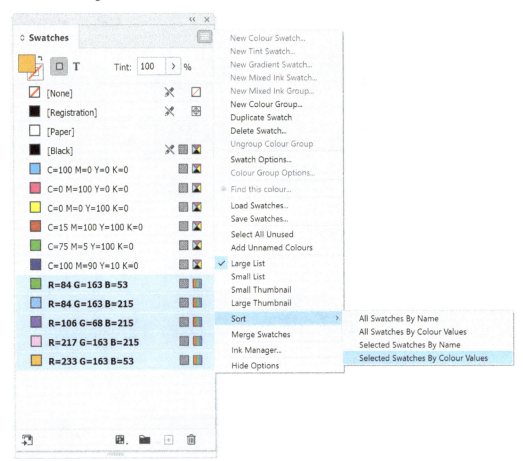

Figure 8.7: The Swatches panel with the last five sorted by color value

3.   Having sorted the swatches by color value, we now want to move the last swatch – in my case, a light orange color – to the top of the five swatches. First, deselect the five swatches if they are still selected by simply clicking another swatch, then click on the last swatch and drag it up the list. When the black line, which indicates its new position, is above the other four swatches, simply let go of the mouse button:

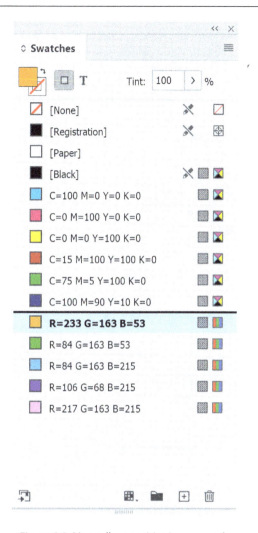

Figure 8.8: Manually repositioning a swatch

4. Having reordered the swatches into the order we want, I would now like to group them in a
    color group. To do this, select the five swatches again and click the **New Colour Group** icon
    (marked *A* in *Figure 8.9*); you will see that it not only creates a **New Colour Group**, but also
    puts the selected swatches into it automatically.

When you create a **New Colour Group** like this, the sort order of the swatches is reset back
to the original order that they were created in, and it doesn't respect any re-sorting that you
might have done since. This can be seen in *Figure 8.9*, where the sort order has reverted to
the original sort order seen in *Figure 8.6* and not the order we had set them to in *Figure 8.8*.

It is also worth noting that you can create an empty color group by clicking the **New Colour Group** icon without first selecting any swatches, and can then easily drag and drop existing swatches into it:

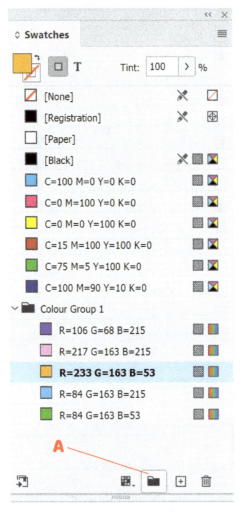

Figure 8.9: Swatches grouped into a color group

Note

At the time of writing this book, color groups cannot be positioned above regular color swatches in the **Swatches** panel and will always appear at the bottom of the list of swatches in the **Swatches** panel.

5. Having sorted our swatches into a color group, I would now like to rename the color group –
    by default, it is called **Color Group 1**. To do this, you can either right-click on the color group
    name in the **Swatches** panel or select it and then go to the **Swatches** panel menu and choose
    Color Group Options. This will bring up a small dialog box, as seen in *Figure 8.10*, where you
    can rename the color group:

Figure 8.10: The Edit Colour Group dialog box

6. Having renamed the color group, it would be useful to also rename the swatches within it. To do
    this, right-click on the first swatch and choose **Swatch Options**; this will bring up the **Swatch
    Options** dialog box for that color swatch. Here, you can edit any of the properties of the swatch,
    including its color type, color mode, and other attributes. In my case, I will deselect the **Name
    with Colour Value** checkbox (*A* in *Figure 8.11*) and rename the swatch **Brand Purple**. I will
    also do the same with the other four swatches in the color group, renaming them according to
    their colors, also seen in *Figure 8.11*:

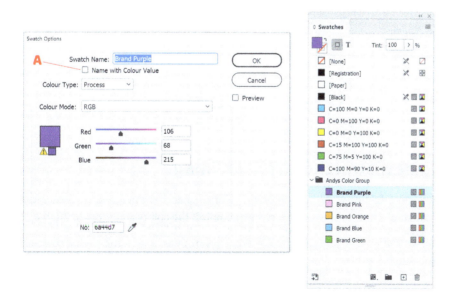

Figure 8.11: The Swatches panel and the Swatch Options dialog

7.   Having renamed all the swatches within the group, I would now like to quickly sort them by name. To do this, select all five swatches in the group, go to **Sort**, and then choose **Selected Swatches by Name**. You will now see the swatches sorted by name:

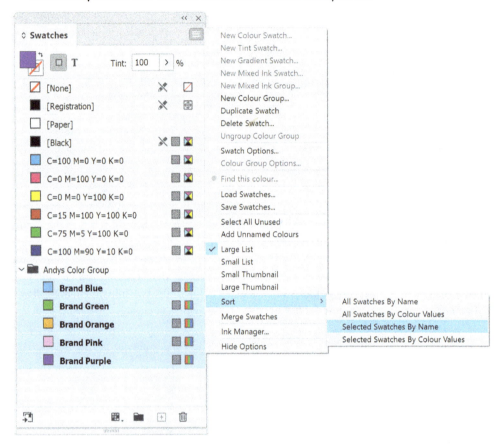

Figure 8.12: Swatches in the group sorted by name

Creating new swatches from an image

In many cases, you might be working with brand colors that are very precisely defined. However, in some cases, you might just want to create colors that reflect the colors and tones in an image.

In this recipe, we will look at generating color swatches from an image and saving them as a color group in your swatches panel.

Getting ready

To complete this recipe, simply open InDesign on your system and create a new document with 12 pages and the intent set to **Print**, as shown in the *Creating a new document* recipe in *Chapter 1*. You should already be comfortable *Placing images in InDesign*, as covered in *Chapter 5*.

How to do it...

To create color swatches from an image, just follow these steps:

1. Start by placing an image on your page in InDesign, then switch to the **Colour Theme Tool** option (marked *A* in *Figure 8.13*):

Figure 8.13: Colour Theme Tool

2. Having switched to the **Colour Theme** tool, click once anywhere on the image; the tool will pick up a selection of five colors from the image, as seen in *Figure 8.14*:

Figure 8.14: Color Theme Tool in use

3. Now, we want to add the second color in the theme to our **Swatches** panel as a single-color swatch. To do this, click the color on the bar (*A* in *Figure 8.14*) and then, while holding down the *Alt* (Window)/*Option* (Mac) key, click the **Add this theme to swatches** button (*B* in *Figure 8.14*). You should now see the color at the bottom of the **Swatches** panel.

4. Having looked at the five colors in the theme that InDesign has generated, they aren't exactly what I wanted and I would like to see some alternatives. To do this, simply click on the flyout menu (*A* in *Figure 8.15*); you will see that there are another four alternative themes to choose from. In my case, I will select the **Bright** theme:

Figure 8.15: Color theme options

5. I would now like to add all five colors from the **Bright** theme to my **Swatches** panel as a color group. Click the **Add to Swatches** icon without holding down any other keys; a new color group will appear at the bottom containing all five colors from the color theme.

    When creating swatches with the color theme tool, by default, the color mode of the new swatches will be based on the document intent that was chosen when you created the new document. In my case, it was **Print**, so the swatches have been created in **CMYK**. If the intent had been **Web**, they would have been in **RGB**. Next, we'll look at how to control this manually.

6. With the **Colour Theme Tool** selected, double-click on the **Colour Theme Tool** icon in the **Tools** panel. This will open the **Colour Theme Options dialog box** shown in *Figure 8.16*:

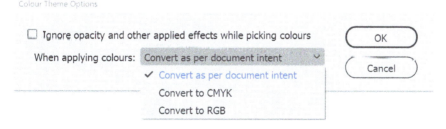

Figure 8.16: The Colour Theme Options dialog box

The panel contains a tick box that can be checked if you want the color theme tool to ignore the impact of effects, including opacity, when creating color themes. As we haven't used any effects, we can ignore this completely.

The other setting here is the **When applying colours** dropdown, which has three options:

- **Convert as per document intent**: The color mode will be set based on the document intent that was chosen when you created the document.

- **Convert to CMYK**: Colors will be automatically converted into the CMYK color mode.

- **Convert to RGB**: Colors will be automatically converted into the RGB color mode. I will set it to this.

7. Having set the tool to convert colors into RGB, click on the **Add this theme to swatches** button again; you should see a second color theme group containing five colors in the **Swatches** panel. This time, though, the colors will all be in RGB rather than CMYK:

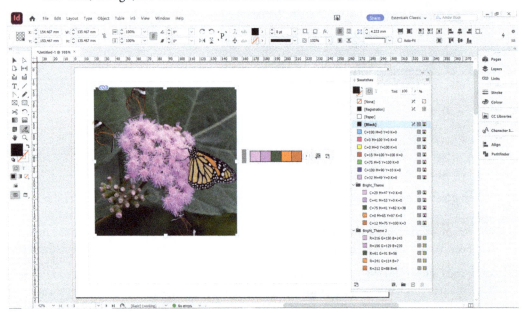

Figure 8.17: Second color theme added to the Swatches panel

Saving and loading swatches

When you are working with InDesign, it is quite common that you will want to use the same colors on more than one document. For example, the colors that appear in corporate brand guidelines should always be the same and shouldn't change every time they are used in a different document. Reusing your color swatches across multiple documents is a good way to ensure this consistency.

In this recipe, I'll show you how to export your color swatches from InDesign as an **Adobe Swatch Exchange File** (.ase) and how to reload the .ase file back into another document. We will also look at a useful trick for setting up default swatches that appear in every new document by default.

In addition to their use for quickly loading and sharing colors, ASE files can also be useful for keeping a backup of your brand colors, which can be useful should you ever have system issues.

Getting ready

To complete this recipe, simply open InDesign on your system and create a new document with 12 pages and the intent set to **Print**, as shown in the *Creating a new document* recipe in *Chapter 1*. You should already be comfortable with creating new color swatches, as covered earlier in this chapter.

How to do it...

To save and load color swatches, just follow these steps:

1. First, start by opening the **Swatches** panel and creating four new process color swatches. It doesn't matter whether these are RGB or CMYK as the process works the same for both color modes.

2. Now, select all four of the new color swatches in the **Swatches** panel by clicking on them while holding down the *Ctrl* (Windows)/*Command* (Mac) key. Then, go to the **Swatches** panel menu and select **Save Swatches...** (marked *A* in *Figure 8.18*). Choose a location to save your .ase file and hit **Save**:

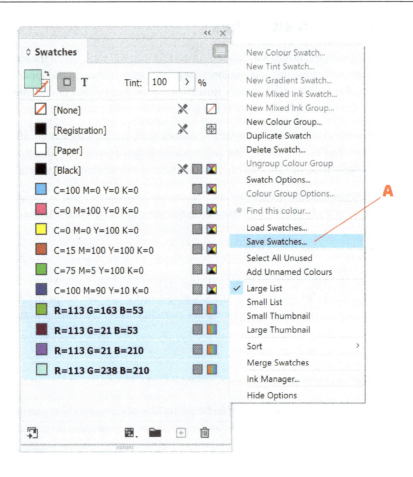

Figure 8.18: Save Swatches… in the InDesign Swatches panel

Your color swatches are now saved within the ASE file, which can be loaded back into any copy of InDesign, Photoshop, or Illustrator.

Note

ASE files in InDesign are designed for reusing solid process and spot color swatches but do not support things such as gradients or tint swatches. If you wish to save this type of file, see *Chapter 12, Using and Collaborating with CC Libraries*.

Having created an ASE file, let's load this back into a different InDesign document.

3. Open a new blank document and then open the **Swatches** panel. There, select **Load Swatches** (found above the **Save Swatches** option we used in *step 2*). Navigate to the ASE file we created, select it, then click **Open**.

    The color swatches will now be loaded into the **Swatches** panel and should appear at the bottom of the list. If the same swatches exist with the same name, the new copy will have the word copy added after the name.

> **Note**
>
> If you want certain color swatches to appear every time you start a new document, simply load them back into the **Swatches** panel or create them there, while no documents are open. These will then become your default color swatches in InDesign for all your new documents going forward.

Applying colors within your document

Having learned how to create color swatches earlier in this chapter, we are now going to take a look at applying swatches to content on the page. We will do this from both the **Swatches** panel and the **Control** panel, allowing you to be as efficient as possible. In addition, we will look at how you can apply custom colors to an object without the use of a swatch, for those occasions where you just want to use a one-off color.

Getting ready

To complete this recipe, simply open InDesign on your system and create a new document with 12 pages and the intent set to **Print**, as shown in the *Creating a new document* recipe in *Chapter 1*. You should already be comfortable with creating new color swatches, as covered earlier in this chapter.

How to do it...

To apply colors within your document, just follow these steps:

1. First, let's create a couple of CMYK color swatches in our document, then create a new text frame on our page containing some text.

2. Select the text using the **Type** tool. Then, from the **Control** panel at the top of the page, select the **Fill** color dropdown (marked A in *Figure 8.19*). If you don't see the **Control** panel, which is a large panel typically found underneath the menus at the top of the screen, you can enable it from the **Window** menu:

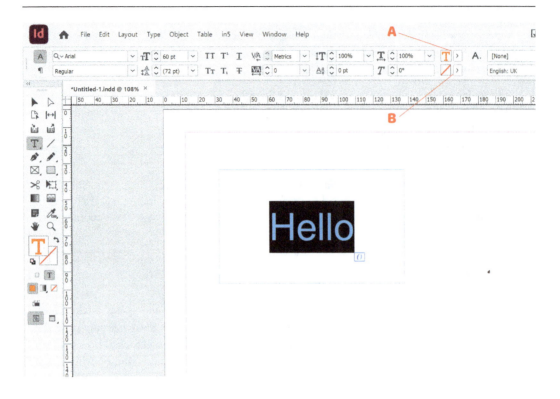

Figure 8.19: Applying a Fill color to text

3. If you wish to give the text a different color stroke, simply leave the text selected and select the **Stroke** box (marked *B* in *Figure 8.19*) and change this to a different color instead.

    Having changed the color of the text from the **Control** panel, we are now going to change the color of the frame itself, but this time using the **Swatches** panel.

4. Select the frame using the **Selection** tool and open the **Swatches** panel. As we have selected the frame already, **Frame** should be selected (marked *A* in *Figure 8.20*) in the **Swatches** panel as opposed to **Text** (marked *B* in *Figure 8.20*). In our case, we want to change the fill color for the frame, so ensure **Fill** is selected (marked *C* in *Figure 8.20*) as opposed to **Stroke** (marked *D* in *Figure 8.20*) on the **Swatches** panel, then click a color swatch from the list:

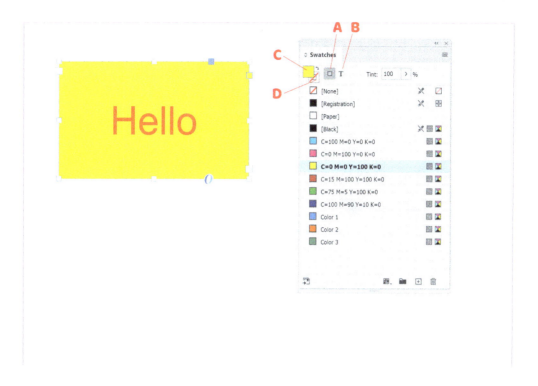

Figure 8.20: Changing colors in the Swatches panel

Having looked at how to apply color swatches to items, let's now look at how to apply a custom color to items.

5. Create another new frame and add some text, then select the text using the **Type** tool. Next, double-click on the **Fill** color icon (marked *A* in *Figure 8.21*) on the **Tools** panel to bring up **Colour Picker**. Here, you can change the color using the following options:

- Manually, by clicking in the box (marked *B*) to pick colors and dragging up and down on the value slider (marked *C*), which increases or decreases the value of the RGB color channel (marked *D*) currently selected.

- Numerically, by adjusting the values. You can do this using a variety of color modes, including the following:

  - **HSB** (marked *E*): Hue, saturation, and brightness.

  - **RGB** (marked *D*): Red, green, and blue. This is the standard color mode used by screen devices.

  - **LAB** (marked *F*): (L) lightness, (A) green to red, and (B) blue to yellow. This large color gamut is based more on how humans see color and is used by tools such as Photoshop to convert between RGB and CMYK.

- **CMYK** (marked *G*): Cyan, magenta, yellow, and key (black). This is the standard color mode for printing. In our case, we will use this mode, setting the values to **80**, **10**, **50**, and **0**, respectively.

- **Hexadecimal** (marked *H*): This is a hexadecimal representation of the red, green, and blue values that make up the color and is commonly used by web designers:

Figure 8.21: Changing color with the color picker

Having changed the **Font** fill color using **Colour Picker**, we will now change the **Text Frame** fill color using the **Colour** panel.

6. Select the text frame with the **Selection** tool and check that the **Fill** box on the **Tools** panel is in front of the **Stroke** box (*A* in *Figure 8.22*), ensuring any changes you make are being applied to the fill and not the stroke of the frame. Now, open the **Colour** panel from the **Window** menu under the **Colour** section.

The **Colour panel** lets you choose numeric values for the color by either using the sliders or typing in the color values. You can switch color modes from the panel menu (*B* in *Figure 8.22*), as well as add a color to your swatches if you wish. Additionally, you can switch between changing the color of **Fill** (*C*) or **Stroke** (*D*) of **Text** (*E*) or **Frame** (*F*):

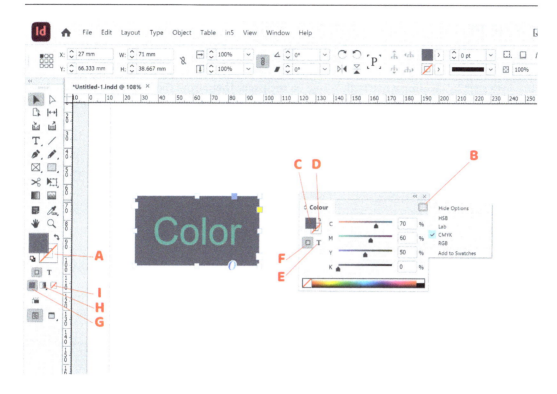

Figure 8.22: The InDesign Color panel

7. Finally, it's worth noting that if you wish to remove a color completely and simply apply transparency, this can be done from the bottom of the **Tools** panel below the **Fill/Stroke** icons. Here, three small icons allow you to switch between applying **Solid Colors** (*G* in *Figure 8.22*), **Gradients** (*H*), or **Transparency** (*I*).

Creating gradients and saving them as swatches

Gradients can be a nice way to draw attention to items in your document and add an element of depth as they transition from one color to another. They can be as simple or as complex as you want and can be designed to flow in a particular linear direction or outwards radially from a central point.

In this recipe, we will take a look at creating both linear and radial gradients, editing your gradients, and saving gradients to your **Swatches** panel for easy reuse within your InDesign documents.

Getting ready

To complete this recipe, simply open InDesign on your system and create a new document with 12 pages and the intent set to **Print**, as shown in the *Creating a new document* recipe in *Chapter 1*. You should already be comfortable with creating new color swatches, as covered earlier in this chapter.

How to do it...

To create gradients and save them as swatches, just follow these steps:

1. Let's start by creating a rectangle frame on the page. Then, from the **Window** menu, under **Colour**, open the **Gradient panel**. Select the frame with the **Selection** tool and make sure you are currently working on **Fill** (*A* in *Figure 8.23*), not **Stroke**:

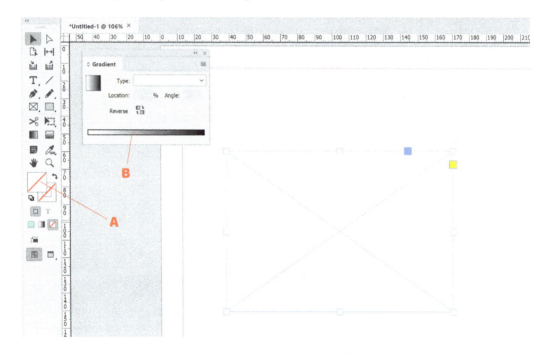

Figure 8.23: Rectangle selected with the Fill box active

2. Next, click on the white-to-black bar on the **Gradient** panel (*B* in *Figure 8.23*); you will see that a white-to-black **linear gradient** is applied to the rectangle. In the **Gradient** panel, you should also see the following options:

    *   **Location**: This allows you to set an exact position for individual color stops (*C* in *Figure 8.24*). We will discuss this more in *step 3*.

    *   **Angle**: This allows you to alter the angle where the gradient is applied. We will set this to **90** degrees (*A* in *Figure 8.24*).

    *   **Reverse** (*B* in *Figure 8.24*): This allows you to reverse the gradient so that it flows in the opposite direction. We don't need to do this.

If you don't see these options, click the **Gradient** panel menu (*D* in *Figure 8.24*) and select **Show Options**:

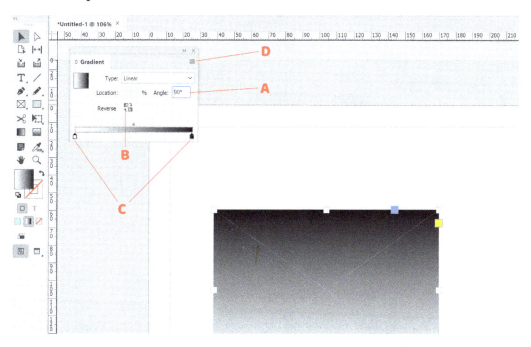

Figure 8.24: Default linear gradient applied to the rectangle

3. Having created our black-to-white linear gradient, I would now like to adjust the colors. Within the **Gradient** panel, click once on the white color stop (marked *A* in *Figure 8.25*) on the left of the gradient bar. Then, double-click the fill box (marked *B* in *Figure 8.25*) on the toolbar to bring up the color picker. Select the color you wish to use within your gradient and then click **OK** to apply it. You should see the color stop that was previously white now change color to the color you chose in the color picker:

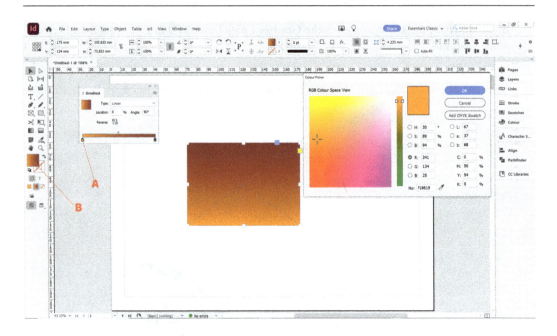

Figure 8.25: Changing colors in a gradient

Let's do the same with the black color stop on the right of the gradient bar and apply a different color to replace the black color stop.

4. Having changed the two default **color stops**, we would now like to add a third color, and I'd like to do so using one of my existing color swatches from the **Swatches** panel. Open the panel, click on an existing color swatch, and drag it across to the **Gradient** panel, positioning it in between the two existing color stops. You should see the cursor change when you are over the gradient (marked *A* in *Figure 8.26*); once you've done this, you can release the mouse button. This will create a new color stop from the chosen color:

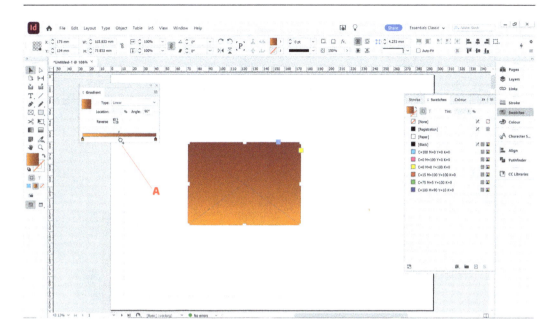

Figure 8.26: Adding a color stop to the gradient

5. Having created a third color stop, we can now fine-tune its position by clicking on the new color stop in the **Gradient** panel and adjusting the location value. In our case, we will set the location value to 33% so that the color stop is roughly a third of the way across the gradient.

    It's worth noting that you can also adjust the color stops manually by dragging them left or right on the gradient bar.

Note

If you are adjusting a gradient on a selected object, the object must remain selected while you're doing so. If you accidentally deselect the object, your changes to the **Gradient** panel will not be applied to it.

---

6. Having created a color stop from an existing color swatch, I would also like to add an additional color stop to the gradient manually. Simply click in the gray area (marked *A* in *Figure 8.27*) just below the gradient bar; you will see a new color stop appear. You can then select it and double-click the color picker to choose the color settings that we saw in *step 3*:

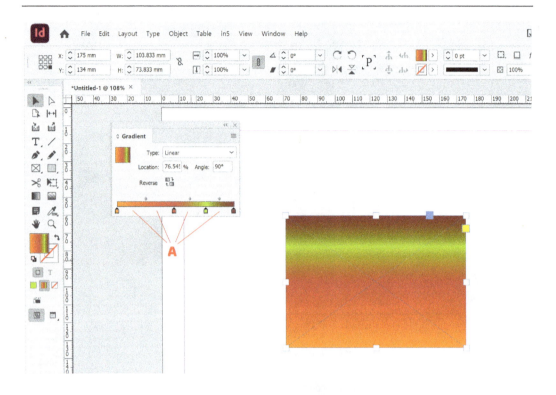

Figure 8.27: Adding color stops manually

7. Having created a four-color gradient, I would now like to adjust the midpoint between my new color stop and the two color stops on either side of it. The midpoint between two colors in a gradient is represented by the small diamond (marked *A* in *Figure 8.28*) that sits just above the gradient bar. The midpoint can be moved so that it is between 13% and 87% of the way through a gradient, allowing you to adjust the balance of color in the gradient.

    In my case, I want the new color to be a small thin strip, so I will drag the midpoints on either side closer to the new color until they are as close as possible, meaning the location of the midpoint is at 87% and 13% from the adjoining colors, respectively:

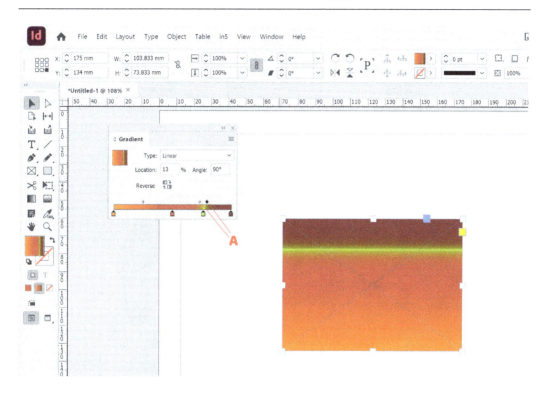

Figure 8.28: Adjusting the midpoints to narrow a particular color within the gradient

8. Having finished creating my linear gradient. I would now like to save it so that I can reuse it on other objects. To do this, right-click on the gradient within the **Gradient** panel, then select **Add to Swatches**. You will see your new gradient swatch appear at the bottom of the **Swatches** panel, from where it can be applied like any other color swatch.

    Having created a linear gradient and saved it as a swatch, we will now look at creating a **radial gradient**. Much of the functionality is the same as with linear gradients but the effect is quite different.

9. Let's start by creating an ellipse frame (you can use a rectangle frame if you prefer), and with the frame selected, click on the gradient bar on the **Gradient** panel. By default, this will apply a **Linear** gradient to the frame; we will change the gradient type to **Radial** from the **Type** drop-down menu. You will see a black-to-white radial gradient applied to the ellipse frame, as shown in *Figure 8.29*:

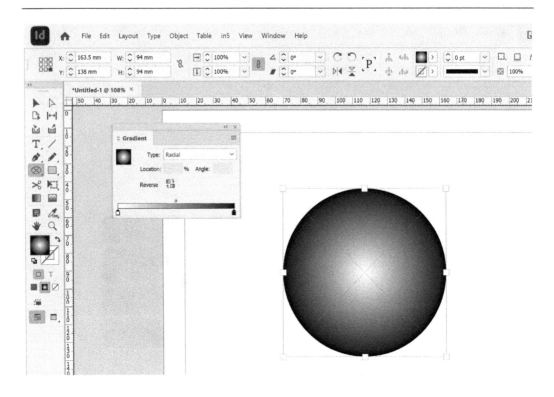

Figure 8.29: Basic Radial gradient applied to the ellipse frame

10. Next, we will customize the existing color stops and add two new colors to the gradient, exactly as we did in *steps 3* and *6* with the linear gradient. In my case, I will use the colors red, blue, green, and cyan, resulting in the following gradient:

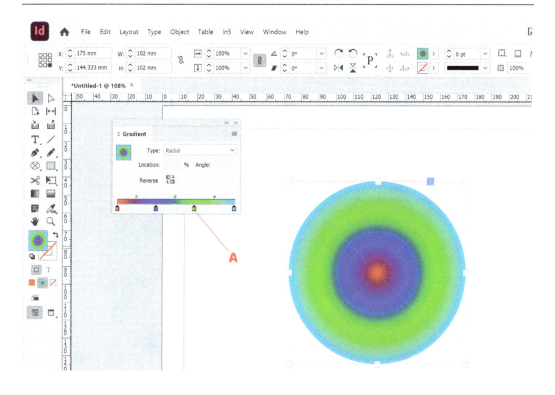

Figure 8.30: Radial gradient with four color stops

11. Having created the radial gradient, I'm not happy with it and would like to remove the green color stop (marked *A* in *Figure 8.26*), leaving us with just a three-color gradient. To delete the green color stop, simply click on it and drag it off the **Gradient** panel before letting go of your mouse; the result can be seen in *Figure 8.31*. If you wish to remove any other colors from the gradient, simply repeat this process with those colors:

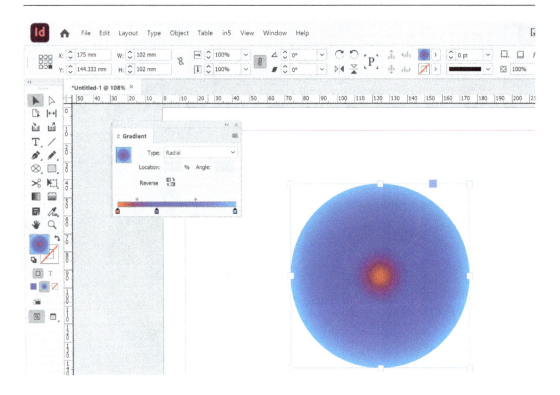

Figure 8.31: Gradient after the color stop has been removed

Merging colors

Sometimes, you might find yourself in a situation where you want to merge colors. A good example of this would be when you have multiple separate colors, which you would like to merge into a single color for consistency.

In this recipe, we will look at a couple of different ways to merge colors in InDesign, giving you complete control of your color swatches.

Getting ready

To complete this recipe, simply open InDesign on your system and create a new document with 12 pages, as shown in the *Creating a new document* recipe in *Chapter 1*. You should already be comfortable with creating new color swatches, as covered earlier in this chapter.

How to do it...

To merge color swatches in your document, just follow these steps:

1. First, let's create several color swatches. I am going to start by creating six color swatches – three different shades of blue and three different shades of red. I will then create six rectangle frames and apply one color to the fill of each frame, as seen in *Figure 8.32*:

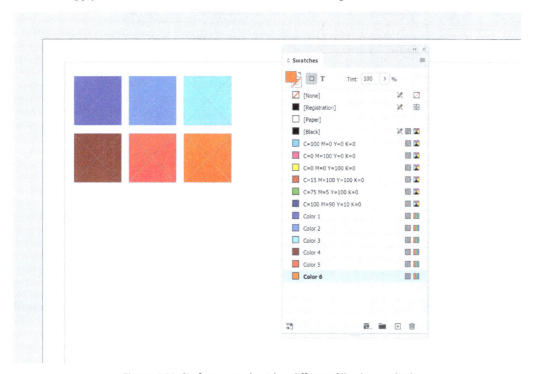

Figure 8.32: Six frames each with a different fill color applied

2. Having done this, I will now select **Color 2**, then, while holding down the *Ctrl* (Windows)/ *Command* (Mac) key, also select **Color 3** and **Color 1**. From the right-click menu, I will choose the **Merge Colours** option, which will merge the three colors into a single color swatch (marked *A* in *Figure 8.33*). This swatch will be the first color swatch we selected – in our case, **Color 2** – and the other color swatches will have been removed. Any objects that were using any of the other selected color swatches (marked *B* in *Figure 8.33*) will have been updated to use the one remaining color swatch instead:

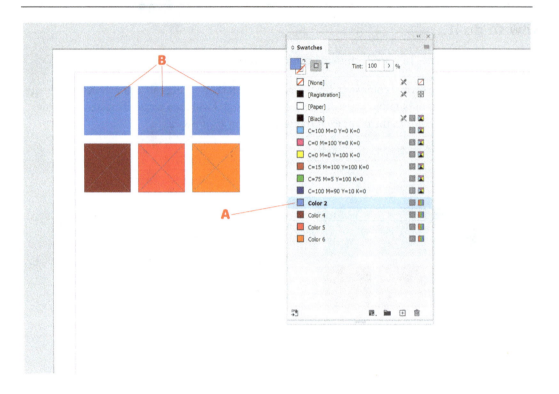

Figure 8.33: Merging swatches with a right-click

Having merged two color swatches into one, next, we would like to simply delete a single color swatch, at the same time replacing all uses of it with one of the other color swatches.

> **Note**
>
> Many of InDesign's options can be found in more than one place. For example, the **Delete Swatch** and **Merge Swatches** options can be accessed by right-clicking on the swatches, or through the **Swatch** panel menu.

3. Select **Color 5** in the **Swatches** panel and click the delete icon (marked *A* in *Figure 8.34*). This will bring up the **Delete Swatch** dialog box shown in *Figure 8.34*. Here, we can choose from one of two options:

    • **Defined Swatch**: Selecting this option will allow you to choose one of the other existing color swatches to be used throughout the document, in place of the swatch you are deleting. We will choose this option and select **Color 6** (marked *B* in *Figure 8.34*)

    • **Unnamed Swatch**: Choosing this option will delete the swatch from the **Swatches** panel. Any objects that use it will continue to use the same color but as an unnamed color, and it will not appear in the **Swatches** panel:

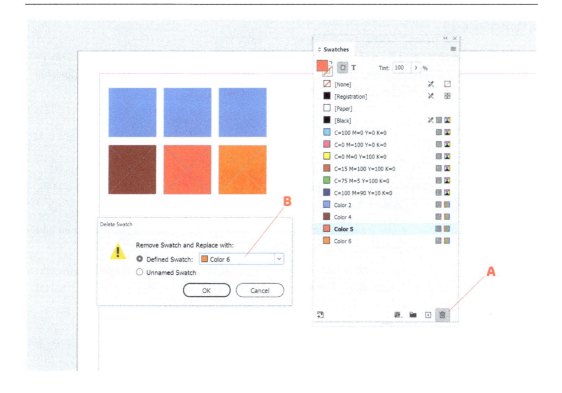

Figure 8.34: Deleting and replacing a color swatch

Having chosen **Color 6** in the **Delete Swatch** dialog box, we can now click **OK** to delete **Swatch 5** and replace all instances of its use with **Swatch 6**.

Finding colors within your document

Sometimes, you might want to identify content that uses a particular color swatch, for example, to change all or just some of the content to a different color. If you have used a color swatch repeatedly throughout a document, it can be useful to do this quickly and easily in a single place.

In addition to this, though, you might want to identify exactly where a particular color channel or spot color will be used within your document. One example of where this could be useful is when you're deciding whether to convert the spot colors into process colors at output time and, as a result, reduce the time and cost (and color precision) of a print job.

In this recipe, we will run through finding and changing color swatches, including within different types of content, as well as identifying where specific color separations are being used within the document.

Getting ready

To complete this recipe, simply open InDesign on your system and create a new document with 12 pages, as shown in the *Creating a new document* recipe in *Chapter 1*. You should already be comfortable with creating new color swatches, as covered earlier in this chapter.

How to do it...

To find and change colors in your document, just follow these steps:

1. In our new document, start by creating three new color swatches – these can be RGB or CMYK – and naming them **Color 1**, **Color 2**, and **Color 3**.

    Next, create two rectangle frames, an elliptical frame, and a text frame on the page, then add some text to the text frame.

    Finally, apply **Color 1** as the fill to one of the rectangle frames, the elliptical frame, and the text within the text frame. Next, apply **Color 2** as the fill to the other rectangle frame and the text frame itself (as opposed to the text within it), as shown in *Figure 8.35*:

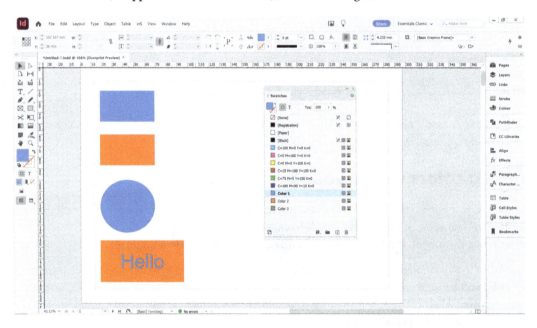

Figure 8.35: Content using Color 1 and Color 2

2. Now, we would like to identify all the places **Color 1** is being used in the document. To do this, right-click on **Color 1** in the **Swatches** panel and select **Find this colour**. This will bring up the **Find/Change dialog box**, as seen in *Figure 8.36*:

Figure 8.36: The Find/Change dialog box

3. The **Find/Change** dialog box is not specific to color but because we accessed it via the **Swatches** panel, it has defaulted to the **Colour** tab. There are several options:

- **Find Colour** (*A* in *Figure 8.36*): Here, we can select the specific color swatch we want to find in the document. In our case, this should be set to **Color 1**.

- **Tint Range** (*B* in *Figure 8.36*): If you have used tints from the **Colour** swatch, this allows you to limit the tints you search for to a certain range; if you prefer, you can leave it set to **0% - 100%** to search for all tints. In our case, we haven't applied any tints, so will leave this set to **0% - 100%**.

> **Note**
>
> A **tint** is a variation of a color that is created by adding white to the color. As more white is added, the tint becomes lighter and less saturated.

- **Change Colour** (*C* in *Figure 8.36*): Here, you can choose the color swatch you would like to replace the color with. In our case, we will set this to **Color 3**, which is the swatch we wish to use, instead of the **Color 1** swatch.

- **Tint** (*D* in *Figure 8.36*): If you wish the replacement color to be a tint, you can set the tint percentage here. In our case, we will leave this blank.

- **Search** (*E* in *Figure 8.36*): Here, we will leave this set to **Document**, which only searches the current document, as opposed to **All Documents**, which would search all the documents that are currently open.

- **Type** (*F* in *Figure 8.36*): Here, you can choose what type of content to include in the search. The available options are as follows:

  - **All Frames**: This includes all the frames in the search (we will choose this option)

  - **Text Frames**: Only includes **Text Frames** in the search

  - **Graphic Frames**: Only includes **Graphic Frames** in the search

  - **Unassigned Frames**: Only includes **Unassigned Frames** in the search

- Finally, at the bottom, there are a series of icons, as follows:

  - **Include Locked Layers and Locked Objects** (*G* in *Figure 8.36*): This allows you to **Find** the color swatch in locked layers and locked objects, but you cannot apply **Change** to them unless you first unlock them. We will leave this disabled.

  - **Include Locked Stories**: (*H* in *Figure 8.36*): This allows you to **Find** the color swatch in locked stories, but you cannot apply **Change** to them unless you first unlock them. We will leave this disabled.

> **Note**
> A **story** is a collection of two or more text frames that are threaded together to allow the text to flow as though they were a single frame.

  - **Include Hidden Layers and Hidden Objects** (*I* in *Figure 8.36*): This allows you to **Find** the color in **Hidden Layers** and **Hidden Objects** and **Change** them to a new color if you wish. We will leave this disabled.

  - **Include Parent Pages** (*J* in *Figure 8.36*): This allows you to **Find** the color swatch on **Parent Pages** (formerly known as master pages) and if it has been used there, **Change** it to another color swatch if you wish. By not selecting this, **Parent Pages** will be exempt from the search. We will leave this disabled.

- **Include Footnotes** (*K* in *Figure 8.36*): This allows you to **Find** the color swatch in footnotes and if it has been used there, **Change** it to another color swatch if you wish. We will leave this disabled.

Having chosen our settings, we can now decide what we want to do. The following options are available:

- **Find Next** (*L* in *Figure 8.36*): Click this to **Find** the next item in the document that matches the settings chosen.

- **Change** (*M* in *Figure 8.36*): Click this to **Change** the currently selected item as per the settings currently chosen.

- **Change All** (*N* in *Figure 8.36*): Click this to **Change All** items that match the settings selected using the settings currently chosen. We will click this option.

- **Change/Find** (*O* in *Figure 8.36*): Click this to **Change** the currently selected item as per the settings currently chosen, and then immediately **Find** the next item that matches the settings.

- **Fewer Options** (*P* in *Figure 8.36*): If the **Fewer Options** button is visible clicking it will hide some of the options in this dialog box, if the button says **More Options**, clicking it will reveal those hidden options.

In our case, since we clicked the **Find/Change** option, we will see that all the items that previously used **Color 1** are now using **Color 3**.

4. In addition to finding and changing individual color swatches within your document, you might also want to identify areas where a specific primary color/ink is being used within the document. This might be handy if you were considering a three-color print run (instead of four) or wanted to see where a particular spot color was being applied in the document. To do this, open the **Separations Preview** panel (shown in *Figure 8.37*) from the **Window** menu under the **Output** section.

> **Note**
>
> **Color separations** are the individual color components that make up a color. For example, when printing on a four-color press, these would be cyan, magenta, yellow, and key (usually black), which are the four primary colors that make up a CMYK color. In the case of screen colors, these are created using red, green, and blue, which combine to create RGB colors.

5. In my case, I would like to see which items on the page are using colors that contain cyan. So, in the **Separations Preview** panel, I will choose the **Separations** option from the **View** dropdown (marked *A* in *Figure 8.37*). Having done this, I can now disable the separations I wish to hide, in this case, **Magenta**, **Yellow**, and **Black**, by clicking the eye next to them (marked *B* in *Figure 8.37*) so that the eye disappears and hides those specific primary colors anywhere they are used. As

you can see in *Figure 8.37*, the items on the page (marked *C* in *Figure 8.37*) are now shown in a shade of gray, which is proportional to the amount of **Cyan** (in this example) being used in that area. Black means cyan is at 100%, while white means cyan is at 0%:

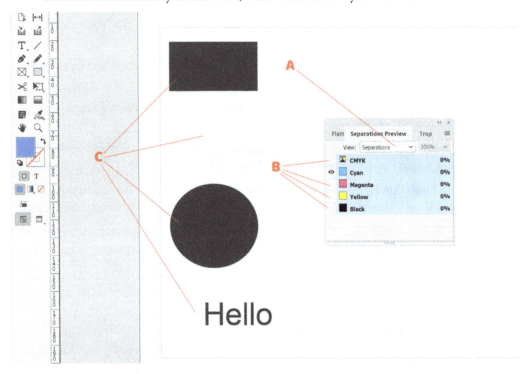

Figure 8.37: The InDesign Separations Preview panel

You will notice that the second object down on the page uses a color that contains no cyan and, as such, appears to disappear completely, as does the fill color for the frame of the fourth object, although the text of the object is in a color that does use cyan, hence it can be seen still. These items that appear to have disappeared are still there, just hidden, and as soon as you re-enable the other colors in the **Separations Preview** panel, you will see them once again.

Customizing strokes

Sometimes, it can be useful to be able to customize strokes in your document to create a particular look and feel. You might want to change the border around a frame to create a specific effect or maybe adjust the stroke on a line to turn it into an arrow that points at something.

In this recipe, we will look at the options for customizing the stroke, putting a dashed line around a frame, and applying an arrowhead effect to a line.

Getting ready

To complete this recipe, simply open InDesign on your system and create a new document with 12 pages, as shown in the *Creating a new document* recipe in *Chapter 1*. You should be comfortable creating new color swatches, as shown in the *Creating new color swatches* recipe, as well as applying colors, as shown in the *Applying colors within your document* recipe, both of which can be found in this chapter.

How to do it

To customize strokes on document items, just follow these steps:

1. Create a rectangle frame on your document and apply a black stroke to it. Now, open the **Stroke** panel; it should look similar to what's shown in *Figure 8.38*. If you only see the first option for **Weight**, just click the **Stroke** panel menu and select **Show Options**; you should now see the other options:

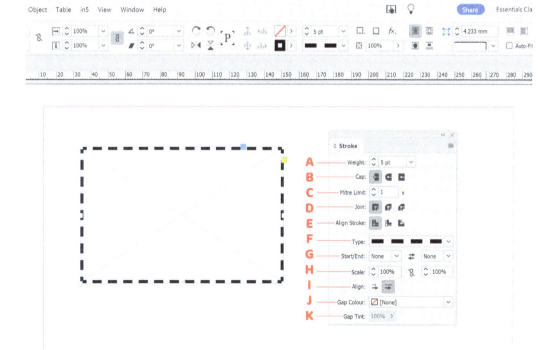

Figure 8.38: The Stroke panel

2.   The **Stroke** panel contains a wide range of options, as follows:

- **Weight** (*A*): This setting controls the width of the stroke. We will set this to **5 pt**.

- **Cap** (*B*): This controls the type of end on an open path (that is, where the two ends of the path don't join together). In our case, we won't change this, but the options here are as follows:

  - **Butt Cap**: This creates a square end in line with the end of the line

  - **Round Cap**: This creates a rounded end on the line

  - **Projecting Cap**: This creates a square end like **Butt Cap**, but it projects beyond the end point by a value equivalent to half of the weight setting

- **Miter Limit** (*C*): This value determines at what point **Miter Join** will automatically switch to become **Bevel Join**.

- **Join** (*D*): This controls the type of join used when two segments of a path meet, and it can be set to either **Miter**, **Round**, or **Bevel**.

- **Align Stroke** (*E*): This controls the alignment of the stroke to the path's **Center, Inside**, or **Outside**.

- **Type** (*F*): Here, you can choose from a range of predefined stroke types. We will choose **Dashed 3 and 2**.

- **Start/End** (*G*): This option allows you to apply an arrowhead to the start/end of an open path.

- **Scale** (*H*): This allows you to adjust the scale of the **Start/End** arrowheads.

- **Align** (*I*): This allows you to align the arrowhead so that it is positioned either beyond the end of the path or in line with it.

- **Gap Color** (*J*): If you have chosen a stroke type that has gaps, you can adjust the color of the gap here.

- **Gap Tint** (*K*): This setting lets you adjust the tint of **Gap Color**.

> **Note**
> What is a path? When we draw shapes in InDesign, such as a rectangle frame, we are drawing vector paths and you can see and edit the anchor points and the paths that make up the shape. While doing this is beyond the scope of this recipe, those who already edit vector shapes in Illustrator should find this relatively easy to do.

Having set the properties for **Weight** and **Type**, our frame should now have a stroke that looks like the frame in *Figure 8.38*.

Having applied a custom stroke to a frame, let's now look at applying it to a simple path.

3. Use the **Pencil** tool to draw a line on the page, then apply a black stroke and transparent fill to it. Now, open the **Stroke** panel and apply the following properties:

    - **Weight**: **4 pt**

    - **Type**: Thick – Thick

    - **Start/End**: Circle Solid/Triangle Wide

    - **Scale**: **100%/300%**

    - **Gap Color**: Cyan

    The middle of your line should now be cyan, and it should have an arrowhead and tail, as seen in *Figure 8.39*:

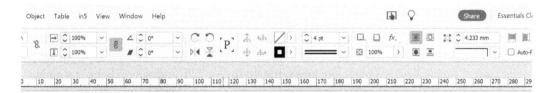

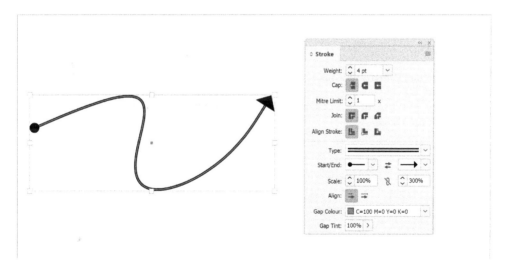

Figure 8.39: Stroke settings applied to a line

Setting color management settings

Good **color management** is important for maintaining consistent and accurate color reproduction across different devices and platforms, and it plays an especially important role in achieving accurate print results. By setting your color management settings properly, you can ensure you avoid any nasty surprises when it comes to the colors in your document.

For those who only use InDesign, color management settings can be configured within the InDesign application itself. If you are also using other Creative Cloud apps such as Photoshop or Illustrator, however, it is better to set your color management settings within Adobe Bridge, which causes Creative Cloud to synchronize the settings across the various Creative Cloud applications, including InDesign.

In this recipe, we will look at how to set up color management in both InDesign and Adobe Bridge, allowing you to ensure accurate color reproduction when working with InDesign.

Getting ready

To complete this recipe, simply open InDesign on your system. We are going to start by setting the color management settings in InDesign, though if you also use other Creative Cloud apps, you may prefer to install Adobe Bridge and simply jump straight to *step 2*. In addition to being a simpler process, this also ensures that the color management settings are synchronized across the whole suite, not just in InDesign.

How to do it...

To set your color management settings, just follow these steps:

1. In InDesign's **Edit** menu, select **Colour Settings** to open the **Colour Settings dialog box**, as shown in *Figure 8.40*:

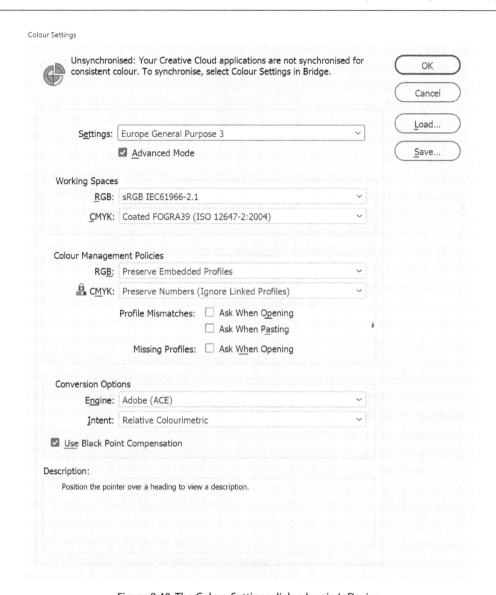

Figure 8.40: The Colour Settings dialog box in InDesign

2. The **Colour Settings** dialog box has several options, as follows:

- **Settings**: Here, you can choose from a range of presets, which will populate the fields beneath it with different settings. Which preset you choose will depend on the region you are in, and the type of output you are intending, so it is worth speaking to your printer to get their recommendations. In my case, I am based in the UK, and producing documents for screen use with some occasional digital print, so I will select the **Europe General Purpose** preset.

- **Working Spaces**: Depending on the preset you chose in the **Settings** dropdown, RGB and CMYK working spaces will be automatically selected from the list. The working space is the range of colors that can be reproduced. In my case, the RGB working space has been set to **sRGB IEC61966-2.1**, while the CMYK working space has been set to **Coated FOGRA39 (ISO 12647-2:2004)**.

- **Colour Management Policies**: This controls how color management is handled when the document is opened. I won't change this setting, but the options are as follows:

  - **Off**: This turns off color management for the document.

  - **Preserve Embedded Profiles**: This preserves any existing embedded profiles within the documents. This has been selected for RGB in my case.

  - **Convert to working space**: This converts a newly opened document to the working space set here.

  - **Preserve Numbers (ignore Linked Profiles)**: This allows the color values (for example, the CMYK values) to be used while ignoring any linked color profiles. This has been set for CMYK in my case.

- **Profile Mismatches**: In this section, you can control what happens when there is a mismatch between color profiles in the document and InDesign:

  - **Ask When Opening**: When checked, you will be notified if the embedded color profile does not match the current working space. This has been deselected in my case.

  - **Ask When Pasting**: When checked, you will be notified if the color profile does not match the current working space when importing colors via pasting or drag and drop. This has been deselected in my case.

- **Missing Profiles**: Here, you can control what happens when opening a document with no embedded color profile:

  - **Ask When Opening**: When this is checked, you will be notified if you're opening a document without an embedded color profile. This has been deselected in my case.

- **Conversion Options**: This section controls the options that are used when converting colors:

  - **Engine**: This specifies the color-matching method used to convert colors. This has been set to **Adobe (ACE)**.

  - **Intent**: This specifies the method used to map colors between color spaces. This has been set to **Relative Colourimetric**.

- **Use Black Point Compensation**: When turned on, this can result in better reproduction of details in darker shadows. This has been enabled.

While changing your color management settings in InDesign is fine if you only use this one application, for those also using Photoshop and Illustrator, it is better to set these settings in Adobe Bridge, which we will look at next.

3. Open Adobe Bridge and, from the **Edit** menu, select **Color Settings**. Unlike in InDesign, you won't see any of the settings here, only the presets (shown in *Figure 8.41*). If you don't see the color preset you are looking for, tick the **Show Expanded List of Color Setting Files** box. In my case, I will choose the **Europe General Purpose 3** preset and then click **Apply**:

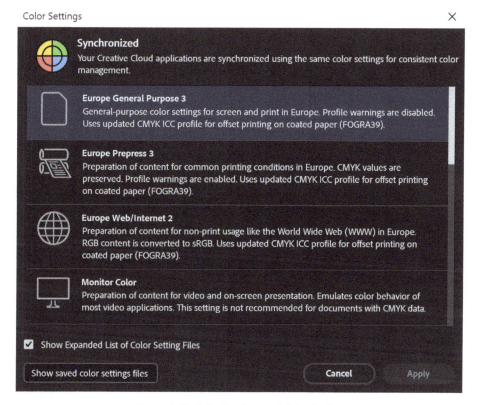

Figure 8.41: Color Settings in Adobe Bridge

With this, your color management settings have been set and synchronized across the different Creative Cloud applications. If you reopen the **Colour Settings** dialog box in either Adobe Bridge or Adobe InDesign, you will notice it now says **Synchronized** at the top of either of the dialog boxes, which means the same color management settings are being used across the different Creative Cloud applications.

Formatting with Paragraph and Character Styles

In this chapter, we will look at paragraph styles and character styles, which are used to ensure rapid and consistent text formatting within your InDesign documents. In addition to assisting with text formatting, InDesign styles are also an essential component in using numerous more advanced features within InDesign, such as tables of contents, indexes, and cross-references.

When working with paragraph styles and character styles in InDesign, there are a number of important features to first understand in order to ensure you are working with the correct type of style. The first thing is to understand that:

- **Paragraph styles** format entire paragraphs. If you select a single character in a paragraph and apply a paragraph style, it will apply to the whole of that paragraph.

- **Character styles** format individual characters. If you select a single character in a word and apply a character style to it, it will apply only to that one character and nothing else.

In addition to this, it's also important to understand that character styles will automatically override paragraph styles if both are applied to the same text, irrespective of what order you apply them in. For example, if you apply a paragraph style to your text that sets the font face to Arial and the font size to 12 pt, but then also apply a character style to the same text which sets the font size to 18 pt, your formatting will end up as Arial 18 pt. If you apply character styles first and then paragraph styles, the result will be exactly the same.

My golden rule when using text styles in InDesign is to always use paragraph styles by default unless you have a good reason why you need to use character styles. It's not that character styles aren't useful, but if you use a character style to format all of your content, you eliminate your ability to do a wide range of things including:

- Use styles to format individual elements within the content differently. You can't apply a character style on top of another character style, but you can apply a character style on top of a paragraph style. Imagine a paragraph with a hyperlink in the middle of it. You might want to make the hyperlink blue with a line under it, but you can't use a style to do this if you have already formatted the whole paragraph with a character style.

- Create an automated table of contents. This can only be done using paragraph styles.

- Format text automatically within an object style. This can only be done using paragraph styles.

- Format text automatically within table styles and cell styles. This can only be done using paragraph styles.

- Work with nested styles. This can only be done using paragraph styles and is something we will look at in the *Using nested styles* section of this chapter.

These are just a few examples of things that can be done with paragraph styles but not with character styles. With this in mind, you should work primarily with paragraph styles and then use character styles to highlight specific elements within a paragraph, or in conjunction with InDesign features that support them such as the hyperlinks panel.

> **Note**
> Before we get started, it is worth noting the difference between starting a new line with the *Return* key by itself, which starts a new paragraph, versus starting a new line with the *Shift + Return* key, which applies a line break but does not start a new paragraph. When you apply paragraph styles, they continue to be applied through to the end of the paragraph and a line break does not qualify as the end of a paragraph.

The recipes we will cover in this chapter include:

- Creating and applying paragraph styles
- Identifying and clearing overrides
- Redefining styles
- Grouping styles
- Creating and applying character styles

- Using nested styles
- Using Next Style
- Importing text styles
- Finding and replacing styles

Technical requirements

To complete this chapter, you will need a PC or Mac, with a copy of Adobe InDesign installed. You should be comfortable adding content to your documents and formatting it as shown in *Chapter 1* through *Chapter 4*.

Creating and applying paragraph styles

When it comes to creating paragraph styles in InDesign, there are a few different approaches. In this recipe, we will look at creating a paragraph style from some existing content, as well as setting up a new paragraph style from the dialog box. We will also look at a useful trick for setting default styles that will automatically appear in every new document you create going forward.

Getting ready

In order to complete this recipe, simply open InDesign on your system and create a new document with 12 pages, as shown in the *Creating a new document* recipe in *Chapter 1*.

How to do it

In order to create paragraph styles, just follow these steps:

1. Create a text frame and fill it with placeholder text. Select some text in the first paragraph and format it differently. In my case, I will change the font face to **Arial**, the font size to **14 pt**, the alignment to **Left aligned**, and the text color to **Dark blue**.

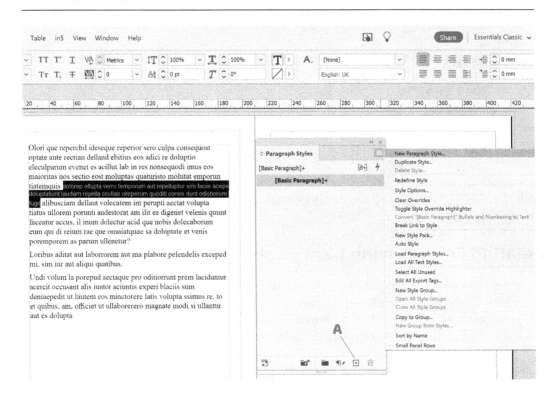

Figure 9.1: Creating a paragraph style from selected text

2. With the text still selected, open the **Paragraph Styles** panel, which can be found in the **Window** menu under **Styles**. From the panel menu, select **New Paragraph Style…** (shown in *Figure 9.1*). This will bring up the **New Paragraph Style dialog box** (shown in *Figure 9.2*). Alternatively, this can also be done by holding down the *Alt* key on PC or the *Option* key on a Macintosh and then clicking on the **Create New Style** icon (marked *A* in *Figure 9.1*).

New Paragraph Style

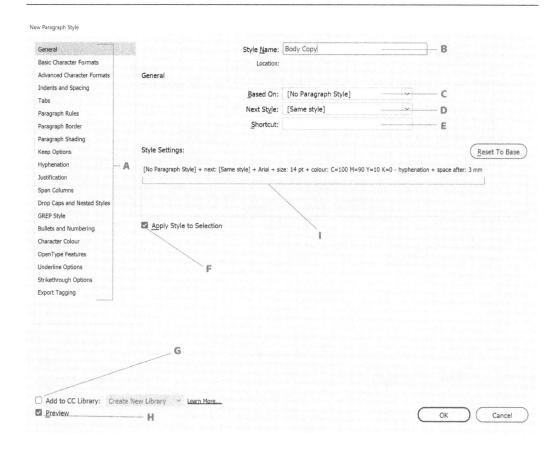

Figure 9.2: The New Paragraph Style dialog box

3. The **New Paragraph Style** dialog box has an extensive range of settings with a total of 20 different tabs (marked *A* in *Figure 9.2*), each containing settings for a different set of paragraph formatting options. By default, you will see the general tab which includes the following options:

    -   **Style Name** (*B* in *Figure 9.2*): You can give your style a custom name which will show up in the **Paragraph Styles** panel, as well as within other InDesign tools that use the paragraph styles. I will call mine **Body Copy**.

    -   **Based On** (*C* in *Figure 9.2*): This allows you to choose another paragraph style to base your new style on, allowing it to inherit the properties of that style as its starting point. We will leave this set to **No Paragraph Style**.

    -   **Next Style** (*D* in *Figure 9.2*): This is another style that you will be switched to automatically if you hit the *Return* key. We will leave this set to **Same Style**. We will look at the **Next Style** setting in the *Using Next Style* recipe.

- **Shortcut** (*E* in *Figure 9.2*): This allows you to create a shortcut for rapidly applying the style to content; for example, you could select some text and hit the shortcut keys to apply the style. The shortcuts available include holding down either the *Shift* key or the *Ctrl* (PC) / *Cmd* (Mac) key and using numbers *1* to *9*. To set a shortcut, just click this box and apply the shortcut (i.e. don't try to type it in the box).

- **Apply Style to Selection** (*F* in *Figure 9.2*): When this is ticked, upon creation of the style, it will be automatically applied to the currently selected text. If this is not ticked, the style will be created but will not be applied to the currently selected text. We will tick this box.

- **Add to CC Library** (*G* in *Figure 9.2*): When selected, the new paragraph style will be automatically added to the selected CC library upon creation. We will look at CC libraries in *Chapter 12, Using and Collaborating with CC Libraries*.

- **Preview**: (*H* in *Figure 9.2*) When this is checked, any changes you make to the settings in the **New Paragraph Style** dialog box, will be immediately visible in the page content as you are making them.

It is worth noting that because we already had some text selected when we started creating our new style, the formatting from that text has been automatically incorporated into the new style. Those settings can be seen in the **Style Settings** area (marked *I* in *Figure 9.2*). As such, we don't need to change any additional settings in the **New Paragraph Style** dialog box.

4. Having created the **Body Copy** style, we now want to apply it to the remaining text. To do this, select the text you want to apply it to (or at least a minimum of one character in each paragraph), and then, in the **Paragraph Styles** panel, click on **Body Copy**. You should immediately see the formatting change for the text, and the **Body Copy** item will now have a light blue background on it in the **Paragraph Styles** panel, which shows that it is being applied to the currently selected text.

5. Having created a paragraph style from some existing text, we are now going to create a new style based on some predefined brand guidelines. To do this, we must first ensure we have no text selected by clicking the grey pasteboard at the side of the document with the selection tool.

> **Note**
>
> While paragraph styles let you control literally hundreds of different properties, in *steps 5* to *11*, we are going to focus on some of the more common elements that most people will want to use rather than attempting to cover every single option available.

In the **Paragraph Styles** panel menu, click the **New Paragraph Style** menu item to bring up the **New Paragraph Styles** dialog box.

Let's start by giving our new style the name of **Brand Header**. We will leave the rest of the settings on this page set to their defaults and then switch to the **Basic Character Format** tab (marked *A* in *Figure 9.3*).

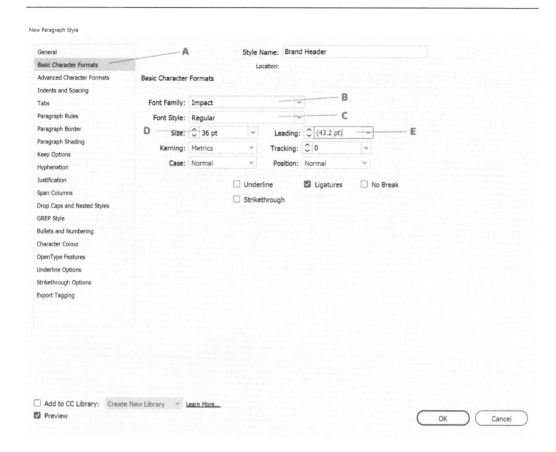

Figure 9.3: Basic character formatting in New Paragraph Style

The settings we will change here include the following:

- **Font Family** (*B* in *Figure 9.3*): We will set this to the **Impact** font.

- **Font Style**: (*C* in *Figure 9.3*): We will set this to **Regular**. The options here will depend on the font being used.

- **Size** (*D* in *Figure 9.3*): We will set this to **36 pt**.

- **Leading** (*E* in *Figure 9.3*): This is set to **Auto** by default, which equates to **Font Size** + 20%. As a result, when we change **Font Size** to **36 pt**, **Leading** automatically updates to become **43.2 pt**.

Now, we will skip the **Advanced Character Formats** tab, which lets you alter **Horizontal Scale** and **Vertical Scale**, **Baseline Shift**, **Skew**, and **Language**.

6. Next, we will go to the **Indents and Spacing** tab, where we will adjust the following settings:

    *   **Alignment** (*A* in *Figure 9.4*): We will set this to **Left**.

    *   **Space After** (*B* in *Figure 9.4*): We will set this to **3 mm**.

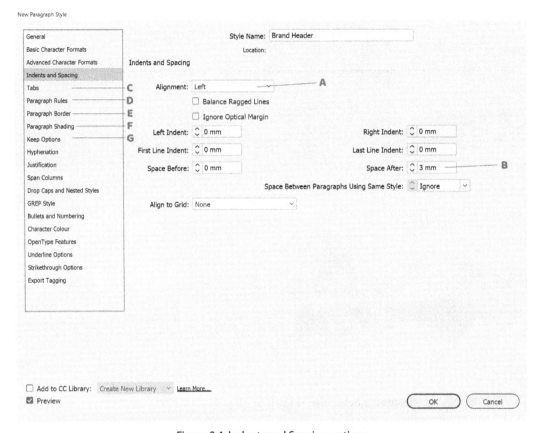

Figure 9.4: Indents and Spacing options

We won't change any other settings on this tab and will now skip over the following sections within the panel:

*   **Tabs**: (*C* in *Figure 9.4*): In this section, you can set tab options for your content

*   **Paragraph Rules** (*D* in *Figure 9.4*): Here, you can create and style paragraph rules

*   **Paragraph Border** (*E* in *Figure 9.4*): Here, you can create and style borders for your paragraphs

*   **Paragraph Shading** (*F* in *Figure 9.4*): This section lets you create and style shading for your paragraphs

*   **Keep Options** (*G* in *Figure 9.4*): This lets you set **Keep Options** to prevent blocks of text from breaking up as they move onto the next line or column

7. We are now going to click on the **Hyphenation** section, where we can control how and when text will hyphenate when using this style

New Paragraph Style

General	Style Name: Brand Header
Basic Character Formats	Location:
Advanced Character Formats	Hyphenation ⟋ A
Indents and Spacing	☑ Hyphenate
Tabs	Words with at Least: ⌃⌄ 8 letters ─── B
Paragraph Rules	After First: ⌃⌄ 2 letters ─── C
Paragraph Border	Before Last: ⌃⌄ 2 letters ─── D
Paragraph Shading	Hyphen Limit: ⌃⌄ 3 hyphens ─── E
Keep Options	Hyphenation Zone: ⌃⌄ 12.7 mm ─── F
Hyphenation	
Justification	Better Spacing ──────O───── Fewer Hyphens
Span Columns	☑ Hyphenate Capitalised Words ☑ Hyphenate Last Word
Drop Caps and Nested Styles	☑ Hyphenate Across Column G
GREP Style	
Bullets and Numbering	
Character Colour	
OpenType Features	
Underline Options	
Strikethrough Options	
Export Tagging	

☐ Add to CC Library: Create New Library ⌄ Learn More...
☑ Preview

(OK)   (Cancel)

Figure 9.5: Hyphenation options in the New Paragraph Style dialog box

> **Note**
>
> **Hyphenation**, in this context, is when a long word is split between two lines. The split is done automatically between two syllables and a hyphen character is inserted, with the rest of the word being pushed onto the next line.

In the **Hyphenation** section, we will set the following options:

- **Hyphenate** (*A* in *Figure 9.5*): We will enable this checkbox to turn on hyphenation.

- **Words with at Least** (*B* in *Figure 9.5*): We will set this to **8** letters, so hyphenation is only applied to words with at least 8 letters in them.

- **After First** (*C* in *Figure 9.5*): This allows you to set a minimum number of letters to appear before the hyphen. We will set this to **2**.

- **Before Last** (*D* in *Figure 9.5*): This allows you to set a minimum number of letters to appear after the hyphen. We will set this to **2**.

- **Hyphen Limit** (*E* in *Figure 9.5*): This is the maximum number of hyphenated lines that can appear consecutively. We will set this to **1**.

- **Hyphenation Zone** (*F* in *Figure 9.5*): This is the maximum amount of white space allowed at the end of a line. If pushing a word down onto the next line would leave more white space than this value at the end of the previous line, the word will be hyphenated instead to prevent too much space from appearing at the end of the previous line. We will leave this setting untouched.

- **Better Spacing/Fewer Hyphens** (*G* in *Figure 9.5*): This slider can be used to adjust the balance between better spacing and a few hyphens appearing. We don't need to touch this.

Finally, there are three checkboxes at the bottom, which we will leave enabled. These control the following:

- **Hyphenate Capitalised Words**: When ticked, capitalized words can be hyphenated

- **Hyphenate Last Word**: When ticked, the last word in a paragraph can be hyphenated

- **Hyphenate Across Column**: When ticked, words can be hyphenated across columns, frames, or pages

8. We will now skip over the following sections within the panel, as we are not going to change settings in these areas

- **Justification** (*A* in *Figure 9.6*): In this section, you can adjust more advanced spacing and justification settings

- **Span Columns** (*B* in *Figure 9.6*): Here, you can force text to span across columns or break up into sub-columns

- **Drop Caps and Nested Styles** (*C* in *Figure 9.6*): This section lets you enable drop caps or work with nested styles. We will look at nested styles in more detail, in the *Using nested styles* recipe

- **GREP Style** (*D* in *Figure 9.6*): This lets you automatically apply a character style to content that matches a specific pattern. For example, you could make all email addresses appear in a different color within any content that uses a particular paragraph style

- **Bullets and Numbering** (*E* in *Figure 9.6*): This allows you to create a paragraph style for formatting numbered or bulleted lists

- **Character Color** (*F* in *Figure 9.6*): Here, you can make changes to the color of the fill or stroke, including adjusting the stroke weight

- **OpenType Features** (*G* in *Figure 9.6*) In this section, you can take advantage of the expanded feature set offered by OpenType Fonts

- **Underline Options** (*H* in *Figure 9.6*): Here, you can format underline settings.

- **Strikethrough Options** (*I* in *Figure 9.6*): Here, you can format strikethrough settings.

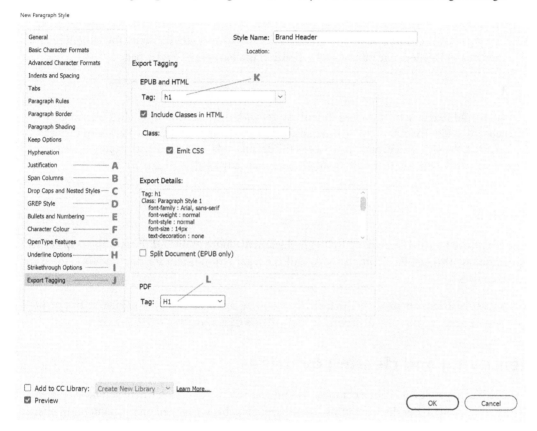

Figure 9.6: Export Tagging in Paragraph Styles

9. Finally, we will open the last section on the panel, which is the **Export Tagging** section (marked *J* in *Figure 9.6*). Here, we are going to set two settings. These will ensure that if the document is exported as an accessible PDF or HTML document in the future, the content styled with this particular paragraph style will be formatted with the correct tag, making it more accessible to those using assistive technologies such as screen reading devices. To change these settings, do the following:

- Under **EPub and HTML**, choose **h1** in the **Tag** drop-down menu (marked *K* in *Figure 9.6*).

- Under the **PDF** section, choose **H1** from the **Tag** drop-down menu (marked *L* in *Figure 9.6*).

The **H1** choice is typically used to denote the primary header on a page, and as this is our main header style, it makes sense to use this. If it had been a secondary header, we would use the **H2**. For regular body copy text, you would set this to the **P** tag.

InDesign Accessibility is an in-depth topic that could take up many pages and is not the subject of this chapter. If it is something you wish to know more about, however, check out the link in the *See more* section.

10. Having created our new style, we can now click **OK** to generate the style. You should see the new **Brand Header** style immediately appear in the **Paragraph Styles** panel.

> **Note**
>
> If you would like to set a style as a **default style**, with the selection tool, click on the grey pasteboard to the side of the page in order to deselect everything. Then, in the **Paragraph Styles** panel, click the style you would like to set as the default style. Next time you create a new text frame in this document, that style should be automatically used.

See also

In the recipe, we touched on making InDesign documents more usable for those with **accessibility requirements**. This can be a complex area and is a legal requirement for documents created in many countries.

If you would like to know more about this topic, the following short course may be of interest: `https://www.highlander.co.uk/course/video-creating-accessible-pdfs`

Identifying and clearing overrides

As you work with styles, it is quite common to find yourself in a situation where you have applied a style to some content, but the formatting has subsequently been changed on the content. In effect, you have a style applied, but you also have some manual formatting overriding elements of your style.

In this recipe, we will look at how to recognize when you have **overrides** active on both specific content and in multiple areas, and also how to clear these overrides by resetting your content back to the original style.

Getting ready

In order to complete this recipe, simply open InDesign on your system and create a new document with 12 pages, as shown in the *Creating a new document* recipe in *Chapter 1*. You should be comfortable creating and applying paragraph styles as shown in the *Creating paragraph styles* recipe.

How to do it

In order to identify and clear overrides, just follow these steps:

1. First, let's create a large text frame and fill it with placeholder text. Next, select the text and format it how you would like it to look. In my case, I will set the font face to **Arial**, the font size to **14 pt**, and fill the color to **Black**. Finally, from this text that you formatted, create a new style called **Body Copy** and then apply the style to the rest of your text.

2. Next, select five or six words in the text and manually change the formatting by applying a different font face, font size and font color to it. In my case, I chose **Times New Roman**, **18 pt** and **Cyan**. If you look at the **Paragraph Styles** panel, you will notice that your style is still highlighted in blue, indicating it is being applied to the paragraph your cursor is in, but if you look closely, you will notice it now has a small + icon on the end of the name (marked *A* in *Figure 9.7*). This indicates it has an override applied to it. In other words, you are using the paragraph style but have overridden some of its properties.

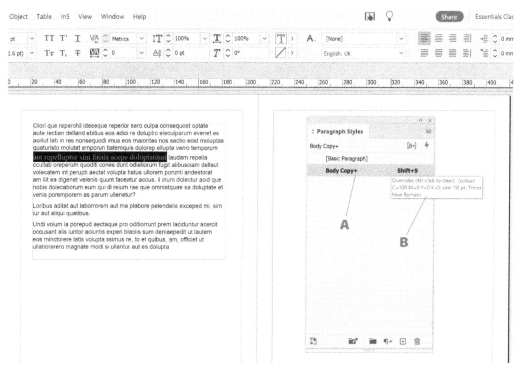

Figure 9.7: Overrides on a paragraph style

Additionally, if you hover over the style, you should see a small tooltip appear on the cursor (marked *B* in *Figure 9.7*) telling you exactly what the override is.

3. You now have to decide what to do with your override, and there are four main options. Do you want to:

    *   Ignore it: It's generally seen as good practice to avoid having overrides. After all, one of the main reasons for using paragraph style is to centralize control of your styling, and overrides affect your ability to do that. Having said that, there are instances where you might decide to leave an override, knowing full well it's there. It will almost certainly cause warnings in the preflighting process, which we look at in *Chapter 13, Preflighting and Outputting*, but that still won't actually prevent you from outputting the document.

    *   **Apply "Body Copy", Clear Overrides**: This will remove the overrides leaving you with the original style, in this case, the **Body Copy** style.

    *   **Redefine Style**: This will update the style to incorporate the override values into it. If you do this, be aware that any other text formatted with this style will be updated to reflect these changes. We will look at this in the *Redefining overrides* recipe.

    *   Create a **New Paragraph Style**: You might decide at this point to create another new style. If you do so be aware that the new style will, by default, be based on the **Body Copy** style and only the override values will be set within the new style. The other formatting settings for the new style will be automatically inherited from the **Body Copy** style unless you subsequently change them within your new style.

    In our case, we want to clear the overrides, so we will right-click on the **Body Copy** style and choose to **Apply "Body Copy", Clear Overrides**. You should see the overrides are now removed and the text now uses just the original **Body Copy** style once again.

> **Note**
>
> If you want some text that has a style applied to continue looking the same but you don't want to use the style, simply select it and then, in the **Paragraph Styles** panel menu, select the **Break Link to Style** option. The selected text will no longer be affected by changes to the style going forward.

4. Next, we are going to identify multiple overrides at once. Select some text near the top of the frame and change the font size to **16 pt**. Now, select some text further down and change the font size to **18 pt,** and also set the color to **Red**. While the second change is fairly easy to identify, the first one is less obvious, and changes like this can easily be missed.

    The good news is we can easily identify overrides anywhere they appear, using a useful tool called the **Style Override Highlighter**. To activate this, click the **Style Override Highlighter** icon (marked *A* in *Figure 9.8*). You will see the areas with the overrides are highlighted in a light aqua color (marked *B* in *Figure 9.8*) making them easy to identify.

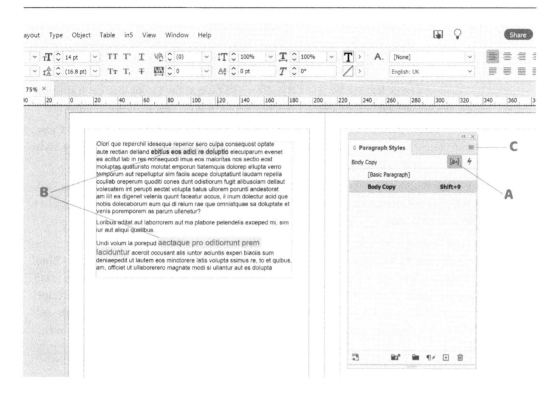

Figure 9.8: The Style Override Highlighter

5. Having identified where the overrides are, we can now select all of the text areas that include both sets of overrides, and then from the **Paragraph Styles** panel menu (marked *C* in *Figure 9.8*), choose the **Clear Overrides** option. This will clear both sets of overrides in one go, removing the need for us to clear them individually.

Redefining styles

When you have created a style, sometimes you will want to update the style later, for example, to change the font face, alter the fill color, adjust the spacing, or alter other properties. This process is known as **redefining the style**.

In this recipe, we will look at how to use overrides to redefine your styles quickly and easily, as well as how to redefine styles quickly from the **Paragraph Style Options** dialog box.

Getting ready

In order to complete this recipe, simply open InDesign on your system and create a new document with 12 pages, as shown in the *Creating a new document* recipe in *Chapter 1*. You should be comfortable creating and applying paragraph styles as shown in the *Creating paragraph styles* recipe.

How to do it

In order to redefine styles, just follow these steps:

1. Start by creating a large text frame. Type My New Title at the top of the text frame, hit the *Return* key to start a new paragraph, then fill the rest of the frame with placeholder text.

2. Select the **My New Title** text and style it up in **Arial**, size **18 pt**, and with text fill color **Cyan**. Then, create a new paragraph style from this called **Header**, ensuring you select **Apply Style to Selection** as you are creating it.

3. Now, select the remaining placeholder text. Format this at **10 pt** in **Times New Roman** with the text color set to **Green**, and create a new style called **Body Copy**, again ensuring you select **Apply Style to Selection** as you are creating it.

4. Having done this, we now want to update the header style. Select the **My New Title** text in the text frame and manually change the font face to **Impact**, the size to **60 pt**, and the color to **Blue**. Having done this, you will notice in the **Paragraph Styles** panel that **Header** now has a small + next to it, telling us there is an override here. We looked at overrides in the previous recipe, *Identifying and clearing overrides*, however this time we don't want to clear the override. Instead, we will right-click the style in the panel and select **Redefine Style** (marked *A* in *Figure 9.9*).

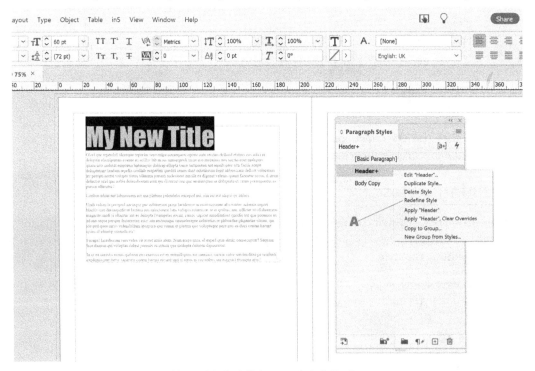

Figure 9.9: Redefining a style in InDesign

The style has now been redefined to incorporate the edits we made, and if it had been applied to other text in the document, those instances would also have been automatically updated when we redefined the style.

> **Note**
>
> Editing the style isn't really redefining it in the InDesign sense of the word, but in the English language sense, that's exactly what you are doing, so it makes sense to include this here.

5. Having redefined the header style on the page, we are now going to redefine the **Body Copy** style, only this time, we will do it by editing the style. To do this, simply right-click on the **Body Copy** style and select **Edit "Body Copy"...** (marked *A* in *Figure 9.10*), which will bring up the **Paragraph Style Options dialog box**.

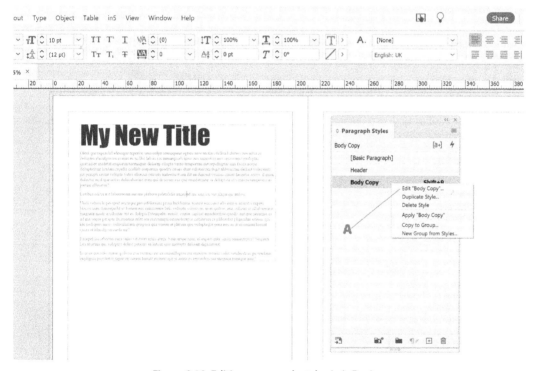

Figure 9.10: Editing paragraph styles in InDesign

Here, we will make the following changes:

- Under the **Basic Character Formats** section, change the font face to **Arial** and the font size to **14 pt**

- Under the **Indents and Spacing** section, set the **Space After** value to **3 mm**

- Under the **Character Color** section, set the **Fill** color to **Black**

Having made these changes, click **OK**, and you should immediately see the changes take effect on any text formatted with the **Body Copy** style.

Grouping styles

In some environments, you may be working with different groups of styles, which naturally belong together. For example, an agency may have a number of different clients each with their own styles, and within a company, you may have multiple brands, each with their own unique styles.

Grouping is a nice easy way for you to keep these styles together and more easily manage them.

Getting ready

In order to complete this recipe, simply open InDesign on your system and create a new document with 12 pages, as shown in the *Creating a new document* recipe in *Chapter 1*. You should be comfortable creating and applying paragraph styles as shown in the *Creating paragraph styles* recipe.

How to do it

In order to **group styles** together, just follow these steps:

1. Start by creating a number of separate paragraph styles with the following names:

    -   **Brand 1 Header**
    -   **Brand 1 Subheader**
    -   **Brand 1 Body Copy**
    -   **Brand 2 Header**
    -   **Brand 2 Subheader**
    -   **Brand 2 Body Copy**

    In the real world, these would all have unique settings, but for this recipe, it doesn't matter what the individual settings are for these styles (they can all be identical if you wish).

2. Now, we will create a new **style group**, but I would like to be able to choose the name for the new one as we create it. To do this, hold down the *Alt* (PC)/*Option* (Macintosh) key, then click on the **New Style Group** icon (marked *A* in *Figure 9.11*). A small dialog box will appear (marked *B* in *Figure 9.11*), allowing us to name the new style group. We will call ours **Brand One** and then click **OK**.

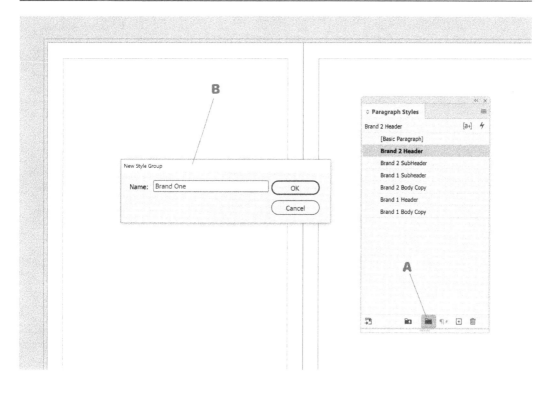

Figure 9.11: New Style Group creation

Having created our **Brand One** style group, we can now drag the **Brand One** styles into it by just clicking on them in the **Paragraph Styles** panel and dragging them onto the **Brand One** style group, which will show at the bottom of the list of styles.

> **Note**
>
> If a style group is already selected when you create a new style, the new style will automatically be created within that style group.

3. With the **Brand Two** styles, we are going to do this in a slightly different way. Switch to the **Selection** tool and ensure nothing is selected in the document by clicking on the grey pasteboard area to the side of the document. Now, select each of the **Brand Two** styles in the **Paragraph Styles** panel by holding down the *Ctrl* (PC) / *Cmd* (Mac) key, and clicking on them to select them.

    With all three selected, go to the **Paragraph Styles** panel menu and select the **New Group from Styles** option (marked *A* in *Figure 9.12*). Give the new group a name, in this case, **Brand Two**, and then click **OK**. This will not only create a new group called **Brand Two**, but it will also automatically move the styles you selected into the new group.

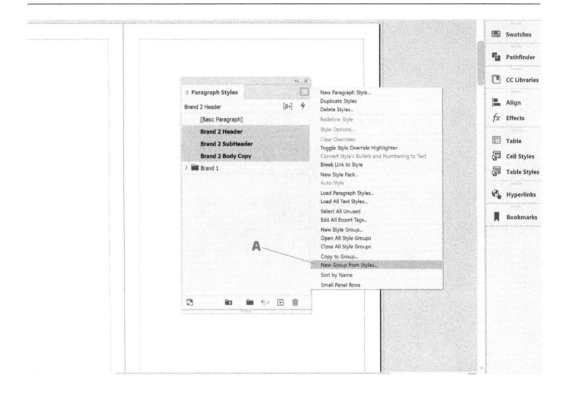

Figure 9.12: Creating a new group from styles

Creating and applying character styles

Paragraph styles are great for formatting the bulk of your text and should be your first-choice style for general text formatting. However, sometimes you might want to simply have a small piece of text in the middle of a paragraph that is formatted differently from the surrounding text. A few examples of this would include email addresses, hyperlinks, and quotes. You can't use a paragraph style for this as they impact the whole paragraph, and while you could use overrides, that would introduce potential problems, not least around the consistency of the formatting.

Character styles offer you a way to consistently format text in this type of scenario without having overrides consistently flagged in your content, and while still maintaining consistency throughout the document.

In this recipe, we will look at creating, redefining, and removing character styles within your document.

Getting ready

In order to complete this recipe, simply open InDesign on your system and create a new document with 12 pages, as shown in the *Creating a new document* recipe in *Chapter 1*. You should be comfortable creating and applying paragraph styles as shown in the *Creating paragraph styles* recipe.

How to do it

In order to use character styles in InDesign, just follow these steps:

1. Start by creating a large text frame and fill it with placeholder text, then format the text with **Arial** at **16 pt** size in **Black**. Then, create a paragraph style called **Body Copy** from the text, ensuring the **Apply Style to Selection** box is ticked as you are creating the style.

2. If the **Body Copy** style isn't applied to all the text, do so now. Then, within the text, add a number of email addresses, which we are now going to format differently from the rest of the text.

3. Position the **Character Styles** panel and the **Paragraph Styles** panel next to each other so you can see both at once, then select one of the email addresses and change the text color to **Cyan** and the font to **Bold**. In the **Paragraph Styles** panel, you will notice the **Body Copy** style now has the + icon next to it (marked *A* in *Figure 9.13*), indicating overrides have been applied to it. With the email address still selected, hold down the *Alt* (PC)/*Option* (Macintosh) key and click the **New Character Style** icon (marked *B* in *Figure 9.13*).

Figure 9.13: New character styles in InDesign

Call the new character style **Emails**, but before you click **OK**, take a look at the **Style Settings** area in the middle of the **New Character Style dialog box**. You will notice it only contains **Bold** and **Cyan** color values. Things like font face and size are not included, as it only includes changes made after the paragraph style was applied. We will now click **OK**.

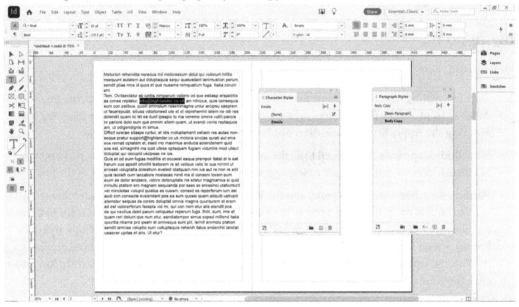

Figure 9.14: Character styles applied with no overrides

Also, you should find that having now created the new character style, the override has disappeared on **Paragraph Styles** and the new **Character Styles** setting is also highlighted in blue to show it is being used. InDesign does not consider character styles as overrides, but rather deliberate changes. As such, those settings won't show up as an override in the **Paragraph Styles** panel.

Finally, apply the new **Character Styles** setting to the other email addresses within the text by selecting them and clicking on **Emails** in the **Character Styles** panel.

4. Having applied our new character style to the other email addresses, we now want to update the **Body Copy** paragraph style to use a different font family and color. Right-click on the **Body Copy** paragraph style in the **Paragraph Styles** panel and click on **Edit "Body Copy"...**, then in the **Paragraph Style Options** dialog under **Basic Character Formats**, change **Font Family** to **Times New Roman**, and under **Character Color**, change the color to **Red**. Now, click **OK** to save these changes to **Paragraph Styles**.

Figure 9.15: Text after Paragraph Styles is updated

You should now see that the text has been updated, including the email addresses, and is using Times New Roman in red. Subsequently, the **Character Styles** have then applied the bold and cyan properties to the email addresses.

Note

If your text with the **Character Style** applied to it now appears to have a pink background, this indicates a **missing font**. In other words, the **Character Style** is trying to make the font bold, but there isn't a bold version installed, so it highlights it in pink as a missing font. In such a scenario, you will need to either install a bold version of the font or choose a different font that has a bold version installed.

---

5. Finally, let's update **Character Styles** by right-clicking on **Emails** in the **Character Style** panel and choosing **Edit "Emails"...** The first thing you will probably notice is there are far fewer options when editing **Character Styles** than with **Paragraph Styles,** as only character formatting options are available here (as seen in *Figure 9.16*). **Paragraph Styles** include all the paragraph formatting options.

    In our case, we are only going to make a simple change under the **Character Color** section by changing the color from **Cyan** to **Blue,** then clicking **OK.** You will now see all the email addresses that were previously cyan in color have changed color to a darker blue color.

Figure 9.16: Editing in the Character Style Options panel

Using nested styles

Nested styles are a useful way of automatically applying character styles from within a paragraph style. If you apply a nested style, it will be applied from the beginning of each paragraph that the paragraph style has been applied to, through to a point that you have set in the nested style settings. If you do more than one nested style, each new nested style will continue from where the last one ended.

In this recipe, we will look at using nested styles to restyle the first word of a paragraph so that the first word and the first letter within it are styled differently from the rest of the paragraph.

Getting ready

In order to complete this recipe, simply open InDesign on your system and create a new document with 12 pages, as shown in the *Creating a new document* recipe in *Chapter 1*. You should be comfortable creating and applying paragraph styles as shown in the *Creating paragraph styles* recipe and character styles as shown in the *Creating character styles* recipe.

How to do it

In order to use nested styles in InDesign, just follow these steps:

1. Start by creating a large text frame and filling it with placeholder text, then format the text with **Arial** at **16 pt** size in **Black**. Create a paragraph style called **Body Copy** from the text, ensuring

the **Apply Style to Selection** box is ticked as you are creating the style. If the style isn't applied to all the text, do so now.

2. Now, right-click on the **Body Copy** paragraph style and select **Edit "Body Copy"...** to bring up **Paragraph Style Options**. Then, select the **Drop Caps and Nested Styles** section. Here, we will click on the **New Nested Style** button (marked *A* in *Figure 9.17*) and then from the drop-down menu above that, (marked *B* in *Figure 9.17*), select **New Character Style**, which will bring up the **New Character Style** dialog.

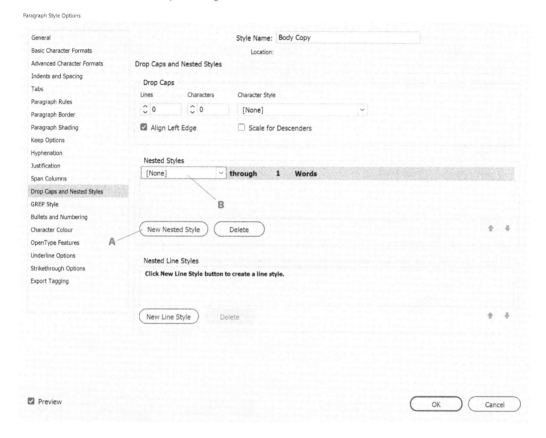

Figure 9.17: The Drop Caps and Nested Styles dialog box

3. In the **New Character Styles** dialog, change the name of the style to **Nested Style 1**. Under the **Basic Character Formats** section, set the following properties:

- **Font Family**: **Impact** (if this font is not installed, you can use an alternative)

- **Font Style**: **Regular**

- **Size**: **36 pt**

Click **OK** to create the new character style and return to the **Drop Caps and Nested Styles** dialog, where you should now see **Nested Style 1** showing in the drop-down box.

Moving to the right, the next three selection boxes are as follows:

- **through/up to** (*A* in *Figure 9.18*): The former will apply the style up to and including the character that denotes the end of the nested style, while **up to** will apply the style up to, but not including, the character that denotes the end of the nested style. We will choose **through** here.

- **Number:** (*B* in *Figure 9.18*): This is the number of items the nested style will be applied either **through** or **up to**. Set this to **1**.

- **Drop-down box** (*C* in *Figure 9.18*): This is where you can choose what item you want to denote the end of the nested style. There is a wide range of options here, including things such as **sentences**, **words**, **characters**, and many more. We will choose **characters**.

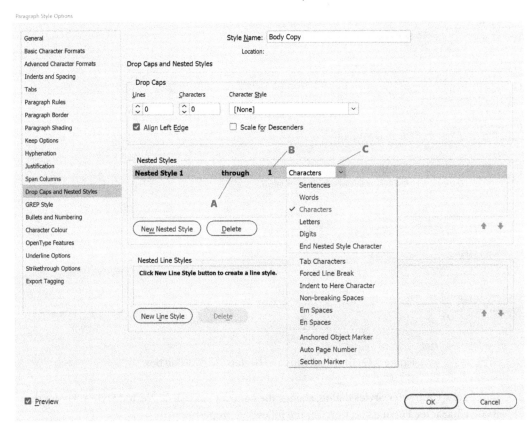

Figure 9.18: A nested style applied in Drop Caps and Nested Styles

You should see the nested style applied live on the document once you have made the changes, but if not, just make sure the small **Preview** checkbox in the bottom left of the **Paragraph Style Options** dialog box is checked.

Having added a nested style, we are now going to add a second nested style. When you add additional styles, they automatically begin from the end of the previous nested style.

4. In the **Paragraph Style Options** dialog box, we are still under **Drop Caps and Nested Styles** (if you clicked **OK** and closed it, just reopen it as we did at the start of *step 2*). Click the **New Nested Style** button, and from the first drop-down menu, select **New Character Style**. This time, we will name the new character style **Nested Style 2**. Under the **Basic Character Formats** and **Color** sections, we will apply the following settings:

- **Font Family**: **Impact**

- **Case**: **Small Caps**

- **Size**: **35 pt**

- **Color**: **Black** with a **70% tint**

Click **OK** to create the new character style and return to the **Drop Caps and Nested Styles** dialog, where you should now see **Nested Style 2** showing in the drop-down box.

We will set the next three selection boxes as follows:

- **through/up to** (marked *A* in *Figure 9.18*): Set this to **up to**.

- **Number** (marked *B* in *Figure 9.18*): Set this to **1**.

- **Dropdown box** (marked *C* in *Figure 9.18*): Set this to **Words**.

Figure 9.19: Multiple nested styles

Your content and **Nested Styles** settings should now look as they do in *Figure 9.19*. Click **OK**.

Using Next Style

Next Style is a simple enough feature in InDesign, which allows you to have the paragraph style automatically switch to a different paragraph style when you start a new paragraph, but it can be quite handy nonetheless. You can use Next Style to do something as simple as automatically switching to your subheader style after typing a header, rapidly creating things like definition lists without the need to keep manually switching styles, or even enabling and disabling it from within object styles for styling text within an object style.

In this recipe, we will look at using Next Style to automatically format a definition list as we type it, which should give you a good idea of how it works.

Getting ready

In order to complete this recipe, simply open InDesign on your system and create a new document with 12 pages, as shown in the *Creating a new document* recipe in *Chapter 1*. You should be comfortable creating and applying paragraph styles as shown in the *Creating paragraph styles* recipe.

How to do it

In order to use Next Styles in InDesign, just follow these steps:

1. We will start by creating two new paragraph styles. The first style will be called **List Item** and will contain the following formatting:

    Under **Basic Character Formats**, set:

    *   **Font Family: Arial**
    *   **Font Style: Bold**
    *   **Size: 20 pt**
    *   **Case: All Caps**
    *   **Underline: Enabled**

    Under **Indents and Spacing**, set:

    *   **Space Before: 5mm**

    The second paragraph style will be called **List Description**. Under **Basic Character Formats** will be the following settings:

    *   **Font Family: Arial**
    *   **Font Style: Regular**
    *   **Size: 18 pt**

2. Having created our two new paragraph styles, we are now going to right-click on the **List Item** paragraph style and choose **Edit "List Item"...**. This will bring up the **Paragraph Style Options** dialog box, where we will set **Next Style** to **List Description** (marked *A* in *Figure 9.20*).

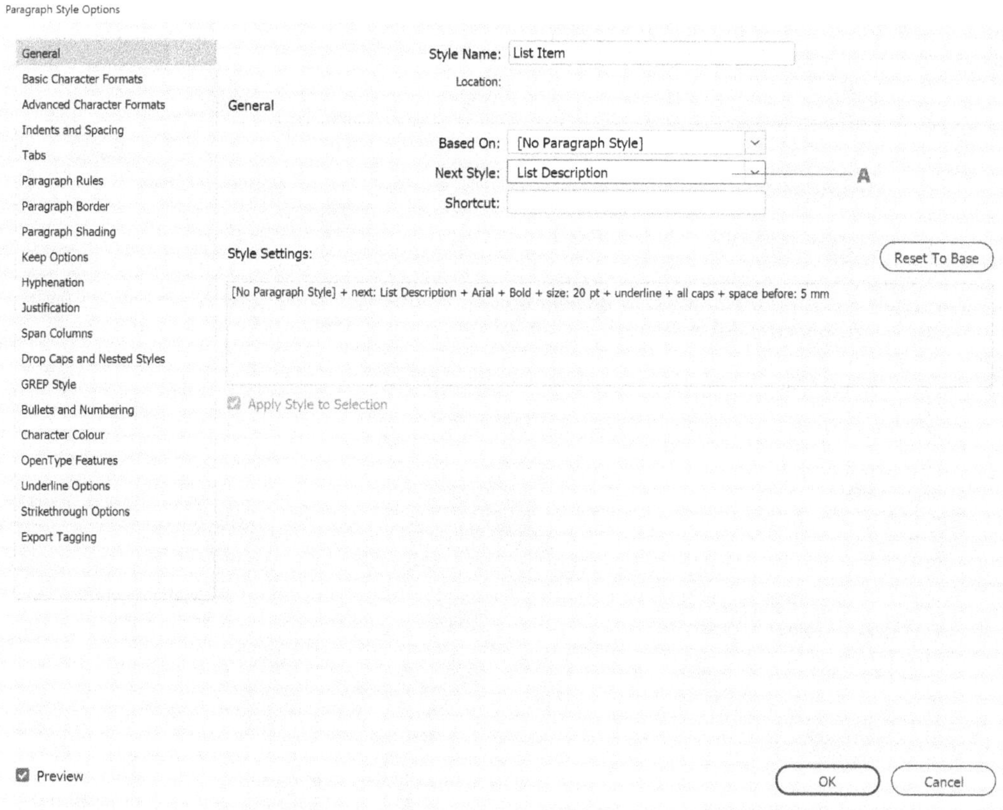

Paragraph Style Options

General	Style Name: List Item
Basic Character Formats	Location:
Advanced Character Formats	**General**
Indents and Spacing	Based On: [No Paragraph Style]
Tabs	Next Style: List Description ——— **A**
Paragraph Rules	Shortcut:
Paragraph Border	
Paragraph Shading	
Keep Options	Style Settings: Reset To Base
Hyphenation	[No Paragraph Style] + next: List Description + Arial + Bold + size: 20 pt + underline + all caps + space before: 5 mm
Justification	
Span Columns	
Drop Caps and Nested Styles	
GREP Style	
Bullets and Numbering	☑ Apply Style to Selection
Character Colour	
OpenType Features	
Underline Options	
Strikethrough Options	
Export Tagging	

☑ Preview   OK   Cancel

Figure 9.20: Applying Next Style in Paragraph Style Options

Click **OK** to save the changes to the **List Item** style. The **List Item** style will now automatically switch to the **List Description** style when you start a new paragraph while using it.

3. Next, right-click on the **List Description** style and select **Edit List Description**. This time, set **Next Style** to **List Item** and then click **OK** to save the changes. This will ensure the **List Description** style will automatically switch back to the **List Item** style when you start a new paragraph while using it.

4. Having configured our styles, let's now create a new blank text frame, type the word `Apples`, and apply the **List Item** paragraph style to it. Now, type the text below with a new paragraph (the *Return* key) at the end of each line:

```
Apples
A red or green fruit
Oranges
A sweet orange fruit
Grapes
A small red or green fruit
Lemons
A yellow sharp-tasting fruit
```

The content should now look like the example in *Figure 9.21*, with no need for you to apply the rest of the styles manually.

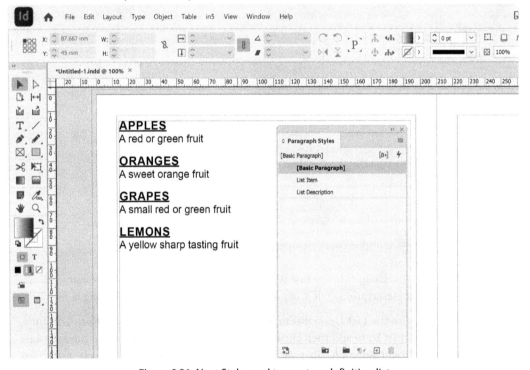

Figure 9.21: Next Style used to create a definition list

> **Note**
>
> If you want to apply a paragraph style containing Next Style to existing paragraphs and want Next Style to be applied, select all the paragraphs. Then, in the **Paragraph Styles** panel, *right-click* on the paragraph style you wish to apply and select **Apply ParagraphStyleName** then **Next Style**.

Importing text styles

Importing text styles is a useful feature in InDesign, allowing you to both save time and ensure consistency across documents. You can import paragraph styles, character styles, or both into a document and easily manage any conflicts in name with any existing styles that already exist. In this recipe, we will look at all of this and even cover useful tricks for setting default styles that will automatically appear in all your new documents going forward.

Getting ready

In order to complete this recipe, simply open InDesign on your system and create a new document with 12 pages, as shown in the *Creating a new document* recipe in *Chapter 1*. You should be comfortable creating and applying paragraph styles as shown in the *Creating paragraph styles* recipe.

How to do it

In order to import text styles into InDesign, just follow these steps:

1. Start by creating a new document with three paragraph styles called **Header**, **SubHeader**, and **Body Copy**, and two character styles called **Char Style 1** and **Char Style 2**. In terms of the settings for these styles, I will go with the following, but feel free to use different values if you wish:

    *   **Header**: Font Family: **Impact**, Size: **36 pt**; Color: **Black**

    *   **SubHeader**: Font Family: **Arial**; Size: **24 pt**; Color: **Black**

    *   **Body Copy**: Font Family: **Arial**; Size: **14 pt**; Color: **Black**

    *   **Char Style 1**: Color: **Red**

    *   **Char Style 2**: Color: **Green**; Underline: **Enabled**

    Save the document to your desktop and call it DocumentwithStyles.indd and then close it.

2. Next, create a new document and add a new paragraph style called **Header**. I will format this using Times New Roman and 24 pt font. Now, click on the **Paragraph Styles** panel menu and select the **Load Paragraph Styles** option. Select the DocumentwithStyles.indd file that we created in *step 1* and click **Open**, which will open the **Load Styles dialog box** seen in *Figure 9.22*.

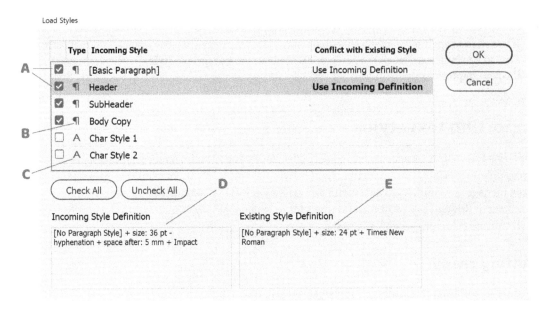

Figure 9.22: The Load Styles dialog box

> **Note**
>
> If you select **Load All Text Styles** instead of **Load Paragraph Styles** from the **Paragraph Styles** panel menu, the same dialog box is opened but **Character Styles** are included by default, in addition to **Paragraph Styles**.

3. The **Load Styles** dialog box lists each style being imported on a separate row under the **Incoming Style** column. Each row contains a number of columns as follows:

    *   **Selection** (*A* in *Figure 9.22*): This controls whether a style is to be imported (ticked) or not (unticked). It's also worth noting the **Check All** and **Uncheck All** buttons below this column, which can be handy when working with larger numbers of styles. We will leave **Paragraph Styles** selected and **Character Styles** unselected.

    *   **Type**: The icon used here denotes whether you are importing a paragraph style (*B* in *Figure 9.22*) or a character style (*C* in *Figure 9.22*), depending on the symbol being used.

    *   **Incoming Style**: This column shows the name of the incoming style.

    *   **Conflict with Existing Style**: A **style conflict** occurs if another style of the same type and name already exists in the current document as a style that you are trying to import. In this scenario, you will be offered two options you can click on to change.

- **Use Incoming Definition**: This will overwrite your existing style with the imported style. In our case, we have a conflict with our **Header** style and will use this setting.

- **Auto-Rename**: The style being imported will be automatically renamed with the word **Copy** added to the end of its name.

Finally, if you click on a style name in the dialog box, you can see the settings for that style in the **Incoming Style Definition** box (*D* in *Figure 9.22*), and if it has a conflict, you can also see the settings for the existing style with that name in the **Existing Style Definition** box (*E* in *Figure 9.22*). This can be useful when deciding which style you want to use.

Having chosen our import settings, we can now click **OK** to import the styles. You should see the styles appear in the **Paragraph Styles** panel.

Top Tip

Do you often use the same styles in different documents? Would you like them to just be there every time you start a new document? Use the exact same process that we followed above in *step 2* and *step 3*, but leave out the bit where we opened a new document and created a new header style at the start of *step 2*. If you load paragraph styles or load all text styles from the InDesign **Paragraph Styles** menu without a document open, they become the default styles that appear for every new document you create going forward.

Finding and replacing styles

Sometimes when working, you just need a quick way to find content using a style. Maybe you want to change it manually or maybe you want to replace it with a different style. In this recipe, we will look at how to find and replace styles in your document quickly and easily.

Getting ready

In order to complete this recipe, simply open InDesign on your system and create a new document with 12 pages, as shown in the *Creating a new document* recipe in *Chapter 1*. You should be comfortable creating and applying paragraph styles as shown in the *Creating paragraph styles* recipe.

How to do it

In order to find and replace styles in InDesign, just follow these steps:

1. Start by creating a new document with two paragraph styles called **Header** and **Body Copy** and two character styles called **Char Style 1** and **Char Style 2**. In terms of the settings for these styles, I will go with the following, but feel free to use different values if you wish:

    *   **Header: Font Family: Impact; Size: 36 pt; Color: Black**
    *   **Body Copy: Font Family: Arial; Size: 14 pt; Color: Black**
    *   **Char Style 1: Color: Red; Font Style: Bold**
    *   **Char Style 2: Color: Green; Font Style: Bold**

    Now, create large text frames on four different pages in your document and apply the styles making sure to use each paragraph style at least once on every page and each character style at least twice per page.

    Finally, let's create one more paragraph style called **New Header**, setting the **Font Family** to **Impact**, **Size** to **36 pt**, and **Color** to **Red**. But don't apply this style anywhere!

2. In the **Edit** menu, select **Find/Change**, which will bring up the **Find/Change** dialog box as shown in *Figure 9.23*.

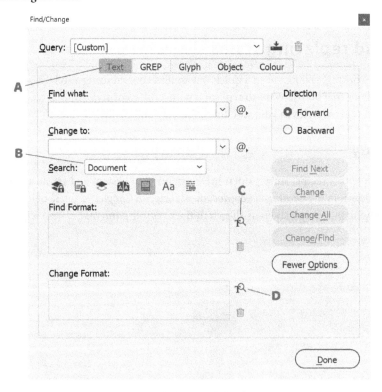

Figure 9.23: The Find/Change dialog box in InDesign

Let's look at the options we will be using:

- The **Find/Change** dialog box includes a wide range of options, and in our case, we need to ensure we are searching for **Text** (*A* in *Figure 9.23*), as opposed to **GREP**, **Glyph**, **Object**, or **Colour**.

- We also want to search the current **Document** (*B* in *Figure 9.23*) as opposed to **All Documents** that are open, so we'll make sure this is set to **Document**.

- Since we are searching for text based on the styles used, we will select **Specify Attributes to Find** (marked *C* in *Figure 9.23*) and **Specify Attributes to Change** (marked *D* in *Figure 9.23*), as opposed to using the **Find What** and **Change To** options, which appear higher up and are used for finding specific text.

3. Click the **Specify Attributes to Find** button, which will bring up the **Find Format Settings dialog box**, defaulting to the **Style Options** section. From the **Paragraph Styles** drop-down menu, select **Header,** then click **OK**. Next, click the **Specify Attributes to Change** button (marked *D* in *Figure 9.23*). From **Paragraph Styles**, use the drop-down menu to select **New Header**, then click **OK**.

Figure 9.24: Find/Change options

We now have a number of options down the right-hand side as follows:

- **Direction** (*A* in *Figure 9.24*): We can set this to search forward or backward in the document.

- **Find Next** (*B* in *Figure 9.24*): This finds the next item that matches the **Find Format** settings.

- **Change** (*C* in *Figure 9.24*): This changes the currently selected content.

- **Change All** (*D* in *Figure 9.24*): This changes all instances that match the **Find Format** settings, telling you how many changes were made. As we wish to update everything using the **Header** style to use **New Header** instead, we will use this option.

- **Change/Find** (*E* in *Figure 9.24*): This changes the currently selected content and finds the next match for the **Find Format** settings.

- **Fewer Options** (*F* in *Figure 9.24*): This hides the options for find/change based on formatting.

4. Finally, we want to change two of the elements that use **Char Style 1**, but first, we need to remove the current format settings that we have just been using from the **Find/Change** dialog. To do this, click the bin icons to the right of the **Find Format** and **Change Format** boxes to delete the current options.

5. Now, click the **Specify Attributes to Find** icon, and this time, we will choose **Char Style 1** from the **Character Styles** drop-down menu. Next, click the **Specify Attributes to Change** icon, and this time, we will choose **Char Style 2** from the **Character Styles** drop-down menu. Click **Find Next** and then click it a second time to jump through to the content we wish to change the formatting on. Now, click **Change/Find** to switch the style for this content to **Char Style 2** and immediately search for the next match. Again, this isn't the content we want to change, so click **Find Next** twice more until we find the right content, then click **Change**.

Having found **Char Style 1** and selectively replaced it with **Char Style 2**, we are now finished, so you can click **Done**.

10

Generating and Updating a Table of Contents

One of the advantages of working in InDesign is that it contains advanced functionality that can be used to automate otherwise slow and laborious tasks, and creating a Table of Contents is a good example of this. By using Paragraph Styles carefully and consistently, you can generate a Table of Contents that can be easily updated, styled, and even reused in other InDesign documents.

In this chapter, we will look at how to generate a **Table of Contents** and the options available when doing so. We will look at styling your Table of Contents so that the styling is maintained when you update it, and we will update and edit an existing Table of Contents. Finally, we will learn how to reuse a Table of Contents across multiple documents, before wrapping up the chapter with a neat little trick by automating story jumps.

The recipes we will cover in this chapter are as follows:

- Generating a Table of Contents
- Formatting the Table of Contents
- Updating the Table of Contents and setting additional options
- Saving and loading Table of Contents styles
- Creating automated story jumps

Technical requirements

To complete this chapter, you will need a PC or Mac, with a copy of Adobe InDesign installed. You should be comfortable adding content to your documents and formatting it, as shown in *Chapters 1 to 4*. You should also be comfortable working with **Paragraph Styles**, as covered in *Chapter 9*.

Generating a Table of Contents

A well-organized Table of Contents can be a great navigational aid in larger documents, allowing users to find their way around the document and get a feel for its structure. In this recipe, we will learn how to format your content ready for a Table of Contents, as well as how to then generate your first Table of Contents from that content.

Getting ready

In order to complete this recipe, simply open InDesign on your system and create a new document with 12 pages, as shown in the *Creating a new document* recipe in *Chapter 1*.

How to do it...

In order to create a Table of Contents, just follow these steps:

1. Let's start by formatting our content with a view to creating a Table of Contents from it. Starting on the third page, create a large text frame that fills the page, and then do the same on the following four pages. In my case, I have threaded these together into a single story. While this is not needed for the Table of Contents functionality, it does make it quicker for me to fill them all with placeholder text, which is what I will now do. In this example, I am going to use the topics of *Fruit* and *Vegetables* as my main headers, with a number of items under each of these as subheadings.

    At the top of the first page, within a new paragraph, we will add the word Vegetables and style it using a new paragraph style called **Header** (marked *A* in *Figure 10.1*). This will be one of your main section headers, so if you wish to adjust the styling and then redefine the style, do so now (I have set mine to *Arial, 40pt, Blue*). Make sure to only use this **Header** paragraph style for content that you wish to include in the Table of Contents.

2. Next, within the first and second pages, we will add some vegetable names scattered around, each within their own new paragraph. I will include Carrots, Potatoes, and Broccoli. These will be formatted using the **SubHeader** style (marked *B* in *Figure 10.1*), which you can now modify and redefine if you wish (I have set mine to *Arial, Bold, 24pt*). Again, only use this paragraph style for content that you wish to have included in the Table of Contents.

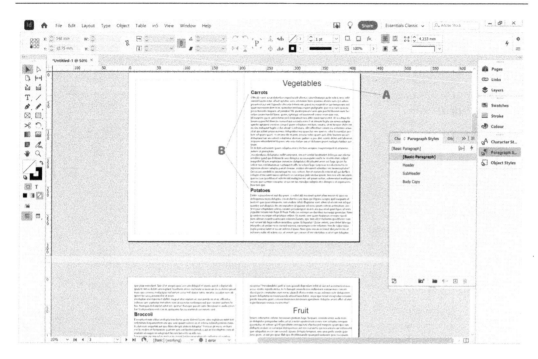

Figure 10.1: Content formatted for a Table of Contents

3. Having formatted our vegetables, we will now do the same for the fruit, adding the word `Fruit` somewhere near the top of the third page and formatting it with the **Header** style. Now, throughout the third and fourth pages, let's add some fruit and format them with the **SubHeader** style; I will include `Apples`, `Oranges`, and `Lemons`.

   Finally, I have added page numbering on the parent pages, as shown in the *Adding content to a parent page including page numbers* recipe in *Chapter 7*. This isn't necessary for the Table of Contents itself, but it just makes it easier to confirm that the page numbers generated are correct and to verify that links are going to the correct pages in your exported PDF.

   Having formatted our content, we are now ready to generate our Table of Contents.

4. On page 2, insert a large text frame and position the cursor in it. Then, from the **Layout** menu, select **Table of Contents**, which will bring up the **Table of Contents dialog box** (*Figure 10.2*).

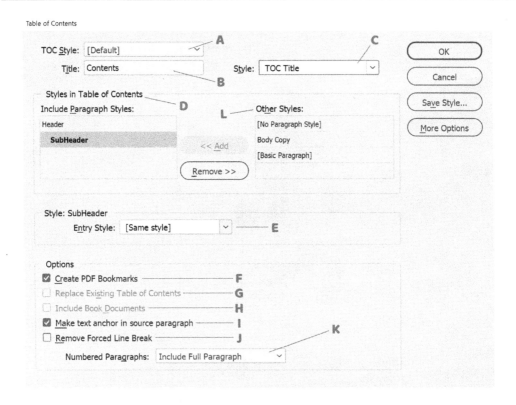

Figure 10.2: The Table of Contents dialog box

In the **Table of Contents** dialog box, you should see the fourth button down on the right saying **More Options**; if it instead says **Fewer Options**, click on it once so it changes to say **More Options**. We will look at **More Options** in a later recipe but, for now, we will look at the settings shown under **Fewer Options**, which are as follows:

- **TOC Style** (*A*): If you have previously created a TOC style, you can reuse it here for rapid Table of Contents creation and formatting. We will leave this set to **[Default]** as we don't have a previously created TOC style; however, we will look at TOC styles later in this chapter, in the *Saving and loading Table of Contents styles* recipe.

- **Title** (*B*): Here, you can set a title for your Table of Contents, which will be positioned at the top of the Table of Contents. We will leave this as **Contents**.

- **Style** (*C*): Here, you can choose a paragraph style to control the look of your title. We will select the **TOC Title** option, which will auto-generate a new paragraph style called **TOC Title** when we click **OK** at the end.

- **Styles in Table of Contents** (*D*): The InDesign Table of Contents works by identifying content that has a specific style applied to it and including that content within the Table of

Contents. This section is where you choose which styles to look for when identifying content to be included in the Table of Contents. We will look at this section in more detail in *step 5*.

- **Entry Style** (*E*): This allows you to set styles for the Table of Contents items, and we will look at this option further in the *Formatting the Table of Contents* recipe.

- **Create PDF Bookmarks** (*F*): If this option is selected, the items that appear in the Table of Contents will also appear in the **Bookmarks** panel in Adobe Acrobat / Acrobat Reader and other PDF readers that support the **Bookmarks** features. This can be useful for document navigation as well as for accessibility purposes, so we will enable this option.

- **Replace Existing Table of Contents** (*G*): This option will be activated once a Table of Contents has been generated and allows InDesign to update/replace existing items in the Table of Contents when making changes. We will therefore want to check that this is enabled at a later point, but at this stage, we are unable to do so as we have not yet created a Table of Contents.

- **Include Book Documents** (*H*): If you are working on an InDesign book, you can check this box to include all items from within the book into a single Table of Contents, as well as renumber the pages correctly. We will leave this unchecked as we are not working on a book here.

> **Note**
>
> An **InDesign book** is a collection of separate **InDesign document files** (**INDD files**), such as chapters of a book that may have been written by different authors, which are then gathered together into a single **InDesign book file** (**INDB file**). This makes it easier to manage, organize, and output your final document, allowing you to use features such as Tables of Contents and Indexes across the whole book, as well as synchronize styles and formatting across the entire book for consistency.

- **Make text anchor in source paragraph** (*I*): This allows you to automatically include a text anchor in the source paragraph (i.e., the content that was copied into the Table of Contents) resulting in the Table of Contents items acting as a hyperlink to the actual page content, provided the document is output correctly. This is a useful feature, which we will enable.

- **Remove Forced Line Break** (*J*): This will remove any forced line breaks you might have applied (*Shift* + *Return*) when formatting your text. As we haven't used any forced line breaks, we will leave this disabled.

- **Numbered Paragraphs** (*K*): If you include a paragraph style that uses numbering within the Table of Contents, you can choose here whether you want the numbering to be included or not in the Table of Contents. This could be useful, for example, when creating a Table of Contents for something like a legal document that may use numbering heavily throughout. The options available include:

- **Include Full Paragraph**: This will include both the numbers and the text
- **Include Numbers Only**: This will include only the numbers
- **Exclude Numbers**: This will exclude the numbers and include only the text

In our case, we can leave this set to **Include Full Paragraph** as we haven't used numbers, so it is irrelevant here.

Having chosen our settings, do not close the dialog box as we will now take a closer look at the **Styles in Table of Contents** section.

5. InDesign identifies what to include within the Table of Contents, based on the paragraph styles that have been applied to the content in the document. In our case, we want to include the content that has been formatted with the **Header** and **SubHeader** paragraph styles. With this in mind, we will click **Header Style** under the **Other Styles** section (marked *L* in *Figure 10.2*) and then click the **Add** button to include it. You should now see **Header Style** move over into the **Include Paragraph Styles** column. We will then do the exact same with the **SubHeader** style too.

If you accidentally move the wrong style across into the **Include Paragraph Styles** column, simply select it there and click **Remove** to move it back into the **Other Styles** column.

Having done this, click the **OK** button on the dialog box, and then click into the blank text frame we created earlier to generate our Table of Contents, as shown in *Figure 10.3*:

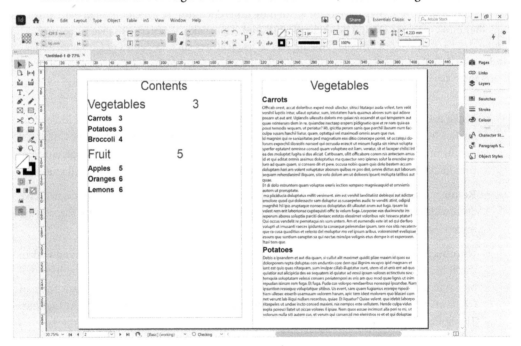

Figure 10.3: Table of Contents generated in InDesign

While we have now created our Table of Contents, you will undoubtedly want to improve its styling. In the next recipe, we will show you how to style your Table of Contents correctly within InDesign.

Formatting the Table of Contents

While you can manually style a Table of Contents or even apply paragraph styles to it in the traditional way, this can be quite labor-intensive as every time the Table of Contents is updated, all this styling will be removed.

In this recipe, we are going to look at how to use paragraph styles within the **Table of Contents** dialog box to automatically apply formatting to your Table of Contents in a way that is not impacted when you update it.

Getting ready

To complete this recipe, open InDesign on your system and create a new document with 12 pages, as shown in the *Creating a new document* recipe in *Chapter 1*. Having done this, create a Table of Contents as shown in the previous recipe, *Generating a Table of Contents*.

How to do it...

To style your Table of Contents, just follow these steps:

1. Having created a Table of Contents, we are now going to look at styling it in a way that won't be overridden when it is updated. Let's start by selecting the Table of Contents content on the page – we can leave out the word *Contents* at the top but select the rest of it, including the page numbers, then format it. I will use the following settings:

   - **Font Family: Calibri**

   - **Font Style: Regular**

   - **Font Size: 18 pt**

   - **Text Fill Color: Black**

   - **Space After: 1 mm**

   - **Align: Left**

Having applied some initial formatting, your Table of Contents should now look like *Figure 10.4*:

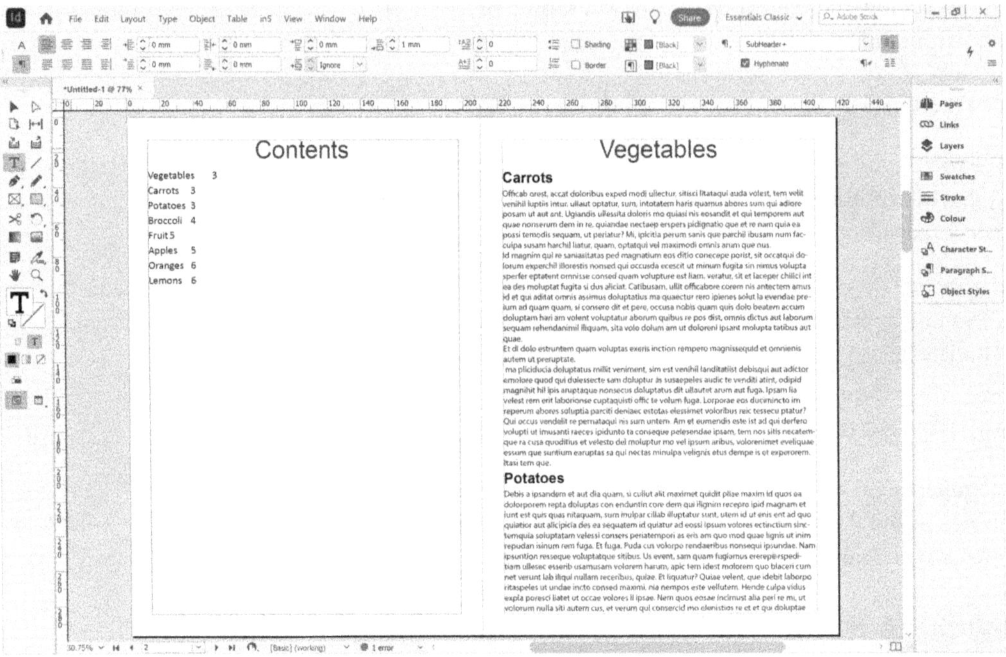

Figure 10.4: Table of Content with initial formatting

2. While this looks slightly better, I would still like to format this further to distinguish between the headers and subheaders. Select the first block of subheaders (in my case, the lines for **Carrots**, **Potatoes**, and **Broccoli**) and apply a **5 mm** left indent. Having done this, go to the **Type** menu and select **Tabs**, which will open the **Tabs** dialog box.

    Select the whole of the Table of Contents once again, and in the **Tabs** dialog box, click the **Right-Justified Tab** icon (marked *A* in *Figure 10.5*). Then click once on the white bar, which can be seen immediately above the ruler within the **Tabs** box. This will set a right-justified tab at the point where you clicked (marked *B* in *Figure 10.5*) and will cause the page numbering to align to that point.

    You can click on this tab (marked *B* in *Figure 10.5*) and reposition it by dragging left to right, but be careful as clicking either side will result in additional tabs being created. If you do this, just drag them off the panel and let go to delete them, as we only need one.

    Finally, I would like to add a **leader** to the page numbering in order to make it easier for readers to visually connect the items with their corresponding page numbers. To do this, simply click on the **Leader** box (marked *C* in *Figure 10.5*) and enter a period character, then hit the *Return* key.

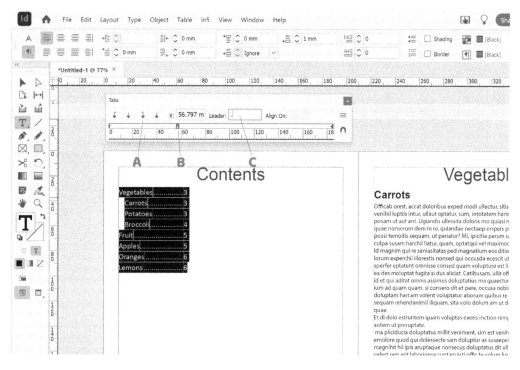

Figure 10.5: Aligning the page numbering with Tabs

I will finish off by selecting the first header line (which starts with **Vegetables**) and changing the font style to **Bold**.

3. Having styled my Table of Contents how I want it to look, I now want to save this formatting as paragraph styles. To do this, select the first line of the Table of Contents and create a new paragraph style, which I will call `TOC Headers`. I will then select the second line (which begins with **Carrots**) and create another new paragraph style from it called `TOC SubHeaders`.

    The temptation at this point is to apply these new styles directly to the Table of Contents on the page and quickly format it. Unfortunately, styles applied in this way will be automatically removed as soon as the Table of Contents is updated, so let's look at where we apply our new styles.

4. With your cursor in the Table of Contents, go to the **Layout** menu and select the **Table of Contents** option, which opens up the **Table of Contents** dialog box. In the **Table of Contents** dialog box, select **SubHeader** in the **Include Paragraph Styles** section (marked *A* in *Figure 10.6*) and then from the section below marked **Style: SubHeader**, set the **Entry Style** dropdown to **TOC SubHeader** (marked *B* in *Figure 10.6*). Having set the styling for the subheader, let's now do the same for the header by selecting the **Header** style in the **Include Paragraph Styles** section, and then from the section below marked **Style: Header**, set the **Entry Style** dropdown to **TOC Header**.

While we are in the **Table of Contents** dialog box, we will also select the **TOC Title** option from the title **Style** drop-down (marked *C* in *Figure 10.6*).

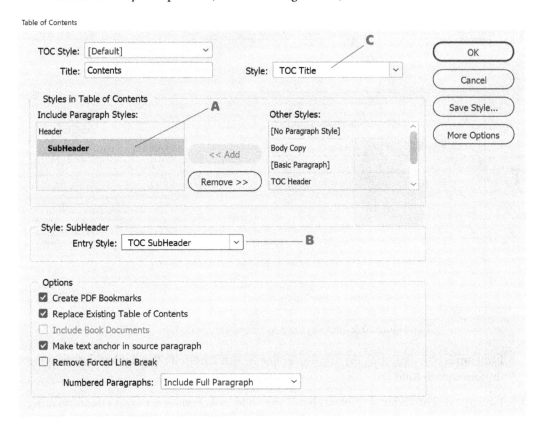

Figure 10.6: Styling the Table of Contents with Paragraph Styles

Having set the styles, click **OK** and your Table of Contents should be formatted using the styles (shown in *Figure 10.7*); best of all, you won't need to reapply styling if you update the Table of Contents.

Figure 10.7: Table of Contents styled correctly

Finally, having finished formatting our Table of Contents, don't forget we applied the **TOC Title** paragraph style to the title, so if you would like to style the title differently, simply edit the paragraph style as shown in the *Redefining styles* recipe in *Chapter 9, Formatting with Paragraph and Character Styles*.

Updating the Table of Contents and setting additional options

Now that you have built a Table of Contents, you need to be able to update it as the content changes in your document with the addition of new content and removal of old content. In addition, you might want to use **More Options**, which is available within the **Table of Contents** panel, to do things such as include hidden content in your Table of Contents.

In this section, we will look at updating your Table of Contents to reflect changes within the content. In addition, we will use the options that appear when you select **More Options**, including sorting entries alphabetically rather than in order of appearance, including hidden text frames within the generated Table of Contents, and using a feature called **Run-in** to force items of the same level to follow on immediately after each other.

Getting ready

To complete this recipe, open InDesign on your system and create a new document with 12 pages, as shown in the *Creating a new document* recipe in *Chapter 1*. Having done this, create and style a Table of Contents as shown in the previous recipes, *Generating a Table of Contents* and *Formatting the Table of Contents*.

How to do it...

To update the Table of Contents and set **More Options**, follow these steps:

1. Having created our initial Table of Contents, we are going to start by adding a new chapter for *Ice Cream* and then updating the Table of Contents. Within your document, add new text frames to both pages on the next empty spread after your existing content. You can thread the frames together if you wish to do so.

> **Note**
> A **spread** is a collection of pages that are viewed as a single unit. For example, when working on magazine layouts, you will typically use facing page spreads, which display the left and right-hand pages side by side.

    Now fill the frames with placeholder text and, at the top of the left-hand page, we will add the words `Ice Cream` and style it with the **Header** paragraph style. We are then going to add some subheaders within the text frames – in my case, I will add `Vanilla`, `Coffee`, and `Coconut` and style these with the **SubHeader** paragraph style.

    Having done this, let's now update our Table of Contents by first clicking into the text frame that contains the Table of Contents and then, within the **Layout** menu, selecting **Update Table of Contents**. You should now see the new content appearing in the Table of Contents.

2. Having added a new section for **Ice Cream**, I now want to add a chapter for *Cheese*; however, on this occasion, I don't wish to have a text header on the page, as I would like to instead use an image as the header.

    Add a suitable image to the top of the next empty spread (add more pages to the end of the document if needed) – in my case, a photo of a selection of cheese. Then add some text frames to fill the rest of the spread and add placeholder text. Within the text frames, add some cheeses (`Stilton`, `Cheddar`, and `Wensleydale`), and format them with the **SubHeader** style. Finally, update the Table of Contents.

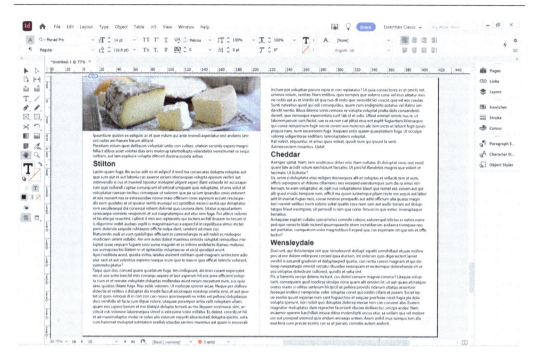

Figure: 10.8: Image used as a header for the chapter

Having added the content, click into the Table of Contents, and from the **Layout** menu, select **Update Table of Contents**. As you can see in *Figure 10.9*, because we don't have a header styled with the **Header** paragraph style at the top of the **Cheese** chapter, the subheaders for that chapter are automatically positioned within the Table of Contents as part of the **Ice Cream** section.

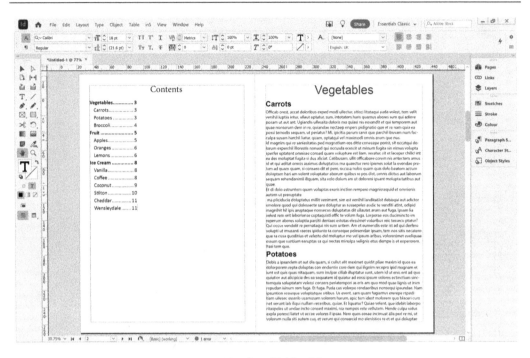

Figure 10.9: Updated Table of Contents

In order to get around this problem, we will create a new text frame containing the word Cheese, which is formatted with the **Header** paragraph style. Position this frame on top of the cheese image and, with the text frame selected, either right-click on the frame and select **Hide** or alternatively, in the **Layers** panel, hide the frame by clicking the small eye icon to the left of that layer.

Having added our hidden text frame containing the word Cheese, formatted in the **Header** style, go to the **Layout** menu and select **Table of Contents** to bring up the **Table of Contents** dialog. Here, check that the button on the right of the panel (marked *A* in *Figure 10.10*) says **Fewer Options**; if it says **More Options**, click on it once. Now, activate the checkbox for **Include Text on Hidden Layers** (marked *B* in *Figure 10.10*) before clicking on **OK**.

You should now see the Table of Contents showing the **Cheese** header with the relevant cheeses included under it (shown in *Figure 10.10*), despite the header being hidden on the page itself.

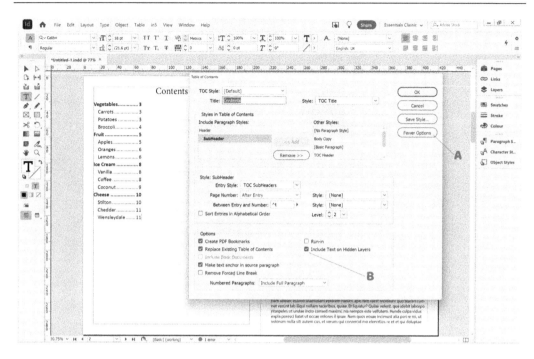

Figure 10.10: Table of Contents with hidden layers included

3. Having added our extra content, I would now like to arrange the **SubHeader** content within each chapter alphabetically in the Table of Contents, while still leaving the chapters themselves in their existing order. To do this, click into the Table of Contents with the **Type** tool; then, from the **Layout** menu, select **Table of Contents**. In the **Table of Contents** dialog box, select **SubHeader** (marked *A* in *Figure 10.11*) under the **Include Paragraph Styles** section and then tick **Sort Entries in Alphabetical Order** (marked *B* in *Figure 10.11*). This will ensure the **SubHeader** items are ordered alphabetically within their respective chapters.

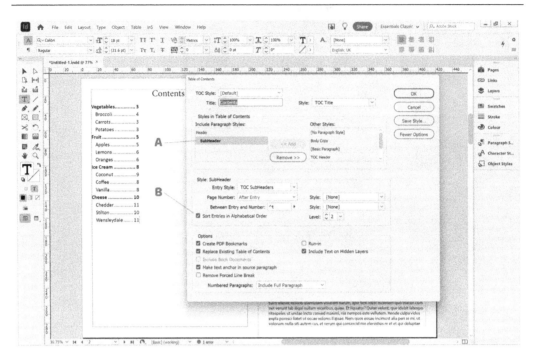

Figure 10.11: SubHeader items ordered alphabetically within the chapters

4. The next thing I would like to do is style page numbering for the chapter headers in cyan to make them stand out a bit. To do this, open the **Table of Contents** dialog from the **Layout** menu, as we have done previously.

    Within the **Table of Contents** dialog, select the **Header** style in the **Include Paragraph Styles** section (marked *A* in *Figure 10.12*). Then, within the **Style:Header** area of the dialog box, click the **Style** dropdown for **Page Number** (marked *B* in *Figure 10.12*) and choose **New Character Style**, which will open the **New Character Style** dialog box.

    In the **New Character Style** dialog box that has now appeared, give your style the name Page Numbers for TOC, and then under the **Color** section, select the **Cyan** color before clicking **OK** to save the changes and close the **New Character Style** dialog. Having done this, you can now also click **OK** on the **Table of Contents** dialog and you should then see your chapter page numbers turn cyan within your Table of Contents. If you need to further edit the style of the chapter page numbers, this can now be done by editing the character style via the **Character Styles** panel, as discussed in *Chapter 9, Formatting with Paragraph and Character Styles*.

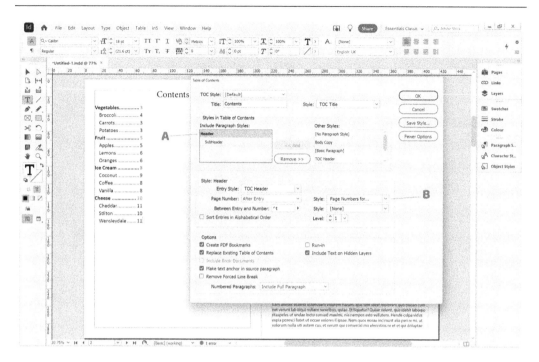

Figure 10.12: Applying a character style to the header page numbering

5.   Finally, there is one last change I would like to make to the Table of Contents. As I am adding more content, I am concerned it won't all fit into a single page, so I would like to use the **Run-in** feature to make consecutive items of the same level follow each other on the same line, rather than a new line for every item.

To do this, go to the **Table of Contents** dialog box and select the **Run-in** checkbox (marked A in *Figure 10.13*) and then click **OK**. You will now see the **SubHeader** items are all following immediately after each other, rather than each being on a new line.

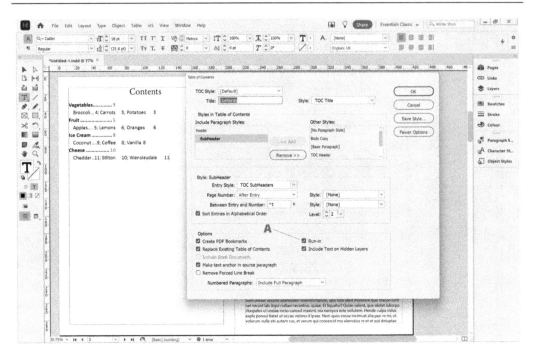

Figure 10.13: Using Run-in on the Table of Contents

As the leader is only applied to the first item, I will finish by disabling this feature as it would look a bit strange visually if we used it this way. To do this, edit the **Tabs** section in the **TOC SubHeaders** paragraph style and delete the leader before then saving the style.

Saving and loading Table of Contents styles

Creating a Table of Contents can take a while and you might not want to have to go through the whole process again every time. By saving a reusable **Table of Contents style**, you can speed up the process allowing you to import the Table of Contents style into new documents along with all the associated paragraph styles.

In this recipe, we will look at how to create a Table of Contents style from an existing Table of Contents, edit the Table of Contents style, and load it back into a new document.

Getting ready

To complete this recipe, open InDesign on your system and create a new document with 12 pages, as shown in the *Creating a new document* recipe in *Chapter 1*. Having done this, create and style a Table of Contents as shown in the previous recipes, *Generating a Table of Contents* and *Formatting the Table of Contents*.

How to do it...

To save, edit, and load Table of Contents styles, just follow these steps:

1. Having created our initial Table of Contents, we now want to save this as a **Table of Contents** style. To do this put the cursor into the Table of Contents, then from the **Layout** menu, select **Table of Contents**. On the right-hand side of the **Table of Contents** dialog box, you will see a button for **Save Style**; select this, and in the **Save Style** dialog box, enter a name for your new Table of Contents style before clicking **OK**. I will call mine `Andys TOC`.

2. Having created a new Table of Contents style, I would now like to make a change to it, as I notice I left the **Run-in** feature enabled. To do this, click on the InDesign **Layout** menu and select **Table of Contents Styles**. This will bring up the **Table of Contents Styles** dialog box (shown in *Figure 10.14*). Here, click the **Edit...** button (marked *A* in *Figure 10.14*), which will load the **Table of Contents** dialog box where we can disable the **Run-in** feature. Then, click **OK** on the **Table of Contents** dialog box and then click **OK** on the **Table of Contents Styles** dialog box.

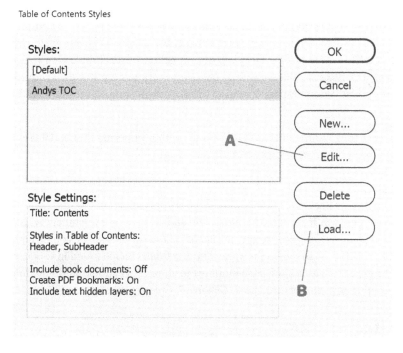

Figure 10.14: Table of Contents Styles dialog box

3. Having created a Table of Contents style, I would now like to reuse this in another document. Save the current document to your desktop and close it before starting a new document. In the new document, go to the **Layout** menu and then select **Table of Contents Styles** to bring up the **Table of Contents Styles** dialog box. Click the **Load…** button (marked *B* in *Figure 10.14*) and select the previous document containing the Table of Contents style and click **Open**. Having now loaded the previous Table of Contents style into the **Table of Contents Style** dialog box, click **OK**. If you look in the **Paragraph Styles** panel, you will notice the various styles used to create the previous Table of Contents have all been loaded here.

4. To create a Table of Contents in your new document, simply style up some content with the relevant **Header** and **SubHeader** styles, and then in the **Layout** menu, select **Table of Contents** to open the **Table of Contents** dialog box. Here, select your style from the **TOC Style** dropdown at the top, and then click **OK** before clicking on to the page to create your Table of Contents.

Creating automated story jumps

In some types of documents, such as magazines or newspapers, you might have a story that jumps to another page later in the document. In order to make it easy for the reader to continue, they will often have a bit of text under a frame saying `Continued on page x`. The problem with manually adding directions for these **story jumps** is they can quickly get out of synchronization with the content. For example, the instructions say `Continued on Page 23` but the story has moved to page 25 because somebody added a double-page spread to the document somewhere between the two parts of the story.

In this recipe, we will look at how to create story jumps with numbering that updates automatically when the different parts of the story move to a different page.

Getting ready

To complete this recipe, open InDesign on your system and create a new document with 12 pages, as shown in the *Creating a new document* recipe in *Chapter 1*. You should also be comfortable threading text frames to create stories, as shown in the *Threading text frames* recipe found in *Chapter 2, Working with Text in InDesign*, as well as adding page numbers to all pages as shown in the *Adding content to a parent page including page numbers* recipe in *Chapter 7, Creating and Applying Parent Pages*.

How to do it...

To create automated story jumps, just follow these steps:

1. Start by creating our first text frame on the second page and then threading it into a new text frame on page 5. If you want to make sure it's properly threaded, simply go to the **View** menu and, under **Extras**, select **Show Text Threads**. If the option says **Hide Text Threads**, that means they are already showing. To see the text threads, simply click either of the frames in the story with the **Selection** tool.

I am also going to add some page numbers to the bottom corner of all the pages by including the current page number marker on the A-Parent pages. This step isn't required for the story jumps or numbering to work, but it is useful to see what page you are currently on when checking whether the markers are updating correctly.

Note

Text threads are hidden if you are in **Preview** mode, as are many other visual indicators such as guides and margins, so make sure you are working in **Normal** mode, which is generally good practice. This is covered in more detail in the *Changing the screen mode* recipe in *Chapter 1*.

---

2. Having created our story, create a new text frame just below the first text frame in the story. In this frame, type the words `Continued on page` with a space at the word `page` for the page number to be placed in, and leave the cursor just after the space. Now, from the **Type** menu, go down to **Insert Special Characters** and, under **Markers**, select **Next Page Number**. Finally, reposition this text frame so its top edge is touching the bottom edge of the first text frame in the story (marked *A* in *Figure 10.15*). You will notice when you do this that the page number changes from the number of the current page to the number of the page where the story is continued.

You can change the styling for these story jump directions however you wish; in my case, I have simply made the text bold.

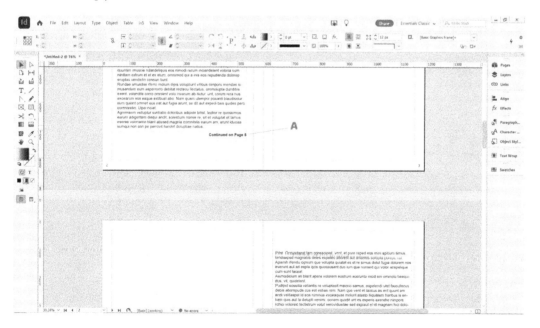

Figure 10.15: Using the Next Page Marker with story jumps

3. Having used a marker to identify the next page for the story, let's now do the same for the previous page. Create a new text frame above the second frame in the story and enter the text Continued from Page with a space at the end, and leave the cursor just after the space. Now, from the **Type** menu, go down to **Insert Special Characters** and, under **Markers**, select **Previous Page Number**. Having done this, move the text frame so the bottom of this new text frame touches the top of the second frame in the story (marked *B* in *Figure 10.16*). You will notice the numbering updates to reflect the location of the previous frame in the story as soon as the frames touch.

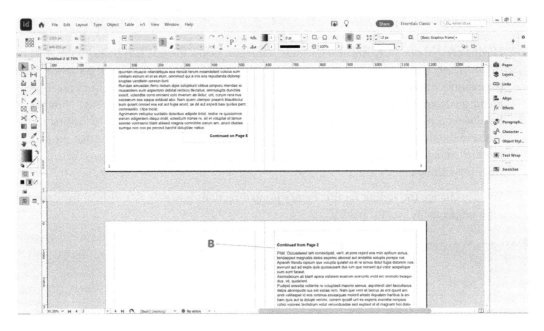

Figure 10.16: Using the Previous Page Marker with story jumps

4. Having set up our story jumps, let's now test them by adding 4 new pages after page 3 from the **Insert Pages** option in the **Pages** panel menu. You should find the Continued on page number has gone from Page 5 to Page 9 automatically. Similarly, if you move the first frame and its corresponding box from Page 2 onto Page 3, you should find the story jump on page 9 will automatically update to reflect this change.

> **Note**
>
> It's worth noting that if the directional frames stop touching the story frames, the numbering will no longer be picked up from the story, and they will revert to merely showing the number of whatever page the box is currently located on.

11
Creating Interactivity and PDF Forms

When it comes to interactivity in InDesign, the choice of which features you can use will be dictated by the choice of output format rather than by InDesign itself.

For example, **interactive PDFs** support basic interactive features such as hyperlinks, bookmarks, and buttons, but they are less reliable when it comes to things such as video or audio, due to differing support in different PDF readers. Alternatively, InDesign's built-in Publish Online capability supports not only all these features but also animation and embedded web content, allowing you to quickly share documents as a link that people can easily view in a web browser.

One of my personal favorites is the **In5 plugin** from Ajar Productions. The In5 plugin gives you support for all of the features mentioned earlier along with more advanced features such as image sequences, flip cards, scrollable text frames, and even responsive design capabilities – all from within InDesign. In5 exports your content as web-compatible HTML5, CSS3, and JavaScript, which can then be viewed in all major browsers and hosted anywhere you like.

In addition to its interactive capabilities, InDesign lets you create complex PDF forms, containing checkboxes, combo boxes, list boxes, radio buttons, signature fields, and text fields. These can then be handed off to third parties for completion, digital signing, and return.

In this chapter, we will focus on the core interactive functionality of InDesign, without using any features that are specific to third-party plugins such as In5. Additionally, we will look at the extensive capabilities of PDF forms. If you wish to look into more advanced interactive functionality, including how to use third-party plugins for InDesign, visit the *Further reading* section at the end of this chapter.

In this chapter, we will cover the following recipes:

- Creating and using hyperlinks
- Including bookmarks

- Showing and hiding items with buttons

- Enhancing navigation with buttons

- Including videos in your document

- Applying page transitions

- Creating PDF forms

Technical requirements

To complete this chapter, you will need a PC or Mac computer with a copy of Adobe InDesign installed. You should be comfortable with adding content to your documents and formatting it, as shown in *Chapters 1* to *5*.

Creating and using hyperlinks

Hyperlinks are a useful tool for making your documents more interactive, allowing you to link to content either within the page or externally, create (but not send) a new email, or jump straight through to a particular page in the document.

In this recipe, we will look at how to use hyperlinks to link to an external website, trigger a new email, and enhance your document navigation, looking at the appearance settings and even using character styles to standardize the look and feel of your links.

Getting ready

In order to complete this recipe, simply open InDesign on your system and create a new document with 12 pages, as shown in the *Creating a new document* recipe of *Chapter 1*.

How to do it...

To create hyperlinks, just follow these steps:

1. Go to the last page of your document and create a text frame at the bottom of the page, then enter the name of the website you want to link to. This doesn't have to be the website URL itself – it could just be a piece of text such as a company name. In my case, I have typed in `Visit our website at www.highlander.co.uk`.

   From the **Window** menu, go down to the **Interactive** submenu, and then select **Hyperlinks** to open the **Hyperlinks panel**.

Select the text we created a moment ago using the **Type** tool. Then, within the **Hyperlinks** panel we just opened, click on the **Hyperlinks** panel menu. The first two options in the panel menu are as follows:

- **New Hyperlink**: This lets you create a new hyperlink and choose all the settings for the hyperlink.

- **New Hyperlink From URL**: If the text you created is a URL, this option can be used to automatically create a new hyperlink from the URL

> **Note**
>
> When creating **New Hyperlink From URL**, ensure the `https://` protocol is included within the selected text. If this is not included, InDesign will automatically insert the protocol as `http://` instead of `https://`, which might result in the page not loading properly. Adobe may update this at some point, but at the time of writing, hasn't done so yet.

Here, we will select the **New Hyperlink** option that brings up the **New Hyperlink dialog box**, as shown in *Figure 11.1*. This can also be done by clicking on the **New Hyperlink** icon (marked as *A* in *Figure 11.1*) at the bottom of the **Hyperlinks** panel:

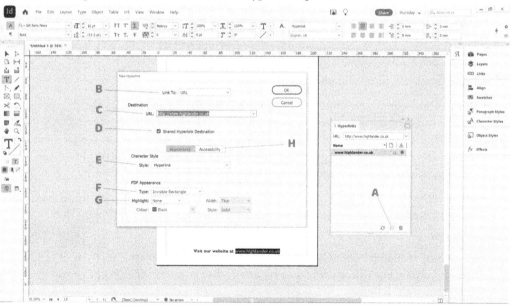

Figure 11.1: The New Hyperlink dialog box in InDesign

2. At the top of the **New Hyperlink** dialog box, you will see a **Link To** drop-down menu (*B* in *Figure 11.1*) that lets you choose the type of hyperlink you wish to create. The following options are available:

    *   **URL**: This is used to create links that open web pages when clicked on. We will select this option.

    *   **File**: This creates the links to a file. If using this, you should bear in mind that the person clicking on the link will need access to the drive where the file is saved for the link to work.

    *   **Email**: This is used to create links that will open the new mail dialog box and fill out the address and subject line via the user's default email software when they click on the link.

    *   **Page**: You can use this option to link to a specific page in either this or another document. If the page is in another document, the person clicking on the link will need access to that document for the link to work.

    *   **Text Anchor**: You can use this to create a link to a text anchor within your document. We will look at creating and linking to a text anchor later in this recipe.

    *   **Shared Destination**: When creating links, you can tick a box to save them as a **Shared Destination**. This means if you wish to link to the same place again, later in the document, you will be able to select the link from this Shared Destination drop-down to reuse it.

    The options shown in the **Destination** section depend upon which **Link To** type you chose. In our case, we have chosen **URL** from the **Link To** drop-down menu. As a result, under the **Destination** section, we will now see the following options:

    *   **URL** (*C* in *Figure 11.1*): This is where you enter the full domain name of the page you wish to link to. InDesign will try to populate the URL field by default and, when doing so, may enter the `http://` prefix as it has here. While a prefix is needed, most modern sites use `https://` instead of `http://`, so with this in mind, I will change this to `https://www.highlander.co.uk`.

    *   **Shared Destination** (*D* in *Figure 11.1*): You can check this option if you wish to make the link a shared destination that can be used again quickly and easily within the document. I will leave this ticked.

    The options available in the **Character Style** and **PDF Appearance** sections of the **New Hyperlink** dialog box will remain the same irrespective of which **Link To** option you choose. The options are as follows:

    *   **Character Style** (*E* in *Figure 11.1*): This allows you to select a **Character Style** option to control the visual appearance of your hyperlink. By default, it creates a new style called **Hyperlink**, and we will leave this option as it has been set.

    *   Under the **PDF Appearance** area, there are a number of settings including the following; however, bear in mind these might not be supported by all PDF readers:

- **Type** (*F* in *Figure 11.1*): This lets you control whether the link will appear as a visible rectangle or an invisible rectangle within a PDF document. We will set this to **Invisible Rectangle**.

- **Highlight** (*G* in *Figure 11.1*): This controls the appearance of the hyperlink when it is being clicked on in the PDF and can be set to **None**, **Invert**, **Outline**, or **Inset**. We will select **None**.

- The options for **Color**, **Width**, and **Style** control the styling of the **Visible Rectangle** option when this is selected as the **Type**. However, as we chose **Invisible Rectangle** here, they are disabled.

- Finally, if you click on the tab labeled **Accessibility** (*H* in *Figure 11.1*), this will bring up the **Alt Text** field, where you can enter a description that will be used as **Alt text** by accessibility devices such as screen readers.

> **Note**
>
> **Alt text** is an abbreviation of *Alternative text*, and is used by accessibility devices such as screen readers that are widely used by those with visual impairments.

Now we have finished configuring our hyperlink and can click on **OK**, at which point our new hyperlink will be created. Having created a hyperlink from some text, next, we are going to turn an image into a hyperlink.

3. Place an image onto the page; in my case, I will place my logo in the middle of the page. The image frame should still be selected, but if not, select it using the selection tool. In the **Hyperlinks** panel, choose the **New Hyperlink** option to bring up the **New Hyperlink** dialog box again.

This time, we will select **Shared Destination** (marked as *A* in *Figure 11.2*), since we are going to link to the same URL that we linked to previously in *step 2*. When we created the URL link in *step 2*, we checked the box to save the destination as **Shared Destination**. This means that upon selecting **Shared Destination** here, you should immediately see the **Destination** section of the dialog box change to display two new drop-down fields. These are as follows:

- **Document** (*B* in *Figure 11.2*): Here, you can pick the name of the document containing the shared destination, which defaults to the current document. If you have additional InDesign documents open, they will be available on this list; however, in our case, we don't, and the current document is exactly what we want.

- **Name** (*C* in *Figure 11.2*): This is where you pick the name of the shared destination, and we should see the shared destination that we previously created in *step 2* listed here. Select this from the drop-down menu:

Figure 11.2: Reusing a shared destination in the Hyperlinks panel

Here, the remaining settings are the same as they were in *step 2*, and we don't need to change them. So, we will simply click on **OK** to finish creating the hyperlink. You will notice that the image frame now has a thicker blue dashed line around it.

> **Note**
>
> You might be wondering about the fact that the **Character Style** setting is still set to **Hyperlink**. As we are creating the link on an image object, this setting will just be ignored and have no impact.

Having turned the logo into a hyperlink, I have decided it would be nice to give users the option to also email me directly from this page, so we will look at that next.

4. Where we added the hyperlink to the text in *step 2*, now let's add an extra line below this that provides email contact details. In my case, this will say, `or email us at info@ highlander.co.uk`. If the last thing on your previous line was the hyperlink, you might find the new line has been automatically formatted with the **Hyperlink Character Style** setting; if so, just manually remove this via the **Character Styles** panel by applying the **None Character Style** setting, as shown in the *Creating and Applying Character Styles* recipe of *Chapter 9*:

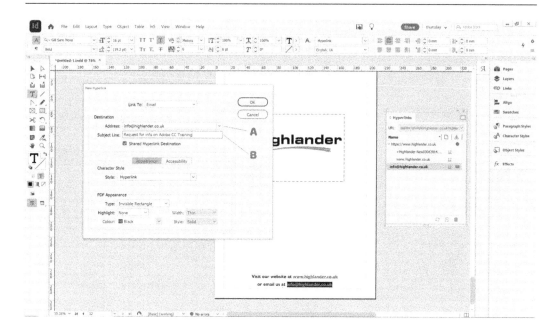

Figure 11.3: Creating an email hyperlink in InDesign

Next, select the email address in your text, and from the **Hyperlinks** panel menu, select **New Hyperlink**. This time, we will choose **Email** as the **Link To** option, and you should immediately see that the **Destination** section of the dialog box changes to display two new drop-down fields. These are as follows:

- **Address** (*A* in *Figure 11.3*): Here, you can enter the email address you would like to include in the new email's **To** field. In my case, I will enter `info@highlander.co.uk`.

- **Subject Line** (*B* in *Figure 11.3*): Here, you can enter a subject line you would like to appear in the new email's "**Subject**" field. I will set the subject line to `Request info on Adobe CC Training`.

Once again, the rest of the fields in this dialog box will remain the same as they were in *step 2*. In our case, we will just check that the **Character Style** setting is still set to **Hyperlink**. If not, set it to **Hyperlink** using the **Style** drop-down box. Other than that we won't change anything else here – click on **OK** to finish creating the email hyperlink.

Having now linked some text to a website, used a shared destination to link an image to the same website, and then created an email hyperlink, we will look at how to create a link to a specific page within the document.

5. Go to **Page 2** in the document, add a new text frame to the page, and type the following text into it: `Full contact details can be found on the back cover`. Then, select the words `on the back cover`, and from the **Hyperlink** panel menu, select **New Hyperlink**:

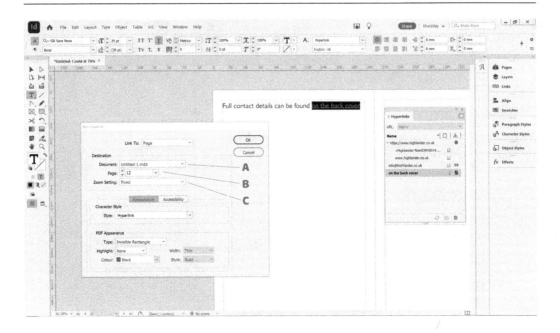

Figure 11.4: Linking to a page within the document

In the **New Hyperlink** drop-down box, set the **Link To** drop-down option to **Page**. You will see three drop-down boxes appear in the **Destination** section, as follows:

- **Document** (*A* in *Figure 11.4*): Here, you can choose which document you are linking to. We will leave this set to the current document.

- **Page** (*B* in *Figure 11.4*): Here, you can select the page number you want to link to. We will select page **12**.

- **Zoom Setting** (*C* in *Figure 11.4*): This controls the zoom appearance of the destination page when you click on the link to go to it. We will set this to **Inherit Zoom**, which means the zoom percentage will remain the same after you click on the link, just as it was prior to clicking on it.

Once again, the rest of the fields in this dialog box will remain the same as they were in *step 2*. In our case, we will just check that the **Character Style** option is still set to **Hyperlink**, and if not, set it to **Hyperlink** from the **Style** drop-down menu. Other than that, we won't change anything else. Click on **OK** to finish creating the page hyperlink.

The final hyperlink we are going to add is a link to an anchor within some text. This is a two-part process where, first, we set the anchor, and second, we create the link to it.

6. Go to **Page 6**, add a large text frame that fills the page, and then insert placeholder text into it. Roughly halfway down the page, I am going to add the word Apples onto a new line as a subheading. Following this, select the word Apples, and in the **Hyperlinks** panel menu, select the **New Hyperlink Destination** option.

This will bring up the **New Hyperlink Destination dialog box**. We will set the **Type** (*A* in *Figure 11.5*) option to **Text Anchor** and the **Name** (*B* in *Figure 11.5*) option should already say `Apples`:

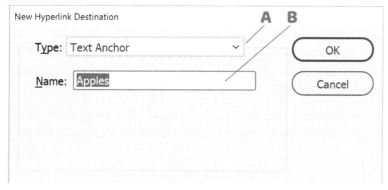

Figure 11.5: The New Hyperlink Destination dialog box

Having created the destination, now we want to create the link to it. Go to **Page 3** of the document, add a small text frame, and enter the following text: `Find out more about Apples`. Now, select the word `Apples`, and from the **Hyperlink** panel menu, select **New Hyperlink**.

In the **New Hyperlink** dialog box, set the **Link To** (*A* in *Figure 11. 6*) setting as **Text Anchor**, and make sure the **Document** (*B* in *Figure 11.6*) setting is set to the current document. Then, check that **Text Anchor** (*C* in *Figure 11. 6*) is pointing to **Apples**; if not, click on the drop-down menu and choose **Apples** from it:

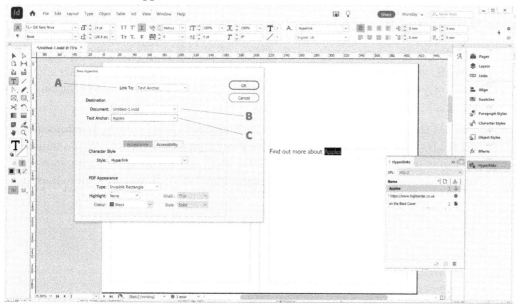

Figure 11.6: Linking to a text anchor

Having created a variety of different hyperlinks, you can now export the document in a wide range of formats that support hyperlinks, including interactive PDFs. If you would like help doing this, please refer to *Chapter 13, Preflighting and Output*.

Including bookmarks

Bookmarks are a handy navigation tool when they are added to PDF documents, but they can be especially beneficial for those with accessibility issues, making it easier for these users to navigate your document quickly and efficiently.

While InDesign's table of contents can automatically generate **Bookmarks**, as we saw in *Chapter 10*, sometimes, you might want to manually generate bookmarks without relying on the table of contents option to do so.

In this recipe, we will look at how to manually create **Bookmarks** within your documents, allowing you to select items within the content and have them show up in the **PDF Bookmarks** panel. Additionally, we will look at how to rename your bookmarks, sort them, organize them in the order they appear, and nest them into logical groups.

Getting ready

In order to complete this recipe, simply open InDesign on your system and create a new document with 12 pages, as shown in the *Creating a new document* recipe of *Chapter 1*.

How to do it...

In order to create bookmarks, just follow these steps:

1. In your document, start by adding some text frames to pages 3 through 6 and filling them with placeholder text. On page 3, we will include the word `Fruit`, on page 4 the word `Oranges`, `Lemons` on page 5, and `Apples` on page 6. I have also styled these words to be bold, but only so we can see them easily in among all the text.

2. Having added our content, now we will open the **Bookmarks** panel from the **Windows** menu under the **Interactive** section. Select the word `Fruit` on page 3. Then, in the **Bookmarks** panel menu, select **New Bookmark** (*A* in *Figure 11.7*). Repeat this process with the words `Oranges`, `Lemons`, and `Apples`, creating separate bookmarks from each of the four words:

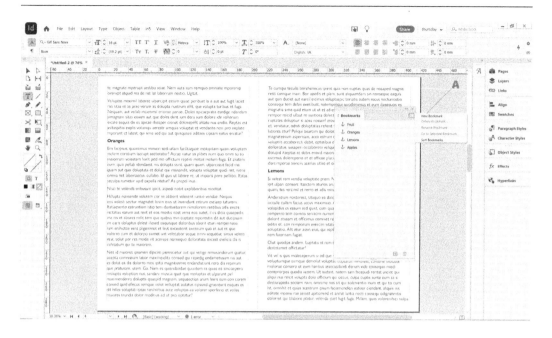

Figure 11.7: The Bookmarks panel menu

3. Having created the bookmarks, I have decided I would like the bookmark called `Fruit` to actually say `Fresh Fruit` when it shows up in the **PDF Bookmarks** panel in Acrobat. With this in mind, I will select the bookmark in the **Bookmarks** panel, and from the panel menu, select **Rename Bookmark**. This will bring up a small box where I can add a new name. It's worth noting that while this changes the name of the bookmark that shows up in the **PDF Bookmarks** panel in Acrobat, it does not change the actual text on the page, which still just says `Fruit`.

4. Having added my four items to the bookmarks, I would like to put them into a more logical order. As *Oranges*, *Lemons*, and *Apples* are all *Fresh Fruit*, I am going to nest them under **Fresh Fruit** within the **Bookmarks** panel. To do this, within the **Bookmarks panel**, individually drag **Oranges**, **Lemons**, and **Apples** onto **Fresh Fruit** within the panel; you will see a small arrow appear to the left of the words **Fresh Fruit** within the panel as they become nested within it. Clicking on this arrow will expand the **Fresh Fruit** category so that you can see the items within it:

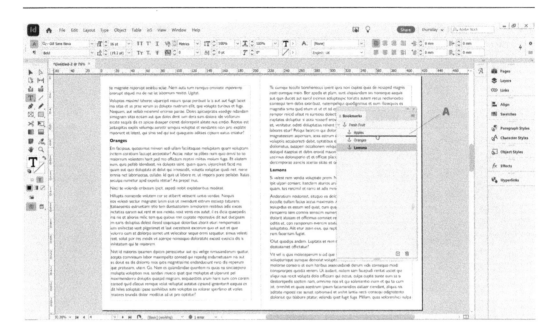

Figure 11.8: Nested items being sorted alphabetically in the Bookmarks panel

5. Having nested the three individual fruits under the **Fresh Fruit** bookmark, now I am going to sort them alphabetically. To do this, simply click on the **Apples** bookmark within the panel and drag it upward so that it is above **Oranges**. Do the same with **Lemons** so that it is also above **Oranges** and below **Apples**. You can tell where you are moving the bookmarks to because a line appears (marked *A* in *Figure 11.8*) as a visual indicator to show you where the bookmark will now be located when you release the mouse button.

6. Having just put the bookmarks into alphabetical order, I have had second thoughts about this – with hindsight, I feel it might be better if the order of the bookmarks matches the order those items appear in the book. With this in mind, I am going to reset all the bookmarks back to the logical order they appear within the document. To do this, click on the **Bookmarks** panel menu and select **Sort Bookmarks**, which will sort all the bookmarks in the order they appear within the document.

Showing and hiding items with buttons

When it comes to creating interactive features in your digital documents, **buttons** are a useful tool, and they are well-supported across a range of different InDesign export formats, including interactive PDFs.

In this recipe, we are going to use buttons to show and hide different images based on which button is being clicked. This is done using the **Show/Hide Buttons and Forms** action, which is just one of many features available within the InDesign **Buttons and Forms panel**.

Getting ready

In order to complete this recipe, simply open InDesign on your system and create a new document with 12 pages, as shown in the *Creating a new document* recipe of *Chapter 1*. You will also need three sample images to use – ideally, all of the same orientation.

How to do it...

In order to show and hide items using buttons, just follow these steps:

1. In your document, create three identically sized rectangle frames side by side, and place a different image in each frame. Next, select the three frames, and while holding the *Alt* (PC)/ *Option* (Mac) key down, click and drag them further down the page using the **Selection** tool, to duplicate all three frames and their contents.

    Having done this, resize the second set of frames to make them smaller and position them centrally beneath the middle frame, as shown in *Figure 11.9*:

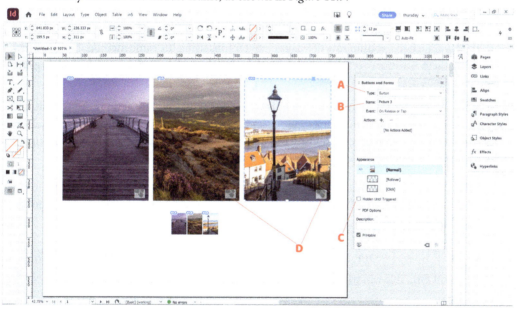

Figure 11.9: The Buttons and Forms panel

2. Go to the **Window** menu. Then, under **Interactive**, select **Buttons and Forms** to open the **Buttons and Forms** panel.

    Select the left-hand frame on the top row. With this frame selected, in the **Buttons and Forms** panel, select **Button** from the **Type** drop-down menu (marked as *A* in *Figure 11.9*). Then, in the **Name** field (marked as *B* in *Figure 11.9*), give the button a name that will allow you to easily identify it later – in my case, `Picture 1`. Since I would also like this button to be hidden until it has been specifically triggered by an action, I will check the **Hidden Until Triggered** checkbox (marked as *C* in *Figure 11.9*). At this stage, I won't change any other settings in the **Buttons and Forms** panel for this button.

Next, I will select the middle frame on the top row and make it a button called `Picture 2`, again checking the **Hidden Until Triggered** checkbox. Then, I will select the right-hand frame on the top row and make it a button called `Picture 3`. However, this time, I will leave the **Hidden Until Triggered** checkbox unchecked, as I want this image to show immediately upon the page loading.

Having turned the top row of images into buttons, I will select all three of them and align the horizontal centers so that they are positioned immediately on top of each other.

> **Note**
>
> When items are turned into buttons, they have a small watermark on them (marked as *D* in *Figure 11.9*). With smaller items, such as the bottom row of images in *Figure 11.9*, you might need to zoom in to see them.

Next, I will turn the bottom row of images into buttons using the same method, but this time, naming them `Button 1`, `Button 2`, and `Button 3`, respectively, and not changing any other options at this stage.

3. Having created all our buttons, we are now ready to start setting the actions on the buttons. First, select the button named `Button 1`, and from the **Buttons and Forms** panel, click on the drop-down option called **Event** (marked as *A* in *Figure 11.10*). Events are used to trigger a corresponding action, and you can choose from the following events:

    *   **On Release or Tap**: This will trigger when the mouse button has been released or when a touch screen has been tapped. This is a commonly used event and the one that we will choose.

    *   **On Click**: This will trigger when the mouse button has been clicked.

    *   **On Roll Over**: This will trigger as soon as the mouse pointer moves over the button.

    *   **On Roll Off**: This will trigger when the mouse pointer moves off the button.

    *   **On Focus (PDF)**: This triggers when the button has been selected, for example, by a user pressing the *Tab* key to move onto the button.

    *   **On Blur (PDF)**: This is the opposite of **On Focus (PDF)**, triggering when the user deselects the button; for example, by hitting the *Tab* key to jump to the next button.

> **Note**
>
> You can apply multiple events to a single button if you wish. For example, you might want one object to appear when you hover the mouse over another object and then disappear when you move the mouse off it. This can be achieved by applying both the **On Roll Over** and **On Roll Off** events to the object you are planning to move the mouse over. To do this, use the **Show/Hide Buttons and Forms** action to show the second object when you roll the mouse over the first object, and then hide the second object when you move the mouse off the first object.

Having selected the **On Release or Tap** event to trigger an action, now we need to control what actually happens by setting the properties of our action. To do this, click on the + symbol (marked as *B* in *Figure 11.10*) next to the **Actions** label, and a long list of potential actions will appear, as follows:

- **Go to Destination**: This action jumps to a text anchor within your document.

- **Go to First Page**: This action jumps to the first page of the document.

- **Go to Last Page**: This action jumps to the last page of the document.

- **Go to Next Page**: This action jumps to the next page of the document.

- **Go to Previous Page**: This action jumps to the previous page of the document.

- **Go to URL**: This action jumps to a web URL.

- **Show/Hide Buttons and Forms**: This action lets you show and hide other buttons on the page. We will select this action.

Additionally, there are a number of actions that will not work in an interactive PDF but are supported in Publish Online, EPUBs, and via InDesign add-ons such as In5. These include the following:

- **Animation**: This action lets you control animations that have been added

- **Go to Page**: This action jumps to a specific page

- **Go to State**: This action jumps to a specific object state when using multi-state objects

- **Go to Next State**: This action jumps to the next object state when using multi-state objects

- **Go to Previous State**: This action jumps to the previous object state when using multi-state objects

- **Sound**: This action lets you control sound with the **play**, **stop**, **pause**, or **resume** options

- **Video**: This action lets you control sound with the **play**, **stop**, **pause**, **resume**, or **play from navigation point** options

Finally, there are some actions that will only work in interactive PDFs, such as the following:

- **Clear Form**: This action will clear all data from the PDF form fields that have been completed.

- **Go to Next View**: This action works in conjunction with the previous view action, allowing a user who has clicked to see the previous view to then subsequently jump back to where they were, prior to having clicked on **Go to Previous View**.

- **Go to Previous View**: This action goes to the last viewed page/zoom.

- **Open File**: This action opens a named file.

- **Print Form**: This action will print a form.

- **Submit Form**: This action allows users to email a form to you. To use this action, enter your email address preceded by the `mailto:` prefix. For example, `mailto:info@highlander.co.uk` will send the form as an email attachment to the email address *info@highlander.co.uk*.

- **View Zoom**: This action will resize the display of the page to the zoom setting you have set:

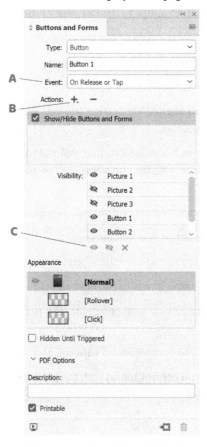

Figure 11.10: The Buttons and Forms panel with Show/Hide Buttons and Forms selected

Having selected **Show/Hide Buttons and Forms**, you will see a new section called **Visibility** appear in which you can see the various buttons that we created earlier listed (you might have to scroll up and down to see them all).

Each item in the visibility list will have one of three icons next to it; examples of each icon are shown immediately below the list (marked as *C* in *Figure 11.10*). To change the state of the individual list items, simply click on the visibility icon next to them and set them to one of the three icons. These icons are as follows:

- **Show**: Triggering this action will make the buttons visible

- **Hide**: Triggering this action will make the buttons invisible

- **Ignore**: Triggering this action will leave the buttons in whatever state they are already in

In our case, we are going to set `Picture 1`, `Button 1`, `Button 2`, and `Button 3` to **Show**, and set `Picture 2` and `Picture 3` to **Hide**.

4. Having set the **Event** trigger, along with the **Action** and **Visibility** settings related to `Button 1`, we will now do the same for `Button 2` and `Button 3`, as follows.

    For `Button 2`, set **Event** and **Action** to be the same as `Button 1`, but set `Picture 2`, `Button 1`, `Button 2`, and `Button 3` to **Show** and `Picture 1` and `Picture 3` to **Hide**.

    For `Button 3`, set **Event** and **Action** to be the same as `Button 1`, but set `Picture 3`, `Button 1`, `Button 2`, and `Button 3` to **Show** and `Picture 1` and `Picture 2` to **Hide**.

5. Now we are ready to export our interactive PDF, which can be done from the **File** menu under **Export**, by setting the export type as **Interactive PDF**. If you have not previously exported an interactive PDF and wish to cover the settings in more detail, please refer to *Chapter 13*.

> **Note**
>
> If the buttons are not triggering properly when the PDF is being tested, usually the main reason is that either the document has not been output correctly as an interactive PDF or the actions are not set to show and hide the correct items on each button. The latter is something quite commonly encountered.

Enhancing navigation with buttons

Buttons are a great way to enhance navigation within a document, allowing you to jump to specific pages, go forward or backward to the next or previous pages, and even jump to a particular anchor within a page.

In this recipe, we are going to add buttons to the parent pages, which will allow you to jump to the next or previous page from any page of the document. Additionally, we will look at how to customize the styling of these buttons, so they change when you hover over them with the mouse.

Getting ready

In order to complete this recipe, simply open InDesign on your system and create a new document with 12 pages, as shown in the *Creating a new document* recipe of *Chapter 1*. In this instance, we will disable **Facing Pages** and create the page using the **Landscape** orientation. A basic understanding of **Parent Pages** is also useful, as covered in *Chapter 7*.

How to do it...

In order to enhance your navigation with buttons, just follow these steps:

1. In your document, go to **A-Parent** by double-clicking on it from the **Pages** panel. **A-Parent** should be applied to all your pages by default, but if not, apply it to them all now.

    As your pages are all blank, let's start by adding a large page number to the middle of each page. This will allow us to easily see whether the navigation buttons are working when we test them. To do this, create a large text frame in the middle of the A-Parent, and with the cursor ready in the text frame, click on the **Type** menu. Then, near the bottom of the frame, choose **Insert Special Characters**, and under the **Markers** section, choose **Current Page Number**. This should show a large letter *A* as we are on the **A-Parent** setting, and I will format this to a larger font size.

    Having added a large page number to identify each page, we will add some navigation buttons next.

> **Note**
> Like many other features, the **Insert Special Characters** options can also be accessed by right-clicking with the mouse when the cursor is active within a text frame.

2. In the lower-right of the **A-Parent** page, we will add a **Text Frame** box and enter the words `Next Page` into it. In terms of formatting the text, I will set mine to the following:

    *   **Font Face: Impact**
    *   **Font Size: 16pt**
    *   **Text Fill Color: Transparent**
    *   **Text Stroke Color: Black**

    If you wish to style yours to look differently, feel free to do so.

    Next, select the text frame with the **Selection Tool** option and open the **Buttons and Forms** panel. In the **Buttons and Forms** panel, set the following:

    *   **Type** (marked as *A* in *Figure 11.11*): Set this to **Button**.
    *   **Name** (marked as *B* in *Figure 11.11*): Enter this as `Next Button`.
    *   **Event** (marked as *C* in *Figure 11.11*): Select **On Release or Tap**.

Following this, click on the + icon (marked as *D* in *Figure 11.11*) next to **Actions**, and select the **Go To Next Page** option.

Finally, from the **Zoom** option (marked as *E* in *Figure 11.11*), I will choose **Fit in Window**. This ensures that if a user is zoomed in when they click on the next page button, the next page will load to fit the window rather than zoom in like the page they were on.

Now we have created our interactive button, and this will work if exported to a format that supports buttons, such as an interactive PDF. However, while we are in the **Buttons and Forms** panel with the button still selected, I would like to adjust the formatting of the button's appearance when it is in a different state:

Figure 11.11: Creating the Next Page navigation button on a parent page

3. By default, we have been editing the **appearance** for the **Normal state**, which is how the button looks by default on the page. But now we are going to create and edit a **Rollover state**, which controls how the button will look when the user moves the mouse cursor over it. To do this, click on the **Rollover** option (marked as *F* in *Figure 11.11*), and you will see that the button thumbnail next to the word **Rollover** changes to look like the thumbnail next to the word **Normal** immediately above it.

Now we are in the rollover state, and any edits we make to the button will specifically affect that state. I am going to switch to the **Type** tool, select the text, change the **Fill** color of the text to black, and set the stroke color of the text to transparent.

Then, I will switch back to the **Selection** tool again, select the button with it, and click on the **Click** state (marked as *G* in *Figure 11.11*). Now I can edit the click state by switching to the **Type** tool, selecting the text, and changing the fill color of the text to blue.

Now we have a button that will, by default, have a black stroke line around it. When hovering over it with the mouse cursor, it will then turn to solid black, and when clicked on, it will briefly turn blue.

> **Note**
>
> It is worth noting that while we have made some simple edits to the color of the text to demonstrate appearance states, it is possible to do more complex edits using tools such as the **Effects** panel. You can even have different text showing for each state if you wish.

4. Having created a **Next Page** button, we now need a **Previous Page** button; otherwise, users will only be able to navigate in one direction. To do this, go to the **Selection** tool, and while holding down the *Alt* (PC)/*Option* (Mac) key, click on the **Next Page** button and drag it to the left-hand side. By doing this, we have not only duplicated the button but all of its properties such as the actions and appearance states. This saves us quite a bit of time, as now there is no need to recreate and restyle the entire button from scratch.

    Select this new button with the **Selection** tool and change the name field within the **Buttons and Forms** panel to Previous Button. The action for this button is currently set to **Go To Next Page**, but we need to change this to the **Go To Previous Page** action. To do this, click on the + icon to add a new action. Select **Go To Previous Page** to add this action. Then, select the **Go To Next Page** action that has already been applied to the button, and hit the – icon to remove it. We will also need to change the **Zoom** setting to **Fit In Window** for this action, just as we did in *step 2* for the **Next Page** button.

5. In terms of its appearance, the **Previous Page** button still has the exact same look and feel as the **Next Page** button that it was created from. With the **Previous Page** button selected, click on the **Normal** state in the appearance section of the **Buttons and Forms** panel. Then, switch to the **Type** tool and change the button text from Next Button to Previous Button. It will only change this for the **Normal** state, so you will also need to do the same thing for the **Rollover** and **Click** states.

6. We have finished creating our **Previous Page** and **Next Page** navigation buttons on the **A-Parent** page, and if we switch back to the regular pages, you should see the buttons at the bottom of every page. To test the buttons, simply export the document as an **Interactive PDF** file, which can be done via the **File** menu under **Export**, by setting the export type as **Interactive PDF**. This is covered in more detail in *Chapter 13*.

> **Note**
>
> If you find your parent items (such as buttons) are appearing behind regular page content and are effectively being hidden, you could move them to a new layer that is higher up the layer stack. This is covered in the *Using layers with parents* recipe of *Chapter 7*.

Including videos in your document

Videos can be a nice way to enhance your interactive documents; however, support can vary depending on the output format chosen and the viewer that is being used to read the file.

Content exported via Adobe's Publish Online or plugins such as In5 will use the native HTML5 video support that has been built into the web browser. As a result, provided that you use a web-compliant video standard such as **MP4**, the playback will generally be reliable and work well.

However, when it comes to PDFs, the experience can vary, depending on the operating system and a number of other factors. The latest versions of Adobe Acrobat Reader can play back something such as an MP4 video file within a PDF, but you might not have access to things such as playback controls. Additionally, there might even be restrictions on the user's system that prevent the video from playing.

In this recipe, we will show you how to embed an MP4 file into your document, as well as how to customize the poster image, set the video to play automatically on page load, and preview the video using InDesign's built-in **EPUB Interactivity Preview** panel. Also, we will look at how to set a navigation point and create a button to jump straight to that point in the video.

Getting ready

In order to complete this recipe, simply open InDesign on your system and create a new document with 12 pages, as shown in the *Creating a new document* recipe of *Chapter 1*. In this instance, we will disable **Facing Pages** and create the page using the **Landscape** orientation. You will also need a sample video. If you don't have any available, simply visit `https://pixabay.com/videos/`.

How to do it...

In order to use videos in your documents, just follow these steps:

1. Placing a video in InDesign is almost identical to placing an image on the page. In your document, from the **File** menu, select **Place**, choose your video file, then click on **OK**. Having done this click and drag on the page to create a rectangle frame containing the video. To fit the video to the frame, right-click on it, and under **Fitting**, select **Fit Content Proportionally**.

2. Now that we have added our video to the page, go to the **Window** menu, and under **Interactive**, select the **Media panel**. If the **Media** panel is currently blank, just click on the video with the **Selection Tool** option, and you should see the settings appear in the **Media** panel.

In the **Media** panel, you will see a preview window at the top of the panel (marked as *A* in *Figure 11.12*) where you can see the video. Below this is a player bar (marked as *B* in *Figure 11.12*) that allows you to quickly scrub through the video. Additionally, you can **Play/Pause** the video or **Mute/Unmute** the audio while previewing, using the two icons below the player bar. You will notice two sets of numbers underneath the player bar on the right-hand side. These numbers are in minutes and seconds, and the left-hand set shows the current position of the play head within the preview window. In the case of *Figure 11.12*, this is 8 seconds. The numbers on the right-hand side of this show the total length of the video, which in *Figure 11.12*, has been set to 12 seconds:

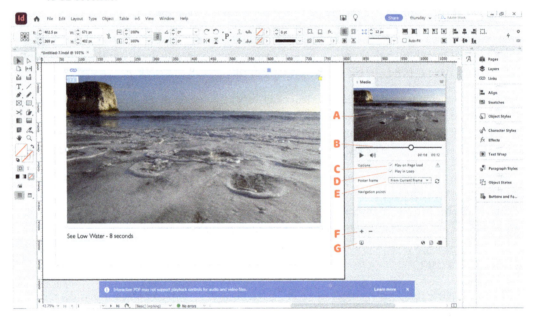

Figure 11.12: The Media panel in Adobe InDesign

Moving down the panel, you will come to the following options:

- **Play on Page Load** (*C* in *Figure 11.12*): Checking this will cause the video to start playing automatically as soon as the page has loaded. If this option is not checked, the user will have to click to play the video. We will leave this checked.

- **Play in Loop**: (*D* in *Figure 11.12*): If checked, this will cause the video to start playing from the beginning again once it reaches the end. We will leave this checked.

- **Poster frame**: (*E* in *Figure 11.12*): The poster frame refers to the image that is shown before the video commences playing. The options that are available here include the following:

  - **None**: This option will display no poster frame.

- **Standard**: This option will display a generic poster based on a file stored in the InDesign installation folder.

- **From Current Frame**: This option allows you to move the play head in the **Media** panel preview area to a specific frame in the video and use that as the poster frame. If you move the play head in the preview area, click on the refresh icon on the right-hand side of the **Poster Frame** drop-down box to refresh the poster. In my case, I have moved the play head to the 8-second mark and set that as the poster.

- **Choose Image**: This option allows you to choose an image file, such as JPG, to use as the poster.

- **Navigation Points** are specific points in time within the video, which can then be used via buttons, as we will see in the next step. In my case, I will move the play head to the 8-second mark and then click on the small + icon (marked as *F* in *Figure 11.12*) to add a navigation point that I will call Low Water.

> **Note**
>
> It's worth noting that the **EPUB Interactive Preview panel**, which renders an HTML-based preview of your document, can provide a useful way of testing interactive features including videos. It can be accessed from the small icon at the bottom of the **Media** panel (marked as *G* in *Figure 11.12*).

Having configured the settings for our video in the **Media** panel, next we are going to add a button to jump straight to the navigation point that we set up in *step 2*.

3. Use the **Type** tool to create a small text frame beneath the video, and enter the words See Low Water - 8 Seconds. Then, open the **Buttons and Forms** panel, which can be found in the **Interactive** section of the **Window** menu. Using the **Selection** tool, select the text frame, and in the **Buttons and Forms** panel, set the following settings:

- **Type** (marked as *A* in *Figure 11.13*): Set the type to **Button**.

- **Name** (marked as *B* in *Figure 11.13*): Set the name to NavPoint1.

- **Event** (marked as *C* in *Figure 11.13*): Set this to **On Release or Tap**.

Next, click on the + icon (marked as *D* in *Figure 11.13*) to create a new action. From the drop-down menu, select **Video** under the **EPUB/Publish Online Only** area. You will see three additional fields appear, as follows:

- **Video** (marked as *E* in *Figure 11.13*): This is the name of the video file that the button relates to. As we only have one video in this document, it should default to our video automatically.

- **Options** (marked as *F* in *Figure 11.13*): You can choose what you would like to happen when the button is clicked. In our case, we will set this to **Play from Navigation Point**, but other options found here include **Play**, **Stop**, **Pause**, and **Resume**.

- **Point** (marked as *G* in *Figure 11.13*): Here, you will see the navigation point that we created in *step 2*. If you created multiple navigation points, they will be listed in the drop-down menu:

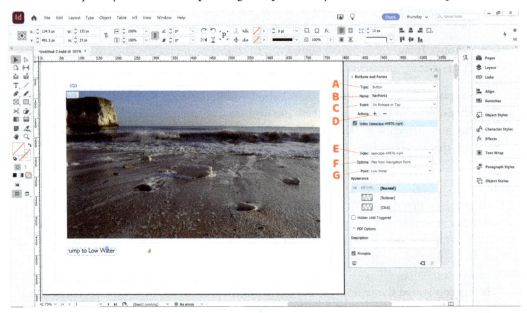

Figure 11.13: Using a button to jump to a navigation point

4. Having finished creating our document that includes a video, as well as a button to jump to a specific navigation point, we can test this in the **EPUB Interactivity Preview** panel. If you are happy it all works, export it with either **Adobe Publish Online** or a plugin such as **In5**. Further details on this process can be found in *Chapter 13*.

Applying page transitions

Page transitions are simple effects that are designed to enhance the process of moving from one page to another within your interactive PDF document. You can apply them directly to a single page or the entire document depending on your preferences.

In this recipe, we will apply a series of different transitions to different pages by selecting the relevant pages in the **Pages** panel and then applying transitions to them via the **Page Transitions** panel. Additionally, we will look at how to apply a single transition to the whole document.

Getting ready

In order to complete this recipe, simply open InDesign on your system and create a new document with 12 pages, as shown in the *Creating a new document* recipe of *Chapter 1*. In this instance, we will disable **Facing Pages** and create the page using the **Landscape** orientation.

How to do it...

In order to apply page transitions in your documents, just follow these steps:

1. Let's start by adding some content to our pages so that we can easily see the transitions. In my case, I will add a large page number to each page. To do this, go to the **A-Parent** page and add a large text frame. With the cursor in the text frame, go to the **Type** menu, select **Insert Special Characters**, and under the **Markers** section, choose **Current Page Number**. On the **A-Parent** page, resize the page number marker to a larger size if needed.

2. Next, let's open up the **Page Transitions** panel from the **Window** menu (under the **Interactive** section) and the **Pages** panel. Select *Page 2* within the **Pages** panel, and then from the **Page Transitions** panel menu (marked as *A* in *Figure 11.14*), select **Choose**. This will cause the **Page Transitions** preview window to appear (marked as *B* in *Figure 11.14*). Within the **Page Transitions** preview window, you can see a visual preview of all of the available page transitions. In our case, we will select the **Wipe** transition by checking the box below it, and then deselect the **Apply to All Spreads** checkbox (marked as *C* in *Figure 11.14*) to ensure the transition is only applied to *Page 2*, before clicking on **OK** in the **Page Transitions Preview** window:

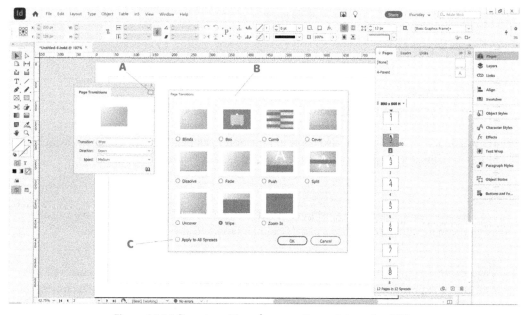

Figure 11.14: Page transitions for exporting as interactive PDFs

3. Next, we will apply a page transition from pages 4 to 8 all in one go. In the **Pages** panel, select *Page 4*, hold down the *Shift* key, and click on *Page 8*. This time, we will do this from the **Page Transitions** panel itself where we will set the following settings:

    - **Transition** (marked as *A* in *Figure 11.15*): This is where you can choose the type of transition. We will set this to **Zoom In**.

    - **Direction** (marked as *B* in *Figure 11.15*): This is where you can set the direction of the transition. We will set this to **Up**.

    - **Speed** (marked as *C* in *Figure 11.15*): Here, you can set the speed that the transition will go at. We will set this to **Medium**:

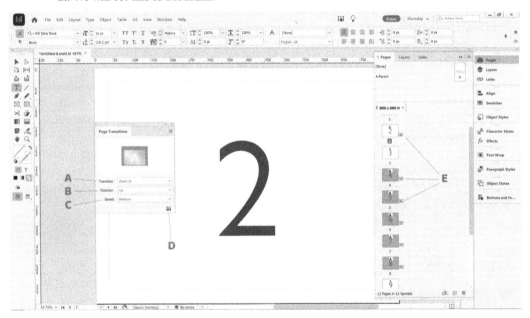

Figure 11.15: Applying the transition, direction, and speed values in the Transitions panel

It's worth noting that you can also apply a transition to all pages in the document from here using the icon at the bottom of the panel (marked as *D* in *Figure 11.15*).

> **Note**
> You can see whether a page has a transition applied to it as the page thumbnail will have a small transition icon next to it in the **Pages** panel (examples marked as *E* in *Figure 11.15*).

4. Page transitions applied in InDesign are supported in documents exported as interactive PDFs. During the export process, the **Page Transitions** option should be set to **From Document**, in order for page transitions created with the **Page Transitions** panel included. This is the default behavior. The export process is covered in *Chapter 13*.

Creating PDF forms

Creating **PDF forms** in InDesign can be a real time saver. You can add a wide range of fields including **Text Fields** that allow users to enter text; **List Boxes** that give you a list of items to choose from, **Checkboxes** that allow users to choose between an on or off state; **Comboboxes** that give you a drop-down list of items to select from; **Radio Buttons** that work as a group and allow you to choose only one option at a time from the group; and **Digital Signatures** that allow users to include a digital signature. In addition, you can add actions to submit the form and check the tab order before exporting. Your forms can then be emailed to users who can complete them and digitally sign them using the free Acrobat Reader before returning them to you to view/export the data.

In this recipe, we will create a sample form using each of the previously mentioned form field types, in addition to which we will include a digital signature field and a submit form button.

Getting ready

In order to complete this recipe, simply open InDesign on your system and create a new document with one or more pages, as shown in the *Creating a new document* recipe of *Chapter 1*. In this instance, we will disable **Facing Pages** and create the page using the **Landscape** orientation. If you don't have it installed already, you will also need a recent version of Adobe Acrobat Professional (not the free Acrobat Reader).

How to do it...

In order to create PDF forms in your documents, just follow these steps:

1. Start by creating some text frames on the page. We will create six small text frames in two columns (three in each column) using the technique covered in the *Creating rectangle and elliptical frames* recipe of *Chapter 4*. If you are using this technique to split the frame up using the keyboard arrows, make sure that you hold down the *Alt* (PC)/*Option* (Mac) key before releasing the mouse; otherwise, all the frames will be automatically threaded together into a single story. Make sure that you keep the frames on one side of the page.

    Now we will use the top-left frame as a descriptive label, so click into it and type in First Name. Do the same with the frames directly beneath it, adding Email Address and Surname, respectively. Next, we will convert the three frames within the right-hand column into text fields.

2. Select the upper-right frame with the **Selection** tool and open the **Buttons and Forms** panel. This can be found underneath the **Interactive** section of the **Window** menu. In the panel, set the following fields/properties:

    -   **Type** (marked as *A* in *Figure 11.16*): Set this to **Text Field**

    -   **Name** (marked as *B* in *Figure 11.16*): Set this to First Name

- **Event**: We will leave this deselected as we are not using an event here to trigger specific actions

- **Actions**: Again, we will ignore this setting as we are not using any actions here

- **Hidden until Triggered**: We will leave this deselected as we do not wish to hide the text field

If you do not see any more options below **Hidden until Triggered**, click on the small arrow (marked as *C* in *Figure 11.16*) next to **PDF Options** to display the remaining options. They are listed as follows:

- **Description** (marked as *D* in *Figure 11.16*): Set this to `Enter your first name here`. The description not only appears when users hover over the field, but it can also be useful for users that have accessibility requirements and use assistive technologies.

- **Printable** (marked as *E* in *Figure 11.16*): Check this to make the field printable.

- **Required** (marked as *F* in *Figure 11.16*): Check this to make this a mandatory field that must be completed within the form. Mandatory fields are displayed with a red border by default in Acrobat Reader and must be completed before the form can be submitted.

- **Password**: We will leave this deselected. When selected, any content that users are typing into this field will be hidden as they are typing it.

- **Read Only**: We will leave this deselected as we do not wish to make the field read-only.

- **Multiline**: In this instance, we will leave this deselected as we do not want the user to use more than a single line.

- **Scrollable**: If checked, when a user enters more text than the text field can hold, a scroll bar will appear instead of the extra text being cut off. We will leave this checked, which should be the default setting.

Finally, in the bottom area of the panel, you can control the **Font Family**, **Font Style**, and **Font Size** settings the user will use to fill out the form. In my case, these settings are **Minion Pro**, **Regular**, and **12pt**, which I will leave unchanged:

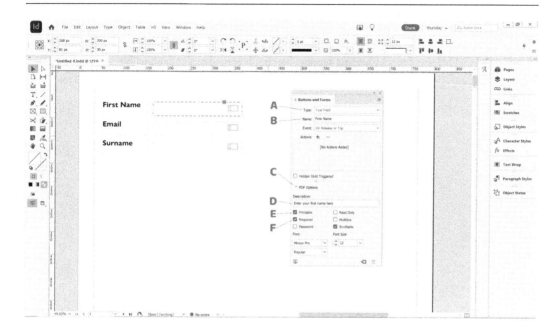

Figure 11.16: Three text fields with descriptive labels

Having done this for the upper-right text frame, we will do the same for the two text frames directly below it using the same settings except for the **Name** field, which will be set to Email Address and Surname, respectively.

Having done this, I would like to reposition the two bottom frames, which are the **Surname** label and the form field, and put them to the right of the **First Name** field at the top. To do this, simply select them together with the selection tool and reposition them by dragging them to the place where you want them.

3. Next, we are going to add a list box for people to choose their location. Using the **Type** tool, create two text frames (unthreaded) side by side beneath the existing fields. The left-hand text frame is the label, and in it, we will type this text: Enter your location.

The right-hand text frame is our list box. Select it using the **Selection** tool, and in the **Buttons and Forms** panel, set the following settings:

- **Type**: **List Box**
- **Name**: Location
- **Printable**: Leave this checked
- **Required**: Leave this unchecked

The only other thing we need to do here is set the actual list items themselves. To do this, type Africa into the **List Items** box (marked as *A* in *Figure 11.17*), then click on the + button (*B* in *Figure 11.17*). Repeat this by adding separate list items for each of the following: Antarctica, Asia, Australia/Oceania, Europe, North America, and South America:

Figure 11.17: Formatting list items in Buttons and Forms

4. The next field we would like to add is a checkbox for people to agree to receive email updates. Create a text field beneath the existing fields and enter the following text: Click to agree to receive email updates. Rather than create a checkbox from scratch, we are going to use InDesign's built-in **Sample Buttons and Forms** tool.

To access it, simply click on the panel menu (marked as *A* in *Figure 11.18*) from the **Buttons and Forms** panel. The first option is **Sample Buttons and Forms**. Click on this and the **Sample Buttons and Forms** dialog box will open. Here, there is a wide range of sample buttons and forms, but we will use the very first sample button, which is a checkbox with a tick in it. Drag it where you would like it on the page, and then close the **Sample Buttons and Forms** dialog box:

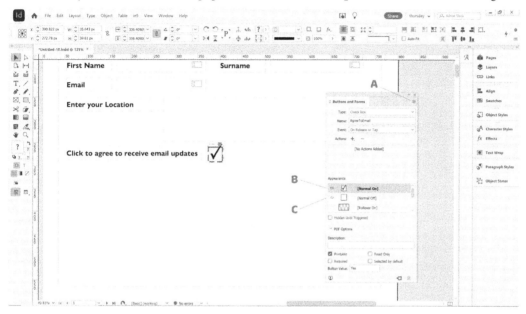

Figure 11.18: Adding a checkbox from the Sample Buttons and Forms dialog box

With the sample button still selected on the page, in the **Buttons and Forms** panel, change the name of the checkbox to AgreeToEmail. You will notice in the **Appearance** section that the **Normal On** appearance (marked as *B* in *Figure 11.18*) has a big tick in it, while the **Normal Off** appearance (marked as *C* in *Figure 11.18*) has nothing in it. These states represent how the checkbox will look when selected or deselected.

5. Next, let's add a combo box. First, add a text field and enter the following text: Which part of the year do you prefer?.

   Add a second field alongside this one and select it with the **Selection** tool. Then, from the **Buttons and Forms** panel, set **Type** to **Combo Box** and **Name** to **Seasons**.

   Now, go down to the **List Items** section near the bottom of the panel and add the following list items in the same way as the list box in *step 3*: Autumn, Spring, Summer, and Winter.

6. The next button we will create is a radio button. First, create a text frame and enter the following text: `How do you prefer to make payment?`. Then, beneath this, create three smaller text frames containing the following text:

    *   `Cash`

    *   `Bank Card`

    *   `Bank Transfer`

    Now, let's open the **Sample Buttons and Forms** box again from the **Buttons and Forms** panel menu. Here, you will see that items 10–24 are **Radio Buttons**, as shown in *Figure 11.19*:

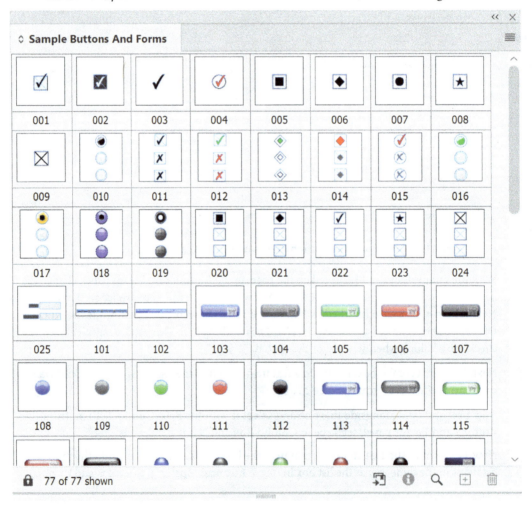

Figure 11.19: Sample Buttons And Forms in InDesign

Drag **item 24** onto the page next to the three small textboxes that we just created.

In the **Buttons and Forms** panel, my radio buttons already have **Type** set to **Radio Button** (this is because we used the **Sample Buttons and Forms** box to create them, rather than doing so manually), and **Name** is currently set to **R10**. Radio buttons work as a group and every time one item is selected, the others are deselected automatically, but this only works provided they have the same name.

I am going to select all three buttons with the **Selection** tool and change the name in the **Buttons and Forms** panel to **Payments**. By doing this to all three at once, I can ensure the name stays the same across all of them.

Now I want to apply an individual **Button Value** field to each button. To do this, select only the top button. Then, in the **Buttons and Forms** panel at the bottom, in the **Button Value** field (marked as *A* in *Figure 11.20*), enter Cash. I will also tick the box for **Selected by default** (marked as *B* in *Figure 11.20*) so that this is the option that is selected by default when a user opens the form:

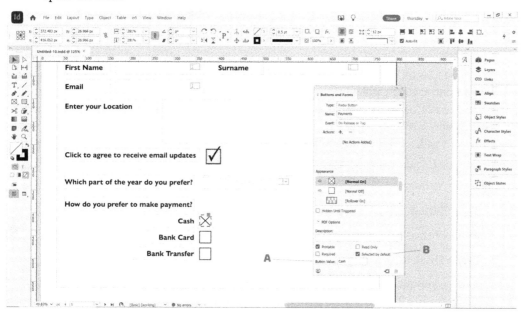

Figure 11.20: Editing radio buttons in InDesign

Set the button value for the next two boxes to **Card** and **Transfer** but leave the **Selected by default** option unchecked on them both.

7. Next, I would like to add a **Signature Field** option to our form so that users can sign the form with a digital signature if they so wish. To do this, add a small text frame to the bottom-left of the page that contains the following text: `Click to Sign`. You can style this however you wish.

    Having done this, select the frame with the **Selection** tool, and in the **Buttons and Forms** panel, change the type to **Signature Field**. I will also change the **Name** to `Signature`.

8. I want to make sure that the form fields we have added can be easily used by keyboard users and via a mouse. To check the tab order of the form fields, go to the **Object** menu, and under **Interactive**, select **Set Tab Order**. This will open the **Tab Order** dialog box, which shows the order in which the fields will be selected when hitting the *Tab* key on a keyboard.

    You can move items up and down easily, and in our case, the **Email** field is in between the **First Name** and **Surname** fields. This means that when a user hits *Tab* with the **First Name** field selected, it will jump to the **Email** field instead of the **Surname** field, which isn't really practical. With this in mind, I will click on the **Email** field in the **Tab Order** dialog box and move it down one place by clicking on the **Move Down** button at the bottom of the dialog box. Having finished changing the tab order, just click on **OK** to save the changes. Now when a user navigates the form using the *Tab* key, it will jump from **First name** to **Surname**, to **Email**, which makes more sense.

9. Before we finish, I want to add one final button to the bottom of the page. This is the **Submit Form** button, which will allow users to easily send the completed form back as an email attachment. Bring up the **Sample Buttons and Forms** dialog box again from the **Buttons and Forms** panel menu. This time, we will drag item **104** onto the bottom-right corner of the page. Click on it with the **Type** tool, and add the following text to the button: `Click to Submit`.

    Select the new item using the **Selection** tool, and in the **Buttons and Forms** panel, choose the following settings:

    - **Type**: Button
    - **Name**: `Submit`
    - **Event: On Release or Tap**
    - **Action: Submit Form**

    URL (marked as *A* in *Figure 11.21*): Here, you can enter the email address you wish the form to be returned to, but this must be prefixed with `mailto:`; for example, `mailto:info@highlander.co.uk` will return the form to `info@highlander.co.uk`:

Figure 11.21: The Submit Form button in InDesign

10. Now we have finished creating our form and just need to make sure that we export it as an interactive PDF. If you have not done this before, go to *Chapter 13*, where we specifically cover the process in the *Exporting to an interactive PDF* recipe.

> **Note**
>
> Historically, older versions of Adobe Acrobat Reader were unable to fill out and save a PDF form unless it had been specifically enabled with Reader Extended Rights from within Acrobat Pro. Newer versions of the Acrobat Reader are no longer restricted in this way, and allow you to fill out forms without the need to enable Reader Extended Rights. It's worth noting though that if users are using a third-party PDF reader, support for forms will depend on that reader.

Further reading

There is a wide range of third-party plugins for InDesign that allow you to create interactive documents containing functionality that goes beyond what can be found in interactive PDFs. For some years now, one of my favorites has been the In5 plugin from Ajar Productions. This reasonably priced add-on for InDesign allows you to export your documents from InDesign as HTML5-based digital magazines, providing a wide range of extra panels to add more advanced interactive functionality. Depending on your plan, you can even output responsive documents that lay out differently for different screen sizes and orientations.

For more details, visit `https://www.highlander.co.uk/blog/creating-digital-magazines`.

12
Using and Collaborating with CC Libraries

Creative Cloud Libraries or **CC Libraries** as they are commonly known, are in some ways the glue that brings the different Creative Cloud applications together. They are a cloud-based storage system for your digital assets that allows you to collaborate with colleagues, easily organize your creative assets, and work seamlessly across the different applications in the Creative Cloud suite.

The range of features supported by CC Libraries is growing all the time, and at the time of writing, CC Libraries in InDesign supports paragraph and character styles, color swatches, color themes, text, InDesign page items, Illustrator artwork, Photoshop layers and layer groups, graphics, Animate animations and symbols, and templates.

Many of these features are supported across multiple Adobe CC products, which makes them even more useful. For example, color swatches added to a library in InDesign can be reused in Photoshop, Illustrator, After Effects, and numerous other Adobe products.

You can have an unlimited number of libraries and can add up to 10,000 assets to a library, with individual assets as large as 1 GB in size supported. These assets can then be made publicly available or shared with up to 1,000 other users.

The CC Libraries work similarly to other cloud-based file storage platforms. When you add items to a CC Library, they are stored in a local **CC Library** folder on your machine; and this folder is automatically synchronized with the Adobe Creative Cloud servers. As you edit, add, or remove files in the library, the changes are synchronized with the Adobe Creative Cloud servers; if you were to log in on a second machine with the same Adobe Creative Cloud account, the existing CC Libraries would be synchronized with your new machine, allowing you to work with the items in these libraries.

If you find that items are not being synchronized, you should check that **Syncing** has not been turned off in the Adobe Creative Cloud Desktop app, a separate application that is installed as part of Adobe Creative Cloud. Since file synchronization requires an active internet connection, your files will not be synchronized when no connection is available. Also, when adding large files such as high-resolution images or videos to the libraries, you should bear in mind that your internet connection speed will affect how quickly the files are added and synchronized. On a fast internet connection, this process is fairly seamless; however, on a slower connection, you may notice a delay occasionally as files are synchronized.

In this chapter, we will look at how to create CC Libraries, add objects, color swatches, styles, and more to them, as well as how to manage our library and share it with other Creative Cloud users.

The recipes we will cover in this chapter are as follows:

- Creating, deleting, and renaming libraries
- Adding and reusing colors via CC Libraries
- Adding and reusing text styles via CC Libraries
- Adding and reusing graphics via CC Libraries
- Adding and reusing text via CC Libraries
- Managing CC Libraries items
- Collaborating with other users
- Backing up and restoring a library

Technical requirements

To complete this chapter, you will need a PC or Mac, with a copy of Adobe InDesign installed. You should be comfortable adding content to your documents and formatting it, as shown in *Chapters 1* to *4*. Some recipes within this chapter will also require a basic working knowledge of Adobe Photoshop, Adobe Illustrator, and Adobe Bridge.

Creating, deleting, and renaming libraries

Libraries are a great way to both collaborate with other users and manage your reusable content. To avoid getting things in a mess, though, you will no doubt want to organize your assets across multiple libraries. There are a variety of different reasons why you might want more than one library, as follows:

- You want to separate your libraries based on different clients or projects
- You want to collaborate with different groups of colleagues in different libraries
- You want to use different libraries to store different types of assets
- You want to use libraries to keep track of different versions of your assets

In this recipe, we will look at creating new CC Libraries within InDesign, as well as how to rename your libraries and delete any libraries that are no longer needed.

Getting ready

To complete this recipe, simply open InDesign on your system and create a new document with 12 pages, as shown in the *Creating a new document* recipe in *Chapter 1*.

How to do it...

To create, delete, and rename CC Libraries, just follow these steps:

1. From the **Window** menu, select **CC Libraries** to open the **CC Libraries panel**. Here, you may see some default libraries listed already; this list will vary, depending on your organization's setup and the Adobe CC subscription plan you are working on:

Figure 12.1: The CC Libraries panel

In our case, we want to create some new CC Libraries to use for storing our assets. Click the **Create New Library** button (marked *A* in *Figure 12.1*); this will bring up a small box where you can choose a name for your new library – in our case, **Library 1**. When you click **Create**, the **CC Libraries** panel will not only create the new library but also automatically open it within the panel. At this time, we don't want to be inside the library, so to exit **Library 1** and return to the main list of libraries, just click the arrow (marked *A* in *Figure 12.2*) to the left of the library's name:

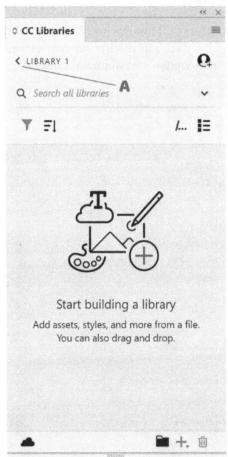

Figure 12.2: Inside a library within the CC Libraries panel

We are now going to repeat this process to create a second library, only this time we will name it **Library 2** instead of **Library 1**.

2. Having created our new libraries, I have decided that I want to use **Library 1** for storing my brand assets, and would like to give it a more descriptive name. Instead of calling it **Library 1**, I would like to rename it **Brand Assets**. To do this, in the list of libraries in the **CC Libraries**

panel, right-click on **Library 1** and select the **Rename Library** option. You can now type the new name, which is **Brand Assets**, into the field that currently says **Library 1** before hitting the *Enter* key on your keyboard to confirm the change.

> **Note**
>
> When you are inside a library within the **CC Libraries** panel, you can change the name of the library by clicking the **CC Libraries** panel menu and selecting the **Rename "Library Name"** option. Alternatively, you can delete a library by selecting the **Delete "Library Name"** option.

3. Having renamed **Library 1** to **Brand Assets**, I have decided I don't need **Library 2** after all since everything can go into the **Brand Assets** library. To delete **Library 2,** right-click on it in the list of libraries in the **CC Libraries** panel and select **Delete**.

Adding and reusing colors via CC Libraries

CC Libraries can be used to save and reuse colors from items on the page, color swatches, or color themes. You can share these colors with colleagues, use them on other documents, and even use them across a variety of different CC applications.

In this recipe, we will look at adding colors to a library from objects on the page, from existing color swatches while creating new color swatches, and via color themes, before applying these colors to other items in our document.

Getting ready

To complete this recipe, simply open InDesign on your system and create a new document with 12 pages, as shown in the *Creating a new document* recipe in *Chapter 1*. Having done this, create a new library – I have called mine **Brand Assets**, as shown in the *Creating, deleting, and renaming libraries* recipe at the start of this chapter. You should already be comfortable with the various skills covered in *Chapter 8, Working with Colors and Gradients*.

How to do it...

To use colors with your CC Libraries, just follow these steps:

1. Let's start by adding a text frame to our new document and giving the frame a fill and stroke color, and the text a fill color. In my case, I have applied a 10 pt red stroke to the frame, a purple fill on the frame, and a green fill for the text. Having done this, I want to add the fill color of both the frame and the text to my CC Library, which is called **Brand Assets**.

    Select the frame with the **Selection** tool, and then, in the **CC Libraries** panel, go to the **Brand Assets** library. Click the **Add Elements** icon (marked *A* in *Figure 12.3*); this will bring up a list of the items within the object that can be added to the library. You should see **Fill color** (marked B in *Figure 12.3*) and **Stroke color** (marked C in *Figure 12.3*) in the list that appears. First, click on the **Fill color** icon; after clicking the **Add Elements** icon to bring the list back up, click the **Stroke color** icon. This will result in both colors being added to the **Brand Assets** library:

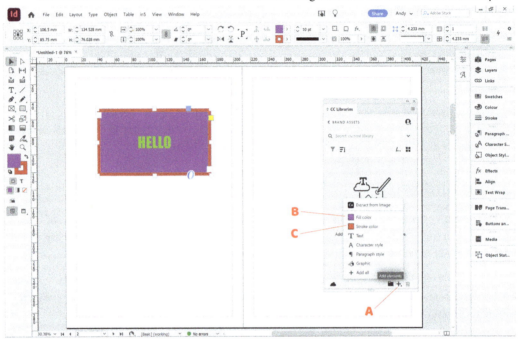

Figure 12.3: Adding colors to a CC Library

In addition to this, I would also like to add the text's **Fill color** to the library. To do this, simply select the text with the **Type** tool; you will see that the list changes to show the text properties. If you previously closed the list of properties, click the **Add Elements** icon again in the **CC Libraries** panel to bring it back up. We can now click **Fill color** in the list to add the fill color of the text to the library.

2.   Having added some colors to my library from an object on the page, I now want to add some colors to the library from my existing swatches. To do this, open the **Swatches** panel and select the colors you would like to add to the library – in my case, I have added a blue swatch and a red swatch. Then, click the **Add selected swatch to my current CC Library** icon (marked A in *Figure 12.4*), which can be found at the bottom of the **Swatches** panel. This will add the swatches to the currently active library in the **CC Libraries** panel, which in our case is the **Brand Assets** library:

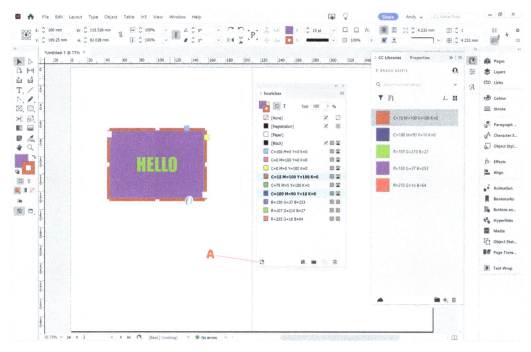

Figure 12.4: Adding existing swatches to a CC Library

Having added two existing swatches to the library, I have noticed there is a missing swatch that I also wanted to add to the library. Let's fix this by creating the new swatch and, at the same time, adding it to the library. In the **Swatches** panel, first, click on another swatch to deselect the two currently selected swatches, then click on the panel menu and choose **New Color Swatch** to bring up the **New Color Swatch** dialog box.

The new swatch I want to create has **Color Type** set to **Process** and **Color mode** set to **RGB**, with **37**, **164**, and **155** as values (marked A in *Figure 12.5*). At the bottom of the dialog box, you will see a checkbox labeled **Add to CC Library** (marked B in *Figure 12.5*) – select this. Then, from the dropdown next to it, choose the name of your library – in my case, **Brand Assets**. Finally, click **OK** to add the new swatch to the **Swatches** panel and **Brand Assets** to the CC Library:

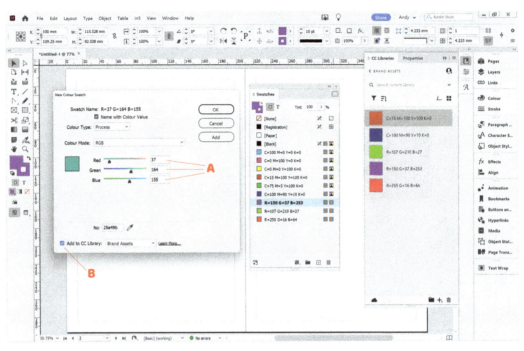

Figure 12.5: Adding a new swatch to the CC Library during creation

Having added colors to our library from an existing text frame, as well as from both existing and new swatches, we are now going to add colors to the library from an image.

3. Place an image onto the page and select it with the **Selection** tool. In the **CC Libraries** panel, click the **Add Elements** icon and select **Extract From Image** to bring up the **Extract from Image dialog box**, as seen in *Figure 12.6*:

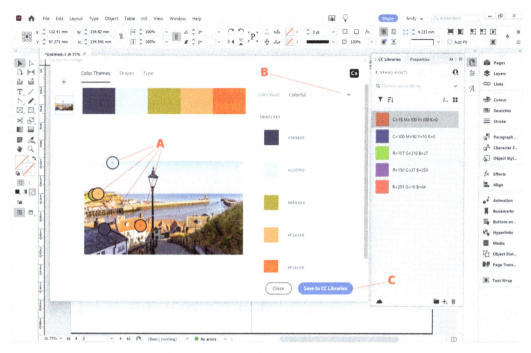

Figure 12.6: Extract from Image in InDesign

When extracting a color theme from an image using this tool, you can fine-tune what colors are selected by adjusting the selection points on the image (marked *A* in *Figure 12.6*). Just click on these points and drag them around to the colors you want to use from within the image to choose different colors for extraction. Additionally, you can adjust **Color Mood** (marked *B* in *Figure 12.6*) and switch between **Colorful**, **Bright**, **Muted**, **Deep**, **Dark**, and **None**. Having adjusted the settings to the colors I want to extract, I can click the **Save to CC Libraries** button (marked *C* in *Figure 12.6*) to extract the color theme and save it to my CC Library.

4. Having created a color theme within our **CC Libraries** panel from an image, I have now decided I also want to add that color theme to the **Swatches** panel. To do this, deselect any items that are currently selected in the document, then right-click on the color theme in the **CC Libraries** panel and select **Add Theme to Swatches**. Your color theme should now appear in the **Swatches** panel.

> **Note**
>
> You can also add individual color swatches from a CC Library to the **Swatches** panel, in just the same way you did with the color theme in *step 4*.

5. Having gathered all the colors I want in the **Brand Assets** library within my **CC Libraries** panel, I am now going to apply them to some content. On a new blank page, create a text frame and add some text to it, formatting it to the size and font you prefer. Select the text with the **Type** tool and make sure **Fill** (marked *A* in *Figure 12.7*) is currently active (on top), not **Stroke** (marked *B* in *Figure 12.7*), which should be behind it in the **Tools** panel. Now, right-click on the color you wish to apply to **Fill** within the **CC Libraries** panel and choose **Set Color** option.

6. Having done this, I would also like to apply a **Fill** color from within the color theme we created to the text frame itself. Select the text frame with the **Selection** tool and hover your mouse over the color theme thumbnail (marked *C* in *Figure 12.7*) in the **CC Libraries** panel, at which point it will become bigger. Simply click on the color within the color theme that you wish to apply to **Fill** and it will be applied:

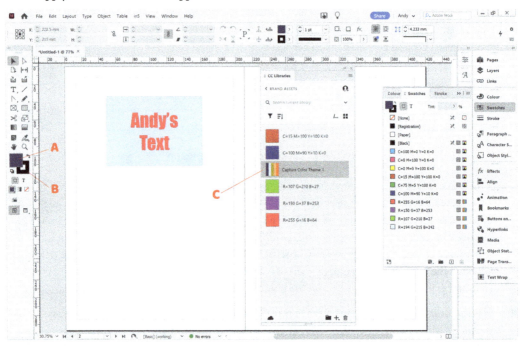

Figure 12.7: Applying colors from the CC Libraries panel to objects

We can now add individual colors and themes to a CC Library and reuse them by applying them to objects within our documents.

Adding and reusing text styles via CC Libraries

Paragraph styles and character styles can save you a lot of time when working in InDesign, and being able to reuse them across documents or share them with colleagues can be an equally big time saver. You might want to include them in a library as you create them, or maybe somebody has handed you a document with existing styles that you want to add to a CC Library, or maybe you already have some styles set up in the paragraph or character styles panels and you now want to add them to a CC Library, for example, to share with colleagues.

In this recipe, we will look at each of these scenarios, as well as how to apply paragraph and character styles from within the **CC Libraries** panel to items in your document, including how to copy styles from a CC Library to your paragraph or styles panels.

Getting ready

To complete this recipe, simply open InDesign on your system and create a new document with 12 pages, as shown in the *Creating a new document* recipe in *Chapter 1*. Having done this, create a new library – I have called mine **Brand Assets,** as shown in the *Creating, deleting, and renaming libraries* recipe at the start of this chapter. You should already be comfortable with the various skills that were covered in *Chapter 9, Formatting with Paragraph and Character Styles*.

How to do it...

To use text styles with CC Libraries, just follow these steps:

1. Let's start by creating some new styles and adding them to our CC Library. Create a new text frame in your document and fill it with placeholder text. Insert a paragraph return after the first four or five words and then select this text. I will format this with the following settings:

    - **Font Family**: Impact

    - **Size**: 30pt

    - **Character Color**: Red

    With the text still selected, I now want to turn this into a paragraph style. From the **Paragraph Styles** panel menu, select **New Paragraph Style** to bring up the **New Paragraph Style** dialog box:

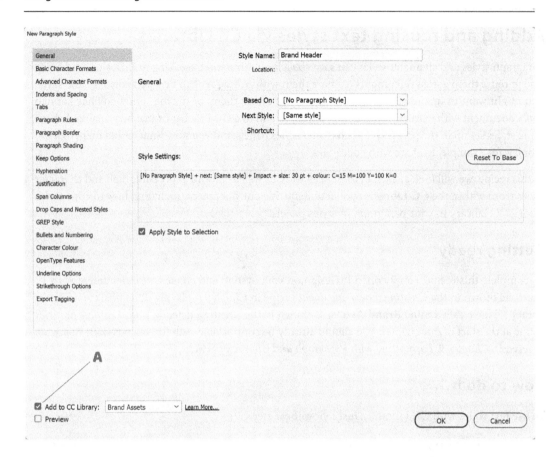

Figure 12.8: The New Paragraph Style dialog box

The settings I applied to the text will have already been incorporated into the style, so I will name the style **Brand Header** in the **Style Name** field and enable the **Apply Style to Selection** checkbox. I am also going to enable the **Add to CC Library** checkbox (marked *A* in *Figure 12.8*) and, from the dropdown, select my CC Library, which in my case is called **Brand Assets**.

> **Note**
> If you are used to creating new styles by clicking the **New Style** icon at the bottom of the **Paragraph Styles** or **Character Styles** panels, rather than from the panel menu, that's fine. Just make sure you hold down the *Alt* (Windows)/*Option* (Mac) key when doing so to bring up the **Style Options** dialog box.

Having created my **Brand Header** style, I am now going to select the rest of the text in the frame and format it using the following settings (if you wish to use a different font, size, or color, that's fine):

- **Font Face**: **Gill Sans Nova**

- **Size**: **14pt**

- **Color**: **Black**

I will save this as a paragraph style called **Body Copy** and check the box for **Apply Style to Selection**, but this time, I will uncheck the box for **Add to CC Library**. As a result, this means the style will appear in the **Paragraph Styles** panel and will be applied to the selected text, but it won't show up in the CC Library.

In *step 3*, we will look at how to add this style to a CC Library from within the **Paragraph Styles** panel rather than during the new style creation process.

2. Next, let's create a new small text frame and add some placeholder text. I will format this using the following settings:

- **Font Face**: **Arial**

- **Size**: **12pt**

- **Color**: **Cyan**

Now, I am going to create a new paragraph style from this and call it **Special Notes**, selecting the **Apply Style to Selection** option but deselecting the **Add to CC Library** option before clicking **OK**.

Having created **Special Notes**, I have decided I would like it in my **Brand Assets** library after all. Fortunately, there is an easy way to add a style that is being used in your document to a library. Select the text on the page that the style was applied to and, in the **CC Libraries** panel, click the **Add Elements** button (marked *A* in *Figure 12.9*) before selecting **Paragraph Style** (marked *B* in *Figure 12.9*) from the list of available elements. Your paragraph style will now appear in the list within the **CC Libraries** panel:

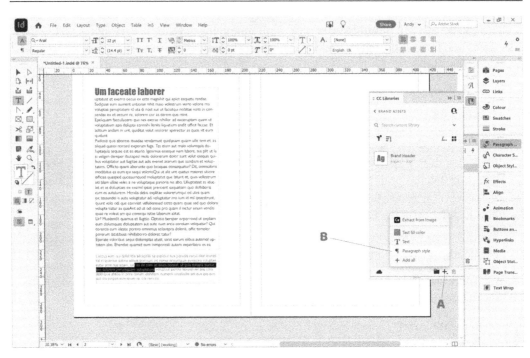

Figure 12.9: Adding a style to a library from selected text

With that, we have added a paragraph style to the CC Library during the new style creation process, as well as added a paragraph style to the library from the document content. Next, we'll look at existing styles.

3.   Open the **Paragraph Styles** panel; you will notice a paragraph style called **Body copy**; this was the style we created toward the end of *step 1*, which we didn't add to the library. I have now decided I would like to include this in the **Brand Assets** library after all. In the **CC Libraries** panel, make sure you are on the library you wish to add the style to – in my case, the **Brand Assets** library. Then, in the **Paragraph Styles** panel, select the style you wish to add to the library and click the **Add selected style to my current CC Library** button (marked *A* in *Figure 12.10*). Your style should now show up within the CC Library:

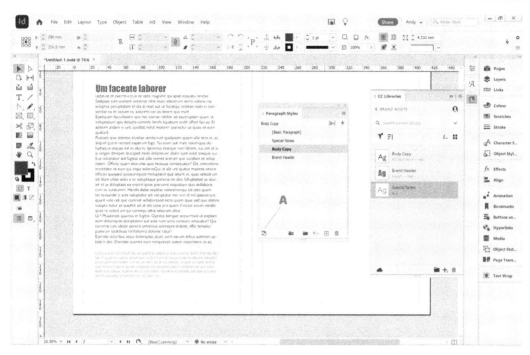

Figure 12.10: Adding an existing style to the current CC Library

It's worth noting that the techniques we demonstrated in *steps 1* to *4* work the same with character styles.

> **Note**
>
> The techniques shown in *steps 1* to *4* work the same whether they are done with a paragraph style or a character style. The main difference is that the **Paragraph Styles** panel is used when working with paragraph styles and the **Character Styles** panel for character styles, in addition to which some of the properties that are supported will vary, depending on the type of style being used. If you are unsure of the difference between paragraph styles and character styles, I recommend reading through *Chapter 9, Formatting with Paragraph and Character Styles*, and in particular the introduction to *Chapter 9*, which will clarify the difference.

4. Select a few words within the large text frame and change the formatting. In my case, I will change **Color** to **Magenta** and **Font Style** to **Bold**. These are the only properties that will be controlled by the character style that we are about to make:

Figure 12.11: Adding a character style from formatted text to a CC Library

Select the text we just applied the formatting changes to and click the **Add Elements** button (marked *A* in *Figure 12.11*); then, select **Character style** (marked *B* in *Figure 12.11*). Even though we didn't create a character style previously, the **CC Libraries** panel is capable of creating a new style from the selection and adding it to the current CC Library, all with one click. You will also find that doing it this way means the style appears in the **CC Libraries** panel, but is not added to the **Character Styles** panel and is not applied to the text.

5. Having done this, I have now decided it would be quite useful to include this style in the **Character Styles** panel after all. To do this, right-click on the style within the **CC Libraries** panel and select the **Add to character styles** option (in the case of a paragraph style, the option would say **Add to paragraph styles**).

6. Finally, having created our styles in the **Brand Assets** library, we are going to apply these to another document. If you want to save the current document, do so now and then close it. Start a new document and then create a text frame and fill it with placeholder text.

    To apply our styles, it is simply a case of selecting the text we wish to apply the style to and then, in the **CC Libraries** panel, right-click on the relevant style and select either **Apply character style** or **Apply paragraph style** from the options.

Alternatively, if you want to add the style to the **Paragraph Styles** or **Character Styles** panel for the document without actually applying it at this point, you can do so using the **Add to character styles** or **Add to paragraph styles** options that appear in the right-click menu. This will add the style to the relevant panel without actually applying it to the page.

Adding and reusing graphics via CC Libraries

CC Libraries can be a useful way to reuse graphics within your documents and they support a wide range of file types, including AI, PSD, TIF, SVG, JPG, PNG, GIF, PDF, BMP, HEIC, HEIF, and DNG. Individual items in a CC Library can be as large as 1 GB in size, and you can add images to your library from several different places, including Adobe desktop apps, such as Photoshop, Illustrator, and Bridge, via Adobe's mobile apps such as Adobe Capture, and through the Adobe Stock website.

In this recipe, we will look at adding graphics to the library from a variety of places, including Photoshop, Illustrator, Bridge, and Adobe Stock, as well as how to then reuse those graphics in your document and fix issues that might arise around linking.

Getting ready

To complete this recipe, simply open InDesign on your system and create a new document with 12 pages, as shown in the *Creating a new document* recipe in *Chapter 1*. Having done this, create a new library – I have called mine **Brand Assets** – as shown in the *Creating, deleting, and renaming libraries* recipe at the start of this chapter.

You should already be comfortable with the various skills that were covered in *Chapter 5, Working with Images in Your Document. steps 1 to 4* in this recipe will involve adding images to your document using Photoshop, Illustrator, and Bridge, respectively, and assume you have a basic level of knowledge of these programs, as will *step 9*, which assumes you have some basic Photoshop skills. It is worth noting that many elements of the interface work the same in these programs as they do in InDesign – for example, all the panels can be found under the **Window** menu. You will also need these programs installed to complete these steps, so if you are unable to install them or do not intend to use them, simply skip the relevant steps.

How to do it...

To use graphics with **CC Libraries**, just follow these steps:

1. Let's start by adding an image to our library using Photoshop. I am going to use one of the images we worked with back in *Chapter 5* to demonstrate this but feel free to use a different image if you wish.

Having opened the image in Photoshop, I am going to apply a simple change to it. From Photoshop's **Window** menu, select **Adjustments** to open the **Adjustments** panel. Then, within the **Adjustments** panel, click the **Black & White** adjustment icon (marked *A* in *Figure 12.12*). This will create an adjustment layer called **Black & White 1** (marked *B* in *Figure 12.12*), turning the image black and white:

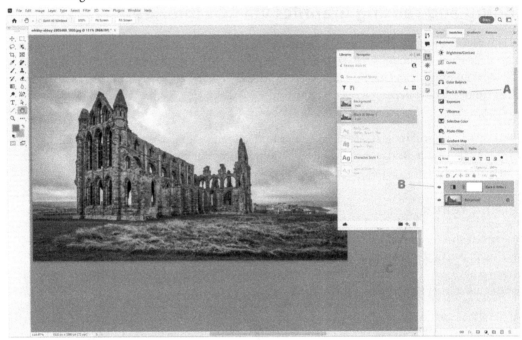

Figure 12.12: Adding an image to CC Libraries in Photoshop

Having made these changes to my image, I am now going to save two versions of the image to the **Libraries** panel – one with the adjustment layer included and one without it included. When you add graphics to a library in Photoshop, only the layers selected at the time are included. With this in mind, select the **Background** layer only in the **Layers** panel; then, in the **Libraries** panel (found under the **Window** menu), go to the **Brand Assets** library and click the **Add Element** icon (marked *C* in *Figure 12.12*), then select **Graphic**. This will add a version of the image without the **Black & White** adjustment applied as we did not select that layer.

Having done this, select both layers in the **Layers** panel, then select **Add Element** and choose **Graphic**. This time, you will notice that the thumbnail in the **Libraries** panel is different, reflecting the fact that the image that was added is in **Black & White** as both layers have been included within it this time.

2. Having added an image to the **Brand Assets** library from within Photoshop and controlled the layers that are included when it is added, we are now going to add multiple images at once from within Adobe Bridge:

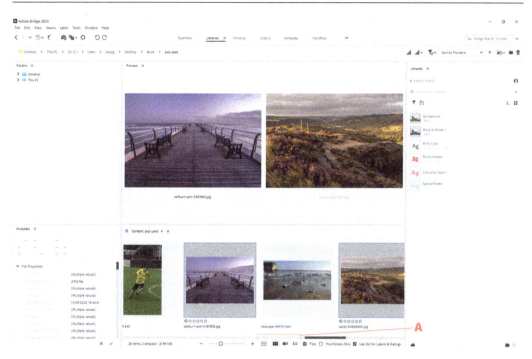

Figure 12.13: Adobe Bridge library workspace

Open Adobe Bridge. Then, from the **Window** menu, under **Workspace**, select **Libraries**. The **Libraries** workspace in Adobe Bridge will bring up several panels, including the **Libraries** panel on the right-hand side, the **Folders** panel on the left, with the **Metadata** panel beneath it, and the **Content** and **Preview** panels in the middle.

> **Note**
>
> It is worth noting that when working in Adobe Bridge, you can temporarily expand and contract individual panels by first clicking on them to select them, and then double-clicking on the panel tab that contains the panel name at the top of the panel. This will expand the panel so that it fills the screen. When you have finished working inside the panel, simply double-click the panel name tab again to shrink it back to its previous size.

First, within the **Libraries** panel, make sure you are currently viewing the **Brand Assets** library (if not, switch to it). Next, within the **Folders** panel, navigate to the folder containing your images and, in the **Content** panel, select the various images that you wish to add to the library. The buttons across the bottom of the **Content** panel (marked *A* in *Figure 12.13*) will allow you to change how you display the images within the **Content** panel, which can make it easier to find and select items. Select the images you wish to add to your library in the **Content** panel and then, with your mouse, drag them onto the library in the **Libraries** panel to add them to the library.

Having added items to the library in Photoshop and Bridge, next, we will add a vector logo from Illustrator.

3. Open Illustrator and then open some vector artwork you want to include in your library, such as a logo. If you don't have any existing vector artwork, you could download a vector from `https://pixabay.com/vectors/`.

> **Note**
>
> **Vector** artwork is resolution-independent artwork that is often used for things such as logos and icons, or in industries where the artwork may need to be scaled, such as the fashion or signage industries. It does not contain any pixels and is instead made up of dots (known as anchor points) with lines joining them (known as paths). These points and paths are mathematically calculated and can be scaled to any size without a loss of quality, unlike pixel-based images. In many respects, it is made up like the "join the dots" drawing that children often do.

To add your vector artwork to the library, open the **Libraries** panel and navigate to the **Brand Assets** library. Having done this, on your artboard, select all of the artwork you wish to add to the library, and then drag it onto the **Brand Assets** library to add it. Alternatively, you can select the artwork and click the **Add Elements** icon at the bottom of the **Libraries** panel, then select **Graphic** from the list (just as we did in *step 1* with the same panel in Photoshop).

Having added graphics to the library from Photoshop, Bridge, and Illustrator, we are now going to add some content from Adobe Stock to the library.

> **Note**
>
> **Adobe Stock** is a paid service where you pay to license a wide variety of assets for use in your projects, so be careful not to accidentally purchase items unless you intend to do so.

4. Open your preferred web browser and go to the Adobe Stock website (`stock.adobe.com`). If you aren't already logged in, do so now using your CC login details. On the Adobe Stock website, you can search for a wide range of images. In my case, I have searched for images of *York, UK*. When you find an image you want to use, hover your mouse over the image; you will see three small icons appear. The heart icon (marked *A* in *Figure 12.14*) allows you to add a watermarked copy of the image to your CC Libraries. Select an image and then click this icon to add the image to your current library:

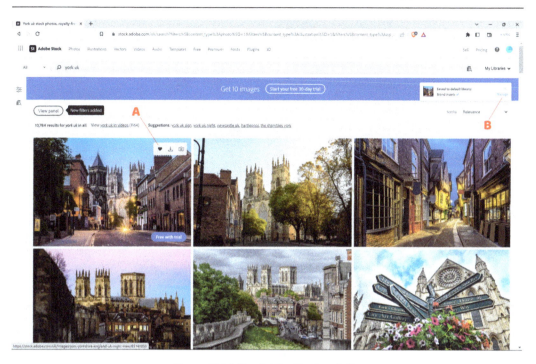

Figure 12.14: The Adobe Stock website

After adding the image to the current library, you will see a small white panel fly out in the top right of the web page – it tells you which library the image has been added to and contains a link called **Manage** (marked *B* in *Figure 12.14*). If the link has been added to the wrong library, you can click on the **Manage** link and select the correct library from the list that appears.

It is worth noting that while we have added the image to the library, this is a low-resolution watermarked preview version of the image. It is designed to let you see how the image looks in your design before you decide whether or not to license and use it. If you decide to use the image, you can license it easily from within the **Libraries** panel by right-clicking on the image and selecting **License Image**, at which point you will be charged a fee for **licensing** the image (if you have existing credits on your Adobe Stock account, these will be used). When you license the image, all instances of the low-resolution preview image will be replaced with the full-quality image.

5. Having added images from a variety of places to our library, let's quickly review what images we have added to our library. Open the **CC Libraries** panel in InDesign:

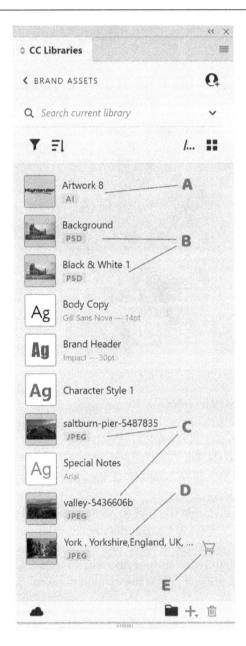

Figure 12.15: CC Libraries contains a variety of assets

The **Brand Assets** library now contains the following image assets:

- Adobe Illustrator (AI) artwork (marked *A* in *Figure 12.15*).

- Photoshop (PSD) files (marked *B* in *Figure 12.15*).

- JPEG files (marked *C* in *Figure 12.15*).

- An unlicensed Adobe Stock preview image (marked *D* in *Figure 12.15*). You will notice that this item contains a small icon of a shopping cart (marked *E* in *Figure 12.15*) that you can click on to quickly pay to license the image.

Now, let's have a look at how to use these various image assets in our document.

6. I would like to start by placing the first PSD file within the library onto the page. To do this, just click on the image (marked *A* in *Figure 12.16*) in the **CC Libraries** panel and drag it over the page, then release the mouse button. You can now either click and drag on the page to place the image at a specific size, or click into an existing frame on the page to place the image into it.

    This image has been placed as a linked image, which is the default behavior when placing an image from **CC Libraries**. This means any edits that are made to the original image in the CC Library will also affect the image within the document. You can tell an image is linked to a CC Library from the small icon at the top of the image (marked *B* in *Figure 12.16*), as well as from the icon next to it in the **Links** panel (marked *C* in *Figure 12.16*):

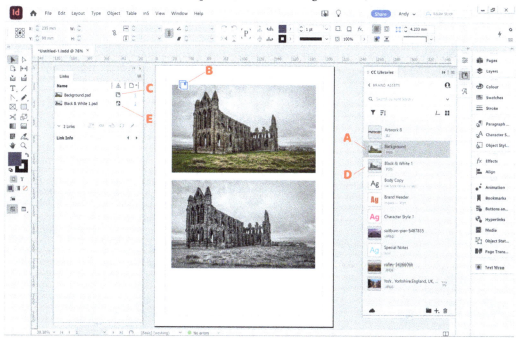

Figure 12.16: Images placed from the library, one linked and one embedded

I would also like to place the second PSD file (marked *D* in *Figure 12.16*) in this document, but this time, I am going to place it as an embedded image (that is, not linked) so that the whole image will be copied into this InDesign document and changes to the original won't affect it. To do this, click and drag the image from the **CC Libraries** panel onto the page, but this time, make sure you are holding down the *Alt* (Windows)/*Option* (Mac) key when you are releasing the mouse button. Now, click on the page and drag; your image will be placed as an embedded image, which means changes to the original image won't affect it. You can tell the image is embedded because there is no icon on the image itself this time; also, in the **Links** panel, the embedded image icon appears next to the image (marked *E* in *Figure 12.16*).

Having placed a PSD file that is linked to the CC Library, and also a copy of a PSD file that is embedded in the document, we will now look at placing a JPG file using a different method.

7. Create a blank rectangle frame on a page in your document and select it. Now, in the **CC Libraries** panel, right-click on the image you wish to use, which in my case is the first JPG image in the list. Within the right-click menu, you should see the **Place linked** option (marked *A* in *Figure 12.17*), which places a linked version of the image, and the **Place copy** option (marked *B* in *Figure 12.17*), which places an embedded copy of the image. In this instance, I will select **Place linked** to place a linked copy of the image. This image will be placed onto the page; you will see the CC Libraries linked image icon in the top left of the image, as identified in *step 6*:

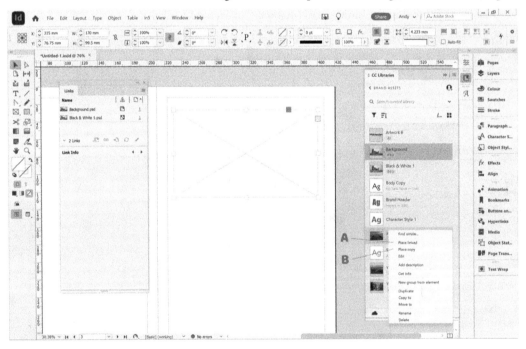

Figure 12.17: Place linked in the CC Libraries panel

Having placed an image by dragging it from the **CC Libraries** panel onto the page, and also by right-clicking on it in the **CC Libraries** panel, we are now going to place an image that is in the CC Library from the **File** menu.

8. Create a blank rectangle frame on a page in your document and select it. This time, click the **File** menu and go down to **Place from CC Libraries**. When you select this option, you should notice that the **CC Libraries** panel automatically hides any items that can't be placed, such as text styles or color swatches, and only shows you the items available to place:

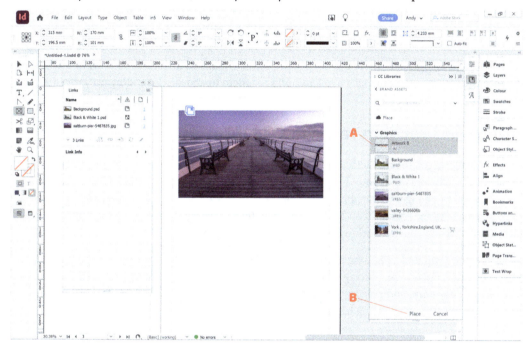

Figure 12.18: Placing an SVG from the CC Libraries panel

This time, I am going to choose the SVG file (this method works just the same with other image types) that I added to the library in Illustrator earlier (marked *A* in *Figure 12.18*), and will then click the **Place** button (marked *B* in *Figure 12.18*) at the bottom of the **CC Libraries** panel. The image will be added to the selected frame, although it will need some fitting applied to it.

> **Note**
>
> Remember that if your images look very pixelated, that is down to a combination of the **display performance** settings and how InDesign handles images. It doesn't necessarily reflect the quality of the output image in your final document, as discussed in *Chapter 5*.

9. Finally, we are going to look at how you can edit an image from the **CC Libraries** panel and the impact this has on a linked image. I am going to use the first image I placed back in *step 6*, which in my case was a color photo of Whitby Abbey. To edit this image, right-click on the image in the **CC Libraries** panel and select the **Edit** option. As this is a PSD file, it should open in Photoshop automatically (if it doesn't, you may need to change your default application for opening PSD files in your operating system's settings).

    Make the edits to the image that you want to make in Photoshop. In my case, I am going to apply a **Photo Filter** adjustment from the **Adjustments** panel, to give the image a red color filter adjustment, and then, from the **File** menu, click **Save**.

    If you go back to InDesign now, you should see the edits appear there, both in the **CC Libraries** panel and on the page where the image was placed as a linked image. If you don't immediately see these changes, it may take a few minutes for them to appear, depending on your internet connection speed.

Adding and reusing text via CC Libraries

CC Libraries allows you to reuse text, as well as all the usual text formatting attributes, including styles. This text can then be reused in your documents and can be placed as an independent text element that is not impacted by changes to the library item, or it can be placed as a linked element that is affected by changes made to the library item. Text items in the library can also be reused in Illustrator as well, which is useful when you are working between the two programs.

In this recipe, we will look at adding text to the library both with and without styles applied, reusing that text in a new document, placing it both as a linked and unlinked item, as well as the impact of editing the library item, and placing it with and without styles. We will finish by looking at how to place text inline within an existing text frame.

Getting ready

To complete this recipe, simply open InDesign on your system and create a new document with 12 pages, as shown in the *Creating a new document* recipe in *Chapter 1*. Having done this, create a new library, as shown in the *Creating, deleting, and renaming libraries* recipe at the start of this chapter. I have called mine **Reusing Text**. You should be comfortable creating and applying paragraph styles, and have a basic understanding of the techniques covered in *Chapter 9, Formatting with Paragraph and Character Styles*.

How to do it...

To use text with your CC Libraries, just follow these steps:

1. Let's start by creating a small text frame and adding some placeholder text. Apply the formatting that you want. In my case, I have used the following:

   - **Font Face**: **Gill Sans Nova**
   - **Size**: **18pt**
   - **Color**: **Red**
   - **Case**: **All Caps**

   If you have formatted yours differently to this, that's fine. Navigate to the **Reusing Text** library within the **CC Libraries** panel, then click the **Add Elements** button (marked *A* in *Figure 12.19*) and select **Text** to add the text to the current CC Library:

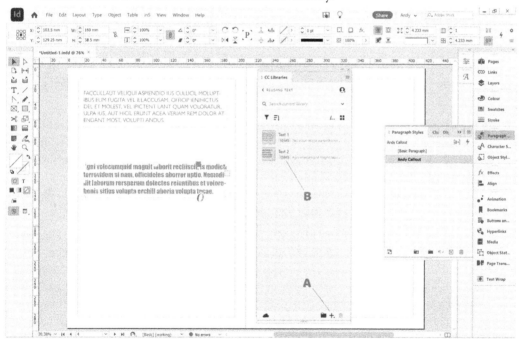

Figure 12.19: Adding text elements to the CC Libraries panel

2. Having done this, create a second text frame on the page and format it how you wish. In my case, I will set **Font Face** to **Impact**, **Size** to **22pt**, and **Color** to **Cyan**. Now, select the text and create a new paragraph style in the **Paragraph Styles** panel, applying it to the text as you do so. I will call my paragraph style **Andy Callout**.

Having created our new paragraph style and applied it to the text, we are now going to add this to our **Reusing Text** library, as we did in *step 1*, by simply selecting the text frame with **Selection Tool** and clicking the **Add Elements** button in the **CC Libraries** panel, then selecting **Text**.

You may notice that the items are added to the library with an **IDMS** extension (marked *B* in *Figure 12.19*). This stands for **InDesign Markup Snippet** and is an Adobe file type that's used for storing objects. Its properties include styles and information on their location relative to each other.

> **Note**
> Effects that are applied through the **Effects** panel are a property of the object rather than the text, and as a result, are not included when adding text to a CC Library. To get around this, you can add the object to the library as a graphic object, rather than as text. Unfortunately, while the effects would then be included, you would lose the ability to place the item as a linked object and will only be able to place a copy.

Having created our library items, we will now close the document and start a new blank 12-page document.

3. In this new document, open the **CC Libraries** panel and navigate to your library – in my case, the **Reusing Text** library – where you should see the two text snippets that we added to the library in *steps 1* and *2*.

   In the **CC Libraries** panel, select the first text item and right-click on it, then select **Place Copy**. Now, click and drag to where you would like to place a copy of the text snippet. This is an independent copy of the text frame that can be edited and altered with no impact on the original snippet in the library. Similarly, if the snippet in the library is edited later, it won't impact this text frame, which has already been placed on the page. This is reflected in the fact that no new link shows up in the InDesign **Links** panel.

4. Having placed an independent copy of the snippet, let's place a linked version. In the **CC Libraries** panel, select the snippet again and right-click on it, only this time, choose **Place Linked**. Now, click on the page and drag to add the snippet to the page. This version of the snippet is linked to the original library item and will update in the future if that changes. If you look in the **Links** panel, you will see a new link listed (marked *A* in *Figure 12.20*); this is the link between the item on the page and the snippet in the library. Similarly, the item on the page also has a small icon at the top left of it (marked *B* in *Figure 12.20*), indicating that it is a linked library item:

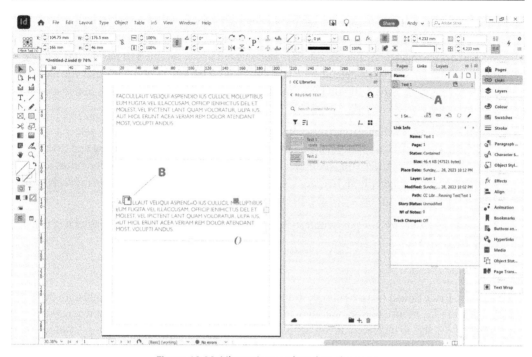

Figure 12.20: Library items placed on the page

5. So far, we have reused the snippet on the document twice, once linked and once not linked. Now, I would like to update the snippet to change the font color and font face. To do this, select the snippet in the **CC Libraries** panel and right-click on it, then select **Edit**. This will open the snippet as a new document so that you can edit it.

   Change the font face, color, and any other properties you wish. In my case, I will set **Font Face** to **Arial**, change **Color** to **Blue**, and disable **All Caps**, then close the document, saying **Yes** when asked if I want to save the changes.

   You should now be looking at your previous document again, where, after a few seconds (or minutes, depending on your internet connection), you should see both the thumbnail in the **CC Libraries** panel and the linked version of the snippet on your page update to reflect the changes you made. The snippet on the page that you placed as a copy won't be altered at all since it is not linked to the library item.

   Having done this, let's go to another blank page in the document. Here, we will use our other snippet, which contains a paragraph style.

6. In the **CC Libraries** panel, select the second snippet, which contains a paragraph style, and then right-click on it and select the **Place without styles** option. Click it and drag it onto your page; you will notice that the text is placed there but without any formatting. It has used the **Basic Paragraph** style, which is a default style that comes with InDesign, and any other formatting has been removed. Equally, if you look in the **Paragraph Styles** panel, you will notice that no new styles have been created.

7. Having done this, I will now place a second copy of the text snippet. This time, select it in the **CC Libraries** panel, right-click on it, and then select **Place linked** before clicking and dragging it onto the page. This time, you will notice that all of the formatting has been included, and if you look in the **Paragraph Styles** panel, you will see that the **Andy Callout** paragraph style that we created back in *step 2* has also been added and applied to the text.

   If you used **Place copy**, the paragraph style will also be included in the same way as it is when using **Place linked**.

Note

You can also **Place linked** items by simply dragging them from the **CC Libraries** panel onto the page, releasing the mouse button, and then just clicking and dragging on the page where you would like the object to be placed. If you do this while holding down the *Alt* (Windows)/*Option* (Mac) key as you drag from the **CC Libraries** panel, it will **Place copy** instead of **Place linked**.

---

8. While we have reused text from the **CC Libraries** on the page, we haven't looked at how to insert that text into existing text on the page yet. Create a new text frame on the page and type some text into it. In my case, I will type `This text is in front. This text is behind.`

   Then, I will click into the space between these two sentences. In the **CC Libraries** panel, select the second text snippet, right-click on it, and select **Place inline**. You will see the text appear in the middle of your existing text, retaining its formatting (marked *A* in *Figure 12.21*):

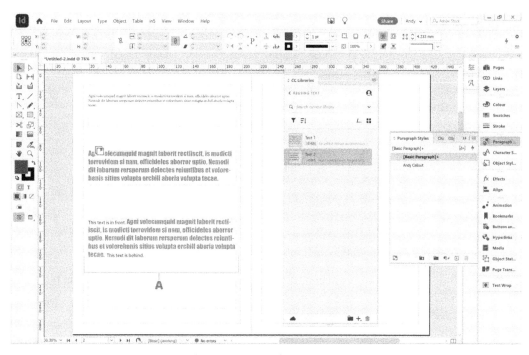

Figure 12.21: Placing inline text from the CC Libraries panel

In this instance, I used the snippet with a paragraph style applied; as a result, it will import the paragraph style to the **Paragraph Styles** panel if it doesn't already exist. However, the paragraph style is not applied to the text as that would alter the existing text (remember, paragraph styles apply to whole paragraphs). Instead of applying the paragraph style, it has used the **Basic Paragraph** style, which is already being used by the existing text, and then applied the formatting as an override.

> **Note**
> Text added to CC Libraries in InDesign can also be used in Adobe Illustrator, where the paragraph and character styles are also supported.

Managing CC Libraries items

The CC Libraries are powerful resources and little actions such as adding descriptions or viewing item information can often make your life much easier when working with them. Additionally, the ability to search for items by name, filter by different types of assets, or change the sort order of items can make you more efficient and speed up your workflow.

In this recipe, we will look at how to do all of this, as well as group items within a library for organizational purposes, and even move or copy items into a different library.

Getting ready

To complete this recipe, simply open InDesign on your system and create a new document with 12 pages, as shown in the *Creating a new document* recipe in *Chapter 1*. Having done this, create a new library, as shown in the *Creating, deleting, and renaming libraries* recipe at the start of this chapter. I have called mine **Brand Assets Library**.

You should also add a mix of items to the new library, including two images, a text snippet, two color swatches, and two paragraph styles, as shown in the previous recipes in this chapter. If you also have other items in the library, that's fine – the idea here is to give you enough items to practice things such as filtering and sorting.

How to do it...

To manage your library items in your CC Libraries, just follow these steps:

1. Let's start by checking the information about some of the assets in our document and making sure it matches what we want. I will start by right-clicking on one of the color swatches and selecting **Get Info**. As this is a color swatch, it shows me the following information:

    - **Type**, which is a **Process** color (*A* in *Figure 12.22*)

    - The **RGB**, **CMYK**, and **HEX** color values (*B* in *Figure 12.22*)

    - The **Created** date for the color swatch (*C* in *Figure 12.22*)

    - The **Modified** date (*D* in *Figure 12.22*)

    - The **Library** area it is in (*E* in *Figure 12.22*)

    To stop looking at the information for this individual asset and return to the library, simply click the small arrow (marked *M* in *Figure 12.22*)

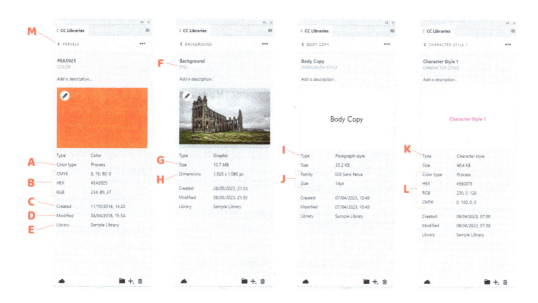

Figure 12.22: The Get Info results for various asset types in the CC Libraries

The information shown will vary for different types of assets. Graphic objects, for example, will show the file's **Type** (marked *F* in *Figure 12.22*), its **Size** (marked *G* in *Figure 12.22*), and the image's **Dimensions** (marked *H* in *Figure 12.22*). In the case of **Text Styles**, you will see the style's **Type** (marked *I* and *K* in *Figure 12.22*), as well as the properties that make up the style (marked *J* and *L* in *Figure 12.22*).

Having checked the properties for my library assets, I am happy that they are what I expected, and I don't need to edit or change any of them. However, I would like to add a description to some of them to make it a little easier for me and others to identify them in the future.

2. Select one of the paragraph styles in the **CC Libraries** panel, then right-click on it and choose **Add Description**. A small box will appear in which you can enter a **Description** value of up to 130 characters and then click **OK**. This description will now appear in the **CC Libraries** panel in InDesign and other programs when you hover your mouse over this item.

   In my case, the description I used was `Main Brand Header Style`. I applied this to the main brand header style in the **CC Libraries** panel. Repeat this for any other assets in your library that you wish to identify more clearly.

3. While adding a description is useful, it requires users to hover over the item to see the description. Sometimes, you might just want to rename an item, to have a more immediate visual cue that can be seen immediately in the **CC Libraries** panel.

   In my case, the main logo I imported from Illustrator is currently called **Artwork 8**. This tells me nothing about it and isn't especially helpful when I'm trying to distinguish it from other artwork there. To rename it, I am going to select the item in the **CC Libraries** panel, then right-click on it and select the **Rename** option. The **Name** field for the asset will now become active, and I can replace the name with a new name before hitting the *Enter* key to save the changes.

4. Having added several items to our library, I want to be able to search for a word that appears in either the **Name** or **Description** field. In my case, I am going to search for the word **Brand**, so I will type this into the search bar (marked *A* in *Figure 12.23*) and click the small arrow to the right (marked *B* in *Figure 12.23*). A dropdown will appear that allows us to choose where we want to search from:

   - **Current library**: This will search within the **Name** and **Description** fields of items in your current library.

   - **All libraries**: This will search within the **Name** and **Description** fields of all the items in all of your libraries.

   - **Adobe Stock**: This will search within the Adobe Stock website for items that match the search word(s) and bring up relevant results:

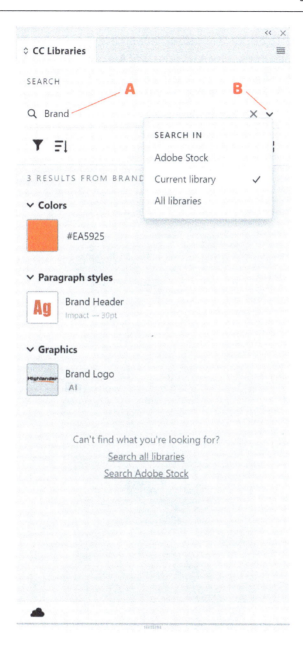

Figure 12.23: Searching within a library in the CC Libraries panel

At the moment, I am searching in **Current library** but I am unable to find what I want, so I will switch to **Adobe Stock** in the dropdown. You will see a list of items appear from the Adobe Stock site. As you hover over them, you will see icons appear to either **Licence and save to Brand Assets Library** (marked *A* in *Figure 12.24*) or **Save Preview to Brand Assets Library** (marked *B* in *Figure 12.24*). The **License** option will charge you a fee to license the image, while the **Save Preview** option will save a watermarked low-resolution version of the item to your current library, which can then be licensed later from within the **CC Libraries** panel (as shown in *step 5* of the *Adding and reusing graphics via CC Libraries* recipe earlier in this chapter):

Figure 12.24: Searching Adobe Stock in the CC Libraries panel

Having searched Adobe Stock and found a graphic that does what I need, I will click the **Save Preview to Brand Assets Library** icon. The panel will now refresh and display my **Brand Assets** library with the Adobe Stock image preview included.

5. I now have quite a few items in my library and would like to be able to find things quickly without having to search for a specific word every time. To do this, I will click the **Filter** icon (marked *A* in *Figure 12.25*), which will let me filter the library to show one or more specific types of content. In *Figure 12.25*, I have filtered this to show only **Graphics** assets and, as such, **Paragraph styles**, **Character styles**, **Colors**, and other items are temporarily hidden in the library. If you wish to see all items again, simply click the **Clear filters** link (marked *B* in *Figure 12.25*):

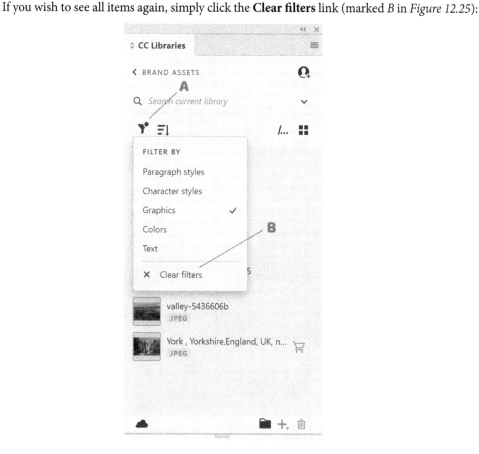

Figure 12.25: Applying filters in the CC Libraries panel

6. Being able to sort by the type of file as we did here is useful, though sometimes, you might want to be able to create custom groups to organize things in. You can do this by selecting the assets you wish to include and then clicking the **New Group** icon (marked *A* in *Figure 12.26*), which will allow you to create **New Group** and, at the same time, automatically include the items you selected. Alternatively, with nothing selected, click the **New Group** icon and create an empty **New Group** that you can then drag items into in the **CC Libraries** panel. If you wish to remove items from a group, you can simply drag them out of the group and into the area marked **Not Grouped**.

In my case, I will select both my **Paragraph styles** and **Character styles** and then click the **New Group** icon and create a new group called **All Styles**. I will then create another new group called **Colors and Logos** that includes my color swatches and logos:

Figure 12.26: Custom groups in CC Libraries

Having created a couple of new groups, I can now choose whether I want my library to **Group By** the asset's **Type** or the new custom groups I have created. To switch the **Group By** choice, click the **Sort Options** icon (marked *B* in *Figure 12.26*); here, you can select **Type** (marked *C* in *Figure 12.26*) or **Custom group** (marked *D* in *Figure 12.26*). In my case, I will choose **Custom group**. When grouping by **Type**, you will be able to sort using either **Name** (marked *E* in *Figure 12.26*) or **Date Modified** (marked *G* in *Figure 12.26*). In my case, I chose to group by **Custom group**, which allows me to sort by either **Name** (marked *E* in *Figure 12.26*), which will sort the groups alphabetically by name, or **Custom Order** (marked *F* in *Figure 12.26*), which allows me to reorder the groups in whatever order I prefer by dragging them up and down within the **CC Libraries** panel. I will sort **Custom Groups** by **Name**.

7. While a library can technically hold up to 10,000 items, it's more likely that you will want to spread assets among several different libraries and may even want to move or copy an asset into more than one library. One reason for doing this would be if you wanted to share some of the assets in a library with colleagues but not others. In such a scenario, you could copy the assets you wish to share into a new library and then collaborate with other users on that library, something we will look at in the *Collaborating with other users* recipe.

    In my case, I would like to do this with my text styles, which I want to share with a third party who also uses InDesign. To do this, I will select the items I wish to copy in the **CC Libraries** panel, and then right-click on one of them and select the **Copy selected item to** option. This will bring up the **Copy to** dialog box:

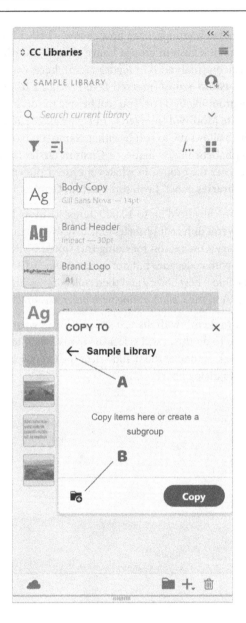

Figure 12.27: Moving items between CC Libraries

The **Copy to** dialog starts by showing your current library, but by clicking the small arrow (marked *A* in *Figure 12.27*), you can view a list of all your other libraries. If the library you want to copy to already exists, you can click it here, but if not, click the small **Create new library** icon (marked *B* in *Figure 12.27*). Here, you can enter a name for your new library – in my case, **Brand Text Styles** – before clicking **Create**. The **Copy to** dialog box will automatically switch to this new library. At this point, you can click **Copy** to copy your selected items into it.

> **Note**
>
> If you would rather move your assets to another library, without leaving a copy in the original library, the process is the same as the copy process shown in *step 7*, except you must replace the word **Copy** with the word **Move** everywhere it appears in *step 7*.

Collaborating with other users

The CC Libraries are a powerful tool for reusing content, moving it between different documents and applications, and backing up your assets, but they are even more powerful when used to collaborate between different users.

In this recipe, we are going to look at sharing our library with other CC users, allowing them to have view-only access and editing capabilities. We will also look at how to generate a link that can be shared with anybody you wish, allowing them to see the contents of your library through a browser.

Getting ready

To complete this recipe, simply open InDesign on your system and create a new document with 12 pages, as shown in the *Creating a new document* recipe in *Chapter 1*. Having done this, create a new library (I have called mine **Brand Ideas Library**) and add a few sample items to your library, such as color swatches, graphics, or text styles, as shown in the earlier recipes in this chapter.

How to do it...

To collaborate with other users in CC Libraries, follow these steps:

1. Having created a library and added some items, we want to share these with two other users. The first user is the Junior Designer, who I wish to grant access to use items from the library. However, I don't want them to be able to edit or change the library. The second is the Brand Manager, who should have editing capabilities as they are responsible for the brand:

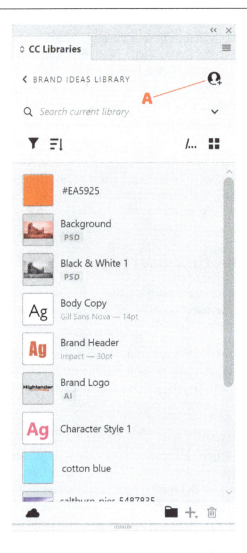

Figure 12.28: The Invite to library icon in the CC Libraries panel

To do this, click the **Invite to library** icon in the **CC Libraries** panel (marked *A* in *Figure 12.28*). This will open the **Creative Cloud Desktop application** and bring up the **Invite to Library** dialog box.

In the **Invite to Library dialog box**, I can add the email address for the Junior Designer in the field marked *A* in *Figure 12.29*, and I can then type a message in the message box (marked *B* in *Figure 12.29*) telling them exactly what the link is. Then, I need to give them **Can View** permissions (marked *C* in *Figure 12.29*) to allow them to be able to only view the library but not edit it, before clicking the **Invite** button (marked *D* in *Figure 12.29*):

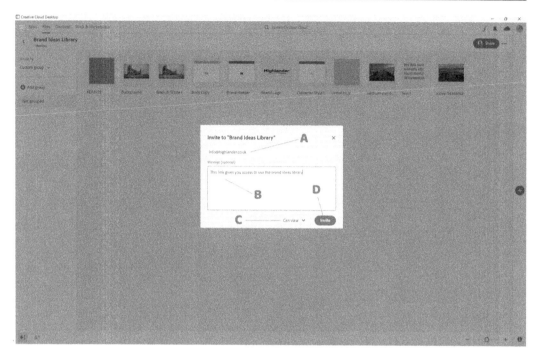

Figure 12.29: The Invite to Library dialog in the Creative Cloud Desktop app

Having added the Junior Designer, I will now add the Brand Manager. Again, I will add their email address and any message, but this time, I will choose **Can edit** from the permissions dropdown (marked *C* in *Figure 12.29*) before clicking the **Invite** button.

Both users will be sent an email containing a link advising them that either **Andy Gardiner has invited you to view and use** the **CC Brand Ideas Library** or **Andy Gardiner has invited you to collaborate on the Brand Ideas library**, depending on whether I chose **Can View** or **Can Edit**. To start using the library, the user just needs to click the link in the email and log in to their CC account to accept the invitation. The library will then show up in the **CC Libraries** panel on their machine.

2. Having sent invites to the users we wish to collaborate with, we might need to manage their access permissions, or even just check if they have accepted the invite. To do this, open the **CC Libraries** panel in InDesign and click the **Invite to library** icon that we used in *step 1*. This will open the CC app again, showing the library. It should also open the **Invite to Library** dialog box However, if it doesn't do so automatically, you can click the **Share** button (marked *A* in *Figure 12.30*) to open this:

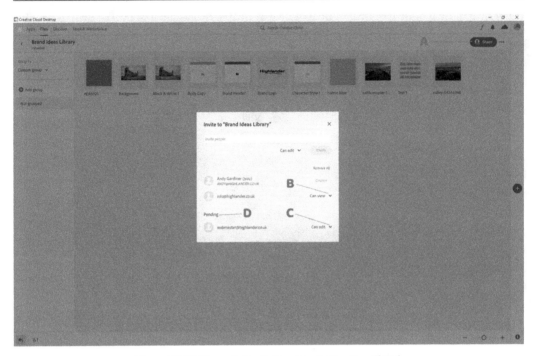

Figure 12.30: Managing collaborators in Creative Cloud

This time, in the **Invite to Library** dialog, you will see the collaborators we invited previously. The **Junior Designer** with **Can View** permissions (marked *B* in *Figure 12.30*) has accepted the invite and appears in the top half of the dialog box; however, the **Brand Manager**, who we gave **Can Edit** permissions (marked *C* in *Figure 12.30*), has not yet accepted the invite and is still showing up under the **Pending** section (marked *D* in *Figure 12.30*). Now that I am aware of this, I can speak to them and remind them to accept the invite. While there isn't currently an option to send a reminder, I can also remove their access here and invite them again, which will, in turn, resend the invite to them.

If you wish to change the permissions for any users, click the small arrow to the right of the **Can edit** or **Can view** options for the user. You will see both of these options in the dropdown that appears, as well as a **Remove** option, which can be used if you wish to remove a user's access to the library completely.

3. In addition to giving other CC users collaborative access to the CC Libraries, we can also share a public link to the library. To do this, in the **CC Libraries** panel, navigate to the respective library and, in the panel menu that appears, click the **Get link** option. This will bring up the Creative Cloud Desktop app with the **Share Link to Library** dialog box open.

Here, we can enable the following settings:

- **Allow Save to Creative Cloud** (marked *A* in *Figure 12.31*): When enabled, this allows anybody with the link to save a copy of the library to their libraries, where they can then edit it as an independent library. They will no longer receive any updates. I will leave this disabled.

- **Allow Follow** (marked *B* in *Figure 12.31*): When enabled, this allows users to follow the library and receive updates automatically when you make changes to it. They cannot edit the library. I will enable this:

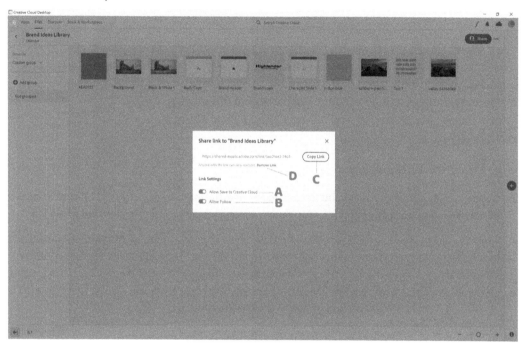

Figure 12.31: Public link settings for a CC Library

Once you have set these settings, you can use the **Copy Link** option (marked *C* in *Figure 12.31*) to get a copy of the link, which can then be sent by email, placed on a public website, and so on so that it can be shared with others. If you decide you no longer wish to share the library with others, use the **Remove Link** option (marked *D* in *Figure 12.31*). In my case, I am going to email this link to a few other people that have a vested interest in the new **Brand Ideas** library but don't need to be actively involved in the creation process itself.

If you have closed the **Share Link to Library** dialog box and wish to come back to it at any point, just use the **Get Link** option in the **CC Libraries** panel again, which we used at the start of *step 3*, to bring it back up.

Backing up and restoring a library

With many of your assets stored in a CC Library, it makes sense to back it up. However, this can also be a useful way to move libraries between accounts. Libraries can be exported as .cclib files, which can then be imported into the **CC Libraries** panel in not only InDesign but also a range of other Adobe CC apps.

In this short but important recipe, we will look at creating a backup of a library and how to restore it from within the **CC Libraries** panel in InDesign.

Getting ready

To complete this recipe, if you don't already have a library with some content in it, create one now. I have called mine **Brand Ideas Library** and added a few sample items, including color swatches, graphics, and text styles, as shown in the earlier recipes in this chapter.

How to do it...

To export and import your CC Libraries, just follow these steps:

1. Open the **CC Libraries** panel in InDesign and navigate to your library. In the **CC Libraries** panel menu, select the **Export** option for your library, which in my case is **Export "Brand Ideas Lib."**.

    You should now see the **Export library** dialog box appear at the top of the **CC Libraries** panel. Here, you can choose a location for your backup file. To do this, click the **Select folder** icon (marked *A* in *Figure 12.32*) and navigate to the folder you would like the .cclib file to be saved in. If you wish to also change the filename, you can; I will leave mine set to Brand Ideas Library.cclib and save it to the **Desktop** folder:

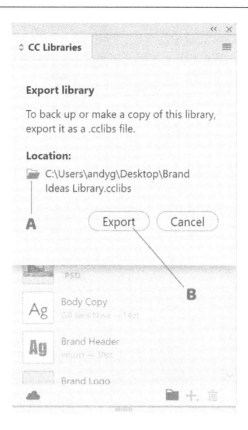

Figure 12.32: The Export library dialog in CC Libraries

Having chosen the folder and filename for the backup, I will now click the **Export** button (marked *B* in *Figure 12.32*) to export my library to a file called Brand Ideas Library.cclib.

Note

When you export a CC Library to a **.cclib** file, it collects all of the included assets and embeds them into a single file, together with a manifest file that details the contents. This is not dissimilar to the process of using a ZIP program to zip up multiple files into a single ZIP file.

2. Having exported my library, I might want to restore it from the backup or give it to a third party so that they can restore it to their account. To restore a library from a .cclib file, go to the **CC Libraries** panel and, from the panel menu, select the **Import Library** option. This will bring up the **Import library dialog box**, where you can select the necessary file and click the **Import** button.

13
Preflighting and Outputting

In this chapter, we will look at preflighting and outputting your documents to a range of different formats.

Preflighting is a useful process that you can undertake before outputting your document to ensure that everything will output as required and ensure there are no hidden problems. The preflight requirements will vary depending on the type of document you are outputting; for example, if you are outputting a print-ready PDF, you will want to ensure your images are all of a high enough resolution for print, while in a small file size digital PDF, you would want to aim for a lower resolution to help bring the overall file size down.

In this chapter, we will run through the options available when creating preflight profiles, look at importing and exporting profiles, and learn how to switch between your profiles for different document types. We will then move on to look at common exporting options such as print-ready PDFs, digital PDFs, and interactive PDFs, and the options available for each of these formats. Then, we will look at how to create a package for backup or handing your document off to a third party, as well as the Publish Online feature that is included with InDesign.

While these jobs will naturally feel like a process you undertake at the end of your work, the opposite is true in some cases. Preflighting, for example, is something that is active as you work on the document, hence it is known as **live preflighting**, and it makes sense to set your preflight profile up at the start of your document, allowing you to receive ongoing warnings as you are working on the document. It is also worth noting that preflighting is a checklist, and ignoring items in it will not prevent you from saving your document to file formats such as PDFs (outputting), which are compatible with other software, albeit it might result in errors in your document.

The recipes we will cover in this chapter are as follows:

- Creating a custom preflight profile
- Exporting and importing a preflight profile
- Switching preflight profiles and embedding a profile
- Reviewing and identifying preflight warnings

- Saving your InDesign file
- Creating a package
- Outputting to a print-ready PDF
- Outputting a small digital PDF
- Outputting an interactive PDF
- Outputting with Publish Online

Technical requirements

To complete this chapter, you will need a PC or Mac, with a copy of Adobe InDesign installed. At a minimum, you should be comfortable adding content to your documents and formatting it, as shown in *Chapters 1* to *4*, and a familiarity with the other features of InDesign will be of benefit.

Creating a custom preflight profile

Preflighting is a powerful way of automatically checking your document for a wide range of potential problems, but it is only as good as the profile you create – set up the profile wrong or use the wrong profile, and you will either be missing potentially serious problems that will affect your document or you will be seeing lots of errors listed for things that aren't necessarily a problem.

In this recipe, we are going to set up a custom preflight profile for checking your document. I am going to create a **preflight profile** for a print-ready PDF document, but as we do this, I will also flag the settings for other types of documents too.

Getting ready

In order to complete this recipe, simply open InDesign on your system and create a new document with 12 pages, as shown in the *Creating a new document* recipe in *Chapter 1*.

How to do it...

In order to create a custom preflight profile, just follow these steps:

1. Let's start by opening the **Preflight** panel, which is found in the **Window** menu under **Output**. Then, from the **Preflight** panel, select **Define Profiles**, which brings up the **Preflight Profiles** dialog box. This is where you can create, edit, import, and export preflight profiles.

   In our case, we want to create a new preflight profile, so we will click the **New Preflight Profile** icon (marked *A* in *Figure 13.1*).

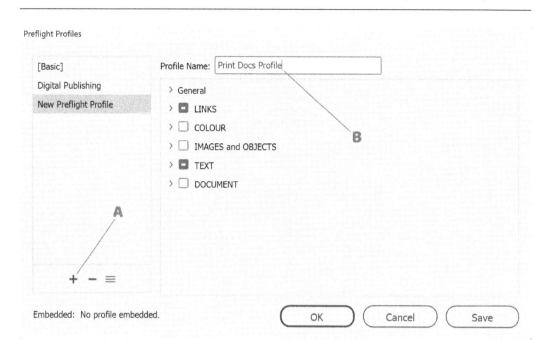

Figure 13.1: Preflight Profiles panel

Having done this, give the new profile a name in the **Profile Name** field (marked *B* in *Figure 13.1*) – I will call mine **Print Docs Profile** as I intend to use it for checking print documents before sending them off for print. Then, click **Save**.

> **Note**
>
> If you click **OK** instead of **Save**, don't panic (we've all done it); to bring the **Preflight Profiles** dialog box up again, just go back to the **Preflight** panel menu and click **Define Profiles** again.

The **Preflight Profiles** dialog box is broken into six distinct sections, and in *steps 2* to *7* we will go through each section one at a time.

2. The first section is **General**, and it is also the easiest as it only contains one thing: the **Description** field. If you don't already see the **Description** field, just expand the **General** section with the small arrow (marked *A* in *Figure 13.2*) next to the word **General**. Type a suitable description of the profile in the **Description** field (marked *B* in *Figure 13.2*), and then click **Save**.

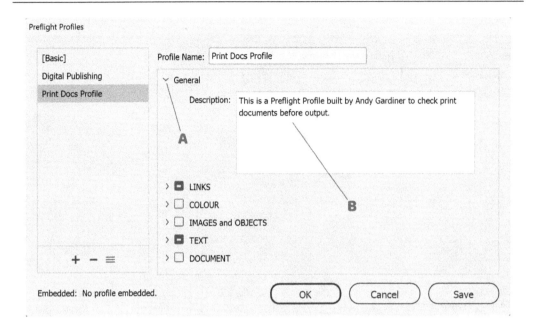

Figure 13.2: The Preflight Description

Having done this, click the small arrow again to contract the **General** section.

3.   Next, we will check the **LINKS** section:

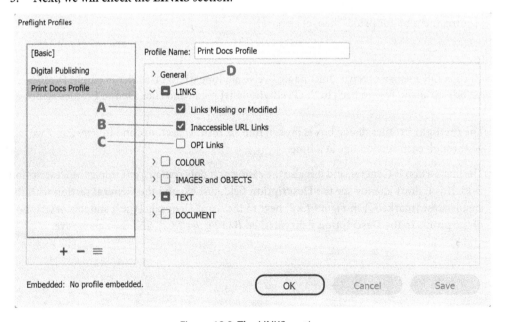

Figure 13.3: The LINKS section

Click the small arrow next to the **LINKS** section to expand it so we can see the options available. These options are as follows:

- **Links Missing or Modified** (*A* in *Figure 13.3*): If selected, missing or modified links (which are typically found in the **Links** panel) will be displayed as errors in the preflight. We will select this option.

- **Inaccessible URL Links** (*B* in *Figure 13.3*): When selected, this will check the hyperlinks in your document to ensure they are valid and accessible. We are creating a print document, so don't specifically need this setting, but there is no harm in leaving it enabled.

- **OPI Links** (*C* in *Figure 13.3*): We will leave this unchecked, as it is rarely used anymore. OPI links allowed the use of low-resolution images, which were replaced with high-resolution images during output, somewhat similar to the proxy functionality available in tools such as Premiere Pro.

> **Note**
>
> It is worth noting the line through some of the checkboxes for the sections – for example, **LINKS** (marked *D* in *Figure 13.3*). This indicates that some of the options in that section are currently selected.

Having looked at the **LINKS** section, we will now contract it by clicking the accompanying arrow, and take a look at the next section, which is **COLOR**.

4. Expand the **COLOR** section by clicking the arrow next to it:

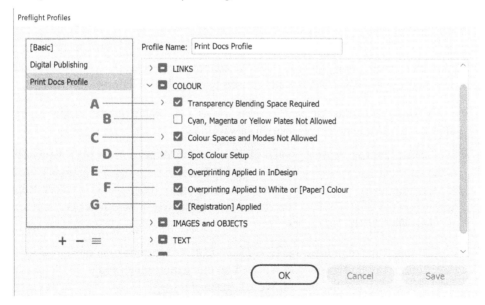

Figure 13.4: COLOR in InDesign Preflight Profiles dialog

You will see the following options:

- **Transparency Blending Space Required** (*A* in *Figure 13.4*): InDesign allows the placing of both **RGB** and **CMYK** objects within a document. If an object contains transparency, it is important to ensure it is using the correct color space when blending with other objects beneath it; in this case, we are creating a print document so will select the checkbox and then expand the section to set this to **CMYK**, as opposed to **RGB**, which would be used for a screen-only document.

- **Cyan, Magenta or Yellow Plates Not Allowed** (*B* in *Figure 13.4*): In some cases, you may not require certain color plates to be used. In our case, we are outputting for a four-color print run (i.e., Cyan, Magenta, Yellow, and Key (black)), so will leave this unselected.

- **Color Spaces and Modes Not Allowed** (*C* in *Figure 13.4*): This check allows you to make sure that all the objects in your document are using the correct color mode and color space for the intended output. In our case, we are outputting a document for four-color print, so we will expand this section and select the other color modes, leaving only **CMYK** deselected.

> **Note**
>
> Bear in mind that preflighting is a checking process, designed to provide you with a warning list of items that might be potential problems, and while it is generally good practice, it is not obligatory to fix the issues identified. In the case of **Color Spaces and Modes Not Allowed**, we are checking for everything except **CMYK** objects; however, we may have included RGB objects in our document with the intention of converting them to CMYK during the output process. These objects will trigger a preflight warning, but in such a scenario, we can ignore the warning on the basis that we are going to convert the color mode of the RGB objects to CMYK during output.

- **Spot Color Setup**: (*D* in *Figure 13.4*) As we are not using spot colors, we will leave this unchecked, but when enabled, this allows users to control the following:

  - **Maximum Spot Colors Allowed**: This lets you set a maximum number of spot colors to allow in the document before triggering a warning.

  - **Predefined Spot Colors Must:** Should either be **Use Lab Values** or **Use CMYK Equivalents** when set, otherwise a warning will be triggered. These days, spot colors commonly use lab values rather than CMYK equivalents. One advantage of this is that spot colors defined with lab values will typically be previewed more accurately on screen devices than those defined with CMYK equivalents.

- **Overprinting Applied in InDesign** (*E* in *Figure 13.4*): Overprinting can cause overlapping colors to come out differently than expected, so this setting allows you to check for items where overprinting is being applied. We will enable this.

- **Overprinting Applied to White or [Paper] Color** (*F* in *Figure 13.4*): As with the previous setting, this allows you to check for overprint applied specifically to White or Paper color. We will enable this too.

> **Note**
>
> **Overprinting** is a printing technique where two or more ink colors are printed on top of each other, creating a new color. It is achieved by printing one color over another color, allowing the two colors to mix and create a third color. For example, if you print yellow ink on top of blue ink, the resulting color will be green. Overprinting can be used to create a range of colors, textures, and effects in printed materials such as books, posters, and packaging.

- **[Registration] Applied** (*G* in *Figure 13.4*): When enabled, this checks whether the Registration color swatch has been applied in your document in place of the Black swatch. The Registration color swatch is made up of 100% on all four color channels that make up the CMYK color mode, while the Black swatch comprises 100% Black (although InDesign does have options to alter this to Rich Black, which includes a small amount of Cyan, Magenta, and Yellow). Using Registration within your design would cause issues in print, so we want to identify any such issues and, therefore, will enable this check.

Having looked at the **COLOR** section, we will now take a look at the next section, which is **IMAGES and OBJECTS**.

5. Expand the **IMAGES and OBJECTS** section and you will then see the following options available:

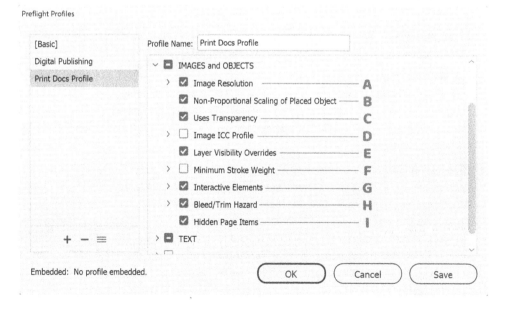

Figure 13.5: IMAGES and OBJECTS section in InDesign Preflight Profiles dialog

Let's take a look at each one:

- **Image Resolution** (*A* in *Figure 13.5*): Here, you can check for images that don't meet the required resolution. In our case, we are creating a profile for print documents, so I will enable this, and then set the **Minimum** value for **Color** and **Grayscale** images to **300** PPI (pixels per inch) and **Maximum** to **1200** PPI. As far as **1 bit** images are concerned, I am not intending to use any and will leave the **Minimum** value set to **800** PPI and the **Maximum** value deselected.

Any images with an effective resolution outside of these ranges will then be flagged as a preflight warning.

- **Non-Proportional Scaling of Placed Objects** (*B* in *Figure 13.5*): This is something we will enable as it checks for objects where the width and/or height have been scaled independently of each other, meaning the object has been stretched.

- **Uses Transparency** (*C* in *Figure 13.5*): This allows you to identify any objects that contain transparency, which might potentially cause printing issues. We will enable this although, in this instance, I don't have any transparent objects.

- **Image ICC Profile** (*D* in *Figure 13.5*): As we are intending to convert the document (including all images) to the relevant CMYK color profile when we export it to a print-ready PDF, we can disable this section.

- **Layer Visibility Overrides** (*E* in *Figure 13.5*): This will check for any images where you have overridden the image's own layer visibility – for example, by using the **Object Layer Options** from the **Object** menu. We will check for this.

- **Minimum Stroke Weight** (*F* in *Figure 13.5*): This allows you to check for any items where the stroke width is below a defined size. We don't need to check for this.

- **Interactive Elements** (*G* in *Figure 13.5*): This allows us to check for common types of interactive content in our document, which is useful in this instance, as we are outputting for print. I will therefore enable all of the options in this section, so we are warned if there is any interactive content and, that way, we don't end up trying to print a video, for example, without realizing it.

- **Bleed/Trim Hazard** (*H* in *Figure 13.5*): When enabled, the **Bleed/Trim Hazard** area lets you add values for **Live Area (inset from Trim)** for **Top**, **Bottom**, **Left/Inside**, and **Right/Outside**. The Live Area is an area around the inside edge of the page, and any colors or images that intrude on this area should be extended past the page edge to the bleed line. If items enter this area and are not extended out to the bleed line, it will trigger a preflight warning. We will set **Live Area (inset from Trim)** to **6.35 mm** on all 4 sides, meaning that an item that is positioned, for example, 6 mm from the edge of the page will trigger a preflight warning.

- There is a checkbox included with the **Bleed/Trim Hazard** settings for **Check for Objects Near Spine**. If this is enabled, the **Bleed/Trim Hazard** checks will also be applied to objects near the spine. We will leave this disabled as we don't want to check objects that are near the spine.

- **Hidden Page Items**: (*I* in *Figure 13.5*) This checks for items on the page that are hidden and alerts you to their presence. I will enable because if there are hidden items on the page, I would like to be aware of them.

Having set the **IMAGES and OBJECTS** settings, we now contract this section and will next take a look at the **TEXT** settings.

6.   Expand the **TEXT** section and you will see the following options available:

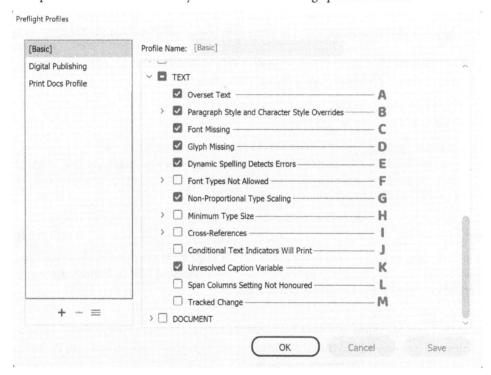

Figure 13.6: TEXT section in InDesign Preflight Profiles dialog

These options are as follows:

- **Overset Text** (*A* in *Figure 13.6*): We will select this to ensure any overset text (text that doesn't fit into the text frame and therefore is being hidden) is identified.

- **Paragraph Style and Character Style Overrides** (*B* in *Figure 13.6*): We will select this to ensure overrides on paragraph and character styles are identified during preflighting. In some cases, they may be deliberate, but often they are accidental, so it is useful to be able to check through them all before exporting. When this is enabled, there are a number of sub-checkboxes allowing us to control this further. We will leave these all deselected; however, they include the following:

    - **Ignore Font Style Overrides**: This will allow us to ignore overrides to the fonts set in styles

    - **Ignore Kerning/Tracking Overrides**: This will allow us to ignore overrides to the **Kerning** or **Tracking** values set in styles

    - **Ignore Language Overrides**: This will allow us to ignore overrides applied to the language set in styles

    - **Ignore Color Overrides**: This will allow us to ignore overrides to the color set in styles

- **Font Missing** (*C* in *Figure 13.6*): We will select this to ensure we are notified if any of the fonts used in our document are missing. I will select this.

- **Glyph Missing**: (*D* in *Figure 13.6*) We will select this to ensure we are notified if any of the glyphs used in our document are missing. I will select this.

- **Dynamic Spelling Detects Errors** (*E* in *Figure 13.6*): This option will identify whether **Dynamic Spelling** is not enabled (it is enabled in the **Edit** menu under **Spelling** by selecting **Dynamic Spelling**). If it is enabled, spelling mistakes in the document are underlined. I will enable this so I will select this.

> **Note**
> **Dynamic Spelling** settings can be customized in the InDesign **Preferences** panel, in the **Spelling** section, where you can change the underline color for **Misspelled Words**, **Repeated Words**, **Uncapitalized Words**, and **Uncapitalized Sentences**.

- **Font Types Not Allowed** (*F* in *Figure 13.6*): Here, you can choose which font types you do not wish to allow within the document. We will leave this disabled; however, the options when this is enabled include the following:

    - **Protected fonts**

    - **Bitmap**

    - **OpenType CFF CID**

    - **ATC (Adobe Type Composer)**

    - **TrueType**

- **OpenType CFF**

- **OpenType TT**

- **Non-Proportional Type Scaling** (*G* in *Figure 13.6*): This will identify any text that has been scaled disproportionately (i.e., the width and height were not kept in proportion to each other). We will select this.

- **Minimum Type Size**: (*H* in *Figure 13.6*): When selected, this allows you to set **Minimum Type Size** as well as choose **Limit to Text with Multiple Inks or Whites**. In my case, I am happy with the size of the fonts I have used so will leave this setting disabled.

- **Cross-References** (*I* in *Figure 13.6*): As we haven't used any cross-references in this document, I will leave this unchecked, but when enabled, this lets you check whether the following apply:

  - **Cross-References Are Out of Date**

  - **Cross-References Are Unresolved**

- **Conditional Text Indicators Will Print** (*J* in *Figure 13.6*): This check will identify whether conditional text indicators are set to print or not. If they are, this might be something you would want to change; in our case, we didn't use **Conditional Text** at all, so don't need to enable this.

- **Unresolved Caption Variable** (*K* in *Figure 13.6*): This will identify whether any captions have been generated that use variables that are not being resolved and will trigger a warning if so. I don't recall using any captions but will leave this checked just in case.

- **Span Columns Setting Not Honored** (*L* in *Figure 13.6*): This check will identify instances for a manual check where the **Span Columns** setting appears to have not been applied properly. As I haven't used the **Span Columns** setting, I can leave this option disabled.

- **Tracked Changes** (*M* in *Figure 13.6*): This will identify where changes have been tracked and flag this for a manual check so that you can identify any issues in the changes. I haven't enabled changes so can leave this disabled.

Now that we have completed the **TEXT** settings, we can contract this section, and we will next take a look at the **DOCUMENT** settings.

7. Expand the **DOCUMENT** section and you will see the following options available:

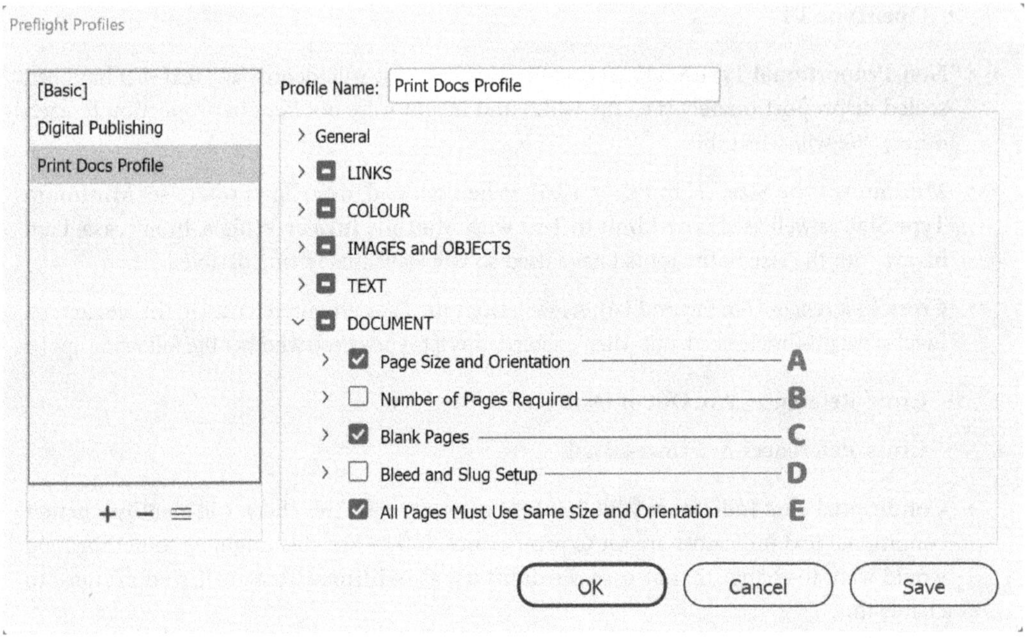

Figure 13.7: DOCUMENT settings in InDesign Preflight dialog

These options are as follows:

- **Page Size and Orientation** (*A* in *Figure 13.7*): This check allows you to ensure all pages are the same size by setting the **Width** and **Height** properties. There is also an optional checkbox for **Ignore Orientation,** which means pages can be positioned in landscape or portrait orientation, as long as the dimensions are correct. I will set this to 210 mm x 297 mm as I am creating an A4 document; if you are working on a different document size, your page dimension will need to reflect that.

> **Note**
>
> It's worth noting that the **Page Size and Orientation** check looks at the page dimensions as set in the **Document Setup** to ensure they match the preflight requirements; however, manually adjusting the dimensions of a single page with the **Page** tool does not trigger the preflight warning.

- **Number of Pages Required** (*B* in *Figure 13.7*): We won't use this option, but this check lets you set the number of pages required to one of the following:

  - **Exactly**: This will ensure the document contains exactly this number of pages.

  - **At least**: This will ensure the document contains a minimum of this number of pages.

- **At most**: This will ensure the document does not contain more pages than the number set.

- **Multiple of**: This will ensure the document contains a multiple of this number of pages. For example, when creating booklets or magazines, you will typically be working in multiples of 4.

- **Blank Pages**: (*C* in *Figure 13.7*) This check lets you identify any blank pages that might have been missed by accident. This could happen, for example, if you leave a page blank with the intention of placing content there from a third party (for example, an advert in a magazine), but the third party then doesn't provide the content. There are also two additional options available for fine-tuning the **Blank Pages** check when it is enabled:

  - **Consider pages empty if they only contain parent page items**

  - **Consider pages empty if they contain non-printing items**

  I will select all the settings here.

- **Bleed and Slug Setup** (*D* in *Figure 13.7*): Here, you can check that the **Bleed** and **Slug** settings match the values you wish to use. While the two checks are set independently of each other, the options are the same, allowing you to set the **Bleed** and **Slug** values for **Top**, **Bottom**, **Left**, and **Right** to one of the following options:

  - **Exactly**: When selected, this will check that the bleed or slug is exactly the value set for the respective sides

  - **Minimum of**: When selected, this will check that the bleed or slug is a minimum of the value set for the respective sides

  - **Maximum of**: When selected, this will check that the bleed or slug is a maximum of the value set for the respective sides

  In my case, I am happy these have been set correctly so don't feel the need to check this.

- **All Pages Must Use Same Size and Orientation** (*E* in *Figure 13.7*): When selected, this will trigger a warning unless all pages use the same size and orientation. I will select this as all my pages should be A4 in size.

Having customized the settings for our preflight profile, we can now click **Save** to save the changes, before then clicking **OK** to close the dialog box.

See also

It is worth noting that while we have created a new custom preflight profile, this is not yet being used. If you are unsure how to switch between profiles and check preflighting, take a look at the other recipes in this chapter, in particular, the *Switching preflight profiles* and *Reviewing and identifying preflight warnings* recipes.

Also, there are a number of options you can check for when creating a custom preflight profile that we haven't covered in this book, such as *Cross-References* or *Tracked Changes*. If you would like to know more about these options, I discuss some of them on my blog at `https://www.highlander.co.uk/blog`.

Exporting and importing preflight profiles

When using preflight profiles, it can be useful to be able to **import and export the profiles**. Maybe you want to export a copy of a preflight profile to give it to a colleague for them to preflight their own documents, or you might want to import a copy of a preflight profile provided by your printer. In either case, the ability to export and import profiles can come in useful and potentially save you quite a bit of time.

In this recipe, we will look at how to export a preflight profile from the **Preflight** panel as well as how to import a profile back into the panel.

Getting ready

If you are intending to export a preflight profile, then you should be comfortable creating a preflight profile as shown in the previous recipe, *Creating a custom preflight profile*. If you are looking to import a preflight profile that you have been provided with, you can skip straight to *step 3*.

How to do it...

In order to import and export preflight profiles, just follow these steps:

1. We will start by exporting an existing preflight profile. Open the **Preflight** panel from the **Window** menu in the **Output** section, and then from the **Preflight** panel menu, select **Define Profiles**.

2. In the **Preflight Profiles** dialog box, select the preflight profile that you wish to export, and then select the **Preflight Profile** menu (marked *A* in *Figure 13.8*) and choose the **Export Profile...** option. In the **Save Preflight Profile As** dialog box that appears, you can give your preflight profile a name and choose a location to save it to, before clicking **Save**.

Preflight Profiles

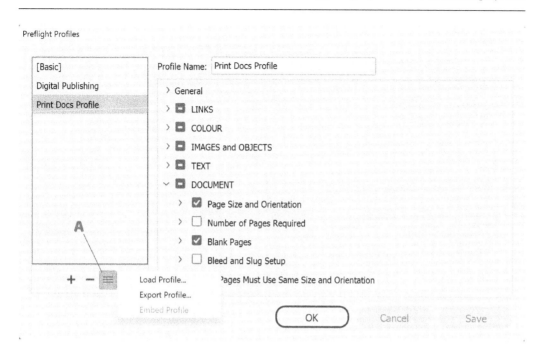

Figure 13.8: Preflight Profiles menu options

Having looked at how to export a preflight profile, let's now look at how to import a profile, or **Load Profile** as it's known in InDesign.

3.   Open the **Preflight** panel and go to **Define Profiles**. Click the **Preflight Profiles** menu (marked *A* in *Figure 13.8*) and select the option for **Load Profile…**. Select the preflight profile file (an IDPP file) that you wish to load and then click **Open**. Your loaded profile should now show in the list of profiles in the **Preflight Profiles** dialog box.

Switching preflight profiles and embedding a profile

When working with preflight profiles, you may end up with a number of different profiles for different types of documents. In a print document, you may want to check that the bleed is configured correctly, that no interactive objects are being included, and that images have a minimum resolution of 300 PPI, while in an interactive digital PDF, you might be more interested in checking for inaccessible URL links or making sure images don't go above a certain resolution.

In this recipe, we are going to look at where you can switch between preflight profiles and also how to embed a preflight profile into your document.

Getting ready

In order to complete this recipe, simply open InDesign on your system and create a new document with 12 pages, as shown in the *Creating a new document* recipe in *Chapter 1*. If you haven't yet created a preflight profile, see the previous recipes on *Creating a custom preflight profile* and *Exporting and importing preflight profiles*.

How to do it...

In order to switch between preflight profiles and embed a profile into your document, follow these steps:

1. Open the **Preflight panel** where you will see the **Profile** dropdown (*A* in *Figure 13.9*). You can use this dropdown to select a preflight profile from those that have already been created.

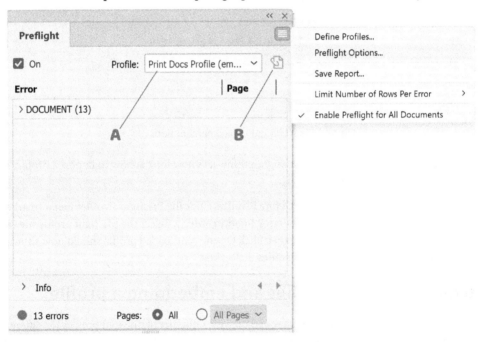

Figure 13.9: Switching the preflight profile

Upon switching the profile, you might see changes to the number of errors detected by preflighting. This is because preflighting is live and it updates constantly as you work on the document and do things such as switch profiles. In my case, I am going to switch to the *Print Docs Profile* that I created in the first recipe of this chapter.

2. Having switched to the *Print Docs Profile*, I am now going to embed the profile into the document. This means that when I send the document to somebody else, they will also get the preflight profile included with it and can use that to check for errors.

To embed the currently selected profile into the document, within the **Preflight** panel, you can just click to embed the current profile using the icon marked *B* in *Figure 13.9*. The profile is now embedded into the document and will be saved with the document when that is saved. If another user opens the document, the embedded profile should be used by default, provided they haven't previously changed their InDesign **Preflight Options** settings to **Use Working Profile**.

InDesign preflighting is configured to **Use Embedded Profile** (marked *A* in *Figure 13.10*) by default when opening documents. If you do not want it to do this, you can switch it to instead **Use Working Profile** (marked *B* in *Figure 13.10*) from **Preflight Options**, which is accessed from the menu on the **Preflight** panel (shown previously in *Figure 13.9*).

Figure 13.10: InDesign Preflight Options

Having embedded the *Print Docs Profile*, the printer I am going to send this to has now asked me not to bother embedding a profile as they will use their own preflighting profiles. As a result, I now want to unembed the profile. To do this, go to the **Preflight** panel menu and click **Define Profiles**. In the **Preflight Profiles** dialog box, click on the menu (marked *A* in *Fig 13.11*) and select the **Unembed Profile** option.

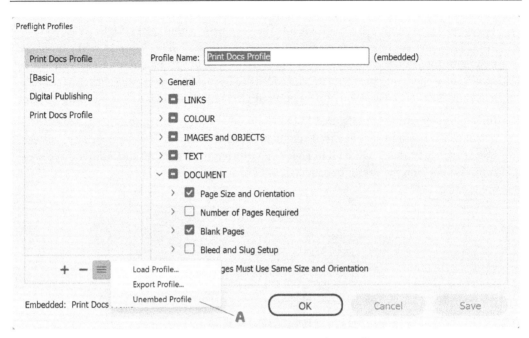

Figure 13.11: Unembed Profile in Define Profiles

This means that when you save the document, the profile will now be no longer be embedded into it.

Reviewing and identifying preflight warnings

Working through preflight errors is an efficient way to ensure your document is properly output and problems are not caused by errors that could have been easily fixed. Provided you use a properly configured preflight profile, you can simply work down the checklist one item at a time, resolving any problems and ignoring items listed that you know are not going to cause an issue.

In this recipe, we will look at how to review and identify errors in preflighting, fixing some example errors to show how the list updates live, and preflighting specific pages instead of the whole document.

Getting ready

In order to complete this recipe, simply open InDesign on your system and create a new document with 12 pages, as shown in the *Creating a new document* recipe in *Chapter 1*.

You should be comfortable adding content to your documents in InDesign and, for this recipe, I will deliberately add some content with errors, including a text frame with overset text and a paragraph style with an override applied. While you do not need to specifically add this content, you will need a document to run preflighting on, and having some errors to identify in the document will make the recipe more relevant.

In addition, it is assumed that you are already comfortable creating a custom preflight profile and switching to it, as shown in the previous two recipes of this chapter.

How to do it...

In order to review and identify errors when using preflight, just follow these steps:

1. The first step to preflighting is having the right profile and switching to it; otherwise, you are going to be checking for the wrong errors. In my case, I am going to switch to the *Print Docs Profile* that I created in the *Creating a custom preflight profile* recipe earlier in this chapter. You can use your own custom preflight profile if you prefer, but I would recommend not using the **[Basic] (working)** profile for this recipe, as it is designed to only identify the most obvious errors.

    Having switched profiles, you should now hopefully see some errors listed. If not, it is either because your document has no errors or your preflight profile is not configured to detect those errors.

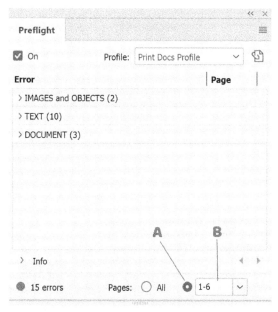

Figure 13.12: List of errors in the Preflight panel

2. By default, you will be seeing all errors for the document; however, in my case, I only want to preflight pages 1 to 6 because pages 7 onward contain placeholder content and I haven't finished designing them yet (hence they will generate a lot of errors). To do this, go to the bottom of the **Preflight** panel and check the box marked *A* in *Figure 13.12*, and then replace the text in the box to the right (marked *B* in *Figure 13.12*) with **1-6**.

Having chosen which pages we are going to preflight, we can now look at the errors.

3. To expand the **Error** categories, click the small arrow next to them (marked *A* in *Figure 13.13*). Then, to see the list of instances (where relevant), expand an error to show the individual instances of a particular error by clicking the arrow next to it.

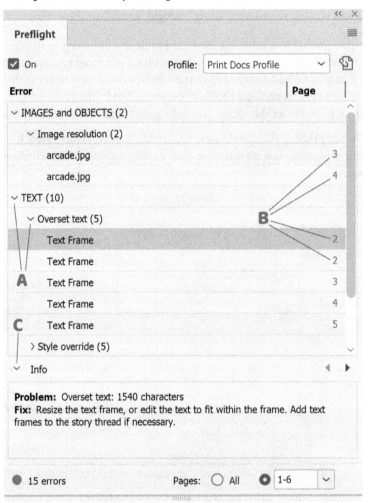

Figure 13.13: Expanding categories and instances of errors

Alongside the instances, you can see the number of the page where the error can be found (marked *B* in *Figure 13.13*). Click on one of the errors (in my case, I will click on the text frame for the overset text error) and next, we will look at the details of the error.

4. To see details on the selected error, expand the information section at the bottom of the panel (marked *C* in *Figure 13.13*), which contains two distinct sections:

   • **Problem**: This section explains exactly what the issue is. In my case, I have selected one of the overset text errors and the problem is therefore showing as **Overset text: 1540 characters**.

   • **Fix**: In terms of the recommended fix, it suggests the following solution – **Resize the text frame, or edit the text to fit within the frame. Add text frames to the story thread if necessary.**

5. I will now click the page number next to the error in the **Preflight** panel and this will jump me straight to the relevant page in the document and automatically select the text frame in question. In this instance, I can simply resize the text frame so that there is no overset text, and you will notice that once done, this instance of the error disappears from the **Preflight** panel. If there was only a single instance, the error itself will also disappear.

   You can now repeat *steps 4* and *5* as many times as required until the errors are either all resolved or you are happy to ignore those remaining. It is worth reiterating that there is no requirement to fix preflight errors and you can ignore them if you are happy that they are deliberate.

Saving your InDesign file

Saving files in InDesign is a pretty straightforward process, but there are a few different file types, and understanding the difference and using the right one can be a useful thing to know.

In this recipe, we will learn how to save a standard InDesign (INDD) file as well as how to save an **InDesign template (INDT)**. We will also look at why, when, and how to save a file to the **InDesign Markup Language (IDML)** format and how to save a copy of your InDesign file.

Getting ready

In order to complete this recipe, simply open InDesign on your system and create a new document with 12 pages, as shown in the *Creating a new document* recipe in *Chapter 1*.

How to do it...

In order to save your file from InDesign, just follow these steps:

1. With your file open, go to the **File** menu and select **Save As**, which will bring up the **Save As** dialog box. Navigate to the folder you wish to save the file to, and then from the **Save as type** (*A* in *Figure 13.14*) dropdown, select **InDesign 2023 document**. This is the default InDesign document file type, an INDD file, which can be opened up on the version of InDesign that was used to create it or a newer version, but it cannot be opened on an older version. Give the file a name in the **File name** field (*B* in *Figure 13.14*) and then click **Save** (*C* in *Figure 13.14*).

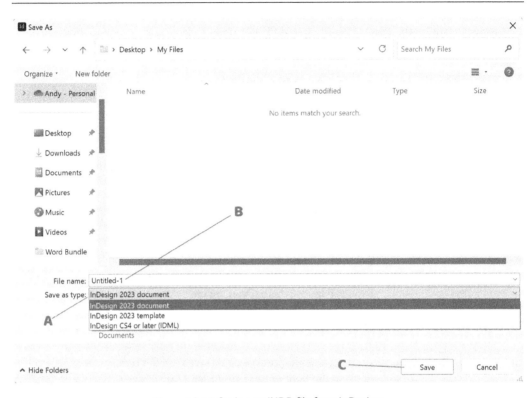

Figure 13.14: Saving an INDD file from InDesign

> **Note**
>
> INDD files cannot be opened on an older version of InDesign than the version used to create them. In *step 3*, we will look at IDML files that can.

In addition to saving an INDD version of my file, I would also like to give it to some colleagues to use as a template from which to start new documents. I am concerned though that if I give them an INDD file, they might change things in the original, and before long, new documents would no longer be brand compliant. Let's look at how to avoid this next.

2. With the document open, return to the **File** menu and select **Save As**, but this time, we will choose the option for **InDesign 2023 template** from the **Save as type** dropdown. The advantage of saving the file as an INDT file is that when a user opens it, hitting **File** and then **Save** will not automatically overwrite the document. In the case of an INDT file, it will ask the user to give the file a new name and save it, as though they were saving the document for the first time.

    Having saved an INDD and an INDT version of the document, I now want to ensure users on older versions of InDesign can open the document if needed. Let's look at how to ensure this.

3. From the **File** menu, go to the **Save As** option, but this time, choose the **InDesign CS4 or later (IDML)** option. This will allow you to save the document using IDML, which is an XML-based format developed by Adobe to ensure compatibility across different versions of Adobe InDesign. An IDML file can be opened on any version of InDesign from CS4 onward regardless of which version it was created on.

> **Note**
>
> While an IDML file allows the document to be opened on older versions of InDesign and ensures constant reproduction of page layouts, images, text, styles, and various other design elements, some features of InDesign will not be fully supported depending on the version being used. For example, if you are opening an IDML file on InDesign CS4, features such as alternate layouts, images in table cells, text hyperlinks, intelligent text wrap around subject, or SVG file support did not exist in that version and would not be supported.

Finally, having now saved the document to INDD, INDT, and IDML files, I want to save a copy of the document with a new name before I carry on working on the existing document.

4. From the **File** menu, go to **Save a Copy**. You can give your copy a new name if you want in the **File name** field (marked *A* in *Figure 13.15*) before hitting **Save**.

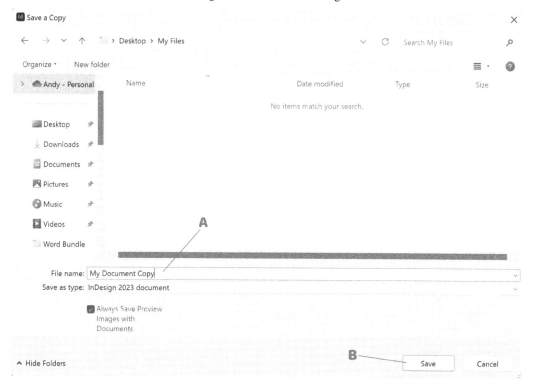

Figure 13.15: Save a Copy dialog box

The advantage of **Save a Copy** is when you hit **Save** (*B* in *Figure 13.15*), it does not open the document you just saved and make it the active document; instead, you can just continue working on your existing document.

Creating a package

While saving your InDesign file is useful, it's worth bearing in mind that doing so only saves the InDesign file and not any linked files, such as images or fonts, that have been used in the document. If somebody opens the file on a different machine, these related files will show as broken links or potentially missing fonts. Also, you may find, even when opening up the file on the same machine sometime later, that there may be missing fonts or broken links as, over time, you may have removed assets that were present when the document was created – for example, by having a clean out of your image assets and deleting some.

In this recipe, we will look at creating a **package** that allows you to collect together the document, as well as copies of all of its assets such as fonts and images into a single directory, which can then be used either for backup purposes or to hand everything off to a third party.

Getting ready

In order to complete this recipe, simply open InDesign on your system and create a new document with 12 pages, as shown in the *Creating a new document* recipe in *Chapter 1*. You should place at least a couple of images somewhere in the document, and use at least two different fonts to format some text in the document.

How to do it...

In order to create a package from your document, just follow these steps:

1. With your file open, start by saving the file if you haven't already done so since you last made changes (InDesign requires all changes to be saved to the document before creating a package file). Now, go to the **File** menu and select the option for **Package** to bring up the *Package dialog box* (*Figure 13.16*).

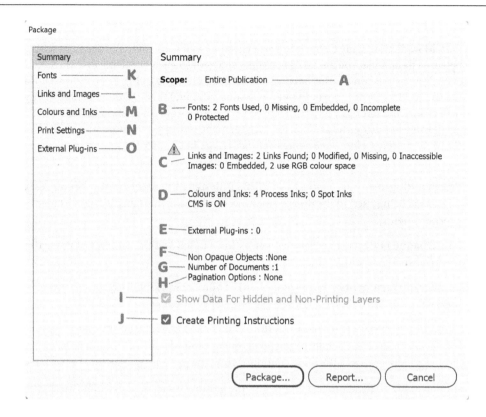

Figure 13.16: The Package dialog box in InDesign

2. When the **Package** dialog box first opens, you will be shown the **Summary** screen, where you can see a summary of the properties of the package that you will create. This is designed to let you check for any problems or missing items before creating the package. The options include the following:

    - **Scope: Entire Publication** (*A* in *Figure 13.16*): This is the default setting when creating a package from within InDesign.

    - **Fonts** (*B* in *Figure 13.16*): This will summarize the number of **Used**, **Missing**, **Embedded**, **Incomplete**, and **Protected** fonts.

    - **Links and Images** (*C* in *Figure 13.16*): This is a summary of the number of **Found**, **Modified**, and **Missing** links, **Inaccessible Images**, **Embedded** images, and Images that **use RGB color space**.

    - **Colors and Inks** (*D* in *Figure 13.16*): This is a summary of the number of **Process Inks** used, **Spot Inks** used, and whether the **CMS** (**Color Management System**) is **ON**.

> **Note**
> While the CMS will most likely be on, it is worth checking that your color management settings are set up correctly and that you are using the right color profile when exporting to CMYK/RGB. This can be done by selecting **Color Settings** under the **Edit** menu in InDesign; however, this only edits the settings for InDesign. I would recommend doing this in Adobe Bridge instead as that will ensure the settings are synchronized across InDesign, Photoshop, and Illustrator, ensuring all three are using the same color management settings. For more information on this, refer to the *Setting Color Management Settings* recipe in *Chapter 8*.

- **External Plug-ins** (*E* in *Figure 13.16*): This is designed to identify whether any external plugins are being used in the document; however, it is worth noting it does not identify all external plugins.

- **Non-Opaque Objects** (*F* in *Figure 13.16*): This will tell you the number of items that are using transparency within your document.

- **Number of Documents** (*G* in *Figure 13.16*): If you are working with a book that contains multiple documents, this will tell you the number of documents.

- **Pagination Options** (*H* in *Figure 13.16*): When working with a book containing multiple documents, this will detail how pagination is being handled – for example, is page numbering within each document in the book continued from the previous document or does it restart?

In addition to the notifications just mentioned, the **Summary** page also contains two checkboxes toward the bottom that allow you to control the following:

- **Show Data For Hidden and Non-Printing Layers** (*I* in *Figure 13.16*): Here, you can decide whether you want to show data for hidden or non-printing layers or exclude it from the information displayed. I will leave this selected to include such data.

- **Create Printing Instructions** (*J* in *Figure 13.16*): Selecting this adds an extra step to the packaging process allowing you to include a text file within the package, which is created from a number of predefined fields that you can complete once you click **Package** (don't do this yet). The fields you will be asked to fill out at that stage will include the following:

  - **Filename**
  - **Contact**
  - **Company**
  - **Address**
  - **Phone**
  - **Fax**

- **Email**

- **Instructions**

If you wish to include a text file containing these details within the package, select the checkbox now as I have.

Finally, the **Report** button allows you to generate a text file containing full details on the package being created, including all of the advanced details covered in *step 3*.

3. The additional tabs in the **Package** dialog box provide more details on the individual categories, including the following:

   - **Fonts** (*K* in *Figure 13.16*): This section expands on the basic fonts information provided in the **Summary** section by allowing you to see more details on your fonts including **Name**, **Type**, **Status**, and whether the font is **Protected**. You can also find/replace fonts from here.

   - **Links and Images** (*L* in *Figure 13.16*): In this section, you can get more extensive information on your links and images including **Name**, **Type**, **Page**, **Status**, and whether the file has an embedded **ICCProfile** or not. You can also click on an item in the list to see more details under the **Current Link/Image** section including **File Name**, last **Link Updated** date, the **File Last Modified** date, **Actual PPI**, **Effective PPI**, information on **Layer Overrides**, **Complete Name**, and file path.

   - **Color and Inks** (*M* in *Figure 13.16*): Here, you can see details on the individual inks used in the document including **Name and Type** of the ink, **Angles**, and **Lines/Inch**. **Angles** refers to the orientation of halftone dots on a grid in the printing process; the standard angles in a traditional printing setup are C=15°, M=75°, Y=0° or 90°, and K=45°. **Lines/Inch** is a measure of how close together the rows of dots in a halftone grid are; the higher the LPI, the more detail in the output.

   - **Print Settings** (*N* in *Figure 13.16*): This section shows you a wide range of information on the print settings that are configured for the document.

   - **External Plug-ins** (*O* in *Figure 13.16*): Here, you can see details on external plugins used by the document. It is worth noting, however, that not all external plugins are identified.

   In our case, we can see that everything is fine from the **Summary** screen and we don't need to expand any of these tabs, so we will continue to create a package now.

4. Click the **Package** button to bring up the **Package Publication** dialog box. Here, you can navigate to the folder where you would like to create the package and then enter a folder name (*A* in *Figure 13.17*).

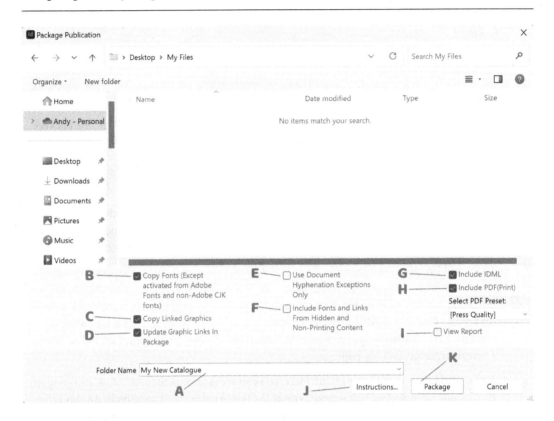

Figure 13.17: Package Publication box in InDesign

The **Package Publication** dialog creates a number of checkboxes including the following:

- **Copy Fonts (Except activated from Adobe Fonts and non-Adobe CJK fonts)** (*B* in *Figure 13.17*): This will include font files in the package, reducing the risk of missing font issues when reopening the document. We will enable this; however, it should be noted that the receiving party will need to ensure they have obtained any licenses needed to use these fonts.

- **Copy Linked Graphics** (*C* in *Figure 13.17*): This will copy any linked graphics into the package, reducing the risk of broken links when reopening the document. We will enable this.

- **Update Graphic Links in Package** (*D* in *Figure 13.17*): This ensures that the links to any graphics that are copied into the package are updated to point to the graphics within the package.

- **Use Document Hyphenation Exceptions Only** (*E* in *Figure 13.17*): Selecting this will help prevent the document from reflowing when somebody opens it on a machine with different hyphenation and dictionary settings. I will leave this disabled; however, I would typically turn it on if sending the package to a printer.

- **Include Fonts and Links From Hidden and Non-Printing Content** (*F* in *Figure 13.17*): Select this option if you wish to include content from hidden layers and non-printing content. As I have none, I will leave this disabled.

- **Include IDML** (*G* in *Figure 13.17*): Selecting this will include an IDML version of the document within the package, ensuring it can be opened on older versions of InDesign. We will select this.

- **Include PDF(Print)** (*H* in *Figure 13.17*): With this selected, you can select PDF presets from the drop-down box. The default options include the following:

  - **[High Quality Print]**: Creates PDFs for quality printing on desktop printers and proofing devices.

  - **[PDF/X-1a:2001]**: An older standard that requires all fonts to be embedded and color to appear as CMYK, spot colors, or both. It is unlikely you will ever use this preset.

  - **[PDF/X-3:2002]**: This preset creates a PDF based on the ISO standard PDF/X-3:2002. It is unlikely you will ever use this preset.

  - **[PDF/X-4:2008]**: This preset creates ISO PDF/X-4:2008 files that support live transparency and ICC color management, and outputs to the PDF 1.6 standard. Adobe recommends the PDF/X-4:2008 preset as the optimal PDF file format for reliable PDF print publishing workflows. We will select this option.

  - **[Press Quality]**: Creates PDF files for high-quality print production, but does not create files that are PDF/X-compliant, focusing instead on high quality. This preset uses PDF 1.4 and can typically be used as an alternative to the **[PDF/X-4:2008]** preset for outputting PDFs for professional print.

  - **[Smallest File Size]**: Creates PDF files for displaying on the web, an intranet, or for email distribution. This set of options uses compression, downsampling, and a relatively low image resolution. It converts all colors to sRGB and embeds fonts. This preset is fine for documents intended for screen use, but should not be used for documents you intend to print.

If you chose **Create Printing Instructions** in *step 2*, you can now check the **View Report** checkbox (*I* in *Figure 13.17*) to automatically open the report. If you want to further adjust the printing instructions at this stage, simply click the **Instructions…** button (*J* in *Figure 13.17*) to do so.

To finish creating your package, simply click the **Package** button (*K* in *Figure 13.17*) to complete the process.

Outputting to a print-ready PDF

While exporting your print-ready documents is a fairly straightforward process, it is important to get the steps right – failure to do so could seriously impact the quality of your printed documents. It is good practice to preflight your document before output and it is important to ensure that your document is output to the correct PDF standard, with the relevant settings applied.

In this recipe, we will run through the common things to check before going on to configure your document for output to a standards-compliant, print-ready PDF, all ready to hand over to your print service provider.

Getting ready

In order to complete this recipe, simply open InDesign on your system and create a new document with 12 pages, as shown in the *Creating a new document* recipe in *Chapter 1*.

Step 1 requires you to be comfortable with creating a preflight profile and reviewing errors as detailed in the *Creating a custom preflight profile* and *Reviewing and identifying preflight warnings* recipes.

If you wish to output your document without preflighting it first, you could skip straight to *step 2*; this is not something I would advise, however, as you may end up with errors in your document.

How to do it...

In order to output a print-ready PDF from your document, just follow these steps:

1. Before exporting your document, it's important that you first ensure it is ready for output. We looked at how to create a preflight profile already in the *Creating a custom preflight profile* recipe, so we won't go through the actual profile creation process again, but when you create a profile to check your print documents it is important that it runs the right checks. The main things you will want to check for on a print-ready document include the following:

    *   Missing or modified links.

    *   Registration is not being used instead of black.

    *   Image resolution. This depends on the type of printing involved – handheld print will typically require an effective resolution of 300 PPI for images, while formats that are viewed from a distance such as signs or posters can have a lower resolution. I would recommend asking your printer what resolution they recommend for the type of print involved.

    *   Non-proportional scaling of placed objects.

    *   Interactive objects, as these will almost certainly be an issue when printing.

    *   Bleed trim hazards to ensure objects near the page edge are properly bled.

- Hidden page items.

- Overset text.

- Paragraph and character style overrides.

- Missing fonts or glyphs.

- Spelling errors.

- Any blank pages.

- Pages are all the right size and orientation.

Having created a profile that checks for all of these, you should then preflight your document and fix any errors, as described in the *Reviewing and identifying preflight warnings* recipe.

2. With preflighting completed, we are now ready to output the document. From the **File** menu, select **Adobe PDF Preset** and then **PDF/X-4:2008**, which will bring up the **Export** dialog box. Navigate to the folder where you want to save the document and enter a filename into the **File name** field before clicking the **Save** button, which brings up the **Export Adobe PDF** dialog box (shown in *Figure 13.18*).

Figure 13.18: The General section of the Export Adobe PDF dialog box

As we started from the **PDF/X-4:2008** preset, the **Export Adobe PDF** dialog box will be automatically populated with settings that are best suited to exporting a print-ready PDF. There are, however, a small number of fields that we might want to change.

By default, the **PDF/X-4:2008** preset exports all pages; however, if you wish to export a particular page range, you can do so by checking the **Range** checkbox (marked *A* in *Figure 13.18*) and then entering numbers/ranges into the **Options** box (marked *B* in *Figure 13.18*). You can enter either individual page numbers or ranges of pages, separated by commas – for example, entering 2,6-10,12 would export pages 2, 6, 7, 8, 9, 10, and 12.

In my case, I want to export all pages so will select **All Pages**.

Having set the **General** settings, we don't need to make any changes to the **Compression** settings so will go next to **Marks and Bleeds**.

3. Switch to the **Marks and Bleeds** section by clicking the **Marks and Bleeds** tab (marked *A* in *Figure 13.19*).

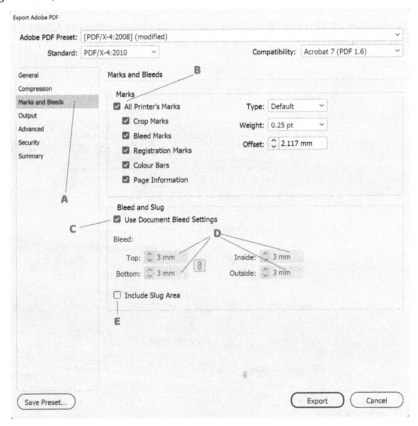

Figure 13.19: Marks and Bleed settings in PDF Export Settings

Click on the checkbox for **All Printer's Marks** (marked *B* in *Figure 13.19*). Checking this will turn on all of the printer's marks, including the following:

- **Crop Marks**: This checkbox allows you to enable or disable crop marks, which identify where the page should be trimmed by the printer

- **Bleed Marks**: This checkbox allows you to enable or disable bleed marks, which are small lines in each corner that indicate how far beyond the page edge the bleed area is

- **Registration Marks**: This checkbox allows you to enable or disable registration marks, which are alignment marks used by the printer

- **Color Bars**: This checkbox allows you to enable or disable color bars, which appear outside the page edge and allow the printer to fine-tune the inks when preparing for print

- **Page Information**: This checkbox allows you to enable or disable page information at the bottom-left of the pages, including the filename, page number, date and time of output, and color separation name.

In the **Bleed and Slug** section, you can choose whether or not to use the document bleed settings that were set when initially creating the document. To do this, simply check the **Use Document Bleed Settings** box (*C* in *Figure 13.19*), which I will do. If you didn't set a bleed when initially creating the document, you can alternatively set the **Bleed** settings manually, with individual value fields for **Top**, **Bottom**, **Inside**, and **Outside** (*D* in *Fig 13.19*).

Include Slug Area is used if you wish to include a slug using the values defined when the document was created; you can do so by selecting this checkbox (*E* in *Fig 13.19*). The slug is an area that can be designated outside the bleed area and can be used to contain any notes you wish to include that won't appear on the final document. I will leave this unselected.

4. Next, we will select the **Output** tab on the dialog box (*A* in *Fig 13.20*) to bring up the **Output** settings. These settings are an important step in ensuring your document is ready for professional print, as it controls things such as how RGB colors are going to be handled.

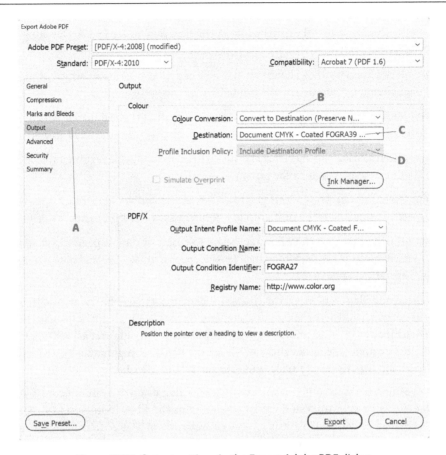

Figure 13.20: Output settings in the Export Adobe PDF dialog

There are some choices to make here and they depend on the geographical region you are in and the print service provider you are working with.

> **Note**
>
> It is worth noting that if your document contains RGB colors, they will be converted to CMYK at some stage during the printing process. This is not optional, and the only question is when and where the conversion occurs. Is it something you will undertake during the export of the document or will you leave the RGB colors intact for the printer to convert later? By speaking to your print service provider, you should be able to decide the answer to this question and, as such, the best approach to take when choosing settings here.

The first area in the **Output** section is the **Color** area, which contains the following dropdowns:

- **Color Conversion** (*B* in *Figure 13.20*): This controls whether colors will be converted during the export and includes the following options:

- **No Color Conversion**: Colors will not be converted during export. If you want your printer to handle all color conversion, you would select this option; however, I would strongly recommend confirming with your printer that they are comfortable with this.

- **Convert to Destination**: This will convert all colors to the color profile set in the **Destination** dropdown below.

- **Convert to Destination (Preserve Numbers)**: This option converts colors to the profile set under **Destination**, but only if they have a different embedded profile to the **Destination** profile or are RGB colors. It will ignore things such as CMYK color swatches created within the document. If you wish to convert RGB colors to CMYK at this stage, select this option now. I will select this option.

- **Destination** (*C* in *Figure 13.20*): If you selected one of the **Convert to Destination** options just mentioned, this is where you can choose the profile your document will be converted to during output. There are a wide range of options here and what you choose will vary from region to region. I would generally recommend having a conversation with your printer about which destination profile is best in your case. In my case, I am based in the UK and going to choose the **Document CMYK – Coated FOGRA39** profile. Users based in other regions will likely need to choose different profiles, and your printer should be able to advise on the best option to choose here.

- **Profile Inclusion Policy** (*D* in *Figure 13.20*): If you selected **No Color Conversion** under **Color Conversion**, then set **Profile Inclusion Policy** to **Don't Include Profiles**. If, however, you selected one of the **Convert to Destination** options under **Color Conversion**, then you should select **Include Destination Profile** here.

5. Having gone through the **Output** section, we are now ready to finish exporting the document. To do this, click the **Export** button at the bottom of the dialog box to create your print-ready PDF.

See also

If you haven't already done so, I would recommend setting up your color management settings for Creative Cloud. Further details on doing so can be found here: `https://www.highlander.co.uk/blog/setting-up-color-management-CC`.

Outputting a digital PDF

Outputting a print-ready PDF, as we did in the previous recipe, is great for handing off the file to a professional printer. The problem is it will normally result in a large file size, which is not going to be practical if the intended audience is downloading the document to view it on screen devices.

In this recipe, we will look at outputting a version of the PDF specifically for use on screen devices, focusing on outputting a smaller file size with an RGB color mode for a wider range of colors that can be viewed on screens.

Getting ready

In order to complete this recipe, simply open InDesign on your system and create a new document with 12 pages, as shown in the *Creating a new document* recipe in *Chapter 1*.

Step 1 requires you to be comfortable with creating a preflight profile and reviewing errors, as detailed in the *Creating a custom preflight profile* and *Reviewing and identifying preflight warnings* recipes.

If you wish to output your document without preflighting it first, you could skip straight to *step 2*; this is not something I would advise, however, as you may end up with errors in your document.

How to do it...

In order to output a digital PDF from your document, just follow these steps:

1. Before exporting your document, it is important to preflight your document to check for any errors. With this in mind, you should first set up a custom preflight profile, as shown in the *Creating a custom preflight profile* recipe, and then run it to check for the following:

   - Missing or modified links.
   - Image resolution is too low. With a screen document, you will typically be working with lower resolution images; however, it is worth checking for any documents with an effective resolution below 72 PPI with a view to replacing them with a better quality image.
   - Non-proportional scaling of placed objects.
   - Minimum stroke weight should typically be 1 pt for screen documents.
   - Interactive objects, as we are exporting this as a small file size PDF and not an interactive PDF.
   - Hidden page items.
   - Overset text.
   - Paragraph and character style overrides.
   - Missing fonts or glyphs.
   - Spelling errors.
   - Non-proportional type scaling.
   - Minimum type size – I would recommend between 10 pt and 12 pt as a minimum.
   - Blank pages.
   - Right page size and orientation.

   Having created a profile that checks for all of these errors, you should then preflight your document and fix any errors, as described in the *Reviewing and identifying preflight warnings* recipe.

2. From the **File** menu, go to **Adobe PDF Presets** and select the [**Smallest File Size**] option. This will open the **Export** dialog box where you can give your file a name and navigate to the folder you would like to save it in. When you click **Save**, this will bring up the **Export Adobe PDF dialog box** (*Figure 13.21*):

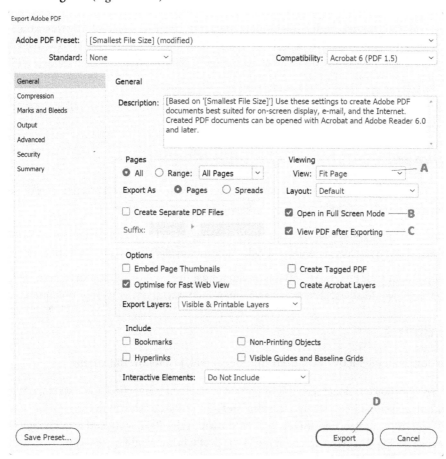

Figure 13.21: Export Adobe PDF dialog

As the **Smallest File Size** preset is already designed for a small digital document, most settings will be well-optimized for our needs. There are, however, a couple of options I want to adjust.

I want to change the **View** setting (*A* in *Figure 13.21*) to **Fit Page**, ensuring the pages are zoomed to fit into the available space.

In addition, I would like to select the checkbox for both **Open in Full Screen Mode** (*B* in *Figure 13.21*) and **View PDF after Exporting** (*C* in *Figure 13.21*). The first option will ensure that the document opens up hiding all toolbars and menus, while the latter will ensure the PDF is automatically opened upon completion of the creation process, allowing us to check it.

3. Having set these options, I will now click the **Export** button at the bottom of the dialog box (marked *D* in *Figure 13.21*) to export our small file size PDF.

Outputting an interactive PDF

Sometimes, you want to make a document more engaging, and one way of doing this would be to add more interactive functionality. Hyperlinks, bookmarks, digital form fields, interactive buttons, cross-references, and page transitions are all examples of features that can be included within an interactive PDF.

In this recipe, we will look at outputting an **interactive PDF**, which can support all of these features and make your documents more engaging for users.

Getting ready

In order to complete this recipe, simply open InDesign on your system and create a new document with 12 pages, as shown in the *Creating a new document* recipe in *Chapter 1*.

Step 1 requires you to be comfortable with creating a preflight profile and reviewing errors, as detailed in the *Creating a custom preflight profile* and *Reviewing and identifying preflight warnings* recipes.

If you wish to output your document without preflighting it first, you could skip straight to *step 2*; this is not something I would advise, however, as you may end up with errors in your document.

How to do it...

In order to output an interactive PDF from your document, just follow these steps:

1. Before exporting our document, it is important to preflight it and check for any errors. With this in mind, you should first set up a custom preflight profile, as shown in the *Creating a custom preflight profile* recipe, and then run it, as shown in the *Reviewing and identifying preflight warnings* recipe. The items to check for in the preflighting would be the same as *step 1* in the *Outputting a digital PDF* recipe, except there is no need to check for interactive objects this time.

   Having checked our document and fixed any problems, we can now export it.

2. In the **File** menu, select the **Export** option, which will bring up the **Export** dialog box, as shown in *Figure 13.22*.

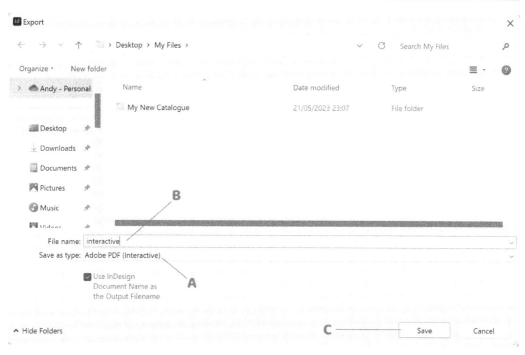

Figure 13.22: Export dialog box

Navigate to the folder where you would like to create your PDF, then select **Adobe PDF (Interactive)** from the **Save as type** drop-down box (*A* in *Figure 13.22*), before giving the file a name in the **File name** dialog box (*B* in *Figure 13.22*). Having done this, click **Save** (*C* in *Figure 13.22*), which will open the **Export to Interactive PDF** dialog box.

3. By default, the settings in **Export to Interactive PDF** (shown in *Figure 13.23*) are configured with the optimal settings for outputting an interactive PDF; however, there are some options you may want to customize.

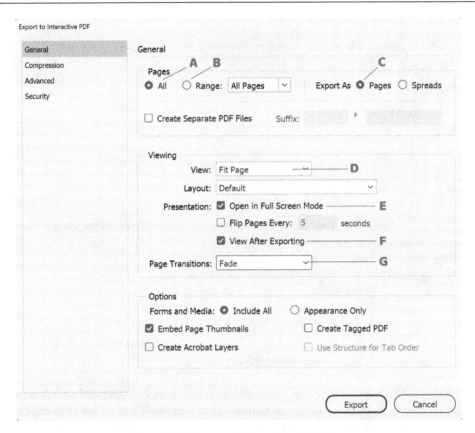

Figure 13.23: Export to Interactive PDF dialog

In my case, I am going to output all pages by ticking the **All Pages** checkbox (*A* in *Figure 13.23*); however, if you prefer to output a specific range of pages, simply check the **Range** box (*B* in *Figure 13.23*) where you can enter either individual page numbers or ranges of pages, separated by commas – for example, 2 , 6 - 1 0 , 12 would export pages 2, 6, 7, 8, 9, 10, and 12.

By default, the **Export to Interactive PDF** process outputs your document as spreads; however, in my case, I would like to export the document as individual pages. To do this, I will check the **Pages** checkbox (*C* in *Figure 13.23*).

I am going to set the **View** setting to **Fit Page** (*D* in *Figure 13.21*) to ensure the document is optimized for the viewer, and I will enable the checkbox for **Open in Full Screen Mode** (*E* in *Figure 13.23*). I will also enable the checkbox for **View After Exporting** (*F* in *Figure 13.23*) to ensure the document is opened with program menus and controls hidden.

In terms of **Page Transitions**, these are set by default to **From Document**; however, I haven't set any transitions in the document and would like to apply a **Fade** transition as users move between pages. With this in mind, I will select **Fade** from the **Page Transitions** drop-down box (*G* in *Figure 13.23*).

The rest of the default settings here are optimal for an interactive PDF and do not need to be changed, so I will now switch to the **Compression** section.

4. Click the **Compression** tab (*A* in *Figure 13.24*) to switch to the **Compression** section.

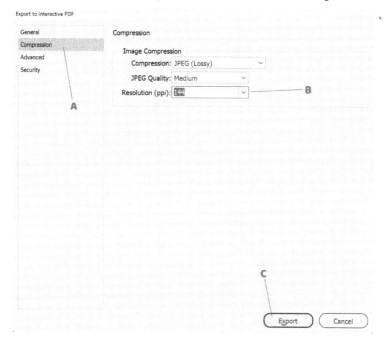

Figure 13.24: Compression options in the Export to Interactive PDF dialog

The default **Resolution (PPI)** (*B* in *Figure 13.24*) is set here is *72 PPI* as this was the standard pixel density for most monitors some years ago. These days, however, the majority of screen devices are set to a far higher value, with many mobile devices now displaying over 300 PPI. While it is tempting to set the **Resolution (PPI)** value nice and high, we also have to allow for the fact that this will increase the PDF file size significantly. With this in mind, I will set this value to **144** PPI, which is a good compromise between quality and file size.

5. Having finished customizing our settings, we will now click the **Export** button (*C* in *Figure 13.24*) to finish exporting our interactive PDF.

Outputting with Publish Online

Adobe **Publish Online** is a built-in Creative Cloud feature that allows you to publish your document to Adobe's server, allowing users to then view the document by simply visiting a web URL through their browser. The system is compatible with different screen sizes and devices, resulting in a consistent viewing experience across desktops, laptops, mobiles, and other devices. Additionally, Publish Online offers support for a number of interactive features including hyperlinks and interactive buttons.

In this recipe, we will look at the process for exporting your document through Publish Online, including the option to update a previously published document, how to include a downloadable PDF link, how to include a custom cover thumbnail, and adjusting image settings.

Getting ready

In order to complete this recipe, simply open InDesign on your system and create a new document with 12 pages, as shown in the *Creating a new document* recipe in *Chapter 1*.

How to do it...

In order to publish your document online, just follow these steps:

1. In the **File** menu, select the **Publish Online** option, which will bring up the **Publish Your Document Online dialog box** (shown in *Figure 13.25*).

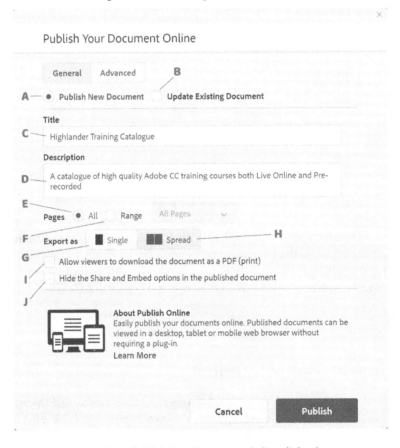

Figure 13.25: Publish Your Document Online dialog box

The dialog box contains a number of settings that we will need to set as follows:

- **Publish New Document** (*A* in *Figure 13.25*): Selecting this allows you to publish a new document. We will select this.

- **Update Existing Document** (*B* in *Figure 13.25*): Selecting this allows you to replace a document that was previously published (rather than publishing a new document). We have already opted to publish a new document, and therefore we won't select this.

- **Title** (*C* in *Figure 13.25*): Here, we can set a title for the document, which will appear in the browser title. The title will also be shown in the **Publish Online Dashboard** where you can manage documents that have been published online. Set an appropriate title for your document here.

- **Description** (*D* in *Figure 13.25*): The description set here is included within the code for the document and is used in the Publish Online dashboard as well as by Facebook if the document is shared there. Set an appropriate description for your document here.

- **Pages**: Here, you can choose to either output all pages by selecting the **All Pages** checkbox (*E* in *Figure 13.25*) or output a range by selecting the **Range** field (*F* in *Figure 13.25*) and entering a range in the dialog box. You can enter either individual page numbers or ranges of pages separated by commas – for example, 2,6-10,12 would export pages 2, 6, 7, 8, 9, 10, and 12.

- **Export as** (*G* in *Figure 13.25*): Choose either **Single** pages or **Spread** (*H* in *Figure 13.25*). In my case, I will select **Spread**.

- **Allow viewers to download the document as a PDF (print)** (*I* in *Figure 13.25*): Selecting this will ensure a PDF download link is included within the Publish Online interface for users who would prefer to download a PDF version. I will leave this deselected.

- **Hide the Share and Embed options in the published document** (*J* in *Figure 13.25*): Selecting this means the buttons allowing users to share the document with others or to embed the document into a web page will be unavailable in the published document. I will leave this deselected.

Having completed the **General** options, let's now take a look at the **Advanced** options.

2. Click the **Advanced** tab (*A* in *Figure 13.26*) to switch to the **Advanced** settings.

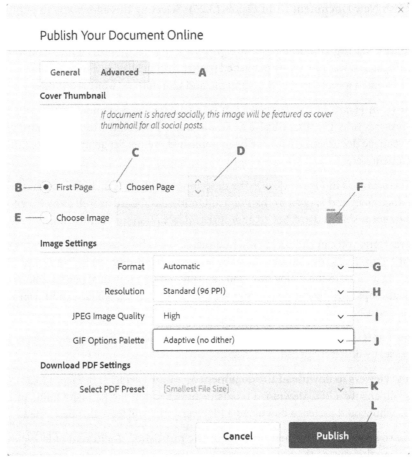

Figure 13.26: Advanced settings in Publish Online

Here, you will find a range of options for fine-tuning a range of settings for your document, including the following:

- **Cover Thumbnail**: This area allows you to set a cover thumbnail for your document, which will be used if the document is shared on social networks. You can choose between three options when setting a cover page:

  - **First Page** (*B* in *Figure 13.26*): Selecting this option will use an image from the first page of the document as the cover thumbnail. I will select this option.

- **Chosen Page** (*C* in *Figure 13.26*): Selecting this option will allow you to generate an image of a specific page from the document as the cover thumbnail. You can select the page from the dropdown (*D* in *Figure 13.26*).

- **Choose Image** (*E* in *Figure 13.26*): Selecting this option allows us to upload a custom cover thumbnail in either GIF, JPEG, or PNG format. If choosing this option, select the *folder* icon (*F* in *Figure 13.26*) to choose an image for the cover thumbnail.

Having set the cover thumbnail, we will now customize **Image Settings** for images included in the document. The options available here include the following:

- **Format** (*G* in *Figure 13.26*): This setting controls what format the images should be exported in, with the following available options:

  - **Automatic**: This is the recommended option as it will allow InDesign to decide the optimal format for the images. I will select this.

  - **JPEG**: A web-compatible format that is good for photographs.

  - **GIF**: A web-compatible format that can support animation.

  - **PNG**: A web-compatible format that can support transparency.

- **Resolution** (*H* in *Figure 13.26*): This setting controls the resolution that the images will be output to and includes the following options:

  - **Low (72 PPI)**: This will result in low-resolution images that may not look as good on higher-resolution screens.

  - **Standard (96 PPI)**: This will result in a compromise between quality and size, resulting in an image that is of reasonable quality while maintaining a reasonable file size. This will help with page load speeds as users are viewing the document. We will select this option.

  - **HiDPI (144 PPI)**: This will result in higher quality images that will also be larger in size and, as a result, may cause slower page loading for viewers of the document. If you are creating a document where high-quality images are a priority, this may be a good option.

- **JPEG Image Quality** (*I* in *Figure 13.26*): This option dictates the quality of any JPEG images that are created and can be set to **Low**, **Medium**, **High**, or **Maximum**. We will choose **High**.

- **GIF Options Palette** (*J* in *Figure 13.26*): This setting allows you to control the color palette used when the system converts images to the GIF format. The available options include the following.

  - **Adaptive (no dither)**: This will create a custom color palette by sampling colors from the color ranges most commonly used in the image. We will select this option.

  - **System (Mac)**: This uses the standard macOS color palette.

- **Web**: This uses the standard web color palette.

- **System (Win)**: This uses the standard Windows OS color palette.

- The final setting here is the **Select PDF Preset** setting (*K* in *Figure 13.26*), which is only available if you enabled the **Allow viewers to download the document as a PDF (print)** checkbox in the **General** settings section. If you did, the options available here will include all of the presets available from the **File** menu under **Adobe PDF Presets**. As we did not enable this setting in the **General** settings section, the option will not be available.

Having chosen our settings, we can now click the **Publish** button (*L* in *Figure 13.26*). Upon clicking the **Publish** button, the document will be exported to a web-compliant format and uploaded to Adobe's Publish Online servers. This will take from a few seconds to a few minutes depending on the document size. The **Publish Online** dialog box should then update to reflect the fact that your document was successfully uploaded.

3. Once you have uploaded your document, you should see a new dialog box, as shown in *Figure 13.27*:

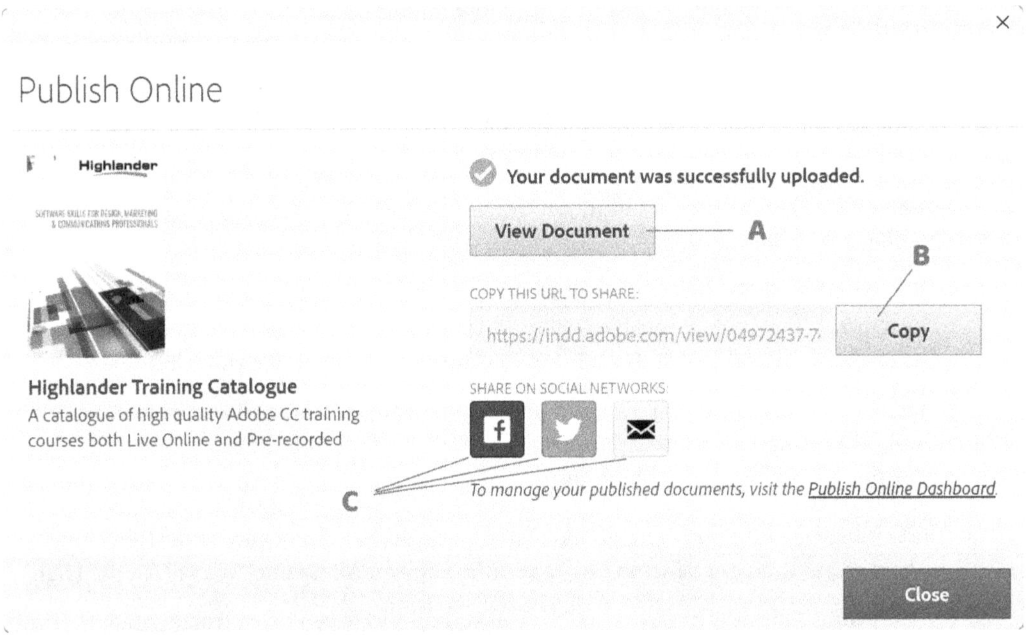

Figure 13.27: The Publish Online dialog after a successful upload

The options available here include the following:

- **View Document** (*A* in *Figure 13.27*): Clicking this button will open your newly published document in the default web browser.

- **Copy** (*B* in *Figure 13.27*): Clicking this button allows you to copy the URL that users can visit to view the document. The URL can then be shared, for example, via email or as a hyperlink on your website.

- Sharing links for *Facebook*, *Twitter*, and *Email* (*C* in *Figure 13.27*): Clicking these will allow you to share the document link via each of these different methods.

When you have finished here, you can click the **Close** button to return to your document.

Your document is now published through the Adobe servers and you can share the URL for the document with anybody you would like to be able to view it. The document can potentially be accessed by anybody with the URL, so be aware of this if you are looking to publish any confidential information.

Appendix

InDesign Tools Panel
at a Glance

When you are working in InDesign, it is important to know which tools you are looking for; this section is designed to help you identify the tools in the InDesign **Tools** panel more easily.

Some tools are grouped together, and where this is the case, I have listed the names of all tools in the group. To access grouped tools, either right-click on the tool, click and hold down the mouse button, or hold the *Alt* (PC)/*Option* (Mac) button down and click until you get to the correct tool.

A: The **Selection** tool

B: The **Direct Selection** tool

C: The **Page** tool

D: The **Gap** tool

E: The **Content Collector** and **Content Conveyor** tools

F: The **Type** and **Type on a Path** tools

G: The **Line** tool

H: The **Pen, Add Anchor Point, Delete Anchor Point**, and **Convert Direction Point** tools

I: The **Pencil, Smooth**, and **Erase** tools

J: The **Rectangle Frame, Ellipse Frame**, and **Polygon Frame** tools

K: The **Rectangle, Ellipse**, and **Polygon** tools

L: The **Scissors** tool

M: The **Free Transform, Rotate, Scale**, and **Shear** tools

N: The **Gradient Swatch** tool

O: The **Gradient Feather** tool

P: The **Note** tool

Q: The **Colour Theme, Eyedropper**, and **Measure** tools

R: The **Hand** tool

S: The **Zoom** tool

T: The **Default Fill & Stroke** and **Swap Fill & Stroke** options

U: The **Fill** option

V: The **Stroke** option

W: The **Formatting Affects Container** and **Formatting Affects Text** options

X: The **Apply Colour, Apply Gradient**, and **Apply None** tools

Y: **View Options**

Z: The **Normal, Preview, Bleed, Slug** and **Presentation** screen modes

Index

www.packtpub.com

Subscribe to our online digital library for full access to over 7,000 books and videos, as well as industry leading tools to help you plan your personal development and advance your career. For more information, please visit our website.

Why subscribe?

- Spend less time learning and more time coding with practical eBooks and Videos from over 4,000 industry professionals

- Improve your learning with Skill Plans built especially for you

- Get a free eBook or video every month

- Fully searchable for easy access to vital information

- Copy and paste, print, and bookmark content

Did you know that Packt offers eBook versions of every book published, with PDF and ePub files available? You can upgrade to the eBook version at packtpub.com and as a print book customer, you are entitled to a discount on the eBook copy. Get in touch with us at customercare@packtpub.com for more details.

At www.packtpub.com, you can also read a collection of free technical articles, sign up for a range of free newsletters, and receive exclusive discounts and offers on Packt books and eBooks.

Other Books You May Enjoy

If you enjoyed this book, you may be interested in these other books by Packt:

Adobe Acrobat Ninja

Urszula Witherell

ISBN: 978-1-80324-817-2

- Use Adobe Acrobat Pro efficiently through shortcuts and preferences
- Expand your knowledge of the functions that you already use
- Understand the connection between PDFs, Acrobat, and other applications
- Find out about unique settings in Adobe InDesign to create high-quality fully featured PDFs
- Address legal concerns for information published in a digital format
- Confidently move away from the use of ink and paper and help preserve physical resources

Express Your Creativity with Adobe Express

Rosie Sue

ISBN: 978-1-80323-774-9

- Learn how to create stunning social media graphics without having any prior design skills
- Repurpose graphic content and convert them to animations
- Create a beautiful responsive web page or marketing splash page, without coding knowledge
- Create once and repurpose the content in different aspect ratios for all the social media platforms
- Repurpose video for various social media uses and adhere to the aspect ratios for each platform
- Create compelling eye-catching content for your audience to engage with
- Create a landing page to collect leads

Packt is searching for authors like you

If you're interested in becoming an author for Packt, please visit authors.packtpub.com and apply today. We have worked with thousands of developers and tech professionals, just like you, to help them share their insight with the global tech community. You can make a general application, apply for a specific hot topic that we are recruiting an author for, or submit your own idea.

Share Your Thoughts

Now you've finished *Designing the Adobe InDesign Way*, we'd love to hear your thoughts! Scan the QR code below to go straight to the Amazon review page for this book and share your feedback or leave a review on the site that you purchased it from.

https://packt.link/r/1-801-07443-7

Your review is important to us and the tech community and will help us make sure we're delivering excellent quality content.

Download a free PDF copy of this book

Thanks for purchasing this book!

Do you like to read on the go but are unable to carry your print books everywhere?

Is your eBook purchase not compatible with the device of your choice?

Don't worry, now with every Packt book you get a DRM-free PDF version of that book at no cost.

Read anywhere, any place, on any device. Search, copy, and paste code from your favorite technical books directly into your application.

The perks don't stop there, you can get exclusive access to discounts, newsletters, and great free content in your inbox daily

Follow these simple steps to get the benefits:

1. Scan the QR code or visit the link below

https://packt.link/free-ebook/9781801074438

2. Submit your proof of purchase
3. That's it! We'll send your free PDF and other benefits to your email directly

www.ingramcontent.com/pod-product-compliance
Lightning Source LLC
Chambersburg PA
CBHW081451050326
40690CB00015B/2756